HQSTA.

Letters of Emma and Florence Hardy

Letters of Emma and Florence Hardy

Edited by

MICHAEL MILLGATE

CLARENDON PRESS · OXFORD

1996

Oxford University Press, Walton Street, Oxford OX2 6DP

Oxford New York
Athens Auckland Bangkok Bombay
Calcutta Cape Town Dar es Salaam Delhi
Florence Hong Kong Istanbul Karachi
Kuala Lumpur Madras Madrid Melbourne
Mexico City Nairobi Paris Singapore
Taipei Tokyo Toronto
and associated companies
in Berlin Ibadan

Oxford is a trade mark of Oxford University Press

Published in the United States
by Oxford University Press Inc., New York

British Library Cataloguing in Publication Data
Data available

Library of Congress Cataloging in Publication Data
Hardy, Emma Lavinia Gifford, 1840–1912.
Letters of Emma and Florence Hardy / edited by Michael Millgate.
p. cm.
Includes index.
1. Hardy, Emma Lavinia Gifford, 1840–1912—Correspondence.
2. Women poets, English—19th century—Correspondence. 3. Hardy,
Florence Emily, 1881–1937—Correspondence. 4. Authors' spouses—
Great Britain—Correspondence. 5. Authors, English—19th century—
Biography. 6. Authors, English—20th century—Marriage. 7. Hardy,
Thomas, 1840–1928—Marriage. I. Hardy, Florence Emily, 1881–1937.
II. Millgate, Michael. III. Title.
PR4739.H77Z48   1995   820.9'008—dc20   [B]   95-38304
ISBN 0-19-818609-6

1 3 5 7 9 10 8 6 4 2

Typeset by Graphicraft Typesetters Ltd., Hong Kong
Printed in Great Britain
on acid-free paper by
Bookcraft Ltd.,
Midsomer Norton, Bath

Acknowledgements

I HAVE consulted many libraries and librarians during my pursuit of Emma and Florence Hardy letters and am especially grateful to the following institutions and their staffs for permitting access to relevant materials (by no means all of them reproduced in the present volume) and for advice and assistance of many kinds: BBC Written Archives Centre; Beinecke Rare Book and Manuscript Library, Yale University (especially Vincent Giroud); Albert A. and Henry W. Berg Collection, New York Public Library, Astor, Lenox, and Tilden Foundations; Birmingham University Library; Bodleian Library; Bristol University Library; British Library (especially Sally Brown and Elizabeth James); University of British Columbia Library; British Museum Central Archives; Brotherton Collection, Leeds University Library (especially Christopher Sheppard); Bryn Mawr College Library; Cambridge University Library; Central Zionist Archives, Jersualem; Colby College Library, Waterville, Maine (especially Patience-Anne W. Lenck and Nancy S. Reinhardt); Dorset County Library, Dorchester, Dorset; Dorset County Museum, Dorchester, Dorset (especially Roger Peers, Richard de Peyer, and Lilian Swindall); Eton College, School Library (especially Michael Meredith and Helen Garton); Fawcett Library; Fisher Rare Book Library, University of Toronto (especially Richard Landon and Kathryn Martyn); Folger Shakespeare Library; Harry Ransom Humanities Research Center, University of Texas (especially Cathy Henderson); Houghton Library, Harvard University (especially Jennie Rathbun); Huntington Library, San Marino, California (especially Sara S. Hodson); Keble College, Oxford (especially Marjory Szurko); King's College Library, Cambridge; National Library of Iceland; National Library of Wales; National Trust, Stourhead (especially Derek Brebner and Peter Cornick); Princeton University Library; Royal Literary Fund; University of St Andrews Library; Wiltshire County Record Office (especially Penelope Rundle).

I owe a particular debt to the collectors and private owners who graciously allowed me to see and reproduce manuscript materials in their possession, notably Frederick B. Adams, Celia Barclay, Gertrude Bugler, Alan Clodd, Henry Gifford, Ronald Greenland, David Holmes, Bill and Vera Jesty, Barbara Jones, Henry Lock, Mrs Michael MacCarthy, Richard L. Purdy, Gordon N. Ray, Mme Romain Rolland, Carola Shephard, Lilian Skinner, and Daphne Wood.

Essential to the completion of the edition have been the permissions for

v

the publication of Emma and Florence Hardy letters granted by the copyright holder, the Miss E. A. Dugdale Will Trust, through the helpful agency of Alan P. Gardner, and the generous financial support received in the form of research grants from the Social Sciences and Humanities Research Council of Canada.

For hospitality, advice, and assistance of all kinds I should like especially to thank Thomas H. Adamowski, Ellen Adams, Frederick and Marie-Louise Adams, Henry Auster, Sabar Balsara, Celia Barclay, C. J. P. Beatty, Alan Bell, Robin Biswas, Naomi Black, Tony Bradbury, Eleanor Cook, Jane Cooper, Peter W. Coxon, Graham Dalling, Dudley Dodd, Gillian Fenwick, Simon Gatrell, James Gibson, Henry Gifford, Desmond Hawkins, Robert H. Hirst, David and Barbara Holmes, Linda Hughes, Heather Jackson, J. R. de J. Jackson, Barbara Jones, W. J. Keith, Ronald D. Knight, Peter Lennon, Charles Lock, Michael Meredith, Lawrence Miller, D. S. Millgate, W. W. Morgan, Alan W. Nineham, Christine O'Connor, Norman Page, David Pam, Michael Rabiger, J. M. Robson, Barbara Rosenbaum, S. P. Rosenbaum, Carola Shephard, Anthony Thwaite, Brenda Tunks, John Tydeman, Wentworth Walker, Keith Wilson, Donald Winslow, J. M. Wraight, and Marjorie G. Wynne. I have also benefited greatly from the excellent research assistance provided at different periods by Adrian Bond and Ian Dennis, and from the astute editorial skills of Lesley Mann.

Catharine Carver and Ann Thwaite have been constant sources of encouragement and constructive advice; Frances Whistler has once again demonstrated editorial tact and expertise of the highest order; Pamela Dalziel has generously taken time from her own scholarly work to give the entire edition an invaluably close and critical reading; I continue to be profoundly indebted to the work and example of the late Richard Purdy, in whose collection so many of these letters once reposed; and I have, as always, depended throughout on the professional skills, practical assistance, and personal support of my wife, Jane Millgate. Vera Jesty has responded with cheerfulness and impressive success to innumerable queries about Dorset places, personalities, and events, and I take particular pleasure, finally, in voicing my deepest thanks to her and to Bill Jesty for their wholehearted friendship over so many years. I should like to think, indeed, that the present volume might stand as a modest tribute to the Jestys' long and benign custodianship of Max Gate and their continuing contribution to Hardy studies.

M.M.

Toronto
December 1994

Contents

Introduction   viii

Editorial Procedures   xxiii

Abbreviations   xxv

LETTERS OF EMMA HARDY   I

LETTERS OF FLORENCE HARDY   57

Index   351

Introduction

THERE are three major presences in this volume, those of the two remarkable though very different women, born Emma Lavinia Gifford and Florence Emily Dugdale, who actually wrote the letters, and that of their famous
husband, Thomas Hardy, whom they so often wrote about. Unquestion-
ably, there is a particular fascination in what the letters show or suggest of
Hardy's personality, relationships, and working habits, and of day-to-day
life at Max Gate, the house on the outskirts of Dorchester in which he lived
with his first wife from 1885 to her death in 1912 and with his second wife
from 1914 until his own death in 1928. But Emma Hardy and Florence
Hardy are of interest and importance in themselves, and the edition seeks
throughout to represent them as fully and fairly as the surviving documents
permit and to allow their own distinctive voices to be heard. As Diana
Johnson has nicely observed in *The True History of the First Mrs Meredith and
Other Lesser Lives*, 'a lesser life does not seem lesser to the person who leads
one. His life is very real to him; he is not a minor figure in it.'[1]

Ideal representation of Emma and Florence Hardy has, however, been
severely inhibited by the nature and scope of the available material and
especially by the extraordinary discrepancy between the number of Emma
Hardy's letters that have survived and the number of Florence Hardy's.
Diligent searches—including hundreds of letters to libraries world-wide—
have turned up a mere 120 or so items written and signed by Emma Hardy,
only one of them to a relative and only two (both of them postcards) to her
husband. Of these roughly a third have been included in the present edition,
supplemented by a few letters to newspapers that seemed to provide ampler
and more considered expressions of her most cherished views and opinions
than could be found in any of the private correspondence. Florence Hardy's
letters, on the other hand, have surfaced in large numbers, and it was
originally envisaged that the present volume would be entirely devoted to
them—or even to the single extended series of letters to Sir Sydney Cockerell.
The eventual decision to include a selection of Emma Hardy's letters was
made on the assumption that there would never be enough of them to
justify publication in a separate volume. If the resulting edition seems
disproportioned, with much less space being devoted to the first Mrs Hardy
than to the second, it remains true that Emma Hardy's letters, though far

---

[1] Johnson, *The True History of the First Mrs Meredith and Other Lesser Lives* (New York: Knopf, 1972), p. xiii.

outnumbered by Florence Hardy's, in fact represent a considerably higher proportion of those that actually survive.

Of even greater editorial concern has been the apparent non-survival of *any* letters written by Emma Hardy prior to the year 1890—apart from occasional letters of her husband's that she either wrote out for his signature or copied for purposes of record. Yet it does not seem that she was an inactive correspondent. Following Florence Hardy's death in 1937 her executor, Irene Cooper Willis, came across a mass of the first Mrs Hardy's incoming correspondence that had sat undisturbed in her former attic retreat at Max Gate ever since her own death twenty-five years earlier. It would be good to know precisely what was there, but Cooper Willis destroyed by far the greater part of the papers she came across, selecting for preservation only a small group of letters that she thought interesting in themselves or representative of significant correspondences. From these items, now in the Dorset County Museum, it is possible to infer that Emma Hardy did exchange letters over the years with a good many different people, among them an early friend named Margaret Hawes, some former neighbours from the period she and Hardy spent at Sturminster Newton, her brother Walter Gifford, Hardy's sisters Mary and Katharine, and a particular friend of her later years, a Cambridge classicist named Alfred Pretor. From the same source, supplemented by information from the sale catalogue of the Max Gate library,[2] it appears that she also corresponded with such friends or admirers of her husband's as Florence Henniker, Rebekah Owen, Lady Hoare, Edmund Gosse, J. M. Barrie, Rudyard Kipling, and Henry James.

It seems possible only to guess at the reasons why so few of Emma Hardy's own letters are now extant, but she was sometimes an abrasive correspondent, in her later years she was often regarded as a faintly ludicrous figure, and in her earlier years her status as Miss Emma Gifford or even as Mrs Thomas Hardy might well have been insufficient to ensure that her letters would be kept and treasured. After all, only a meagre proportion of Hardy's own surviving letters date from before 1890, and of those few the great majority are business letters indifferently preserved among the records of publishing houses.

Most glaringly absent, of course, are Emma Hardy's letters to Hardy himself. The couple were only occasionally together during the four and a half years that intervened between their romantic first meeting in Cornwall in March 1870 and their marriage in London in September 1874, and it is beyond question that they exchanged many letters during that period. It

[2] Hodgson & Co., cat. 16 of 1937–8, lots 299 and 303.

appears, however, that both sides of the correspondence were burned in the garden of Max Gate by Emma Hardy herself during the unhappy later stages of the marriage.[3] The only remains of Emma Gifford's letters to her fiancé—indeed, of her entire personal correspondence prior to 1890—are the two fragments, one from 1870 the other from 1874, that Hardy copied down at the time and then recopied some fifty years later when searching back through his old notebooks prior to their destruction. Those fragments, included here, perhaps reveal little in themselves, except in so far as a curiously poignant and premonitory note is struck by Emma Gifford's lament, written just two months before her marriage: 'My work, unlike your work of writing, does not occupy my true mind much . . . Your novel seems sometimes like a child all your own & none of me.' They do, however, tend to suggest that Emma Gifford's literary ambitions and enthusiasms may genuinely have served to enhance not just her own initial responsiveness to Hardy but his to her; at the same time, they scarcely seem sufficient to endorse Hardy's claim, made after the destruction of the correspondence, that it had been comparable to the famous courtship letters of Robert Browning and Elizabeth Barrett.

A number of Hardy's letters to his first wife have been preserved and published, the earliest dating from 1885, and while they are for the most part concerned with domestic details—once married, the Hardys were rarely apart for more than a week or two at a time—those very details constitute evidence that the marriage, despite its many difficulties, was at least kept up, right to the end, as a functioning daily domestic operation within which meals were eaten, conversations engaged in, and guests entertained—if sometimes in unintended ways. If, as is sometimes suggested, there was a major rift in the marriage in the early 1890s, or some sort of crisis or personality change experienced by Emma Hardy herself, then it becomes all the more regrettable that the lack of earlier letters should rule out the possibility of assessing differences in attitude and tone. Even so, the available documents extend over more than twenty years, projecting a strong sense of Emma Hardy herself as she was in her fifties, sixties, and early seventies, and illuminating, from her point of view, the later stages of her marriage.

What further skews the record is the fact that by far the largest of Emma Hardy's surviving correspondences is with the American Hardy enthusiast Rebekah Owen, who made with her sister Catharine the first of several 'pilgrimages' to Dorchester in the summers of 1892 and 1893 and later moved permanently to England, taking a large house in the Lake District. Hardy,

---

[3] Florence Hardy to Howard Bliss, 10 January 1931 (Princeton). Footnote identifications in this introduction are confined to documents not included in the edition itself.

by no means as famous as he later became, was at first amused and a little flattered by Miss Owen's admiring interest in his work and in himself, but he soon wearied of her relentless inquisitiveness and delegated the correspondence—and, in effect, the relationship—first to Emma Hardy and later to her successor. Rebekah Owen's sheer activity as a correspondent and as a hoarder of documents has given her a prominence in Hardy studies that she scarcely in herself deserves, and in reading the letters addressed to her from Max Gate it is important to keep in mind that their authors neither understood nor greatly liked her and found her persistent curiosity at once a burden to be borne and an intrusion to be resisted. Emma Hardy seems none the less to have found in the correspondence some kind of compensation for the loneliness she experienced as a result of a worsening marital estrangement and a lack of local friendships. Since she was rarely aiming at real communication, she tended to write to Rebekah Owen with even more than her usual inconsequentiality, filling her letters with whatever came most readily to hand, typically household trivia or brief comments on whatever she was currently reading or worrying about. Her rapid flitting from topic to topic does have a certain birdlike charm, but again and again—as in her letter of 19 February 1897—the thought sequences slide through several abrupt shifts of direction into what had already become a familiar groove of domestic grievance.

Although Emma Hardy's letters to Rebekah Owen are the most persistently peppered with negative comments about her husband, she was in the end no respecter of correspondents. Once launched upon a topic she deeply cared about—religion, animals, Zionism, women's suffrage, the iniquities of her husband and of the male sex generally—she became too intensively engaged to retain any real sensitivity to individuals or to situations. She wrote sternly to Hardy's friend Edward Clodd on 29 March 1897 about the godlessness of his Darwinian views on evolution, fired off on 16 June 1908 an angry condemnation of Rebekah Owen's conversion to Roman Catholicism, and on 3 November 1902 informed Desmond MacCarthy's mother, innocently seeking advice as to her son's prospects for a literary career, that she personally was 'prejudiced against authors—living ones!— they too often wear out other's lives with their dyspeptic moanings if unsuccessful—and if they become eminent they throw their aider over their parapets to enemies below, & revenge themselves for any objections to this treatment by stabbings with their pen!' When the copy of Lady Grove's *The Social Fetich* arrived at Max Gate Emma Hardy responded on 9 December 1907 by pointing to what she saw as its grammatical infelicities—doubtless in the knowledge that her husband had read and commented on the proofs—

and then offering her own somewhat eccentric prescriptions for correct English usage.

It is not difficult to imagine the amused head-shaking, and worse, with which such letters were received: Clodd brushed off the criticisms of himself as 'a curious mixture of sentiment and ignorance'.[4] But it must have been different with the truly destructive response Emma Hardy made to an appeal for advice on marriage received from the new but by no means youthful bride of Kenneth Grahame, the author of *The Wind in the Willows*: her letter of 20 August 1899 warned that as the wife of an author her correspondent could expect 'neither gratitude, nor attentions, love, nor *justice*, nor *anything* you may set your heart on'. It seems impossible to identify the precise sources of such bitterness, let alone assess the respective degrees of responsibility as between Hardy and herself. There can be little doubt, however, of the extent of Emma Hardy's emotional secession from her marriage—or of the embarrassment Hardy must have been caused by such letters and by his wife's parallel proclivity for openly criticizing him on social occasions. And while these particular documents were preserved by their recipients, it's not difficult to appreciate why Emma Hardy's letters might not always have been welcomed or treasured—to suspect, in short, one possible reason for their surviving in such small numbers.

But Emma Hardy did have another voice, one that chiefly made itself heard in her public letters and published articles. Among her most attractive qualities was her capacity not just for passion but for passionate action in addressing the issues she really cared about—Hardy himself especially admired the courage with which she would intervene whenever she saw animals suffering mistreatment—and she wrote to the newspapers with characteristic vehemence about the slaughter of skylarks for food, about the cruelty involved in training animals for performance, about house flies and their status as creatures too, not to be wilfully destroyed. She also wrote, more substantially, about the importance of everyone's becoming what she called a maker of happiness and especially about women's rights and women's suffrage, of which she became and remained an active supporter—though not to the point of condoning the use of violence, the issue over which she resigned from the London Society for Women's Suffrage in 1912. Most striking, perhaps, is the long letter published (probably after some editorial polishing) in *The Nation* of 6 May 1908 in which she advanced a claim for the equality of women that saw the achievement of the vote as a mere incident along the way of the future.

---

[4] Edward Clodd's diary (Alan Clodd).

Emma Hardy died suddenly on 27 November 1912, and on 10 February 1914 Hardy was married for a second time. In 1874 Emma Lavinia Gifford, aged thirty-three, had married a man only five months older than herself who was still in the early stages of a financially uncertain career; forty years later Florence Emily Dugdale, just turned thirty-five, was marrying an immensely famous and securely affluent man of seventy-three. As with her predecessor, the second Mrs Hardy's literary interests and enthusiasms were directly contributory to her marriage—it was she who seems first to have approached Hardy, writing as a hitherto unknown admirer of his work to ask if she might call upon him at Max Gate.[5] But whereas Emma Gifford had been virtually without occupation—or, indeed, education—prior to her marriage, Florence Dugdale had for many years been earning her own living. The second of the five daughters of a junior school headmaster and his wife (a former governess), she was herself trained as a teacher, and when that career proved not only uncongenial but physically beyond her powers she became variously, and perhaps a little desperately, typist, companion, journalist, and author of children's stories.[6] The occasional secretarial work she did for Hardy while Emma Hardy was still alive—typing up, for example, the 'Postscript' he added to the Preface to the Wessex Edition of *Jude the Obscure*[7]—expanded to a major daily chore following her marriage, but she also continued, perhaps as a kind of compensation, to publish pieces of her own in national newspapers and magazines.

In so doing she was consciously challenging her husband's displeasure. Hardy, as Pamela Dalziel has admirably shown,[8] had gone to a good deal of trouble to foster the writing career of Miss Dugdale, but it is clear (e.g. from the letter of 22 July 1914) that he felt altogether differently about publishing wives. His first wife had only rarely had her work printed, but his second—typically billed as 'the wife of our greatest novelist'—made several appearances in the Sunday tabloids of the day, publishing unabashedly patriotic stories in the *Sunday Pictorial* during the war year of 1915[9] and

---

[5] See *The Collected Letters of Thomas Hardy*, ed. Richard Little Purdy and Michael Millgate (Oxford: Clarendon Press, 1978–88), iii. 179.

[6] She told Rebekah Owen ([21 March 1916?], Colby College) that journalism was 'the most degrading work anybody could take up—typewriting is a lady's occupation by comparison'.

[7] Hardy's holograph is now in the Beinecke Library, together with the envelope, postmarked [20?] November 1911, in which it was originally sent to 'Miss F. E. Dugdale' at her Enfield home.

[8] *Thomas Hardy: The Excluded and Collaborative Stories*, ed. Pamela Dalziel (Oxford: Clarendon Press, 1992), 333–46.

[9] Specifically, '"Greater Love Hath No Man." The Story of a Village Ne'er Do Well', 13 June 1915, 7, and (as Florence E. Dugdale, 'an authoress well known as a very charming writer of short stories') 'War's Awakening: How Duty's Call Came to a Bachelor Girl', 22 August 1915, 7. Colby College library has a cutting of another such story, 'Her Lonely Soldier', evidently dating from late March 1915 but not as yet traced to its source.

articles with such titles as 'A Woman's Happiest Year', 'No Superfluous Women', and 'The Dress Bills of Wives' in the *Weekly Dispatch* of 1922–3.[10] She also kept up for several years her anonymous reviewing of novels for the *Sphere* (see letter of 3 November 1916), although Hardy deplored the time she devoted to the work and doubtless recognized the general vapidity of her observations on the generally vapid novels Clement Shorter chose to steer her way. The mediocrity of most of Florence Hardy's publications, indeed, must often have been troubling to her husband, although from her own standpoint, of course, her persistence in such activities could—and can—be more positively viewed as an assertion of partial independence.

Upon her marriage Florence Hardy became responsible, as her predecessor had been, for the domestic economy of Max Gate, the management of the servants, the planning of meals, and the entertainment of guests. She also performed, as Emma Hardy seems not to have done, a task that became particularly important with the passage of the years—that of reading aloud to her husband each night after dinner. Secretarially, her main role was that of typist, and while she typed skilfully and at a considerable speed it is perhaps of some significance that she almost entirely abandoned the typewriter shortly after becoming a widow. She typed up Hardy's manuscripts—poems, prefaces, the clandestinely written 'Life' of himself that would eventually be published over her own name—and was daily involved in helping him to keep up with the mass of correspondence constantly descending upon him as the most famous writer of his time. Complaints about the burden imposed by such letters—and by the copies of Hardy's own books sent in the hope of securing his autograph—occur frequently in Florence Hardy's own correspondence, especially as each June 2nd brought her husband's birthday round again: 'I am afraid there are still *many* birthday presents & letters unacknowledged,' she told Rebekah Owen in July 1920. 'At the age of eighty it is impossible to keep pace with the kindness of friends. Alas, I am afraid the autograph hunters will be unsatisfied. Every now & then one writes for his, or her, album to be returned (or book) which is done. To see to all this properly requires a permanent paid secretary.'[11] Later on, as the letters and parcels still poured in, a young secretary named May O'Rourke was indeed employed on a part-time basis to assist in such tasks—her signature or initials appearing on many of the letters sent out from Max Gate subsequent to March 1923.[12] This lightening of Florence Hardy's burdens was at best intermittent, however: Miss O'Rourke was

[10] *Weekly Dispatch*, 27 August 1922, 8; 17 September 1922, 8; and 8 April 1923, 2.
[11] Letter of 23 July 1920 (Colby College).
[12] May O'Rourke, *Thomas Hardy: His Secretary Remembers* (Beaminster, Dorset: Toucan Press, 1965), 27.

sometimes ill and often away and Hardy was unwilling to allow access to any other 'stranger' in her place.

Although Hardy still wrote most of his personal letters in his own hand, a different procedure was adopted for letters deemed to be of lesser importance. Using the back or the foot of the incoming letter, Hardy would draft or briefly sketch a reply in his own hand and then pass it on to be typed by either his wife or May O'Rourke. If Hardy had drafted the reply in the first person, he would usually sign the typed final version himself, but such letters were quite often signed 'for Thomas Hardy' either by Florence Hardy (sometimes using only her first initials, 'F.E.') or by May O'Rourke (sometimes as 'M.O'R.'). Just as frequently, however, Hardy's original draft would be in the third person, giving the impression that the letter despatched had been written as well as signed by Florence Hardy or May O'Rourke. Many such drafts survive in the Dorset County Museum—the incoming letters, now bearing Hardy's annotations, having generally been retained for purposes of record—and there also exist, scattered among several collections, a substantial number of actual letters that bear Florence Hardy's signature or initials but were almost certainly composed and perhaps dictated by her husband: many, indeed, begin with the tell-tale phrase, 'I write for my husband'.

Though such items have their own importance, they have been excluded from the present edition for the sake of allowing Florence Hardy as much of her own voice as possible—especially in light of the availability of so many letters unmistakably hers in every respect. It is no derogation of the intrinsic qualities of her letters to suggest that their recipients tended to preserve them for essentially the same reasons as her acquaintance was cultivated during her husband's lifetime: because Hardy was by the end of the first decade of the twentieth century an immensely famous figure, and because his wife, long seen as the doorkeeper of Max Gate, was uniquely placed to write of him with intimacy and even speak on his behalf.

The survival of her correspondence in such quantities does not, however, reflect what she herself would necessarily have wished. Habits of caution and privacy learned from her husband, reinforced by her own chronically low self-esteem, naturally inclined her to dispose of documents rather than retain them, and one of her regular New Year rituals appears to have been the systematic destruction of letters received during the twelve months just concluded.[13] She did, however, keep letters from important literary figures

---

[13] Her letter to Gertrude Bugler of 28 February 1926 (Bugler) begins 'I was burning last year's letters'. She also told Siegfried Sassoon (Thursday, [July 1923], Eton) that she would have burned the letters written to Hardy by Florence Henniker had it not seemed 'an act of treachery to a dead friend'.

and from particular friends, and after her death several groups of such letters were sent to the saleroom along with the bulk of the Max Gate library.[14] A number of Hardy's exceptionally relaxed and intimate letters to her also survived, if sometimes in fragmentary form, but in the very last week of her life she specifically asked her sister, Margaret Soundy, to destroy the letter he had written to her immediately before their marriage—though the empty envelope exists still.[15] Florence Hardy's relatives, indeed, though respectful of her husband's letters—most of them passed on to Richard Purdy over the years—were essentially of one mind in destroying such personal documents of her own as came into their possession, with the result that only a handful of family letters survive, none of them of early date. In fact, the earliest letter of any kind that has as yet been discovered is her 20 November 1906 application for a ticket to the British Museum Reading Room in order to do research for *The Dynasts*. Like her predecessor, therefore, by the time she makes her first appearance in this edition she has already come permanently within Hardy's orbit.

It has been unfortunate for Florence Hardy's posthumous reputation that a little group of letters written by Miss Dugdale to Mrs Hardy in 1910 and 1911 should have been among those selected for preservation by her own solicitor and executor when rooting through the Max Gate attics following her client's death. It is striking, given the many tales of Max Gate bonfires, that Emma Hardy's papers should have survived so long; still more striking, on the face of it, that Florence Hardy, whose 24 February 1934 letter mentions the existence of 'boxes of letters & bills even which belonged to the first Mrs Hardy', should never have looked out and destroyed those letters of her own that have since been deemed discreditable. It seems perfectly possible, however, that she had either forgotten them or remembered them without embarrassment. Awareness of Florence Dugdale's longstanding relationship with Hardy during his first wife's lifetime has undoubtedly served to throw a somewhat lurid light over everything she said and did during that sensitive period, but to suspect her of disingenuousness is easier than to convict her of it.

What the letters show is that Florence Dugdale was 'taken up' by Emma Hardy in the summer of 1910, spent several weeks at Max Gate that autumn, and devoted a good deal of time, both there and back home in Enfield, to typing up the older woman's stories, poems, and religious writings and

---

[14] Hodgson & Co., cat. 16 of 1937–8, lots 297, 300 (122 from Barrie), 301 (6 from Galsworthy), 302, 304 (6 from Masefield), 305, 306, 307 (25 from Charlotte Mew), 308 (25 from Sassoon), 309 (40 from T. E. Lawrence).

[15] Information from the late Richard Purdy; the envelope is in the Beinecke Library.

attempting to get them published. Although occasionally voicing reservations about details of what she was being asked to read and type, she wrote always as an admiring assistant and ally, praising prose and poetry alike and predicting particular 'triumph' for 'The Inspirer', evidently a story about a wife who was in some sense responsible for her husband's literary achievements. But Emma Hardy was by this date already well advanced in eccentricity, and if some degree of pretence was being practised upon her it seems in fact to have been kindly meant. Knowledge, again, of Florence Dugdale's later agnosticism might seem to throw doubt on the readiness with which she seconded Emma Hardy's fervent anti-Catholicism (e.g. in the letter of 11 December 1910), were it not that she was currently conducting an Anglican Bible class in Enfield. Her attraction to Hardy seems in any case to have originated in a sufficiently familiar blend of hero-worship, literary aspiration, and yearning to be of use, admixed with a certain element of self-interest, and while her dealings with Hardy's wife were certainly less than transparent, it is by no means certain that they were complicated by sexual guilt or by any thought of one day becoming the mistress of Max Gate.

Very relevant here are the strikingly indiscreet letters she was writing to Edward Clodd during roughly the same period. Clodd, for many years Hardy's closest male confidant, had entertained Hardy and his 'young cousin' together at his house in Aldeburgh on more than one occasion while Emma Hardy was still alive, and he evidently shared with Florence Dugdale a kind of sympathetic scepticism towards what she on one occasion called 'the Max Gate ménage'. Her letters to Clodd certainly reflect a gradual cooling towards Emma Hardy, who seemed to become steadily 'queerer' even while demanding more and more time and attention, but on 11 November 1910 she could still speak of the older woman's ever-increasing kindness towards herself and exclaim: 'I am *intensely* sorry for her, sorry indeed for both.'

Later letters to Clodd indicate that Florence Dugdale by no means saw marriage to the widowed Hardy as a foregone conclusion, but she certainly spent substantial amounts of time at Max Gate after Emma Hardy's death and allowed herself to become gradually absorbed into its deeply settled rhythms. By June 1913 she had already embarked upon the long correspondence with Sydney (later Sir Sydney) Cockerell that provides, despite so many unavoidable omissions, at once the core and much of the substance of the present edition. Cockerell, director of the Fitzwilliam Museum at Cambridge, had made his first visit to Max Gate in 1911 and immediately succeeded in persuading Hardy to distribute the bulk of his literary manuscripts to selected institutional libraries. Impressed and gratified by so prompt and efficient a resolution of what he had himself seen as a vexing problem, Hardy welcomed

Cockerell at Max Gate on many subsequent occasions, relied increasingly on his experience and expertise, and eventually chose him as one of his literary executors—the other being Florence Hardy herself.

She too learned to turn to Cockerell for assistance of all kinds, from getting a locket made to overseeing the production of her limited-edition pamphlets of Hardy's poems, and her letters to him dwell so often upon practical matters—Hardy's health usually foremost among them—that they constitute for considerable periods almost a day-by-day account of Max Gate events and concerns. They also show an attractive combination of domestic responsibility and personal independence interspersed from time to time with low-spirited complaints about her husband's persistent work-absorption, selective sociability, and occasional stubbornness and tightfisted-ness. The relationship with Cockerell was at one level close and almost conspiratorial, in that Hardy cannot have read or been intended to read much of what passed between them. But there was always an element of tension—Cockerell's low opinion of his correspondent's intelligence playing silently off against her instinctive distrust of his male assertiveness—and once Hardy was dead and the literary executorship in force Cockerell no longer troubled to keep the friendship in good repair.

Another of Florence Hardy's long-running obligations was maintenance of the Max Gate correspondence with Rebekah Owen, but in attempting to cope with the constant flow of inquisitive letters from a woman she scarcely knew she fell promptly into essentially the same traps as her predecessor had done, verbalizing whatever came most handily to mind and often rambling on until she reached and then transgressed the boundaries of discretion. At the same time, she too seems in her isolation—from friends, from parents and sisters, and even from a husband who spent so much of each day secluded in his study—to have found an appropriately solitary if sometimes risky release in the writing of letters, almost irrespective of their intended recipient. It was to Rebekah Owen, a notorious gossip, that she rashly revealed (on 3 November 1916) her instinctive dislike and distrust of Sydney Cockerell, only to reverse her judgements in the next letter and beg that its predecessor be destroyed—as of course it was not. Ironically, it was also in writing to Rebekah Owen that she repeated some relevant advice that Hardy had once given her but that she rarely observed in her own practice: 'Letters, my husband says, are a dangerous medium—one writes things that may be taken in a wrong sense when there is no saving smile, no inflexion of the voice to help. I believe I write most injudiciously to people I like and trust.'[16]

---

[16] Florence Hardy to Rebekah Owen, 25 August 1916 (Colby College).

Where the abundant availability of Florence Hardy's letters to Rebekah Owen and, especially, to Sydney Cockerell has mandated an editorial policy of severe selectivity, quite a different problem has been presented by her letters to Gertrude Bugler—the young and beautiful Dorset actress to whom Hardy became increasingly attracted as she played such parts as Marty South, Eustacia Vye, and Tess Durbeyfield in dramatizations of his novels produced in Dorchester by the so-called 'Hardy Players'. In this instance the gradual development of the relationship between the two women over a period of years has seemed to demand the inclusion of occasional letters (not all of them to Gertrude Bugler herself) primarily for the sake of maintaining a sense of continuity—or of permitting the juxtaposition of the different things Florence Hardy sometimes said to different people at roughly the same moment in time. She does not emerge well from this fuller exposure of the manœuvres by which she succeeded in preventing Gertrude Bugler from appearing in the first London production of Hardy's stage version of *Tess of the d'Urbervilles*. Bewildered by her husband's absorption in the play and in Gertrude Bugler herself, despairing at the contrast between the sexual appeal of her 'rival' and what she perhaps too harshly regarded as her own plainness and charmlessness,[17] terrified not just of ridicule and embarrassment but of actually losing her husband and her function in life, she struck out wildly, bringing to bear a battery of accusations, threats, sisterly pleadings, and invocations of Hardy's health and reputation that the younger woman was simply powerless to resist.

Gertrude Bugler's side of the correspondence has of course disappeared, but it is evident from the drafts and copies she sometimes kept that she had little real awareness of what was going on, either in fact or in Florence Hardy's imagination. Of the latter's behaviour it seems fair to say that its extravagance is significantly illuminated, if hardly excused, by the experience of reading her letters to Gertrude Bugler alongside her other correspondences and within the context of an accumulated sense of life at Max Gate. She also had an opportunity for partial and belated reparation when *Tess* was revived in the West End after Hardy's death and she put herself out to ensure that Gertrude Bugler was not only given the heroine's part but properly paid, suitably accommodated, and discreetly warned of the dangers of theatrical life.

In times of stress—the episodes involving Gertrude Bugler, for example, or the aftermath of Hardy's death—Florence Hardy was distressingly capable of open and sometimes extreme expressions of anger and resentment,

---

[17] '[M]y glass tells me I look painfully plain and old', she told Rebekah Owen on 29 July 1917 (Colby College).

even when writing to her most valued friends. For the most part, however, her letters show her in a happier light—a notable instance being her correspondence with Charlotte Mew, whose poems she admired and whose personal difficulties she deplored and respected and tried unobtrusively to relieve. If a somewhat gushing class-consciousness too often invades her letters to Lady Hoare of Stourhead—at one period a correspondent almost as insistent as Rebekah Owen—she generally demonstrates better judgement as to both content and tone when writing to Siegfried Sassoon and E. M. Forster, although neither man perhaps took her entirely seriously, hence entirely kindly: 'I know how you feel about E. M. Forster,' she wrote to Lady Ottoline Morrell in mid-July 1930. 'I have had *such-like* experiences with so many of T.H.'s friends—so much kindness & sympathy at times, & then silence & long neglect. I often wonder whether selfishness is not at the back of most friendships.' But it is difficult to arrive at any balanced assessment of Florence Hardy as a letter-writer—or, indeed, to judge her in more comprehensive terms—when so few examples are available of her writing in relaxed and confident mood to someone of whose interest, trust, and affection she felt wholly assured. There are no surviving letters to Hardy or to her much-loved parents, a mere half-dozen or so to other family members, and scarcely more to any of her intimate women friends—those to Ethel Inglis, to whom she was particularly close during the early years of her marriage, unfortunately remaining untraced,[18] although they were apparently preserved.

The record of her later correspondence is further depleted by the lack of letters to Sir James Barrie and T. E. Lawrence, the two men who meant most to her in the years following her husband's death. Letters *to* her from both Barrie and Lawrence certainly survive, and in some quantity, but her own letters to Barrie were apparently destroyed, while those to Lawrence seem now to be represented by just three typed transcripts of lost originals. Nor do any personal letters as yet discovered reflect at all adequately her conscientious discharge of voluntarily accepted local responsibilities as a Justice of the Peace, as a member of the Dorchester Hospital Management Committee, and as chairman of the Mill Street Housing Society, although the edition does include one of two letters she wrote to *The Times* about housing problems in general and the progress of the Mill Street scheme in particular.

It is at least clear that Florence Hardy found useful occupation in her widowhood, quite apart from the protection of her husband's literary

---

[18] Apart from a single example at the University of Northern Illinois, kindly brought to my attention by Professor W. W. Morgan.

remains, and that several valued friends did remain faithful, among them Barrie (despite his failure to make the proposal of marriage she seems at one time to have expected), Lawrence, Dorothy Allhusen, and Max and Florence Beerbohm, whom she visited in Rapallo. Even Forster did not completely disappear and Sassoon fitfully kept up a relationship always a little prickly on both sides. Her sense of isolation was further moderated by the development of new friendships—with Stephen Tennant, for example, first introduced by Sassoon, with Sir Arthur Pinero, the dramatist, at times almost lovingly addressed, with Adelaide Phillpotts, Eden Phillpotts' daughter and collaborator, with Wilfred Partington, the literary journalist, her escort to the cinema on at least one occasion, and with John Cowper Powys, the novelist, whom she urged not to delete a single line from the lengthening manuscript of *A Glastonbury Romance*. She was also helpful to and corresponded with several people whom she judged to be seriously interested in her husband's work, chief among them two young transatlantic visitors—Richard Purdy and Frederick B. Adams—whose scholarly interests had happily brought them to Max Gate at a time when house, garden, and Hardy's study all remained very much as they had been in Hardy's lifetime.

Max Gate, indeed, and the never-resolved question of its eventual fate, became a recurring theme of the letters written by Florence Hardy subsequent to her husband's death. She shared repeatedly with the collector Howard Bliss her painful uncertainties as to her responsibilities as custodian of her husband's literary remains—the issue over which her long and complex relationship with Sydney Cockerell finally collapsed into acrimony and silence—and many even of her newest correspondents were directly or indirectly consulted as to whether or not she ought to continue living at Max Gate and how, in any case, she should dispose of it in her will. At that date the Scotch pines Hardy had planted still stood thick and dark around the house and its garden, and while his widow could still be moved by the summer beauty of the place she more often spoke as if in terror of its winter gloom and isolation—which of course meant, since the deaths of Hardy and of the dog Wessex, its aching loneliness. On 26 October 1930 she wrote to John Cowper Powys: 'It is late at night—or what I call late—in this silent house—a clock ticking near me—in the room where we have so often sat together with T.H. & it is rather like a grave. Do you know his poem "The House of Silence", which begins "This is a quiet place"? It described Max Gate then, & even more aptly describes it now—when I am the phantom left alone.' She was sorely tempted to move away altogether and did in fact rent a series of London apartments for limited periods, only

to find that she could not in practice abandon a place so profoundly associated with Hardy and his work—indeed, with her own marriage and everything that had given meaning and purpose to her life.

Nor was her husband the only lingering presence at Max Gate: 'Today
is the 22nd anniversary of the death of E.L.H.', she wrote to Howard Bliss
on 27 November 1934,[19] '& she has been in my mind all day—& I have been
up in the sad little attic where she died—still full of her presence.' Florence
Hardy had always been painfully conscious of her status as a second wife—
telling Sassoon in 1922 that she disliked being called 'Mrs Hardy' because
the name 'always seems to belong to someone else, whom I knew for
several years, & I am oppressed by the thought that I am living in *her*
house, using *her* things—&, worst of all, have even stolen her name'.[20] Nor
could she quite forgive that first wife for becoming, in the 'Poems of 1912–
13', so profoundly and so publicly the object of Hardy's retrospective devotion. In later years, however, she more than once alluded to Emma Hardy
in sympathetic terms, as if increasingly recognizing, during the many backward glances of her widowhood, how much there might be in common,
not so much between her predecessor's fretful vitality and her own tend-
ency to melancholic resignation as between their experiences of marriage
to Thomas Hardy—a great writer whose primary loyalties were to the
work that he so conscientiously pursued to the last days of his long life. To
that extent the two sets of letters in this edition can be seen not only in
terms of their obvious contrasts but as jointly offering a many-sided impression of literary marriage and a poignant demonstration of the rewards and,
more especially, the costs of finding oneself cast—to quote the heading of
one of Florence Hardy's obituaries—as 'the helpmate of genius'.[21]

---

[19] Princeton University.
[20] Letter of 30 June 1922 (Eton College).
[21] *The Times*, 18 October 1937, 16.

Editorial Procedures

THE letters of Emma and Florence Hardy selected for inclusion in this volume have been edited on essentially the same principles—and annotated in at least as much depth—as the documents printed in *The Collected Letters of Thomas Hardy*, edited by Richard Little Purdy and Michael Millgate and published in seven volumes by the Clarendon Press between 1978 and 1988.

The specific policies adopted for the present edition have been to reproduce all documents in their entirety (except where they survive only in fragmentary form), to follow precisely the texts of holograph letters (including all errors and eccentricities of spelling), and to correct only inarguable errors occurring in typed letters, the actual readings (other than omissions of single letters as a result of inadequate key pressure or the mechanical action of the right-hand margin stop) being recorded in the notes. Addresses, dates, salutations, valedictions, signatures, postscripts, and postscript initials are standardized as to position and layout (but not as to wording); stamped or printed letterheads are rendered in small capitals; letterhead elements supplementary to the address (e.g. telephone numbers or alternative addresses) are omitted, as are letterheads recurring on sheets of stationery subsequent to the first; and underlinings are rendered as italics, double underlinings as full capitals, except that no attempt has been made to reproduce lines and flourishes appearing beneath final signatures.

Eccentricities of punctuation (e.g. both Emma and Florence Hardy sometimes open a quotation with a single quotation mark and close it with a double, or vice versa) have been transferred to print as closely as possible, except that Emma Hardy's occasional superscripts are brought down to the line, accidentally omitted periods are silently supplied, and dashes (normally reproduced as such even when only minimally inscribed) are read as periods whenever followed by what seems unmistakably a new sentence beginning with a capital letter. Supplied and speculative dates and other editorial matter appear within square brackets, but when alterations, annotations, or other markings have been made on a manuscript by someone other than its author, such intrusions, although sometimes mentioned in the notes, are not reflected in the edited text. This latter issue arises chiefly with Florence Hardy's letters to Sydney Cockerell, someone—possibly Cockerell himself—having gone through almost the entire series in order to identify, by crayon marks on the documents themselves, the passages to be omitted from any given letter in the event of its publication. Because the resulting texts of the Florence Hardy letters printed in *Friends of a Lifetime: Letters to Sydney Carlyle*

Cockerell, edited by Viola Meynell (London: Jonathan Cape, 1940), are often radically incomplete it has seemed both useful and appropriate to include re-edited texts of several of those same letters in the present volume.

At the conclusion of each letter the copy-text is described and located and the basis specified for any supplied or speculative dating. Explanatory notes, together with any textual notes required, then follow in a single block, keyed to the text not by numbers but by cue-words—thus permitting the letter itself to be kept free of intrusive superscripts. The recipients of letters and other persons mentioned are identified at the time of their first appearance, although those who are at first only mentioned but later reappear as recipients may be further described in a note or headnote to the first letter addressed to them. Location of information relevant to more than one letter is in any case assisted by generous cross-referencing and by the provision of a comprehensive index.

Abbreviations

ELG/ELH	Emma Lavinia Gifford/Hardy
FED/FEH	Florence Emily Dugdale/Hardy
TH	Thomas Hardy
Adams	Personal collection of Frederick B. Adams
Beinecke	Beinecke Library, Yale University
Berg	Berg Collection, New York Public Library
BL	British Library
Bugler	Papers of the late Gertrude Bugler
Colby	Colby College, Waterville, Maine
DCM	Dorset County Museum, Dorchester, Dorset
Eton	Eton College, School Library
Fawcett	Fawcett Library, London
Huntington	Huntington Library, San Marino, California
Leeds	Brotherton Collection, Leeds University
Millgate	Personal collection of Michael Millgate
Texas	Harry Ransom Humanities Research Center, University of Texas
Biography	Michael Millgate, *Thomas Hardy: A Biography* (Oxford: Oxford University Press, 1982)
CL	*The Collected Letters of Thomas Hardy*, ed. Richard L. Purdy and Michael Millgate, 7 vols. (Oxford: Clarendon Press, 1978–88)
Life and Work	Thomas Hardy, *The Life and Work of Thomas Hardy*, ed. Michael Millgate (London: Macmillan, 1984)
Purdy	Richard Little Purdy, *Thomas Hardy: A Bibliographical Study* (London: Oxford University Press, 1954)
Some Recollections	Emma Hardy, *Some Recollections*, ed. Evelyn Hardy and Robert Gittings (London: Oxford University Press, 1961)
Weber	Carl J. Weber, *Hardy and the Lady from Madison Square* (Waterville, Maine: Colby College Press, 1952)
Wessex	Wessex Edition: *The Works of Thomas Hardy in Prose and Verse*, 24 vols. (London: Macmillan, 1912–31)

Letters of Emma Lavinia Hardy

[It is not known exactly when Thomas Hardy and Emma Lavinia Gifford became formally engaged, but their courtship extended for four and a half years, from their original encounter at St Juliot in March 1870 to their marriage in a London suburb in September 1874. Because they were rarely together during those years—ELG remaining for the most part in Cornwall, TH in Dorset or London—letters became of supreme importance, and it is clear that an extensive correspondence passed between them, one that TH in later years thought worthy of comparison with the love-letters of Robert Browning and Elizabeth Barrett. No portion of that correspondence is now extant, but one of TH's surviving notebooks does preserve tiny fragments from two of ELG's letters, one written some five months after they first met, the other just two months before their marriage.]

To Thomas Hardy

[24? October 1870]

. . . This dream of my life—no, not dream, for what is actually going on around me seems a dream rather. . . . I take him (the reserved man) as I do the Bible; find out what I can, compare one text with another, & believe the rest in a lump of simple faith.

Text   Pencil transcription in TH's hand, 'Memoranda I' notebook, fos. 7–8 (DCM).   *Date*   The entry, dated 25 October 1870, refers to 'E's letter of yesterday'.
around me: ELG was living with her sister Helen and Helen's husband the Revd Caddell Holder (1803?–1882) in the Rectory at St Juliot, Cornwall, where TH had met her the previous March; see *Life and Work*, 66–78.   *the reserved man*: evidently a reference to TH himself; see Richard H. Taylor (ed.), *The Personal Notebooks of Thomas Hardy* (London: Macmillan, 1978), 6 and n., and *Biography*, 124, 131. The sentence 'I take . . . faith' was absorbed, slightly revised, into chap. 19 of *A Pair of Blue Eyes* (Wessex, 208–9), serialized Feb. 1873.

To Thomas Hardy

[July 1874]

My work, unlike your work of writing, does not occupy my true mind much. . . .

Your novel seems sometimes like a child all your own & none of me.

Text   Pencil transcription in TH's hand, 'Memoranda I' notebook, fo. 33 (DCM).   *Date*   From date of entry, 'July 1874'.
My work: it is not certain what ELG was doing nor even where she was living at this date; the memorial tablet in St Juliot Church, designed by TH, refers to her residence at St Juliot as ending in 1873.   *Your novel*: *Far from the Madding Crowd*, serialized in the *Cornhill Magazine*, Jan.–Dec. 1874.

[ELG seems to have made a fair copy of the greater part of TH's novel *Desperate Remedies* in the autumn of 1870, and although that particular manuscript has not survived the available manuscripts of other novels provide ample evidence of her having continued after their marriage to assist him in his literary career. Although TH's first wife never acted as his secretary to the extent that his second was later to do, she did from time to time copy out portions of his manuscripts, enter items into his notebooks, make fair copies of letters for his signature, and conduct correspondence on his behalf.]

To Ada Rehan

ALEXANDRA CLUB, | 12, GROSVENOR ST. W.

July 16. 90

Dear Miss Rehan,

Just a word of warm congratulation on last night's success. The papers cannot say too much in praise of your delightful impersonation of Rosalind— I, for my part, was entranced by it. I hope I may see you again in it at some time & that I may have the great pleasure of meeting you.

My husband wishes me to remind you that he said when he came round to see you that it was going to be a success: he had spoken to some of the critics & they were of the same opinion.

Believe me

Yours sincerely

Emma L. Hardy

Do take plenty of rest, & don't let society wear you out as it will try to do.

Text MS. (Max Gate address struck through) Folger Shakespeare Library.
Alexandra Club: a London women's club of which ELH was a member. *Rehan*: Ada Rehan (1860–1916), American actress visiting London as a leading member of Augustin Daly's company. *of Rosalind*: TH and ELH had attended the first night of Daly's production of *As You Like It* at the Lyceum Theatre; ELH's comments upon the occasion are very similar to those recorded, at some length, in TH's *Life and Work*, 238–9.

[Rebekah Owen, a devoted American admirer of TH and his work, first visited Dorchester in company with her sister Catharine in the summer of 1892; later the two women moved permanently to England, taking a large house at Hawkshead in the Lake District. Although Rebekah Owen is treated as a figure of importance in Carl J. Weber's *Hardy and the Lady from Madison Square*, it seems clear that TH himself soon wearied of her inquisitive attentions, leaving it increasingly to ELH—and later to FEH—to keep up the Max Gate side of the connection and its associated correspondence. ELH's use of black-edged stationery for her 1892 letters was an act of mourning, conventional at that period, for TH's father, who died in July of 1892.]

To Rebekah Owen

Max Gate
Aug. 31. | 1892

My dear Miss רִבְקָה,

We will come to tea with you with pleasure on Thursday, *if fine* & then we can talk over the enterprise about Winterbourne. It is one I feel very eager for, & hope nothing will set aside. I am expecting to go to a garden party on Saturday, but the weather may still be in a boisterous mood & prevent my going. Last Monday evening Mr Barnes had donned his *evening suit*, & half-ascended his bycicle, with misgivings in his mind about his *sails* behind interfering with his locomotion when the rain fell suddenly again in torrents, & ended his difficulties & our chance of seeing him that evening. He & his wife will come one afternoon to tea & then you must meet them.

Yours very sincerely
E. L. Hardy

With kind regards to Miss Owen & yourself dear Rebekah.

Text   MS. (correspondence card with envelope, mourning stationery) Colby.
Max Gate: the house, just outside Dorchester, into which TH and ELH had moved in June 1885; it was designed by TH himself and built by his father and brother.   *Owen*: Rebekah Owen (1858–1939), daughter of a New York businessman (Weber, II, 225); named Rebecca at birth, she later preferred what she called the 'Hebrew' spelling, Rebekah (Weber, 19), and ELH on this one occasion made the gesture of employing actual Hebrew characters. *Winterbourne*: a visit was evidently being planned to the Dorset hamlet of Winterbourne (or Winterborne) Came, where the Revd William Barnes, the dialect poet, had been rector until his death in 1886; R. Owen was preparing an index to his poems (Weber, 97).   *Mr Barnes*: Barnes's son, the Revd William Miles Barnes (1840–1916), rector of Winterborne Monkton; his wife was named Emily.   *Miss Owen*: ELH observes correct 'form' in so identifying Catharine Owen (1851–1914, née Catherine), the elder of the two sisters (Weber, 9, 178).

To Rebekah Owen

MAX GATE—
Sept. 10—[1893]

Dear Miss Rebekah Owen,

I am sorry I missed you yesterday afternoon—in fact we *crossed*—as letters do. I shall be home from 4 o'clock to-morrow afternoon—perhaps you & your sister can walk out again. I have engaged the pony-carriage— for Woodbury Hill fair—it seems rather inadequate for the journey, but the waggonette was previously engaged, & we must have mercy on the beast & walk up the hills I suppose. Anyway *he* goes, Old tells me—& he will certainly have a better time with us—at least I think so. This refers to the pony & not the man—& it will be delightful *if fine*.

With kind regards

Yours very sincerely

E. L. Hardy—

Text MS. (70 Hamilton Terrace address struck through: see *CL*, ii. 7 n.) Colby.

missed you: the Owen sisters had walked out to Max Gate the previous day, found ELH away from home, and left a message suggesting an expedition to Woodbury Hill fair, the 'original' of Greenhill Fair in Hardy's *Far from the Madding Crowd*; the fair was always held, just outside Bere Regis, during the week in which 21 Sept. fell.   *Old*: presumably George Old of West Stafford, a blacksmith who also hired out horse-drawn vehicles.

To Mary Haweis

MAX GATE, | DORCHESTER.

November 13. [1894]

My dear Mrs Haweis,

I have been so long replying—but we have the workmen about altering our kitchens & are obliged to stay through it on account of my husband's writing. His interest in the Suffrage Cause is nil, in spite of "Tess" & his opinions on the woman question not in her favour. He understands only the women he *invents*—the others not at all—& he only writes for *Art*, though ethics show up.

I believe it would be quite delightful for me to belong to the Society— but I don't know exactly what the "National Central' has for its object, please do enlighten me—the fee is not a large me.

I am interested in Mrs Ormiston Chant, her proceedings & her faith in the possibility of purifying London—if only she would organize a crusade to clear the young men from the streets—to attack them rather than the women—how she would do it!

We had a very charming entertainment here—A Singing in Character of "Songs of the West"—a collection made by Baring Gould, songs which were supplanted by Music Hall vulgarities—exquisite poetical pieces. The coun- try is so charming if you can keep the sound of London out of it—a sad sweetness & deeper thought is here—& after all—inventions & novelties travel up from the provinces to town & are not *born* there—often.

I wish your party may win. No doubt canvassing shows up character. Don't forget to tell me more about your Society.
Believe me
Dear Mrs Haweis

Yours very sincerely—
Emma L. Hardy.

Text MS. (Alexandra Club address also present: see letter of 16 July 1890) Univ. of British Columbia.   *Date* Year supplied in another hand.
Haweis: Mary Haweis (d. 1898), wife of the Revd Hugh Reginald Haweis, a popular preacher and author; she was an artist of some note and active in women's suffrage and other causes. *"National Central"*: evidently the National Society for Women's Suffrage; for ELH's later involvement in the suffrage movement see letter of 27 Sept. 1909.   *Chant*: Laura Ormiston Chant, née Dibbin (1848–1923), crusader for the social-purity movement and editor of the *Vigilance Record*, was currently campaigning against the parading of prostitutes in the London music-halls; her pamphlet, *Why We Attacked the Empire*, was pub. in late 1894 or early 1895. *entertainment*: a Dorchester performance, by the 'Songs of the West' company, of folk-songs from the Revd Sabine Baring-Gould's collection, *Songs and Ballads of the West*.   *canvassing*: presumably for the London School Board election of 22 Nov. 1894.

[Although its immediate occasion cannot be established—TH was in London by himself at the time and Emma had gone to Brighton to recuperate from an attack of eczema or shingles (*CL*, ii. 111, 112)—the following remarkable letter is powerfully eloquent of the bitter hostility between ELH and TH's family and of ELH's sense that they, even more than her husband himself, were the instigators and perpetuators of her marital difficulties.]

To Mary Hardy

Worthing Sussex
Feb. 22. [1896]

Miss Hardy

I dare you, or any one to spread evil reports of me—such as that I have been unkind to your brother, (which you actually said to my face,) or that I have "errors" in my mind, (which you have also said to me,) and I hear that you repeat to others.

Your brother has been outrageously unkind to me—which is *entirely your* fault: ever since I have been his wife you have done all you can to make division between us; also, you have set your family against me, though neither you nor they can truly say that I have ever been anything but, just, considerate, & kind towards you all, notwithstanding frequent low insults.

As you are in the habit of saying of people whom you dislike that they are "mad" you should, & may well, fear, least the same be said of you; what you mete out to others shall be meted to you again; & I have, heard you say it myself, of people. I defy you ever to say such a thing of me or for you, or any one, to say that I have done anything that can be called unreasonable, or wrong, or mad, or *even unkind*! And it is a wicked, spiteful & most malicious habit of yours.

Now—what right have you to assert that I have been no "help" to my husband? That statement, false & injurious, as it is, you have constantly repeated without warrant or knowledge of the matter.

How would you like to have your life made difficult for you by anyone saying, for instance, that you are a very unsuitable person to have the instruction of young people?

You have ever been my causeless enemy—causeless, except that I stand in the way of your evil ambition to be on the same level with your brother by trampling upon me. If you did not know, & pander to his many weaknesses, & have secured him on your side by your crafty ways, you could not have done me the irreparable mischief you have. And doubtless you are elated that you have spoilt my life as you love power of any kind, but you have spoilt your brother's & your own punishment must inevitably follow— for God's promises are true for ever.

You are a witch-like creature & quite equal to any amount of evil-wishing & speaking—I can imagine you, & your mother & sister on your native heath raising a storm on a Walpurgis night.

You have done irreparable harm but now your power is at an end.

E.

If you will acknowledge your evil pride & spite & change your ways I am capable of forgiving you though I cannot forget or trust your nature but I can understand your desire to be considered cleverer than I which you may be I allow.

Doubtles you will send this on to your brother but it will not affect me, if you do as he will know from me that I have written thus to you—which I consider a duty to myself.

Text   MS. (with envelope) H. E. F. Lock.   *Date* Year from postmark.
what you mete . . . again: cf. Luke 6: 38.   *young people*: Mary Hardy was headmistress of the Bell Street junior girls' school in Dorchester, although she resigned on grounds of ill health in April 1897 (*Dorset County Chronicle*, 8 Apr. 1897).

To Rebekah Owen

MAX GATE, | DORCHESTER.
Feb. 19. 1897

My dear Miss Betty Owen,

What a pleasure it must be to you & your sister to be in your own home again after so long an absence. I am glad you are enjoying some social gatherings or if not enjoying, getting to-gether your perceptions & impressions—perhaps for future use. For my part I have but small energy for our usual spring flitting to London—for dressmakers milliners, luncheons & dinners, though daily invitations call to us to make haste & return to our haunts, perhaps my disinclination may in part be attributable to a recent and somewhat prolonged attack of rheumatism & neuralgia. We are all going frantic this year about honouring the Queen—there is nothing to be named or talked of but "Diamond Jubilee" "Victoria the Good" & Celebrations.' I suppose London will be blocked everywhere & we shall be all staring at each other. "Tess" is to be performed in Philadelphia on March 2nd. Here also in London on the same day in a casual way merely to secure copyright. The play differs fundamentally from the story & T.H. does not much care for it—he goes to Town in a week—so do not I. T.H. has "moved" his Study for the *fourth* time in this house; he goes bit by bit, & book by book, leaving a room unfit for use till the workmen have been!

Our new maid has the footfall of an earthquake! and daily crashes the china—*placidly*! but she is sweet-tempered & sweet to look at. The "boy" who says he has been a page, gapes at the visitors, & hardly gets them in, or out, of the house. You certainly found me at a disadvantage, on account of our travels late in the autumn & so long absence from home. I have been reading John Gabriel Borkman. Ibsen has excelled himself in it—pathetic, powerful & true to the characters in their positions. A friend of ours has sent us some translations of the classics which he has edited—I have always liked latin prose translations from a girl. I shall be a subscriber to *Mudie* in the summer—strangely enough we begin when we are in Town—& not here at all, we have so many books & periodials to read here. You left behind you two pages of the "Outlook." Shall I send them? I have just finished Le Gallienne's "Golden Girl"—which he has *just* published almost the day he married. It is exquisitely poetical at the beginning—crisply amusing in the middle, though somewhat licentious—& very pathetic at the end—which is quite unexpected. But the *plan* is a judicious blending of Sterne's Senti: journey—& T.H's Pursuit of the W. Beloved. Le Gallienne

9

is quite a *beauty* himself with a kind of Shelly face—& he knows this. I wonder what his bride is like. Anent Mrs Shelley she was a little of the minx kind to fly into his arms as she did whilst Harriet was still out of the depths of water (if not of misery). It strikes me that I ought to have an Author's wives *day* occasionally I wonder if we should get mixed in our words & phrases like your Mrs Lister. One thing I abhor in Authors. It is their blank materialism—(neither do I like Corelli-ism) I get irritated at their pride of intellect—& as I get older I am more interested in ameliorations & schemes for banishing the thickening clouds of evil advancing. I do not care for art for art's sake alone. Yet a friend cannot persuade me to get T.H. to write to Zola to bring out a book on antivivisection. I will not because I know that he would n't do it—& I do not want T.H. to be hand in glove with *Zola!* Alas! that *you* are a Jude-*ite* I really ought not to countenance you though you are my New York correspondent. However I will add photographer to my shopping list next summer,

Believe me

Yours very sincerely
Emma Hardy.

My wrist has the gout still.

Kind regards to your sister. I scarcely believe in *your* housekeeping with such a *life-easing* sister as yours.

Text   MS. (with envelope) Colby.

Betty Owen: R. Owen apparently adopted this short form of her name (via 'Becky') in the mid-1890s (Weber, 110).   *spring flitting*: the Hardys were accustomed each spring to rent a London house or flat for two or three months of the 'season', but in 1897, deterred by the high prices generated by the approaching celebration of Victoria's sixty years as queen, they took a house in Basingstoke and travelled to and from the city by train.   *"Tess"*: this dramatization of TH's novel, drastically revised by Lorimer Stoddard from a version prepared by TH himself, was first performed not in Philadelphia but at the Fifth Avenue Theater, New York, on 2 Mar. 1897; on the same date the text was read, for copyright purposes only, at the St James's Theatre, London. See *CL*, ii. 149, 152.   *Borkman*: the English translation by William Archer had just been published.   *friend of ours*: Alfred Pretor (1840–1908), classical scholar, fellow of St Catharine's College, Cambridge; the first vol. of his edition of *The Letters of Cicero to Atticus* was pub. in 1897. His collection of stories, *Ronald and I* (Cambridge, 1899), is dedicated to ELH.   *Mudie*: Mudie's Select Library, the largest of the circulating libraries.   *"Outlook"*: a New York magazine, previously called the *Christian Union*.   *Le Gallienne's*: Richard Le Gallienne (1866–1947), poet, essayist, and novelist; his second marriage (to Julie Norregard in 1897) was later dissolved. In his novel, *The Quest of the Golden Girl* (London: John Lane, 1896), the first-person narrator goes on a 'pilgrimage' in search of 'the mystical Golden Girl' (6) who will be his ideal wife.   *Senti: journey*: Laurence Sterne's *A Sentimental Journey Through France and Italy* (1767).   *Pursuit . . . Beloved*: i.e. the serial version (1892) of the novel, *The Well-Beloved*, which TH had revised and was about to pub. in volume form.　　*Shelly*: i.e. Percy Bysshe Shelley, the poet.　　*Mrs Shelley*: Mary Godwin; Harriet (née Westbrook), Shelley's first wife, committed suicide by drowning.　　*Mrs Lister*: presumably a malapropistic servant.　　*Corelli-ism*: ELH first wrote 'Corellism'; the reference is to the romantic writings of Marie Corelli, the pseudonym of Mary Mackay (1855–1924).　　*Zola*: Émile Zola (1840–1902), the French novelist; ELH evidently shared the popular view of Zola's work as sordid and brutal but knew that TH had joined in protesting against the imprisonment of Henry Vizetelly, Zola's British publisher, in 1888. The suggestion that TH might approach Zola over the anti-vivisection issue apparently originated with Florence Henniker; see *CL*, ii. 148, and (for Henniker) FED's letter of 11 Dec. 1911.　　*a Jude-ite*: an admirer of *Jude the Obscure*, a novel by which ELH had felt personally offended.　　*My wrist . . . still.*: marginal insertion alongside an untidily written portion of the letter's final paragraph.

To Edward Clodd

MAX GATE, | DORCHESTER.
March 29. 1897

Dear Mr Clodd,

Will you pardon my writing to you on the subject of your last book.

The chapters I greatly object to, are those with which you seem to have taken so much pains to say—There is no God—there is no Christ. And you also endeavour to take from the latter his best human as well as divine attributes.

And then—why do you say "a doubtful story" at page 39? It is to be remembered that whatever conclusions Darwin arrived at, he yet never distinctly denied the existence of a Supreme Thought or Word—which we designate God—though he was much pressed to do so.

Of course nothing that a Materialist explains to a Christian on this subject alters his opinion in the least. Once his faith is firmly fixed he stands on the safest altitude possible; & scorn cast upon him could be easily repaid by men of the highest intellectual powers—I need not enumerate them—who have accepted the doctrines of Christianity. However there are so many suffering people, whose wrongs cannot be redressed in this world—& whose weak faith is stricken into heavy despair by such writings coming boldly & continually to the front—though not new—that it must be the duty of others who are strong in their belief to make a protest against writings which cause incalculable distress & misery.

I observe that in speaking of the ancient Greeks you totally ignore the great defect of their character—licentiousness. You also assert that intellect alone atones for defect of character. I, and many others, do not agree with you in this assertion—considering rather that intellect without religion has done, & must always do mischief, & is too *often* allied to injustice insincerity—& other baneful qualities.

You say also—that "ten millions of distinct species would be impossible in a creation". But "nothing is impossible to a framer of creation'. In spite of the theory of evolution, for my part I still believe that man was always man.

We not only never see men being produced from apes however delicately the latter may be treated under the care of the former—but the mental differences between men & apes are insurmountable. They neither laugh, or *weep*, or act with any power of comparison. The missing link theory is a fallacy—I enclose a cutting from The Times supporting testimony against this theory. I do not see why we should have doubts as to immortality, or that we should not be able to rise in *myriads* invisible to such eyes as ours. In the plan of creation there is no permanence of form, size, time, or quantity: all is limitless.

I do not know if I have made my ideas plain to you. Pray forgive my presumption in writing thus but I try to do all I can to stem the torrent of misery hanging over the next generation.

(Yesterday I had a Drawing-room meeting on Anti-Vivisection.)

Yours very sincerely,
Emma Hardy.

Text   MS. Leeds.
Clodd: Edward Clodd (1840–1930), banker, author, and leading rationalist; over a period of some twenty years beginning in the early 1890s TH was present at a number of the convivial yet serious-minded gatherings Clodd liked to host at his house on the seafront at Aldeburgh in Suffolk.   *last book*: Clodd's *Pioneers of Evolution. From Thales to Huxley* (London, 1896), which ELH quotes, misquotes, and summarizes throughout her letter. Clodd's diary for 30 Mar. 1897 (Alan Clodd) reads: 'Letter from Mrs Thomas Hardy about the Pioneers: a curious mixture of sentiment & ignorance.'   *alters his opinion*: ELH first wrote 'alters her faith'.   *You say also*: ELH in fact cites a passage quoted by Clodd from Herbert Spencer.   *"nothing . . . creation*: the absence of closing quotation marks tends to confirm that this is ELH's own assertion.   *cutting*: unidentified.   *invisible to*: ELH first wrote 'invisible now to'.

[ELH, a horsewoman in her younger days, had enthusiastically taken up the newly fashionable sport of cycling in the autumn of 1895; she seems have been a dashing if somewhat accident-prone performer and to have worn on occasion (if Dorchester gossip is to be believed) a green costume of the kind popularized by Mrs Bloomer. TH became a cyclist himself, and he and ELH shared in numerous expeditions into the Dorset countryside; they also holidayed together in Belgium in 1896 and in Switzerland in 1897. The increasing separateness of their daily lives is, however, suggested by ELH's references to her 'little apartment', 'boudoir', or 'attic'—constructed as part of the extensions to Max Gate which provided TH himself with a new and more spacious study—and in her August 1899 letter to the newly married Elspeth Grahame she specifically recommended 'keeping separate' as a way of surviving the rigours of a literary marriage.]

To Rebekah Owen

MAX GATE, | DORCHESTER.
Tuesday Feb. 14. 1899.
a Valentine.

Dear Miss Rebecca Owen

I write during a lull of hurricanes! This is the first real quiet day we have had for some days; I went out for a ten-minutes bicycle canter over the mud this afternoon, & came back with a dread of lapsing into a heavy cold—& wearying-cough-state in which I have lately been doing nothing but thinking. A thrush has just ended his prolongings in the dusk, so very loud his song in the stillness, he was almost a nightingale!—but I have never heard the latter bird. *The Thrush in Feby*—is a perfect subject for poetry.

Our small birds have had a tragedy owing to the tempests. (I shall not be able to get away from the weather subject in this little note—which is going on for a page or two perhaps—if I fancy you good, & not quizzical— T.H. has always so much to say by voice, & pen, that letter-writing is my only resource for having all the say to myself, & not hearing his eloquence dumbly. Revenons a nous *birds*—the tragedy was that the ivy came down bodily from the stable gable one night & the little dears lamented much, near at hand watching the dragging off of their late abodes! Now they come to the house-wall.

Yesterday, we all jumped up together from the tea-table to look out at the windows to see the swirl of the wind buffeting the trees, or the effect thereof. The refrain in my letter, comes in, like some in Mrs Browning's poetry, or an old ballad. Do you like her poetry? I like many myself. Last night I was reading aloud one of Poe's criticisms on them—very humourous! I have read but few novels lately—some sent to us. I am getting on with Rosseau's Julie—queer morals! I should have read it through but I kept it on to read little bits with my morning cup of tea last summer—now I feel I must start a better one. I resemble a cat, liking to go in a certain daily track. I keep two or three old books in reading—at present I am usually painting in oils, small landscapes from pencil sketches which friends say have pretty effects (very slight). I have succeeded in taking the portrait of a handsome young nephew—if I continue I must do young, beau-tiful, care-line free faces—that's weak, you will think. Kindest regards to your sister & accept best thanks for your very kind, & *ample* invitation. I know we should be in clover with four rooms & their lovely views; but I fear we must not promise anything yet about coming. Are you writing anything?

Your delight must be very great getting your beautiful old house in order. There is nothing so interesting & absorbing, & bright—I hope you will enjoy it when in it.

Your account of Ruskin's birthday was fresh & pleasing as we were taking an interest in him. I have cut out his portrait from the Daily Chronicle to hang up in my day-room. (Did I show you my little apartment where not a sound—even the dinner-bell—scarcely reaches me.) Poor Ruskin, How sad it is that his mind is wearing out first; like many other famous brainworkers!

I feel the beauty of your scenery by your descriptions but imagine, from what you say that you pine for something occasionally to use your abundant vitality upon, that is absent there. Just before you wrote I had heard from Mr Moule of your decision about your residence but perhaps a nomadic strain of temperament will lead you this way yet!

I mean to try that lump of fat plan myself. The Hoppies are merged in the general community owing to my being unable to sit out of doors but in the Spring I shall make distinguishing attentions to them. I admire your keepin game to protect them. May you be imitated.

Yours very sincerely

Emma Hardy

In haste to catch the post. I am a bad procrastinating creature.

Text   MS. (with envelope) Colby.

nous birds: ELH presumably meant 'nos' (= our) birds.   *Mrs Browning's*: the Max Gate library contained an 1887 one-vol. edition of Elizabeth Barrett Browning's *Poems* (now in DCM).   *Poe's criticisms*: included in vol. iv of John H. Ingram's 1874–5 edition of *The Works of Edgar Allan Poe*, present in the Max Gate library and now in DCM.   *Rosseau's Julie*: i.e. Jean-Jacques Rousseau's *Julie, ou la nouvelle Héloïse*; ELH's copy, purchased in Geneva in 1897, was in the Max Gate library (present location unknown).   *young nephew*: Gordon Gifford (1877–1952), the son of ELH's brother Walter; he and his sister Lilian spent extended periods at Max Gate both before and after this date.   *invitation*: to Belmount Hall, near Hawkshead, the large Lake District house which the Owen sisters had just rented and were later to purchase.   *Ruskin's birthday*: Belmount Hall was not far from Brantwood, John Ruskin's house, and R. Owen had sent flowers ('Eighty flower sprays for eighty pure and lovely years') on the occasion of his 80th birthday, 8 Feb. (see 'Mr. Ruskin at Home', *Academy*, 22 Apr. 1899, 462–3).   *Daily Chronicle*: of 8 Feb. 1899.   *Mr Moule*: Henry Joseph Moule (1825–1904), curator of the Dorset County Museum; he was the eldest son of the Revd Henry Moule and one of TH's closest friends.   *Hoppies*: ELH's name for the Max Gate sparrows.   *keepin game*: ELH, hurrying, elided the two 'g's.

To Elspeth Grahame

MAX GATE, | DORCHESTER.
Aug. 20. 99

Dear Mrs Graham

It is really too "early days" with you to be benefited by advice from one who has just come to the twenty-fifth year of matrimony. (I knew T.H. in 1870, (April) married Sepr 1874) You are *both*, at present in a "Benedict" state. (Women can be anything in these days.)

Do I know your choice, perhaps I have met him—perhaps not. However it is impossible to give "directions for use"—besides characters change so greatly with time, and circumstances. I can scarcely think that love proper, and enduring, is in the nature of men—as a rule—perhaps there is no woman "whom custom will not stale." There is ever a desire to give but little in return for our devotion, & affection—their's being akin to children's—a sort of easy affectiona*ness*—& at fifty, a man's feelings too often take a new course altogether. Eastern ideas of matrimony secretly pervade his thoughts, & he wearies of the most perfect, & suitable wife chosen in his earlier life. Of course he gets over it usually, somehow, or hides it, or is lucky!

Interference from others is greatly to be feared—members of either family too often are the cause of estrangement. A woman does not object to be ruled by her husband, so much as she does by a relative at his back,—a man seldom cares to control such matters when in his power, & lets things glide, or throws his balance on the wrong side which is simply a terrible state of affairs, & may affect unfavourably himself in the end.

Keeping separate a good deal is a wise plan in crises—and being both free—& *expecting little* neither gratitude, nor attentions, love, nor *justice*, nor *anything* you may set your heart on. Love interest—adoration, & all that kind of thing is usually a *failure—complete*—some one comes by & upsets your pail of milk in the end. If he belongs to the public in any way, years of devotion count for nothing. Influence can seldom be retained as years go by, & *hundreds* of wives go through a phase of disillusion,—it is really a pity to have any ideals in the first place.

This is gruesome, horrid, you will say—& mayhap Mr Graham is looking over the bride's shoulder as bridegrooms often do—but you have asked me. Ah some day we may talk further of these matters—there is so much to say—and to compare. Every one's experience is different—*very*. The *Spartan* style was wise doubtless.

Yet I must qualify all this by saying that occasionally marriage undoubtedly is the happy state—(with Christians always if *both* are) which it was intended to be. There must, of necessity, be great purity in the mind of the *man*, joined with magnanimity, & *justice*, and where, or rather, how often are these qualities to be found combined? Similarity of taste is not to be depended on, though it goes some way, but rivalry, fear, jealousy, steps in—often a love-match has failed completely over, & over again—Christian philosophy is the only oil certain to work the complication. I see that continually.

However let me now give you my congratulations in due form dear Mrs Graham (though I rather congratulate a man in these cases.) If you come into my neighbourhood both, or either, I shall be delighted to see you, do drop into our roadside cottage.

Believe me

Yours very sincerely
Emma L. Hardy

You must enjoy Fowey—what a lovely spot to choose, but best in the winter—I know North Cornll a little.

Text   MS. Bodleian Library.

Grahame: Elspeth Grahame (née Thomson, 1862–1946) was the recently married wife of Kenneth Grahame (1859–1932), Secretary to the Bank of England and author of *The Golden Age* and, later, of *The Wind in the Willows*; for an illuminating account of their courtship and marriage, see Peter Green, *Kenneth Grahame: A Biography* (Cleveland, Ohio: World Publishing, 1959), 202–21. TH had been friendly with her sister, the artist Winifred Thomson, for some years and wrote a faintly flirtatious letter to Elspeth herself in 1898 (*CL*, ii. 186–7).   (*April*): TH and ELH in fact met in March 1870.   "*Benedict*" *state*: ELH seems to be suggesting, not altogether tactfully, that the couple were no longer young and had both seemed to be confirmed bachelors (like Benedict in *Much Ado About Nothing*).   "*whom . . . stale.*": adapted from *Antony and Cleopatra*, II. ii. 234–5.   *relative at his back*: ELH was clearly thinking of Mary Hardy or of TH's strong-minded mother, still alive at this date.   *Spartan style*: the marriage customs unique to ancient Sparta allowed women a considerable degree of independence and even dominance.   *roadside cottage*: i.e. Max Gate.   *Cornll*: i.e. Cornwall, where she first met TH.

To The Editor of the *Daily Chronicle*

Aug. 31. [1899]

Sir,

The scene described in "The Daily Chronicle" as having taken place at the Alexandra Palace is a disgrace to civilisation, and should be held up as such. That an animal (in this case a tiger) should be whipped before the public, because he objects to ascend steps, &c., and attacks his daily tormentor when an opportunity occurs (and how he must hate him, or her!), and that the public should submit to be reprimanded by the exhibitor for showing their disapproval of the whipping, is altogether an outrage against humanity, its sense of unfairness and cruelty, if it has any such natural sentiments left in these days of unprecedented tortures; also it is an outrage against common sense.

Are the public expected to appreciate and become used to the whipping, and to stifle their feelings of mercy and good will to the dumb wild creatures who have been caught for the purpose of these exhibitions? A writer on this subject says that could the public daily witness the training instead of the show they would protest instead of applauding, but it seems the public is to be gradually inured to any amount of torture; hot-ironing may be done before their eyes in the future. And what is it that they go to see?— a wild creature do what its muscles and anatomy were not made by the Creator to do. Why not go to see men walk on the ceiling, and allow another to flog them or prong them if they do not perform satisfactorily? As a matter of fact, walking on the ceiling has been attempted, and men have had the want of common sense to gaze at it.

Shall we never have an Act passed to prevent the exhibiting of performing animals? Why should human beings have the power to lower the national character by such means? Why should children be brought to see and enjoy these senseless, cruel sights (practising a good deal of it at home on their own pets in imitation afterwards)? Why exclaim against the brutality of old times and the bull-fights of today in Spain?

The lie given continually that kindness alone is used to train wild beasts to do unnatural things is manifested by such exhibitions.

I have waited for someone to protest against it—no one does—silence is kept, and approval given, alas, from high quarters!

The hideous-minded continue to earn their living by the agonies of the captivated dumb creatures, and the public are taught to enjoy these exhibitions from infancy.

Yours truly,
PROTEST.

Text Daily Chronicle, 4 September 1899, 4.
Chronicle": in 'The Tiger and the Whip. Narrow Escape of a Lady at the Alexandra Palace', *Daily Chronicle*, 24 July 1899, the audience was reported to have hissed when an animal tamer used the whip on one of his Bengal tigers—which then sprang at the tamer's wife, also participating in the performance. She escaped, but the tamer blamed the incident on 'the uncalled for demonstration on the part of some of the onlookers'. It was of this 4 Sept. letter that ELH claimed authorship when writing to R. Owen, 12 Sept. 1899 (Colby), not of the anti-bull-fighting letter, signed 'An Old-Fashioned Englishwoman', found by Weber (130–1) in the *Daily Chronicle* of 8 Sept. 1899.

[The outbreak of the South African (or Boer) War in the autumn of 1899 precipitated a period of acute military and moral crisis for Britain as a whole, and TH freely acknowledged in letters to friends that he was torn between a hatred of the brutality and barbarism of war and an irresistible fascination with military spectacle and the sheer drama of battles and campaigns. ELH's 27 December 1899 letter to Rebekah Owen reveals the extent to which the entire Max Gate household was caught up in the first excitement of wartime mobilization, her own admirably independent perception of the fundamental issues at stake in the war and the likelihood of future disasters having doubtless been sharpened by the defeats and losses the British forces had already suffered.]

To Rebekah Owen

MAX GATE, | DORCHESTER.

Dec: 27. 99.

Dear Miss Betty Owen.

It really does not matter greatly where one lives this sad Christmas time of warfare; I hear it is gloomy enough in London. We have no snow here but is coming to us soon, so bitterly cold as it is, to day—it quite cripples my energies, I can feel procrastination seizing hold of me with unusual power.

My birds are fed with *regularity also* with crumbs & raspberry & strawberry *Jam*—they are tame, but do not eat out of my hand now as formerly, knowing that I have a Cat: such handsome clean sparrows most of them are, with just a sprinkling of rara avis occasionally. I like to hear of your birds, & your lovely gardens, vistas & avenues. I may appear someday at the other end! No doubt you feel it "deadly dull" at Coniston but its beauty must largely compensate—also its poetical associations—perhaps you will *flit* again some day in this direction! *My* beloved country is Devon—my beloved people the gentle, good-hearted Devonians—without guile any of them, & altogether lovely.

We are engineering the lower lawn: it will be a fine croquet, or tennis, lawn next summer. I have a swing there too, & the trees grow all round it, quite nicely at last.

My nephew is with us till the Spring, & is making good progress with his architecture. I scarcely think I shall care to take a Flat or House in Town next season, it will be so gloomy after the war, though the war may not be over by April at this rate! We rush at the papers by day, & send to Dorchester for telegrams, & read *old* battles at night! (but have no near relatives or friends at the front.) Sir Redvers Buller, we know well, & his portrait, the latest, is on a table to be *signed* when he returns, Lady Audrey says. T.H. writes his war poems, & Gordon talks *"guns"*, on which he is a great authority, & as he is as garrulous as any "old ancient man," he sometimes obtains quite a large part of the conversation, whenever, he thinks he can instruct his elders—, & I finish by reminding him of a conscription coming! we get excited over the news, though it is quiescent enough at this moment. What a burst it will be, when Roberts & Kitchener "get there"! The battles will be on a huge scale, that's certain—& a terrible ending it will all have. But the Boers fight for homes & liberties—we fight for the Transvaal Funds, diamonds, & gold! is it not so? I have all along called the enemy formidable & the country impossible to fight in—no generals can rightly be blamed, if disaster & defeat occur, which is more than probable. Why should not Africa be free, as is America? Peace at any cost of pride, & aggrandisement, is my idea. Well, we gabble all day long about this war. People at home will become indifferent to the news however after much prolongation, & those at the front will experience terrible complication of difficulties.

I do not subscribe to Mudies, but am buying a few books for myself—& I go out very seldom, getting shyer as I get older, as Mrs Lyn Linton once told me *she* did! I think you read a good many, more far than I do. Novels do not appeal to me, as they used to do. I am reading a friends' MS poetry (not Mr Pretor's) but another literary friend. (By the bye *Ronald & I* is selling well, a new edition is coming out.) Much of *this* poetry is good but as he has no copy, I read it in some amount of anxiety, & keep it under my eye in my own room. However, no new books can have a chance of selling at present. Of recent poetry perhaps you admire "The Ivy Wife". Of course my wonder is great at any admiration for it, & SOME others *in the* same collection. Thank you for Omar Kayám I had read it several times before however. What a handy size it is—I wish all books were like it if it were possible, in that respect at least. Of course I think the poetry excellent in style, *remarkably* fine indeed—but in sentiment pernicious, though it is rampant everywhere; such literature being no doubt a factor in the accumulation of despairs, miseries, & sorrows, to be heaped up in the latter days. Christ's words "behold I have told you", (referring to these, as much as to those after his time) are striking when one considers present day events, tendencies & opinions all over the world: it is the beginning of the end, no doubt though indefinite as to date. I still think the Bible *unmatchable*.

We met Mr Meridith's married daughter—he has only *one* though) awhile ago at Mrs Sheridan's, she talked of her baby all lunch-time.

Wishing you & your sister a Happy New Year
Believe me

Yours very sincerely
Emma L. Hardy.

Ah, the name of that blue flower I gave you is lost in antiquity alas! It flourishes here on the chalk wonderfully—blue & pink on same bunch. I have *never* heard its name. I have never seen Miss Holman Hunt that I can remember but *may* have in a galaxy!

Text   MS. (with envelope) Colby.

Coniston: some 4 miles from Belmount Hall; the Owens had taken lodgings there in the past for the sake of its associations with John Ruskin (see letter of 14 Feb. 1899).   *Buller*: Sir Redvers Henry Buller (1839–1908), the general currently—and somewhat unsuccessfully—commanding the British forces in South Africa; the Hardys had met him and Lady Audrey, a daughter of the 4th Marquess Townshend, at London social occasions (see *CL*, ii. 240–1).   *his war poems*: 'Embarcation', 'Departure', etc., subsequently collected in *Poems of the Past and the Present* (1902).   *Gordon talks "guns"*: a drawing by Gordon Gifford of fortifications, artillery, and the shattered words 'Peace on earth, goodwill towards men' seems to have been sent as a Max Gate Christmas card for 1899 (Carola Shephard).   *"old ancient man"*: cf. 'very old aged person', *Far from the Madding Crowd* (Wessex, 72).   *Roberts & Kitchener*: Field-Marshal Lord Roberts, on his way to assume the supreme command in South Africa, and General (later Field-Marshal) Lord Kitchener, his second-in-command.   *Linton*: Eliza Lynn Linton (née Lynn, 1822–98), novelist and writer on social issues; she was on friendly terms with the Hardys *circa* 1890 (see *CL*, vii. 110–11).   *literary friend*: unidentified.   *Ronald & I*: see letter of 19 Feb. 1897; second edition pub. 1901.   *"The Ivy Wife"*: first pub. in TH's *Wessex Poems* (1898); ELH evidently read it personally.   *Omar Kayám*: probably Macmillan's recently pub. Golden Treasury Series edition of *The Rubáiyát of Omar Khayyám* as translated by Edward FitzGerald.   *"behold . . . you"*: an apparent blending of Matt. 28: 7 (where Christ is not the speaker) with Luke 24: 44, 49.   *Meridith's daughter*: George Meredith's daughter Marie, married to Henry Parkman Sturgis.   *Mrs Sheridan's*: Mary Sheridan (d. 1918), one of the Hardys' oldest Dorset friends (see *Life and Work*, 413), was the daughter of the American historian John Lothrop Motley and the wife of Algernon Thomas Brinsley Sheridan of Frampton Court, near Dorchester, descended from Sheridan the dramatist.   *blue flower*: Mrs William Heelis (Beatrix Potter, the author and illustrator of children's books) was a neighbour of the Owens, and when she read ELH's letters after R. Owen's death (see Weber, 229) she suggested that the flower must be pulmonaria, or lung wort (MS. notes, Colby), also known as the bugloss cowslip.   *Hunt*: Gladys Mulock Holman Hunt (1876–1919), the painter's daughter by his second wife, Marion Edith Waugh.

To Rebekah Owen

May 1900

Dear Miss Rebekah Owen,

Some of the roses you were so kind as to send me reached me: the others had a bad journey (I enclose the Post Mem:) They are delicious in colour & perfume—& repose in a blue bowl. (like *June*) Here it is cold—bitter east wind to day, but our trees grow apace—everything is a-bloom—reaching & spreading forth as if it were an undiscovered country & the lower lawn is laid out for croquet. I can just faintly imagine your luxuriance & am very sure that your enjoyment of it is great. Have you *Comfree?* that may not be the spelling). The Lung Wort here is full flowered too—am glad you & your gardener like it—*"well.* I cannot get to town owing to a sprain—& am pulled down very much—though I do not care greatly for the season & the extravagance, & attrition, of society. I could not speak on a platform from shyness even if I had the ability. Mrs Lynn Linton told me *she* was "very shy"—one never knows from manner. How you must enjoy putting those boys to rights. I hope you will get them *quite honest by apple time.* There's a deal of petty larceny sometimes. As to evil-speaking it is on the increase & great unhappiness is caused thereby—people ought to be MUCH punished for it. Catechisms are not learnt as they used to be. Honesty seems an elementary virtue—yet look at the increase of *monopolies.* (coals too). As to *fighting*—men love that I know. The world seems very wicked: I am growing old I suppose.

I am glad that you belong to "Animal" Societies. It makes me ill to think of the Vivisection tortures. Coleridge the animals' greatest champion is a hero to me. As to the New Enclyclopedias—the illustrations & explanations of the insides of us all make one feel very bad & miserable indeed. I would rather not know it. And cleanliness & carefulness for ourselves & others are the chief remedies. The *"throb"* of life cannot & never will be found. Canst thou search out the Almighty? asks Job.

I too like Miss Wilkins' *"Cat"* immensely—'tis *perfectly told.* I am also reading *Eleanor* & *The Mantle of Elija* by Zangwell—it begins cleverly but *Allegra* is almost an exclusive name. I should myself prefer some names in history & fiction to be prohibitive. If Mrs H Ward is merely intending to write about an insane woman the story will lack a *proper* interest but if not—the story is *unpleasant,* & will be so I expect—if the heroine is persecuted there is nothing new in the conception. I am reading Tolstoy's "Ressurrection" in a French trans: It is powerful but unpleasant too. I am fond of the old books—translations of classics—& of poetry—but it seems scarcely allowable for *me* to say what I like or do not like perhaps. I am most busy painting in oils from pencil sketches—but do not excel by any means. My sonnet in the *Sphere* wanted just two words altered in last verse. Alas I did not see their *proof*—nor observe till too late.

Yours very sincerely

E L Hardy.

Kindest regards to your sister.
Who is Nora Hopper?

Text MS. (two correspondence cards) Colby.
Comfree: Comfrey is the English name of *Symphytum officinale*, a tall plant with clusters of bell-shaped flowers.   *Lung Wort*: see postscript (with note) to letter of 27 Dec. 1899.   *to town*: i.e. to London.   *Linton*: see letter of 27 Dec. 1899.   *those boys*: evidently trespassers onto the grounds of Belmount Hall.   *(coals too)*: ELH evidently shared the view that the current European shortage of coal was the result of market manipulation by the mine-owners.   *as to fighting*: the South African War was still in progress.   *Coleridge*: Sir John Duke Coleridge (1820–94), 1st Baron Coleridge, lord chief justice of England, was a passionate anti-vivisectionist.   *asks Job*: Job 11: 7 reads, 'Canst thou by searching find out God? canst thou find out the Almighty unto perfection?'   *New Enclyclopedias*: sic; ELH had perhaps seen an early volume of the *Encyclopaedia Medica*, edited by Chalmers Watson (15 vols., Edinburgh, 1899–1910).   *'Cat'*: 'The Cat', a story by Mary E. Wilkins (later Mary Wilkins Freeman) in the May 1900 issue of *Harper's Magazine*.   *Eleanor*: a novel by Mrs Humphry Ward currently being serialized in *Harper's Magazine*; in the next sentence but one ELH speculates as to its future development.   *Zangwell*: correctly Zangwill (see letter of 30 Apr. 1906); the high-spirited young heroine of his novel *The Mantle of Elijah*, beginning serialization in the May issue of *Harper's*, is called Allegra, a name ELH apparently thought should be permanently reserved to Byron's daughter by Claire Clairmont.   *"Ressurrection"*: correctly *Resurrection*; the translator was T. de Wyzewa.   *My sonnet*: called 'Spring Song', it appeared in the *Sphere*, 14 Apr. 1900, 393, within the 'Literary Letter' section written by the editor, Clement King Shorter (see letter of 15 Sept. 1904).   *Hopper?*: Nora Hopper (1871–1906), poet; her *Songs of the Morning* was pub. by Grant Richards in 1900.

To Rebekah Owen

Max Gate— | Dorchester
April 4. 1901

Dear Miss Rebecca Owen,

   It is good of you to offer to send me flowers again—I think I should be as glad to get them now as later—for we have few here.—the dear little blue flowers are out—those of which I gave you a root, & I suppose yours are in bloom too, & your gardener admiring them—*I* am fond of them—violets & primroses, & blackbirds with their too sweet notes are trying to compensate for the terrible hurricanes, & bitterly cold weather we have experienced. I have put an old last winter's nest—a wren's—in a tree, & am wondering if *they* will use, or scorn it. We are mourning the loss of a fine & dear cat—killed on the railway *terribly* at the level crossing at the bottom of our garden lane. It is remarkable how much one feels for comparatively so small a loss—it has "cast a gloom" over us all. Tom used to carry it to the stable every night, as a rule, & just left it out once to enjoy a fine moonlight when lo! he's gone. (Chopin's funeral March!)

   I will let your sister know if I manage to gird up for Town—& shall be very glad to see her—or you. I hope you have both kept well through the "coldness". I am sorry for you about your dear old nurse—such a faithful servant & friend is not usual in this hard world in these days at any rate—I suffered much at the loss of my mother's old servant. I think the failing of old friends dreadfully sad & solemn—but I trust you will be able to keep yours a long while yet. *I* believe that we shall all meet in the next world—probably animals too—"I know there's a spiritual world because I live in it," has been finely said by a French writer—but we must "BELIEVE" it, or we cant know it, & "press forward" to it it whilst here.

I wonder if I shall muster up courage & energy enough to get to London this summer, I am much afraid of crossing the streets & have narrow escapes now I am old—I fear I am getting apathetic—that's bad. I certainly care little enough for Dorchester, & wish I were back in dear Devon—the people are rougher & more evil-speaking in this county—in fact Devon is *nearly* perfect every way. I believe in the Chinese superstition that *places* affect one's happiness & success—" 'Tis but the fate of place—" W.S. says. Dorchester is building itself "large" however—perhaps you will come to live here some day. Every thing is quiet every body economical lest we *dont remember* war & taxes. I am making an effort to read *Babbs* the Impossible—what an absurd title. The book is a plagiarism from Two on a Tower.

With love to both—

Yours sincerely
Emma Hardy.

Text   MS. (with envelope, mourning stationery—ELH's sister, Helen Holder, having died in December 1900).
blue flowers: see letters of 27 Dec. 1899 and May 1900.   *gird up for Town*: the Hardys took rooms in London for a month only in May-June 1901.   *your dear old nurse*: Caroline Ash; she was ill at this date and died, aged 90, in 1910 (Weber, 133, 154).   *French writer*: unidentified.   *to it it*: ELH's repetition.   *W.S. says*: quotation from Shakespeare's *Henry VIII*, I. ii. 75.   *lest we dont remember*: a joking allusion to the 'Lest we forget' of Kipling's 'Recessional', first pub. 1897.   *absurd title*: Babs the Impossible (London, 1901), a novel by 'Sarah Grand' (Frances Elizabeth MacFall); it resembles TH's novel of 1882 only in using a former watch-tower as one of its principal settings.

[ELH's long 2 September 1901 letter to the *Daily Chronicle*, published there three days later as a contribution to an ongoing correspondence on 'The Decay of Domesticity', is included here as providing an exceptionally full and comprehensive expression of her general outlook on life—a combination of largely negative views of the world immediately around her with a series of extravagantly optimistic prospects for the future.]

To The Editor of *The Daily Chronicle*

Margate,
Sept. 2. [1901]

Sir,

One of your correspondents speaks of vapourings about happiness, but whatever the grievance, we all strive to replace it with happiness. All should try to become makers of happiness. As a cult, as a business, it should be learnt. The reason why happiness is yet unachieved, and the true and only reason why this world is therefore one of unutterable woe for the masses, is that we do not *teach* the way to the young to obtain and secure it.

The knowledge acquired in schools is *not* making for happiness for all, but far otherwise. The gaols, asylums, hospitals, workhouses are crowded with woeful mortality, accidents, afflictions, illnesses are continually produced by want of care, or stupidity, or lack of interest in others' well-being; sins and sorrows, pain, and anguish follow. Even the well-to-do have continual droppings of jealousies, rivalries, bullyings, and worse—wickedness never known, miseries never spoken of. The sales of articles of commerce false in substance and appearance lower the people, avertable poverty produces disease, crimes, madness, terrible deaths, hideous operations on men and animals—the houseless, bedless, ever-comfortless poor should not exist in a *rightly-taught* nation.

Regard attentively the position of infancy. Almost always the plastic minds and hearts are in ignorant hands. Even where a household is well looked after, a woman of the uncultivated class is chosen to attend the children in their early years. Listen to the talk of a nurserymaid, hear the reprimands given by her to a wondering little inmate of a baby-carriage, who wants to get out of it, and feel and see for itself what the world is. What is the child taught? Nothing, or worse, and it often returns home unhappy or dulled. That is a pitiable sight, and it is a most reckless way of saving the family funds and treating human material.

The children of the poor are in greater misery, starved in their bodies, crammed in their minds, morals ignored, religion defied. But now start another way altogether: get instructors as near as you can to the Arnoldian type—that is, get them of a class, high, not for attainments merely, but qualifed by excellence of morals, true and simple religion, and good sense; supplement these if you like by mere learned machines for particular technical learning, but yet place your character instructor in the position of highest authority, and get future instructors by schooling them to the same ideal. The teaching profession of this high stamp should be everywhere, in towns, cities, country villages, and should have an exalted position.

The young people put out to learn trades, professions, arts, sciences, should have persistently inculcated and made plain to them the necessity of considering every other life as important as their own individual one, and that some may be far more important, and that, therefore, their work must be as perfect and reliable as human ingenuity can devise. Human ingenuity is a terrible quality as we now possess it, uncontrolled by any feeling of its awful responsibility, and every young person should be taught determinedly never to sleight or deceive in construction or design of work for other human beings, never to give pain or cause trouble by not using sufficient precautions and preventive measures at any cost of expense or toil, and also to take every conceivable care for the prevention of accidents, illnesses, even disappointments, especially those who have the daily lives and care of others, enforcing on them to remember how valuable such may be, and that others are as ourselves, that all are united by the same feelings, wants, desires. Give to the poor food, clothing, house room, not as the result of politics, but of the law learnt, the law of Love the Conqueror. If a child is found to be persistently irreclaimable, sequestration from other children must be adopted; as generations pass fewer of these would be found.

Women's perplexities and trials would vanish. They it is who would, who must, be the first instructors, paid or unpaid; and women are peculiarly fitted for this work, or would be when themselves are trained aright.

I appeal, unfortunately, to a few! Not to the cynical unbelievers in human possibilities, nor to those who rejoice in iniquities, nor to those who love the world as it is, full of perplexities, wretchednesses, cruelties for the greater number.

I appeal to the few. To the generous, the just, to the ameliorators, to them for the true and wise expenditure of their sympathies, of their money, and of their influence. It may be said that the project is idealistic, crude, impossible, to try to make all happy.

At first sight it may seem so. However, let it be remembered that every other scheme has failed—so let it be tried. Even a fad's career, however absurd, once started, has sway; it may melt if it is of cloud-like nature, or it may remain as a real atmosphere. All other and previous attempts have been weak efforts, because they have begun at the wrong end, and are only partial remedies at best; not preventive of evil, curative merely, and decided failures, through all the Christian charities and ameliorating influences abounding everywhere.

We cannot all be happy! Yet why not? There is no real, unsurmountable obstacle, although revolutions by the sword could not effect it, nor an effort to raise up one section of society and put down another. But when individuals believe that health and happiness are possible for all, when they recognise in the lowest a being of infinite aptitude for happiness, they will not rest with the mere bestowal of pity.

Eliminate evil, stamp it out at its source. Eradicate selfishness, the rage for power and advancement, the accumulation of wealth by others' woes. Expenses will be moderated, violence utilised, punishment abolished; and through every necessary exercise of brain and body a world would be evolved progressing towards perfection from the present chaos. Lives would be prolonged blissfully, and in one or two generations nearly every person would in some way or other be a *maker of happiness*.

Yours, &c.,

E. L. Hardy.

Text   *Daily Chronicle*, 5 September 1901, 3.

Margate: evidently a misreading of 'Maxgate', a form ELH occasionally used.   *it is a most*: the printed text reads 'is is a most'.   *Arnoldian type*: the reference is presumably to Thomas Arnold (1795–1842), headmaster of Rugby, rather than to his son Matthew.

To Louise MacCarthy

MAX GATE, | DORCHESTER.

Nov. 3. 1902

Dear Mrs Mac-Carthy

Thankyou for your kind expressions, I am of course much interested in the contents of your letter. I had partly guessed that your son might be a possible author—for the people who come to see us as strangers are so very often authors, or ready to become so. I can well imagine your interest and anxiety regarding the career of your son as marked out for himself, and can better perhaps imagine it, than you may be able to, what I have felt, & feel, & probably may not sympathise with my point of View. But your relationship to the Author will doubtless make all the difference—To those who *marry* authors, & ask my advice, I say, "Do not help—him—so much as to extinguish your own life—but go on with former pursuits".

I fear I am prejudiced against authors—living ones!—they too often wear out other's lives with their dyspeptic moanings if unsuccessful—and if they become eminent they throw their aider over their parapets to enemies below, & revenge themselves for any objections to this treatment by stabbings with their pen! I have however observed a nicer feeling usually towards the young, and also towards the old—Mothers—especially—&

sometimes gratitude for help in childhood—this is I take it, on account of the absence of contemporaneous feeling & influences.

I shall be greatly interested in your experiences. Trollope's Mother I believe gave her son much help, & also others have done so; certainly it is true that clever men have generally had an early spur from their mothers. For my part I have suffered much, & greatly from the ignorant interference of others (of the peasant class). I seem to know the whole range of classes from the highest to the lowest—& their attitudes of mind & inwardnesses, & am a-weary perhaps, of all of them.

Thank you for kind invitation [*remainder of letter absent*]

Text MS. (Alexandra Club address also present) Mrs Michael MacCarthy.
MacCarthy: Louise Joanne Wilhelmine MacCarthy (née von Chevallerie), widow of Charles Desmond MacCarthy.   *your son*: Charles Otto Desmond MacCarthy (1877–1952), dramatic and literary critic, knighted in 1951; see *CL*, iii. 203, 228, etc.   *able to, what*: ELH evidently intends 'able to imagine what'.   *Trollope's mother*: Frances Trollope (1780–1863), mother of Anthony Trollope (1815–82), was the successful author of *Domestic Manners of the Americans* and of numerous other works.   *of the peasant class*: i.e. TH's family.

[ELH had recommended to Elspeth Grahame the advantages of 'keeping separate' within a marriage, and in the early years of the new century she acted increasingly on her own advice, going off on holiday trips of her own to such English seaside resorts as Brighton, Worthing, and Dover, and even crossing the Channel on two occasions. In November 1903 she departed for Dover with her niece Lilian Gifford, currently making one of many extended visits to Max Gate, only to travel on to Calais—despite the lateness of the season—about a week later.]

To Elizabeth Churchill

Hotel Famille | Rue de la téte D'Or | Calais
Tuesday Nov. 24 [1903]

Dear Bessie

I should *not* certainly like Pixie to be given to the washing-person: I must find a *good* home for her as soon as I can—I may send her to London. I was very glad to hear about Marky. Perhaps Pixie chased her off—& will try to do so again. Probably I shall return about the 1st or 3rd of Dec. or the first week, as far as I know—may be later.

I suppose you have had a picture-card from me—I am greatly surprised to hear about Martha as she had a *good* character or I should not have taken her.

Will you go to Miss Shellabear & inquire for me if she has heard of any suitable person yet?

I am glad to know that you are not leaving Dorchester & that I shall be able to have you out with us sometimes. I hope that Charles is going on all right. Will you ask Mrs Rendel if she will be able to come for some day, or days about Xmas, or Mrs Barrett perhaps.

We are very comfortable here, the people are attentive the cook good, & the weather is not altogether unfavourable—not much sunshine—but warm—usually & rather rainy. I think I shall occupy the East room on my return but have not quite decided.

I shall have been away a three weeks next Saturday—

Yours truly

E L Hardy

Text MS. Millgate.   *Date* Year from internal evidence.

Churchill: Elizabeth (Bessie) Churchill, the Max Gate parlourmaid; she married and left the Hardys' service just over a year later.   *Pixie . . . Marky*: Churchill's letters to ELH of 22, 24, and 29 Nov. 1903 (DCM) contain numerous references to the Max Gate cats, as do TH's letters to ELH during this period (*CL*, iii. 82–7).   *Martha*: Churchill's 22 Nov. letter reported that Martha (surname unknown), another of the Max Gate servants, was expecting her third illegitimate child; by 'character' ELH means 'reference'.   *Miss Shellabear*: the Misses E. and E. Shellabear, fancy drapers, of South Street, Dorchester, also ran a servants' registry .   *Charles*: surname unknown, employed at Max Gate as a 'page'; Churchill said in her 29 Nov. letter that Charles was 'better sometimes than others' and 'very good to amuse the Kittens'.   *Mrs Rendel . . . Mrs Barrett*: evidently local women available for employment as part-time 'helps'.   *We . . . here*: ELH was accompanied by her niece Lilian Gifford, daughter of Walter Gifford and sister of Gordon.   *a three weeks*: ELH first wrote 'a fortnight'.

To Clement Shorter

MAX GATE, | DORCHESTER.

Sepr 15: 1904

Dear Mr Shorter—

This Competition is very interesting and amusing certainly. What a splendid double-page it is, & how finely they have all come out! I admire your diplomacy, & thank you for *your thanks*, feeling highly honoured, and pleased, at my share of the affair—except for anticipations of wrathful mothers (though they will not know which to blame—) and then—of course, I think my *Choices* the best,—also, that the 2nd Prize is far & away, more beautiful than the 1st. Please condone my criticisms because I had considered that little sweet face, expression quite charming—but then there was the *Flower* in hair—that being adsititious. Thankyou for so kindly sending me an extra copy, which I can keep and mark. Everybody here is greatly interested—

also a little envious of my claim to judge beauty—but I say you decided that claim. By the bye—we both think the 3rd prize not a beauty exactly—he looks somewhat cross—but has fine limbs;—please observe that my beau-ties have all,—with one exception—*lovely* chins. The 1st Prize has also like my exception a short chin. How pretty, & interesting it will be to see the other beauties appearing. What *all* of them?

I am going to ask you two favours—do not at all mind not being able to *accede*.

One is—that I should much like to possess photographs of my chosen ones—if the mothers would be flattered by the request for another one. As you know, but may forget—they are these,—*Clarke—Adams-Connor—Nixon Galbraith-Scott—Watts-Russell Needham-Browne—6.*

The other favour is of the nature of an offer—with a condition. I have two rather remarkable-looking Cats, & a most unusual photograph of them to-gether, taken by a friend. I value the Photo:, & should not like it lost by any mischance of post, but I want you to see it & put them in one of your Papers because I think you will like them as much as I do myself. *If so* Kindly return afterwards. Kind regards to Mrs Shorter. We are intending to take a Flat next summer & hopg to see more of you both.

Yours very sincerely

Emma L. Hardy.

Text   MS. (Alexandra Club address struck through) Beinecke.

Shorter: Clement King Shorter (1857–1926), journalist, currently editing the *Sphere*, the *Tatler*, and other illustrated magazines.   *This Competition*: Shorter had been running, in the *Tatler*, a photographic competition to determine the three prettiest children in the United King-dom, with ELH and Lady Conan Doyle (wife of Sir Arthur Conan Doyle) as the judges. ELH's use of 'we both' in the first paragraph suggests that TH had also been consulted. *double-page*: the *Tatler*, 14 Sept. 1904, 417–20, devoted four pages of photographs to the prize-winners and runners-up in 'The Pretty Children Competition'.   *adsititious*: OED accepts this as an alternative spelling of 'adscititious' = supplemental, supplied from without.   *in one of your Papers*: see letters of 3 Oct. 1904 and 23 Apr. 1908.   *hopg*: abbreviation for 'hoping'.

To Clement Shorter

Max Gate. Dorchester

Oct. 3. 1904

Dear Mr Shorter.

We are in great sorrow, for the death, a terrible one, of our beloved Snowdove—Cut-in-two on the railway which runs at the back—& where we have lost several dear Pussies in a horrible manner. You would scarcly, perhaps, imagine what a gloom this event has cast upon us—but he was a personality & worthy of lamentation. His body lies in our little cemetery— here. Will you let him appear? or not? being now dead! It is a week ago— but we are feeling just as bad as at first about it. It does not matter about "Comfy", *thankyou*—& also for the return of photographs—I thank you.

The lovely children in the *Tatler* are a joy. What a *task we had* judging, is seen by these charming ones appearing, as it were defying our judgments. What a pity they should change by time and the world's buffetings, as *we* all have.

Yours very sincerely
Emma Hardy

Text   MS. (correspondence card) Beinecke.
little cemetery: Snowdove's stone—cut by TH himself (*CL*, iii. 137)—is still visible, along with several others, in the pets' cemetery at Max Gate.   *photographs*: see letter of 15 Sept. 1904; a photograph of two of the Max Gate cats did appear in the *Sphere* in 1908 (see letter of 23 Apr. 1908).   *charming ones appearing*: additional photographs submitted to the beautiful children competition were reproduced in the immediately succeeding issues of the *Tatler*.

[ELH had completed the manuscript of a short novel, 'The Maid on the Shore', several years earlier (see FED's letter to her of 18 August 1910), and in her letter to Rebekah Owen of 24 April 1899 she spoke of the writing of poetry as one of her current activities. Whether she wrote from sheer inclination, from a need for leisure-time activities, or from a desire to compete with her husband—or, indeed, from a combination of these—is by no means clear, but the appearance in 1898 of *Wessex Poems*, TH's first volume of verse, coinciding as it did with a decline in trust and intimacy within the marriage, certainly seems to have stimulated—or provoked—her to renew her efforts towards both composition and publication. Nor can she have been unaffected by Hardy's active and romantic interest in the literary endeavours of Florence Henniker and Agnes Grove—women strikingly younger and handsomer than ELH herself, and of better education and higher social class.]

To Clement Shorter

MAX GATE, | DORCHESTER.
Sepr 6. 1905

Dear Mr Shorter

Will you please accept the accompanying verse? I should be so pleased if you will print it. A Cambridge man of attainments living at Wyke to whom I sent it for his approval says it is *very* good, in good style & form for publication—I hope *you* will think so. Otherwise, could you place it anywhere else *soon* for me? I do hope that you & Mrs Shorter will pay us a visit here this autumn. I am coming for a few days to town either when TH. returns from Aldburgh or else beginning of Oct:. Afterwards we shall both be here a good while—we never can leave home at the same time until some sweet spirit acts as caretaker—the last had a stupid careless devil in her, & gave me much trouble to get the house alright again. We had a *"party'* week a while ago—all our neighbours, & two days after *all* the journalists there are in the present creation of the generations & some editors, & a rising generation of daughters & sisters etc—& two beautiful days came to our assistance & made us happy. We had pretty speeches on the lawn after tea in a Marquée but Marky the cat howled in a bowery recess near by, after behaving sweetly at first, & was greatly perplexed at our gathering together our species, also at the disappearance of the magical tent the next day.

I hope you will all have a nice time for the Crabb Commtion. I used to read him as a very young girl for the stories, only, & have a volume still which I used to read then. Kindest regards to Mrs Shorter.

Yours very sincerely

Emma L. Hardy.

(The verse is *private* until published please)

Text   MS. (Alexandra Club address also present) Beinecke.
print it: Shorter apparently did not accept the (unidentified) poem, although he had pub. an earlier poem of hers; see letter of May 1900.   *Cambridge . . . Wyke*: Alfred Pretor (see letter of 19 Feb. 1897) lived at Wyke Regis, now part of Weymouth.   *Mrs Shorter*: see letter of 23 Apr. 1908.   *Aldburgh*: correctly, Aldeburgh, the site later that month of celebrations marking the 150th anniversary of the birth of George Crabbe; see *Biography*, 439.   *journalists*: Max Gate had been visited on 1 Sept. 1905 by some 200 members of the Institute of Journalists.   *Marky*: short for 'Marquise'; if a pun was intended it was undercut by the unwanted accent on 'marquée' (derived from the French 'marquise'). See letter of 24 Nov. 1903.   *Crabb Commtion.*: i.e. Crabbe Commemoration.

To Lady Grove

MAX GATE, | DORCHESTER.

Jan: 23. 06.

Dear Lady Grove.

I have read your lovely little dirge-tale with my woman's heart, twice over. Perhaps, never having had a babe I do not quite comprehend the grief, yet I believe I do too. How many sweet poems have been written about a child's loss! I think I know them all, & Coventry Patmore's is pathetic to a degree most sweet and real, also Tennyson Turner's. I feel I know & love your boy, & his sweet ways, as "Kissing" your "eye-*covers*", I do love children, greatly, *even* poor people's lacking breeding etc. They all know me in the parish here. I have been meaning to write & tell you how beautiful I think the book—but latterly have had little time—for correspondence—what with the management of my lazy household the excitement of the Elections & consequent newspaper-reading—and writings of my own the day never seems long enough. I am so very sorry to hear of your illness, but feel sure consumption cannot be your complaint, nor mine—though I was, as a girl supposed to be going that way, but the doctor said, with *my width* and *shape* of chest it was quite impossible, so I recovered, & how much more must it be so with *your* physique! & then again, when one has the sense to understand one's own constitution and requirements, these occasional complaints can be resisted. I do not think one should sorrow "without hope", no such lovely life can ever be quite lost. I wish you felt as I do; that this is God's world—it *sustains* one to have this faith.

With best wishes,

Yours very sincerely
Emma L. Hardy

(Tom will write to you)
We have looked you out on the *map*.

Text   Typed transcription (by Henry Reed) Millgate; location of original unknown.
Grove: Agnes Geraldine Grove (1863–1926), daughter of General and the Hon. Mrs Augustus Henry Lane Fox Pitt-Rivers and wife of Sir Walter Grove, Bt. TH was much attracted to her when they met at Rushmore, the Pitt-Rivers estate, in 1895 (see *Life and Work*, 286) and subsequently encouraged her aspirations as a writer on social issues; she had visited Max Gate, called on the Hardys in London, and disagreed (in a letter of 20 Mar. 1900, DCM) with ELH's religious views. See Desmond Hawkins, *Concerning Agnes: Thomas Hardy's 'Good Little Pupil'* (London: Alan Sutton, 1982).   *dirge-tale*: 'How Time Began to Count: An Allegory', a 10-page booklet written and privately printed by Grove in memory of Terence, her youngest child, drowned in 1902.   *Patmore's*: presumably Patmore's 'If I were dead' (*The Unknown Eros*, I. xiv).   *Turner's*: several of Charles Tennyson Turner's poems treat of the deaths of children, but ELH was perhaps thinking of Sonnet cccxxviii, 'It was her first sweet child', in *Collected Sonnets* (1880).   *eye-covers*: i.e. eyelids; quoted from 'How Time Began to Count'.   *the Elections*: the General Election of January 1906, in which the Liberal Party won a large majority.   *your illness*: writing to F. Henniker, 11 Feb. 1906, TH reported Lady Grove as being in Adelboden (in the Bernese Oberland) 'on account of a lung complaint' (*CL*, iii. 196).   *'without hope'*: perhaps a reminiscence of Eph. 2: 12, 'having no hope, and without God in the world'.   *on the map*: of Switzerland.

32

To Israel Zangwill

1 Hyde Park Mansions
April 30. 06

Dear Mr Zangwill

My interest in the Jews & their return to Jerusalem dates back from my childhood. My grandmother, a gentlewoman of the olden time & a great reader who lived with us giving me that interest. She possessed the "Apocrapha" & read it duly with the Old Testament each returning Sunday & was never tired of talking about the wonderful people, nor I, of reading & listening; she was great on the prophecies, & I have the same faith that she had, namely that Palestine would receive again its own people & be the home of the banished ones at last when their penance was over. I am a (Protestant) Christian, but I have always loved the Jews & am *sure* that Christ's words were heard by the Father, "forgive them for they know not what they do".

For weeks & months past I have had it in my mind to offer a mite, (I am poor *personally* on account of helping relatives) a small sum it is, but if you can imagine from what I have said, the feeling more than a sentiment, a burning desire, with which I offer it, you will accept it in the spirit I wish, yes, a burning desire to be one in so grand a scheme. I have often found too, that I am fortunate for others—and may I be so now! I have not liked to write before but have decided to do so after reading your article & the letters yesterday but I am an atom beneath the clouds & upper regions you will probably think. Please treat this as *strictly confidential*.

Yours sincerely
Emma L. Hardy.

I enclose a P.O. for 7/-

Text MS. Central Zionist Archives.

Zangwill: Israel Zangwill (1846–1926), author and Zionist, was the founder of the Jewish Territorial Organization (ITO), dedicated to the early establishment of a Jewish homeland elsewhere than in Palestine itself. TH was one of several authors who responded to Zangwill's invitation to comment upon this latter scheme, and ELH had seen that letter as pub., along with the others, in Zangwill's article, 'Letters and the ITO', in the *Fortnightly Review* for Apr. 1906. *My grandmother*: Helen Gifford (née Davie). *"Apocrapha"*: i.e. *Apocrypha*. *"forgive . . . do"*: Luke 23: 34. *confidential*: Zangwill's reply (copy, Central Zionist Archives) was brief and entirely impersonal.

To Rebekah Owen

MAX GATE, | DORCHESTER.
Dec: 26. 1906

Dear Miss Rebecca,

I thank you for your cake—home-made I suppose for it is very pretty & though I have rather lost my cake-taste I still have a remembrance of the delight I used to have in cakes when I see or take any, the very word was delightful. I have been lately dressing dolls a most tedious & impatient occupation but I remember that work as a joy 'ere I was old, ah! woful ere" (a soul-reaching poem that for late years, I learnt it young. I never can think why children love old-feeling poetry but they do. I hope we have not "influenced" each other harmfully—Influenza was so named on account of its raging from one to another, I took your first letter in my pocket to London & read it in the train. I returned home after two or three days bringing it back with me. I had managed to keep well through fogs & rainy weather, but at 4.30 the next afternoon I descended to the drawing-room for tea from my eerie, & doors & windows had been left open all over the house, for it was one of those strange warm days occurring at that time, then a house-breeze caught me, & a draught swept down to my lungs & vitals & laid me up for nearly 3 weeks, I have had a relapse too & now have another & a barking cough and a husband to nurse he has a chill, but it is not a serious one his colds are short usually but the effects linger in liability to get fresh ones, & consequent weakness. I shall I expect keep my cough till summer weather comes, & it is hindering me *much*. So is Xmas I am overpowered with its business, & these complaints only one eye to use, & a shake-cough!

I can sympathize greatly with you & your illness, & that of your old nurse to whom you are so much attached; it is sad to see the difficulty the very old have of throwing off an illness & getting over the after-weakness; that is a dread for the coming years with me, & I have no really *sweet* attentive relatives to sympathize, or have "pious drops" ready. My readings are newspapers chiefly at present, three daily, the political situation is so engrossing. I am concerned about France too, the country I love most after our own—& the one I shall want to fly to perhaps some day or other when fighting comes on here, or our beautiful free land changes its character. About witches. Well you know they always live on *Heaths*, or Moors or desolate plains or Mountains—but have no mediaval ways or any broomsticks etc, but are *modern* evil-*wishers* as the name means, as the French express it "en vouloir," they can throw the odium of their evil doings &

wishings on the innocent. There are, as a matter of fact, many malicious defamers *here* in, ah even, in 'Casterbridge'.

In some of the lovely little out-of-the ways villages too, such as *Batscombe*, what a name! perhaps you know that place the veritable old belief in them complete in all particulars survives as TH. has described, I suppose the idea is not renounced in any country.

My husband sends his best wishes with mine for a Happy New Year—& I hope good health for you all. I was intending to send you a pen & ink sketch of our house at the top of this, but cannot find time (this is the very pen I was going to do it with & may yet, if it is some interest to you to know it!! Kindest regards to both.

Yours very sincerely
Emma L. Hardy

Text MS. (Alexandra Club address also present, with envelope, mourning stationery—occasion unknown) Colby.

'*ere* . . . *ere*": quoted (with altered punctuation) from S. T. Coleridge's 'Youth and Age'.   *eerie*: i.e. 'eyrie'.   "*pious drops*": Thomas Gray, 'Elegy Written in a Country Church-yard', stanza 23.   *political situation . . . France too*: ELH probably had in mind the demise of the British government's education bill and the French government's struggle with the Vatican over issues relating to the separation of church and state.   *evil-wishers*: cf. letter of 22 Feb. 1896.   *Batscombe*: or Batcombe, a Dorset hamlet; 'Conjuror Mynterne' (*Tess of the d'Urbervilles*, Wessex, 170) is said to be buried in its churchyard.

To The Revd R. G. Bartelot

MAX GATE, | DORCHESTER.
Feb 24 07

Dear Mr Bartelott

Two women came here from Fordington to ask help of some sort—one named Cluett—the other Ellory. I had them informed that they must bring a recommendation from you, otherwise you see I should half the parish here begging. Please tell me if they should be helped?, how much in want they are? & if not worthless & unaidable? I thank you for garden-room for my Chair.

Yours sincerely
Emma L. Hardy

Gifford. Mills. Hamilton
Yolland. Mitchell. Randolph
Ireland Rowe Mark. Rolls
Fortune Davie or Davy.

Jenner. Farman. Jeune Hellier.

Ware Gifford original place

Plymouth. Devonport. Bristol

(Some of the names & places of my family.)

Text MS. DCM.

Bartelott: i.e. the Revd Richard Grosvenor Bartelot, vicar (1906–36) of Fordington St George, the parish church for Max Gate and the one which ELH regularly attended.   *Cluett* . . . *Ellory*: not further identified.   *should half*: ELH, eliding 'have' and 'half', intended 'should have half'.   *my Chair*: the Bath chair in which ELH, now 66 and experiencing some difficulty in walking, was sometimes pulled to church by one of the Max Gate servants. *Gifford . . . my family.*): ELH's inscription of this list on the back of her letter was presumably prompted by Bartelot's interest in genealogy; a similar list occurs in her *Some Recollections*, 17. Ware Gifford is a Cornish village about 3 miles south of Bideford.

[Lady Grove had kept up her friendship with TH and appeared with some frequency at the Hardys' London 'At Homes'. In December 1907 she published *The Social Fetich*, a collection of humorous and lightly satirical essays on contemporary speech and manners. TH—as his wife was doubtless aware—had read a set of the proofs (now in the Beinecke), suggested a number of alterations, and even had a hand in the phrasing of the dedication: 'To Thomas Hardy in grateful recognition of timely aid and counsel, and in memory of old and enduring friendship'.]

To Lady Grove

MAX GATE, | DORCHESTER.

Dec. 9. 07.

Dear Lady Grove,

I have been much entertained with your book "The Social Fetich" having observed many of the errors myself which you mention so felicitously & with such gentle consideration. And I have enjoyed the anecdotes, especially in the chapter on *"tips"*. Perhaps you have already dis-covered an inaccuracy to, be corrected in a new edition on page 12. In the use of the word *inculcate* with *into* instead of "with which" & past participle. There is an infelicity in the sentence following the word "wit" which has a different sense from un*wit*tingly. By-the-bye "*wit*ting" is a pretty word but seldom used—never perhaps, neither by you. You may think me hypercritical perhaps but I love words, & pounce upon sentences by early habit having to search for errors & misprints. In the daily papers how many occur! My father allowed us no *slang*, no obsolete words no *affectations* at all—"plain English". He was a fine classical scholar & a courtly man at *home* & abroad! Good-breeding meant simple manners with much stateliness then—a combination never achieved now—all is changed—culture even abhorred by some of the self-educated "'Deportment,' what is that?" they say. There is so much elasticity every way—but the old times seem best to those who knew them. However, I must own to liking a "Cosey" & the *hot tannin* produced under it which benefits me me as St Raphael's wine does invalids—*its tannin* though being COLD. Few people, I know do care for the ingredient, therefore *no* tea-cosey for visitors! I agree with you in a general way, though of course some words have a prounciation which *use* and *euphony* demand. The letter "z" has a more pleasing sound than 's"—with which we make our tongues *hiss* according to foreigners! so let us have z instead of the sibilant, at least in *blouse*. We sound a *"v"*—& not an "f" in ne*ph*ew. After all words were made for man not vice-versa. *Lounge* for "Couch" would be correct for a *one*-end thing—*Sofa*—has two ends—nice old thing—a low-lying-lair! Why do people offer a sugar bowl with a question?—but if any—*like* has a friendly sound. People ought to be well slapped for saying of*ten*. "Chemise" is a pretty word "Shift" is vulgar & is wanted for 'make-shift". People do worry me with their use of prejudice instead of prepossession. About 100 words altogether alone constitute the vocabulary of many even talkers! Ah that lovely word *morning* calling up the best part of a day—especially a winter one to be used so frequently for *mourning* a word for the public notice of grief! People's tongues have lost their flexibility. "Bicycle" is easy, short, pleasing. Americanisms account for a great deal. America's *first* instructors must have had slovenly though rapid intellects. Anyone who has been nurtured upon "distinctive niceties" is distressed by deflections in speech, also more so by *behaviour* especially if in continual daily life. But the disturbing elements of life generally in this present century are of such immensity & *importance* that the use or abuse of words are after all not matters of like importance.

Affectionate regards to Sir Walter & yourself.

Yours Very sincerely
Emma L. Hardy

My sight gets worse & worse for reading & writing.

Text MS. (Alexandra Club address struck through) Beinecke.

Fetich ": *The Social Fetich* (London: Smith, Elder, 1907); see *Biography*, 454–5, and Hawkins, *Concerning Agnes*, 122–5. The copy Grove presented to TH (see *CL*, iii. 284) is at the Univ. of British Columbia.   *inculcate with into*: Grove had good grounds for leaving this passage unaltered in the second 'edition' of 1908.   *infelicity*: on p. 116 Grove uses 'witty' and 'unwittingly' perfectly correctly but in successive sentences.   *My father*: John Attersoll Gifford (1808–90), solicitor; see *Some Recollections*, 22–3.   *"Cosey"*: Grove included 'tea-cosies' among the 'actual possessions' which—together with distinctive expressions and pronunciations—were 'reserved solely for the use of middle classdom'.   *benefits me me*: ELH was turning the page.   *St Raphael's wine*: a French aperitif consisting mostly of fortified

red wine flavoured with quinine.   *blouse*: Grove thought French pronunciation obliga-
tory for 'blouse' and considered 'blowse' unpardonable.   *"Chemise"*: Grove disapproved
of its substitution for 'the homely English "Shift"'.   *"Bicycle"*: if 'bicycle' were to be
shortened, Grove's preference was for the American 'wheel' over either 'bike' or 'cycle'.

To Clement Shorter

MAX GATE, | DORCHESTER.
April 23. [1908?]

Dear Mr Shorter

It is a Cats' cemetery but then there is one Dog's grave. A Tramp did
him to death years ago in our absence & I nursed him in his last hours, (*she*
I mean only I forgot.)

I think the photo: must be returned—as I fear that T.H: will not like it
added to his affairs he has an *obsession* that I must be kept out of them lest
the dimmest ray shoud alight upon me of his supreme story—*"This to please
his family,"* chiefly. He is like no other man—nor himself as *"was."*

Yours sincerely
Emma L. Hardy

I liked Mrs Shorter—*Gipsy Road* very much please tell her this.

Text MS. Beinecke.   *Date* Year inferred from internal evidence.
Cats' cemetery: one of three Max Gate photographs Shorter was about to reproduce in the
Sphere, 23 May 1908 (see letters of 15 Sept. and 3 Oct. 1904).   *Dog's grave*: Moss, 'an
affectionate retriever' (*Life and Work*, 240, and see *CL*, i. 217); her stone is still legible.   *the
photo*: presumably of ELH herself; neither TH nor ELH appears in the photographs actually
used by the *Sphere*.   *Gipsy Road*: i.e. the poem 'Gipsies' Road', by Dora Sigerson Shorter
(née Sigerson, d. 1918), Shorter's first wife; it was first collected in *The Troubadour and Other
Poems* (London, 1910).

[Agitation in support of the women's suffrage movement mounted steadily throughout the United Kingdom in the early years of the twentieth century, and ELH eagerly
involved herself in the struggle both on paper and in person—participating, for
example, in the major London demonstrations of 9 March 1907 and 21 June 1908
and contributing (alongside Millicent Fawcett and Annie Kenney) to a 'symposium'
on the issue published in *The Woman at Home* magazine of March 1907. Her most
significant and extensive statement on the whole question of the rights of women
appeared in the correspondence column of the *Nation*, a political weekly edited by
H. W. Massingham, a prominent liberal who knew TH, had reviewed *Tess of the
d'Urbervilles* in positive terms, and would certainly have been in sympathy with the
general drift of Emma Hardy's views. It seems likely, indeed, that her letter received a
certain amount of editorial attention prior to its actual appearance on 9 May 1908.]

To The Editor of *The Nation*

Maxgate, Dorchester, Dorset,
May 6th, 1908.

Sir,

Mr. Massie, M.P., some time since, writing somewhere against the Woman's Suffrage movement, quoted Mr. Goldwin Smith as saying that "the bed-rock of law is *force*, and *force* is male." Now I venture to assert that this should be an exploded idea for the twentieth century. Law and force should be superseded by a more advanced and complex machinery of the State— that of preventive measures and persuasiveness; and this could chiefly and best be carried out by the gentle, resourceful feminine mind, so used, as it is, to such measures in home life. Some people argue that the world is well managed, yet it would seem that vice, poverty, misery reign still; that prisons, workhouses, asylums, roads are full of the miserable, worthless, vile, poverty, disease-stricken people; hospitals crammed with those who are afflicted with preventible diseases and victims of preventible accidents; towns full of drunken babes, tortured animals, burglaries, suicide—every kind of elementary wickedness, in fact, is rampant.

Mr. Massie refers to women's physical disabilities, but who has not observed a powerful mind overcoming physical disabilities; for instances, the blind Fawcett, the armless and legless Kavanagh, late M.P., a man who was full of infinite physical ability; and though these are men, there are, and have been, also women of like persistent effort and determination, such as Laura Bridgman, Joan of Arc, and others. A human being with brains, though handicapped, is able to be active according to his, or her, temperament, natural ability, and circumstances; indeed, the Nietzsche theories, if carried out in their ruthless cruelty and folly, would be fatal to a community or nation, eliminating some of the bravest brains which are able to serve their centuries. It is a remarkable fact that the weak and afflicted often do what is apparently the most difficult work for them. Men who consider *force* the only power with which to rule should at least remember the *power of thought* which alone rules in the *beginning*, and in the *end* of all things! The physically strong find it easier to rule by *force* than *thought*, but this era is full of strong thoughts leading effectively to great issues, in women as well as in men. At present even the word *virility* is an insult to an active, intellectual feminine mind, as all words of the kind, which cast the woman on one side, proceeding from the pride of the male. Such words are untrue as denoting perfection to be an attribute of the masculine intellect, for a good deal that is carried out as original and finished work has been suggested, and often completely thought out, by a woman, though never so acknowledged. The truth of the matter is that a man who has something of the feminine nature in him is a more perfectly *rational* being than one who is without it, though men who are not possessed of this supreme quality pour contempt on such rare ones as have it; and the reverse holds good, but in a less degree. Sport, of course, spoils the fineness of a woman's temperament; but with the qualities of endurance, concentration, courage added to intellect, she also is a more perfect creature than one who relies entirely on her "woman-hood," for that phase has passed, and both sexes must progress together, emerging from barbarism at the same era to perfection. The "vote for women" movement is a high pyramidal step towards this end, and to this end must she struggle through ploughed difficulties to the summer of her content. The ancient tale of Hercules and Omphale is in direct allusion to this fact; many instances occur in history of this dual nature, comprising strong intellect and firmness with exquisite tenderness in a man, and courage, high and determined, with all the best masculine qualities, in a woman; and without this duality of nature though with intellect many have failed in their careers or suffered damage. Man's pride and woman's forced subjection and crushed condition have hitherto prevented acceptance of the necessity of this completed nature in a world of two sexes but the same humanity. The peaceful and right government of the world can only be carried on by *both*, though the distinct work of each can still be carried out separately, such as home duties for women, and for men heavy labor, science, naval and military affairs, preaching, anything in which they are supreme; but never henceforth should there be permitted a right of government to one sex alone. The time is ripe, women are capable, and their demands of momentous interest and *importance*. Their energetic actions for immediate recognition of this before all other Government business, including that of education and licensing, are of highest and strictest necessity, and more so on account of these debated subjects, with no woman's voice to be heard. Silently, humble to abjectness, she is to wait for the men's decision on what concerns her and the children vitally. Their participation in government is not to supersede men's rule but to share it, standing on the same platform with equal rights. Men cannot continue to hinder this progressive movement or lay down laws for the women of to-day, who must, will, and shall take their place in all councils of the nation—ay! and *every* nation as the world rolls on. Sex prejudice dominates *young* men ludicrously, especially in those just emerged from "infancy."

Women have been sacrificed for ages to men. The absurd idea kept up by them, and hitherto humbly accepted by women, that their manhood is a much higher state for a human being than a woman's womanhood, is allied with tyranny and a fearful calculation as to the real capabilities of women, who are abashed and crushed by their treatment, and obliged hitherto to cringe to the idea of the superiority of the male, whose praise has seldom been for a good woman except safely on a tombstone.—

Yours, &c.,

Emma Hardy.

Text   *The Nation* [London], 9 May 1908, 189, under the heading 'Women and the Suffrage'. *Massie*: John Massie (1842–1925), currently a Liberal MP, was a leading Congregationalist and a former Professor of New Testament Exegesis at Mansfield College, Oxford. His letter in *The Times*, 12 Mar. 1908, 11, quoted Goldwin Smith (1823–1910, historian and polemicist) as saying, 'The bed-rock of law is force, and the force of the community is male'.   *Fawcett*: Henry Fawcett (1833–84), statesman and political economist, husband of Millicent Fawcett, the suffrage leader; he lost his eyesight in a shooting accident in 1858.   *Kavanagh*: Arthur Macmorrough Kavanagh (1831–89), Irish politician, MP 1866–80; although born with only rudimentary arms and legs he travelled widely and practised such physical activities as riding, fishing, shooting, yachting, and painting.   *Bridgman*: Laura Dewey Bridgman (1829–89), an American woman who was rendered blind, deaf, and mute by scarlet fever before the age of two but nevertheless learned to write and to communicate in sign-language.   *Nietzsche theories*: although ELH had already mentioned Nietzsche in a letter to R. Owen of 24 Apr. 1899 (Colby), it is not clear how familiar she was with his writings; for TH's knowledge of Nietzsche see *The Literary Notebooks of Thomas Hardy*, ed. Lennart Björk (2 vols. London: Macmillan, 1985), ii. 511–12.   *Omphale*: in Greek mythology, a queen of Lydia who purchased Hercules as a slave and set him to women's work while she assumed his lion's skin and club.

To Catharine and Rebekah Owen

Max Gate.

May | 20. 08

Dear Miss Owen, & Miss Rebecca.

I find myself unable to get to London for the season—& have taken no Flat or House—but am hoping to go for a very short time next month. The fact is my strength & SIGHT are fast failing & two houses are too much for me now. Mr Hardy is in Town for a short time. I have had a Useful Companion with me but neither her person or *mind* accord with my preconceived ideas on the desirability & restfulness of the plan—& I seem a little better lately—am enjoying the Spring flowers bird-concerts, & absence of grass insects—so till June—when away to Town or elsewhere for a change.

My Eminent partner will have a softening of brain if he goes on as he does
& the rest of the world does—!

With kind regards

Yours ever

E. L. Hardy.

I have a letter in *The Nation*. If you have not seen it shall I send you it?

Text MS. (correspondence card, with envelope) Colby. *Date* Envelope postmarked
19 May 1908.

Useful Companion: unidentified, but presumably a predecessor of Dolly Gale, the personal
maid who was present at ELH's death in 1912. *to Town or elsewhere*: she seems in fact to
have remained at Max Gate until September; see letter of 10 Sept. 1908. *The Nation*: see
letter of 6 May 1908.

[ELH's religious views, though doctrinally eclectic, were always staunchly Protestant,
and she had a profound abhorrence of Roman Catholicism, which she saw as
insidiously extending its presence and influence throughout British society. Her disapproval of Rebekah Owen's conversion to Catholicism in 1908 was expressed with
characteristic forthrightness, and their subsequent correspondence appears to have
been relatively sparse and confined for the most part to the social conventionalities
extorted by Owen's continuing, if increasingly vain, 'pursuit' of TH himself.]

To Rebekah Owen

MAX GATE, | DORCHESTER.

June 16. 08

Dear Miss Rebecca Owen

I expect the Chauffeur is one who will learn experience at a still greater
cost of your bravery, which he may expand further. Gentle reprimands are
too good for him!

I cannot comprehend how the world of 1900 odd can turn again to Roman
Catholicism for Christianity, & accept such a *travesty* of Christ's life, teaching,
& death! The fact that its secret stretching forth for power over the person &
means of the people of our free & enlightened England should have any
success is marvellous nothwithstanding the inundation of nuns, bishops
priests etc.

The "going through the gap" is illustrated—Roman Catholicism is *fashionable*. Ah! if you were English you would hate the thought, and you love
England too, as though you were! Can we forget what has gone before? If
we read *our* Bible (not the *Douay*) we find every statement & practice of the
R. C. in opposition to the teaching of Christ & his disciples. If Xt is *not* our

advocate, our *only* one. If He who "has risen" & has forever sat down in Heaven, is not our Great High Priest, then we are lost & happiness cannot be be permanent. His mother received no authority to be a partaker or advocate in His Salvation "Whatever ye shall ask in *my name*" is plain—not in that of his Mother. "Come to *me*"—not by his Mother. Yet His tenderness for her was very great. No word of praying to Saints, or for the dead—no purgatory—but a plain statement "Where the worm shall never die—or the fire be quenched,"—no "mixing of water with the wine"—or drinking the latter & giving the bread only to his disciples, no infrequent supper for the believers—but "often" no wafer—no command for persecutions, torture or force of any kind, no breaking of the Civil Law, or superseding it.

Consider, would you bear to see a near relative persecuted as a "heretic" with cruelty & say it was your duty to God. The Bible to be taken from you, & traditions & ordinances, & prohibitions of men substituted. Not to read God's truth, not to be permitted to enter a Protestant Church to hear it—not to listen, or to read *this*. Ah if you read the Bible with a prayer The Spirit of Truth will reveal it to you & Satan's guile will be gone. I am losing my sight which was never strong—& reading & writing are difficult, still I hope to get it better again by often resting. I was interested in your letter.

 Believe me

Yours very sincerely

Emma. L. Hardy

Text   MS. (with envelope) Colby.

the Chauffeur: writing to ELH from Paris, 5 June 1908 (DCM), R. Owen reported that her chauffeur had driven into a telegraph pole, run over a dog, and knocked a cyclist 'insensible in a great pool of blood'.   *to Roman Catholicism*: in the same 5 June letter R. Owen reported that she had become a Catholic and was 'intensely happy'.   *the Douay*: i.e. the Catholic Douai (or Rheims and Douai) version of the Bible (New Testament 1583, Old Testament 1609–10), translated into English from the Latin of the Vulgate.   *be be perma-nent*: ELH was starting a new page.   *in my name*: John 14: 13.   *be quenched*: adapted from Mark 9: 44.   *"often" no wafer*: i.e. ' "often", no wafer'.

[Two postcards sent by ELH from Calais in September 1908 are included here not so much for their contents' sake as because they are the only messages from her to her husband known to survive. Since the Hardys had taken no London house or flat for the 1908 'season', TH went to London by himself in late May and June, staying in hotels, complaining of the heat and the crowds, and effectively discouraging his wife from joining him there. In early September, however, when extensive building work at the rear of Max Gate was being put in hand, largely with a view to enlarging and improving her attic rooms, ELH made a sudden decision to go off on holiday, cancelled a garden party to which the guests had already been invited, and left for Dover—only to make another spur-of-the-moment decision to cross over from there to Calais. Following her return to Dorchester she wrote an article, 'In Praise of Calais', which was published in the *Dorset County Chronicle*, 31 December 1908.]

To Thomas Hardy

[10 September 1908]

Just come to Calais straight from London because the channel very smooth I found on arriving at Dover—lovely day, & passage—found Hotel the same as before. Mme Berchier

> Hotel Famille.—
> Rue de Tete D'Or.
> Calais

Text MS. Eton (picture postcard of the Place d'Armes, Calais).   *Date* From postmark. *same as before*: see letter of 24 Nov. 1903.

To Thomas Hardy

[15 September 1908]

X. Top of a little street, leading to the Square where the market is held; is the Hotel Famille. 1st floor, my window nearest the harbour which I can see if I look out. The Harbour comprises many Basins, & is picturesque, & lit up evenings. Send on letters. Our correspondence crossed last time.

Text MS. Eton (picture postcard of the Quai de la Colonne et le Bassin, Calais). *X. . . . Hotel Famille*: overleaf, at the right-hand edge of the photograph, ELH has put a cross and the words 'near here'.

To Madeleine Rolland

MAX GATE, | DORCHESTER.
Aug: 30. 09.

Dear Melle Rolland.

It gives me great pleasure always to hear from *you*—& *such* an *English* letter how delightful it must be to write in another language than your own like that—I wish I could. Sometimes I have attempted it with tolerable but *short* success!

When you are in England let me know what date you you will be able to visit us for we shall both be quite delighted to have you under our roof. September is a nice month—always an improvement on August with its dull foliage—& *dumb* insect life & *dumb* bird-life—& oh! what a miserable month of August we have had here!

Tell me as soon as you can when to expect you—& believe me
Yours most sincerely
Emma. L. Hardy.

I cannot write or do anything much because of a *bad attack* of *neuralgia* which is persistent owing to the wet & cold days we have now as before.

Text MS. Mme. Rolland.

Rolland: Madeleine Rolland, sister of Romain Rolland, the French novelist; her French trans-lation of *Tess of the d'Urbervilles* appeared in 1901. She corresponded with both ELH and TH (there are numerous letters to her in *CL*) and visited Max Gate in Aug. 1907.   *you you will*: ELH was turning the page.   *under our roof*: this visit did not materialize.

[ELH had identified herself since the mid-1890s with the mainstream of the women's suffrage movement as represented by such moderate leaders as Millicent Fawcett and Lady Frances Balfour. Like many others, she was deeply disturbed by the acts of violence performed by the more militant 'suffragettes' and especially by attacks directed against the Prime Minister, H. H. Asquith, a resolute opponent of votes for women.]

To The London Society for Women's Suffrage

MAX GATE, | DORCHESTER.
Sep: 27. 09.

Mrs Thomas Hardy resigns her membership of the London Socty for Women's Suffrage—(at least for the present) though always highly in favour of the movement & impressed with the justice, importance, & wisdom, of it. But is averse to the strongly aggressive attitude of one section, in the attempt to assasinate the Prime Minister, which with the other *very* violent acts of stone-throwing etc: by the *Suffragettes*, who are by the generality of people identified with one-& all the branches of this great movement is very *unchristian*, & *not* likely to bring about a successful result; it would seem better, having made the *demand* in various distinct ways & mild & just attempts at petitioning, to *wait more patiently* till the Country is PERME-ATED with the justice of the cause, carrying on meanwhile a peaceful but continuous assault upon the understanding of opponents. Men's *power* & OBSTINACY being exceedingly great on account of centuries past—but TIME works wonders, & the *future* promises *well* for success.

Text MS. Fawcett Library (annotated 'ackd 29. 9. 09').

violent acts: following Asquith's 17 Sept. 1908 visit to Birmingham several women were imprisoned for throwing stones and other missiles at the police and at the train in which the Prime Minister was travelling.

To Alfred Evans

MAX GATE, | DORCHESTER.
Saturday Morning | Nov. 21. 09.

Dear Mr Evans—

The "Play" quite charmed me—! I thought it most *excellent* in every particular & was much surprised at the briskness of it, and the inclusion by retrospective talk, & frequent allusions of everything at all essential to the comprehension of the whole even by those—who may not have read the story—& probably there were many—though it is thirty-five years old. Its crispness as a play was remarkable! and so was the acting—especially noticeable to one who had seen it muddled & taken liberties with on previous occasions. I never saw a novel so beautifuly put on any stage, so well translated to another sphere, in fact. I fully admired *all the* actors—*you* came out as a veritable "Oak" & even "George" behaved as if he comprehended at last the proceedings & enjoyed it a little.

I was *greatly* delighted with Mrs Evans brightness—& stately *dignifiedness* on right occasions. Please tell her I am intending to come & see her to chat again about it & congratulate her on a most decided talent.

Yours very truly
E. L. Hardy.

Text MS. Berg.

Evans: Alfred Herbert Evans (1862–1946), Dorchester chemist, father of Maurice Evans, the actor; his dramatization of TH's *The Trumpet-Major* in 1907 initiated a series of such productions by the Dorchester Debating and Dramatic Society (later known as the Hardy Players).   *The "Play"*: Evans's adaptation of *Far from the Madding Crowd*; ELH had attended, with TH, the first performance on 17 Nov.   *previous occasions*: ELH had seen the Liverpool and London version of 1882, when TH's script was heavily doctored by J. Comyns Carr, and the Dorchester presentation of dramatized episodes from the novel in October 1907 (see *CL*, iii. 279–81). According to *Life and Work*, 375, TH himself thought Evans's version 'a neater achievement' than Carr's.   *veritable "Oak"*: Evans himself took the part of Gabriel Oak, his wife, Laura, that of Bathsheba; George the sheepdog was played by a sheepdog.

To Madeleine Rolland

MAX GATE, | DORCHESTER.
Feb: 13. 10.

Ma chere Melle Rolland—

J'ai recu la petite carte & je vous en rende remerciements—il me fait voir l'aspect particulier de la inondation a Paris; c'est une terrible calamité veritablement; j'espere que vous-même êtez *toujours* en sécurité—est que le

Vil Fleuve sera soumettre pour l'avenir par le circuit des Canaux—mais les pauvres victimes! il y aura longtemps vive-douleur sans doute causer aux plusieurs *pauvres* gens spêcialement, j'ai beaucoup de chagrin—pour les tous.

Les Magasiniers de Dorchester on donné a Weymouth le "Far from the Madding Crowd" et "The Trumpet Major", les Spectacles tous-les-deux etaient tres beaux—ils etaient jouer *merveilleusement*—d'une facon—inattendu! Il y a la beaucoup de monde—*se serrer*—!!!

Il vous faut venir a voir un de ces jours. N'est pas que *nous-nous* renconterons cet été.

Acceptez mes biens bons souhaits, je vous les envoies avec sincérite, et amitie.

Chere amie—

Emma. L. Hardy.

Text MS. (Alexandra Club address struck through) Mme. Rolland.
inondation a Paris: serious flooding in Paris had begun in mid-Jan. 1910; the 'petite carte' was presumably similar to the 'picture-cards' of the floods acknowledged in TH's letter to Rolland of 1 Feb. 1910 (*CL*, iv. 72–3).   *le circuit des Canaux*: TH's 1 Feb. letter had spoken of the need for a system of canals that would encircle Paris and draw off flood waters.   *Les "Magasiniers . . . Major"*: see letter of 21 Nov. 1909; the two plays were performed at Weymouth on, respectively, 7 and 8 Feb. 1910. Although not all the actors were shopkeepers, ELH's characterization had some validity—as, doubtless, did her implication that their performances gave pleasure in unexpected ('inattendu') and perhaps unintended ways.   *se serrer*: ELH evidently means that the audience was tightly packed.   *Chere amie*: when Rolland wrote a letter of sympathy following ELH's death TH replied, 'As you know, Mrs Hardy was very fond of you, & often said she hoped to see you here again for a longer stay' (*CL*, iv. 255).

To Lady Hoare

MAX GATE, | DORCHESTER.

April 24 1910.

Dear Lady Hoare—

I, also, feel much charm in Bath—for the old literary times there, & for our own visits to it, perhaps you SEE my husband & self pacing along! he is great at hunting up old houses of interest—as you do, fine times once must have been enjoyed doubtless, of dash & jollity!—but I did so like bathing in those baths as if I were a Roman, & seeing imaginatively those oldest times of all; yet anyway there is something of sadness—in one's reflections of the passing of time & times of old. When TH & I were engaged—(1870 to 74) my first visit there was to an old lady & he came to stay near by—it was but a few days we remained but we were highly pleased with the city & all of its romance, & we knew later the Portsmouths of Eggesford—very well—(the *former* ones.) *He* used to boast that he had revived *it*—& so he had—& was often there—the result being however the same as with everyone—that, (as far as I can judge)—the benefit wears off—& once you begin getting "cured" you must go on with the process at intervals always.

My husband's books have not the same kind of interest for me, as for others. I knew every word of the *first* Edition—in MS. sitting by his side—etc etc. So long ago, & so much endured since—in this town in which I have been *unhappy*, that they are bound to be different to me!

I had expected always to live in London with occasional visits to the *country*. (I love the country however). Perhaps you may *understand*!—and perhaps not—that *only Authorship* seldom causes the trouble that undesirable proximity does!

I have returned lately from seeking in London a suitable *place* to dwell in for a few weeks soon—& did not succeed—but came back quickly with an evil cold.

My husband is there for a while—but as the weather has most suddenly changed to bitter cold—I expect he will be back again for a later setting forth. You know we are both *old* now & every kind of change has much consideration.

Recognition here has certainly come somewhat too late to us. I would rather go to the seaside—a quiet—forgotten—kind of one—than to London just yet. I am ensconsing myself in the Study in *his* big chair foraging—he keeps me *out* usually—as *never* formerly—ah well! I have my private opinion of men in general & of him in particular—grand brains—much "power" —but too often, lacking in judgment of ordinary matters—opposed to *un*selfishness—as regards them*selves*!—utterly useless & dangerous as magistrates! & such offices—& to be put up with until a new order of the universe *arrives*, (IT WILL).

Yours sincerely
Emma L. Hardy

Text MS. (with envelope) Wiltshire R.O.; pencil note on verso of final leaf in an unidentified hand.

Hoare: Alda Hoare, née Weston (1861–1947), wife of Sir Henry Hugh Arthur Hoare, Bt., of Stourhead, Wiltshire, was one of ELH's most active correspondents at this period; several of her letters to ELH are in DCM. For her relationships with ELH, TH, and later FEH see Roger Alma, 'Thomas Hardy at Stourhead', *National Trust Studies 1979*, ed. Gervase Jackson-Stops (London: Philip Wilson, 1978), 99–110. Stourhead House and its famous gardens now belong to the National Trust.   *Bath*: Lady Hoare, writing to ELH from Bath (21 Apr. 1910, DCM), had expatiated upon its interest and charm.   *old lady*: Anne d'Arville; see *Life and Work*, 93, 96.   *Portsmouths*: the family of Isaac Newton Wallop (1825–91), 5th Earl of Portsmouth;

see *Life and Work*, 173. Eggesford House, in Devon, was the Portsmouths' country seat.   *My husband's books*: Lady Hoare had reported purchasing all of TH's books.   *in which . . . unhappy*: ELH first wrote 'that I have been unhappy in'.   *seeking in London*: it was TH who eventually found and rented a London flat; see letter of 21 June 1910.   *to the seaside*: ELH did go briefly to Bournemouth (*CL* iv. 85) before joining TH in London early in May.

To London Society for Women's Suffrage

4. Blomfield Court. Maida Vale
21st ins: [June 1910]

Mrs Thomas Hardy would like to have received an official receipt by post for a 10/- sub: to the Secy of the London Society of W. Suff: (Lady F. Balfour). Instead of which she had an unexpected, visit (& UNINVITED) from Miss Bertha Newcombe who asserted in a most ill-bred manner that Mrs. Hardy had previously belonged to the Militant Set—which she certainly did not, & would abhor to belong to—& had worn the wrong colours—which probably inadvertently she *had* some very long time since.

Mrs Hardy wishes to know if this visit was made on behalf of the Society & she were sent by the Sec: or was an independent one—?

Text MS. Fawcett Library.   *Date* See notes below.
4. Blomfield Court: the flat, in Maida Vale, rented by the Hardys for the late spring and early summer of 1910.   *Balfour*: Lady Frances Balfour (1858–1931), daughter of 8th Duke of Argyll, was an active advocate of the women's suffrage cause.   *Newcombe*: Bertha Newcombe, painter and book illustrator; she knew the Hardys well and had stayed at Max Gate in 1900.   *this visit*: the Society's secretary, Philippa Strachey (22 June 1910, DCM), denied that ELH had been seen as a supporter of the militants but indirectly acknowledged that Newcombe's visit had been made on the Society's behalf. ELH's postcard of 23 June (Fawcett Library) again insisted that 'the visit had *no purpose* but to annoy'.

To The Editor of the *Dorset County Chronicle*

Max Gate, Dorchester.
[Early July 1910]

I have been asked to contribute to the Amazon Society, or Women's League of Health, lately started in Fordington with what seems to be a good object; but having glanced through the papers, illustrated and otherwise, I think that it will do some harm in its methods. I write to mention that I am opposed strongly to teaching children to practise cruelty on living creatures, even of the insect kind, unless actually noxious or dangerous to human life, as are mosquitoes and stinging insects when invading our dwellings, which should be killed by instant crushing. In my early years all

49

children were taught not to torture flies, and that house flies were not only harmless, but useful, as scavengers of the air, which contains imperceptible refuse injurious to us. The thorough cleaning out of corners, seldom properly done, would reduce their numbers effectually, and should be imperative on every householder; but on no account should horrible deaths by poison or fly-papers be allowed. Great cleanliness is all-sufficient. Consider the careful brushing of head, legs, and wings in a most curiously diligent manner by these little creatures. It must be remembered that minuteness of organism does not prevent agony, that size is of no account in the scheme of creation. And let me draw attention to Milton's words about summer flies humming—"while this multitude of flies is filling all the air with melody." I have thought that, when in July the birds begin their long silence for the remainder of the year, the melodious hum of flies is charming, and is a kind of singing up a line, and joyous withal in its soft way.

E. L. Hardy.

Text   *Dorset County Chronicle*, 14 July 1910, 3; headed 'FLIES, HEALTH, AND CRUELTY. MRS. THOMAS HARDY'S VIEWS.'
Amazon . . . Health: untraced as a national organization; perhaps a local group only. *Milton's words*: the passage—correctly quoted except for the absence of the line-break following 'flies'—is in fact Wordsworth's, from Book I of *The Excursion*. Florence Henniker, receiving a copy of this letter, understandably acknowledged to ELH (22 July 1910, DCM) that she hadn't known 'Milton's line'; she also confessed that she did think flies a pest.

To John Lane

MAX GATE, | DORCHESTER.

Sep: 20. 1910

Dear Mr Lane,

—You once offered to be my publisher—it sounded a large idea to me, but I have some little M.S.S. lying by & a friend staying with us who is a writer herself, considers some of them might be published, perhaps singly in pamphlet form or altogether—they are somewhat scrappy. Kind regards to Mrs Lane & yourself.

Sincerely yours,

Emma. L. Hardy.

Text   MS. Berg.
Lane: John Lane (1854–1925), the publisher, whom ELH had known for some years; a friendly letter to him of 25 June 1905 is also in the Berg Collection.   *a friend*: Florence Emily Dugdale, whom ELH seems to have met for the first time during the summer of 1910; see headnote to FED's letter of 15 July 1910. One of the MSS. was perhaps 'The Acceptors': see FED's letters of 18 Aug. and 30 Sept. 1910.

To John Lane

MAX GATE, | DORCHESTER.
Sepr. 30/10—

Dear Mr Lane ..

. . . Not hearing from you—after some waiting I have promised my M.S. to another publisher—to consider. I may add it is more prose than poetry—& the latter is but scrappy. I shall think of you another time, & *venture*!

With kindest regards to all

Yours very sincerely
Emma. L. Hardy

Text   MS. Berg.
Lane . . . Not: sic.

To The London Society for Women's Suffrage

Max Gate
18th inst. [May 1911]

Mrs Thomas Hardy is changing some of her "subs" & "dons" this year as she is not able to do so many things as formerly & cannot subscribe or take part in Wms Suffrage movement—though not at all disapproving of it—but nearly her whole attention is given to the Protestant cause—the situation being in such a critical condition by the aggresive attempt of the R. C. Hierarchy to interfere with our simple services & subvert free-flourishing England & *aggressive* attitude of the *Roman* C.s *generally*. The upholding of our *true*, *Bible* faith is paramount for believers, & has to be impressed upon the apathetic. Besides which the pressure of Parliamentary business seems to exclude any chance of success till next year.

Text   MS. (correspondence card) Fawcett Library.   *Date*   MS. annotated 'Ans 19.5.11'.
"subs" & "dons": subscriptions and donations.   *the R. C. Hierarchy*: cf. FED's letter of 11 Dec. 1910.

To Leonora Gifford

MAX GATE, | DORCHESTER.
October 18th [1911]

Dear Cousin Leonie—

—I have not forgotten you. I think it must be delightfull to be an American & an English person in one. I should like to do as you if I were younger—

pack myself on board & sail away to another land. I am not too much devoted to my native land—though I say to myself of dear Devon—"this is my own my native county"—I wish I were a *Continental*! I have always hated the return after journeying. I could not write to you before—there was so much to do, & such a hot summer. I managed to have a *cool* tea-party—under our trees—& windows opened up to full extent by a morning carpenter. I should so like you & your Father to have been here.

All through the summer I have had worries of servants in a state of *unrest* like nations—what with one thing another we all do live in troublous perilous times! I have been scattering beautiful little booklets about—which may, I hope, help to make the clear atmosphere of pure Protestantism in the land to revive us again—in the *truth*—as I believe it to be. So I send you some of them. Do read & *pass them on*.

I have captured a good cook at last—& having given us rather good meals—thinks she does not like it here—we do seem much in the country certainly because of our forest trees secluding us from the road. I should like so much for you to come to see us next week—if you would not mind a small room & a certain amount of vagueness in the house-keeping—for I never know whether the fairies will desert me all at once & leave the kitchen hearth cold. Yes really, the maids might *strike*—so I have provided myself with a particularly nice *chafing-dish* to put on the dining table & cook up cutlets & things!!! whilst I wait patiently for a sensible person—man or woman to consider it a privelege to cook for us.

dear me whatever will you think of all this!—

I have a friend too I am looking up—a fine clever *vegetarian!*—I hope she will come.

This Play, or rather these, *Plays* are drawing more people than ever—from a distance & numbers of people come & take the new houses—*for a while*—but I do not believe they like Dorchester *much* better than I do—the working people are not, as a rule, easy to get on with—

I hope you are none of you the worse for the extraordinary heat of the past summer. I had a horrid *bite* of a most venomous *hot* insect on my instep which laid me up at my Club. Then I went to Worthing—a nice quiet soothing place where I always get well *again*. We have both got old; but feel young still except for occasional prostrating by weakness after unusal exertions inconsiderately undertaken. I learnt when young "Verse a breeze amidst blossoms straying". Coleridge you know; & now I *feel* it *all*. How is it that children love solemn things I wonder?

Dear cousin *once* removed (to be quite *accurate*) do come—before my new cook vanishes—on the 9th & give me some of your ideas.

Believe me

Yours very sincerely & affectionately
Emma L: Hardy

Especial kind regards & affectionate remembrances to my *first cousin*—your dear Father.

Text   MS. Bristol University.   *Date*   From internal evidence.

Gifford: Leonora ('Léonie') Randolph Gifford (1881–1968), elder daughter of ELH's first cousin Charles Edwin Gifford, was apparently planning a visit to the United States.   *"this ... county"*: an adaptation of Scott's 'This is my own, my native land' (*The Lay of the Last Minstrel*, canto VI, st. 1).   *dear ... this!—*: so set out in MS.   *clever vegetarian*: unidentified.   *Plays*: in Nov. 1911 the Dorchester Debating and Dramatic Society presented two plays based on Hardy stories, *The Three Wayfarers*, dramatized by TH himself from 'The Three Strangers', and *The Distracted Preacher*, dramatized by A. H. Evans (see letter of 21 Nov. 1909).   *my Club*: the Alexandra Club.   *to Worthing*: she was apparently accompanied by FED; see the photograph following p. 148 of Robert Gittings, *The Older Hardy* (London: Heinemann Educational, 1978).   *"Verse ... straying"*: the opening line of Coleridge's 'Youth and Age', though omitting the important comma after 'Verse'.   *Dear cousin*: ELH first wrote 'Dear *second* cousin', then opted for the more precise definition of the relationship.

To The London Society for Women's Suffrage

Max Gate
March. 9. 12.

Mrs Thomas Hardy is greatly shocked at the conduct of the Suffragettes' & cannot encourage such illegal proceedings, & can only beg that the donation she has lately sent may be returned to her & her name taken off any book it may be on—as to be even on the *right* side of the movement is still to be identified with the *whole* in a sense—but may add that she considers Miss Violet Markham a *traitor* to the cause of women—who suffer greatly from injustices. It is easy therefore to earn applause from an assemblage of men—an audience ready to endorse her arguments which are not *new*— neither true—& the Times leader—forgets that no people can get complete knowledge & power to use it—when for generations they have been kept *under*.

Text   MS. (correspondence card) Fawcett Library; in the final sentence 'er' in 'power' and 'e' in 'they' have been torn away.

illegal proceedings: i.e. the recent window-breaking campaign in Westminster and other parts of London organized by the Women's Social and Political Union and commonly referred to in newspaper headlines as 'The Suffragist Outrages'.   *donation*: see letter of 14 Mar. 1912.   *Markham*: Violet Rosa Markham (1872–1959), a well-known social reformer, had spoken against the suffrage cause at a large anti-suffrage demonstration held in the Albert Hall on 28 Feb.   *Times leader:* a leading article in *The Times* of 2 Mar. 1912 cited Violet Markham as blaming the scarcity of women in elective positions upon their indifference to public responsibilities.

To The London Society for Women's Suffrage

Max Gate.

March 14th [1912]

Mrs Thomas Hardy certainly wishes the *Donation* sent to L.S.W.S. Feby the 28th to be returned immediately & her name not left on their books, as she does not wish to be identified in any way with the movement as it *now* stands or give any semblance of encouragement to it. She was unaware that any illegal conduct was likely to occur in any of the numerous sections— & withdrew on the previous occasion from being a subscriber—& must *remind* that her own particular feeling & advice was to let the subject— great as it is—& *just*—lie in *abeyance* whilst so much was occupying the Government at present. The beautiful processions were effective as a show of numbers & strength—would not be allowed probably now.

Text   MS. (correspondence card) Fawcett Library.   *Date*   See notes below.
the Donation: a letter sent by the Society on 13 Mar. 1912 (carbon copy, Fawcett Library) assured ELH that the Finance Committee shared her views and suggested that her donation be recorded as an anonymous gift; an annotation on the present MS., however, indicates that a 'private cheque' for ten shillings was sent to her on 15 Mar.

To Evelyn Bartelot

MAX GATE, | DORCHESTER.

23rd [July 1912]

Dear Mrs Bartlott.

   Saturday *certainly* it must be! My idea is to drive to your house in a Brake about 3.30(?) stopping at Max Gate to take up the things we want—& on to Osmington—returning about 6.30.(?). *All* coming into this *house* for light refreshment & the brake returning *through* Fordington to Dorchester. Some such way seems feasable. What do you think of it—*time* etc.? I, if fine shall be in Dorchester in morning about 12—bringing some of the things. If Saturday is a wet day—Monday?

Yours sincerely

E L Hardy.

Text MS. Colby.   *Date* Month and year supplied on MS. in unidentified hand.
Bartlott: i.e. Evelyn Bartelot, wife of the Revd Richard Grosvenor Bartelot (letter of 24 Feb. 1907); she was a daughter of TH's friend Alfred Pope, a Dorchester brewer active in local affairs.   *it must be!*: i.e. a picnic organized by ELH and her niece Lilian Gifford (see headnote to letter of 29 Mar. 1897) for the Children's Guild of Fordington St George. The *Fordington Monthly Messenger* for August 1912 thanked ELH for taking the children to the seaside at Osmington and 'providing the most splendid tea they ever had'.

To The Revd R. Grosvenor Bartelot

Max Gate

Thursday— [1 August 1912]

Dear Mr Grosvenor Bartlott.

Do please read these two little books. One *I* admire—& the other I hope *you* may like—tell me anyway what you may think? Kindly return.

I hope the *Darling* was none the worse for her journey. One child has sent me a sweet grateful note—("*but where are the 9*"?

Excuse haste

Yours sincerely

E. L. Hardy

Text MS. Colby.   *Date* Supplied on MS. in unidentified hand.
Bartlott: correctly Bartelot; see letter of 24 Feb. 1907.   *two little books*: perhaps ELH's own privately printed booklets of verse (*Alleys*, dated Dec. 1911) and religious prose (*Spaces*, dated Apr. 1912), both reprinted in ELH, *Poems and Religious Effusions* (St Peter Port: Toucan Press, 1966).   *the Darling*: i.e. the Bartelots' own daughter, one of the children attending ELH's picnic.   *("but . . . the 9"?*: Luke 17: 17; parenthesis unclosed.

Letters of Florence Emily Hardy

[Florence Emily Dugdale gave different people different accounts of her first meeting with her future husband, but it does seem clear that while on holiday in Weymouth in August 1905 she wrote, as an unknown admirer, to ask if she might call on him at Max Gate. Addressing her as 'Dear Madam', TH replied: 'As you are not going to print anything about your visit I shall be happy to be at home to you some afternoon during this month, if you will send a post card a day or two before you are coming' (*CL*, iii. 179). They must have met again when TH was in London the following spring and summer—he and ELH having rented an apartment on the Edgware Road from mid-April to mid-July—and by the autumn of 1906 she had undertaken to visit the Reading Room of the British Museum on Saturdays and school holidays in order to check historical details related to Part Third of *The Dynasts*, then in progress. She acknowledged many years later that TH had probably invented some at least of these assignments, 'knowing the pleasure I took in "helping" him'.]

To The Superintendent, British Museum Reading Room

River Front. | Enfield.

20. 11. 06.

Dear Sir.

I would be much obliged if you would kindly allow me to have a Ticket of Admission to the British Museum Reading Room.

I wish to verify certain facts concerning the Napoleonic Era, & this for the use, & under the direction of, Mr Thomas Hardy, who, being at Dorchester, cannot look up for himself certain references that he needs for his book "The Dynasts."

I am twenty-six years of age, a school teacher in Enfield, & my abode is at the address given above.

I would strictly observe the rules.

Yours faithfully

Florence E Dugdale.

Text   MS. British Museum Central Archives.

River Front: FED was still living with her parents and sisters at 5 River Front, a substantial semi-detached 'villa' in the London suburb of Enfield.   *Ticket*: annotations on the MS. indicate that authorization was sent immediately, on 21 Nov. FED's sponsor was not TH but a prominent Enfield citizen named John McEwan, a Scottish-born tea-merchant: writing to Edward Clodd 29 Nov. 1911 (Leeds) she referred to McEwan and his wife as friends of hers and great admirers of Clodd's writings. See also note to letter of 30 Jan. 1913.

[It was in 1908 that FED, persistently hampered by a weak throat, finally abandoned the teaching career for which she had been trained and sought instead to maintain herself by writing, secretarial work, and occasional journalism. By the summer of 1910 she had already ended—in disgust—her brief experience as a reporter for the London *Standard* and *Evening Standard*, but the *Standard* nevertheless printed her well-informed profile of TH on the occasion of his seventieth birthday, 2 June 1910. At the end of that same month the *Evening Standard* carried a similar piece of hers on the seventieth birthday of Edward Clodd. TH was intimate with Clodd at this period and took FED with him on visits to Clodd's house on the sea-front at Aldeburgh on a number of occasions from August 1909 onwards.]

To Edward Clodd

5, RIVER FRONT, | ENFIELD.
Saturday morn: [2 July 1910]

Dear Mr Clodd/

I am not nearly so bad as I seem. I telephoned to the Standard office, directly I had your letter, & told them not to set up the article until they heard from me. Then I wrote at once & said it was on no account to be published. The only result was that they rushed it through a day earlier than they intended & then the news-editor sent me the enclosed letter. But if my intentions were good, Mr Hardy's were not. When I told him I had written to stop the article he said what a pity it was I had posted the letter so quickly, & that it would have been so easy to have been too late. As for the purple patches, they were *all* his, I can assure you.

But it was very very kind of you to be so forgiving.

Yours very Sincerely,
Florence E Dugdale.

Text   MS. Beinecke.   Date   From internal evidence.
Clodd: see ELH letter of 29 Nov. 1897.   *the article*: 'Edward Clodd', *Evening Standard and St James's Gazette*, 30 June 1910, 5.   *a day earlier*: Clodd's birthday was on 1 July.   *the purple patches*: according to Clodd's diary for 30 June 1910. (Alan Clodd) these had 'happily' been omitted before publication.

[Although the date when FED first met ELH cannot be precisely determined, she had certainly done so by the early summer of 1910, when she attended two or three of the Hardys' London 'At Homes'—apparently after coming forward to help ELH rearrange the muddled pages of a speech she was delivering at the Lyceum Club, a women's club in Piccadilly to which they both belonged. ELH quickly 'took' to the younger woman, asked her to keep an eye on TH in London after she had herself returned to Max Gate, and invited her to spend a week at Max Gate from 26 July to 2 August 1910 in the overlapping and to some extent conflicting roles of friend, typist, and literary adviser. FED also had typing to do for TH and took some of the work home with her to Enfield, but she was again at Max Gate in September, November, and December 1910, even spending Christmas there.]

To Emma Hardy

5, RIVER FRONT, | ENFIELD.
Friday. [15 July 1910?]

Dear Mrs Hardy,

I am truly grieved to learn how sadly you have been. I trust that you are recovering strength in the country air. You have, I fear, found the past month or two very trying.

I will with pleasure call at the flat as often as I can. I went up this afternoon & all seemed well. The woman had been & attended to the bedroom, etc, but Mr Hardy was taking his meals out.

As you say, he would be better in a hotel, & certainly the anxiety as to how he is cannot be good for you. You will need all your strength for the great campaign which lies before us.

I cannot find words to thank you sufficiently for all your goodness to me. Believe me I am most truly grateful, & if at any time there is anything you wish me to do for you, it will be a great joy.

Trusting that you will soon be well,

Yours very sincerely,
Florence E Dugdale

Text   MS. DCM.   *Date*   This was the only Friday between ELH's departure from London on 12 July and TH's on 20 July.
how sadly you have been: ELH's 'cough' is sympathetically mentioned in FED's letter to her of 23 July 1910 (DCM).   *the flat*: 4 Blomfield Court, currently rented by the Hardys; see ELH letter of 21 June 1910.

To Emma Hardy

5, RIVER FRONT, | ENFIELD.
18th August '10.

Dear Mrs Hardy,

Thank you very much for your kind letter & invitation. I am afraid that should not be able to leave home before the 9th of September. My mother very much wishes to go to a wedding on the 8th, & there is no-one but myself who would be able to go with her. She would not go by herself.

I would very much like to come to you on the 9th, if that will suit you.

I have already typed the 'Acceptors' MS, & yesterday I gave it to a publisher I know & asked him to look throught it & tell me whether, if it were revised, he would be able to publish it. I did not give your name, nor is there any name on the MS. I thought that it would be wiser to get a perfectly unbiassed opinion. However, I roused his curiosity by saying it was written by a well-known lady, a philanthopist & writer. We will see now what happens. I am retyping it to send you a copy.

The more I see of the story—'The Maid on the Shore'—the more I like it. I will type that next. I would have done it before, but I have had to write an article that was ordered, & that took up a great deal of my time.

With most grateful thanks,

Yours very sincerely,
Florence E. Dugdale.

Text MS. DCM.
My mother: born Emma Taylor and said to be related to the John Taylor who edited the *London Magazine* and published Keats.   *on the 9th*: FED apparently did go to Max Gate on 9 Sept. and stay until 29 Sept.; from 2 to 6 Sept., however, she was with TH at Clodd's house in Aldeburgh (Clodd diary, Alan Clodd).   *the 'Acceptors' MS*: one of the short pieces of religious prose included in ELH's *Spaces* booklet of 1912 (see ELH letter of 1 Aug. 1912) bears the title, 'The Acceptors and Non-acceptors'; at this stage, however, the title was apparently being used for a longer piece of writing or for the booklet as a whole.   *publisher*: unidentified.   *on the Shore'*: the novella-length romance with a Cornish setting—'A story of fair passions, and beautiful pities, and loves without stain'—which ELH seems to have begun in the 1870s and finished in the late 1880s; FED's typescript is in DCM.

To Emma Hardy

LYCEUM CLUB, | 128, PICCADILLY, W.
30th September [1910]

My dear Mrs Hardy,

I arrived home quite safely last night—but a little late. Something went wrong with the engine of the train & it had to be changed near Basingstoke. On my arrival at Enfield I went straight off to a French class, & I have been very busy ever since. I have just come up to London & have been rushing round at a great rate. As soon as I get home I am going to start typing 'The Maid on the Shore,' & will just stick to it until it is done. There is rather more of it than I thought—107 pages in all. I do not think I can manage more than 10 pp a day so may possibly take a little over a week to finish. I fancy there are many corrections that must be made. Certain costumes are described fully & these—appropriate as they must have been 21 years ago when the story was written—would only make the story seem ridiculous now. For instance—'a robe of yellow velvet, golden coins hanging over her brow, & dusky hair floating over her shoulders.'

Perhaps all these corrections can be made after.

I am writing a rambling letter & have left until now that which I should have said at first. Thank you so much for your goodness to me during my visit to you. It was so very delightful, & I have such pleasant memories of our talks.

I am quite burning with anxiety to know the fate of 'The Acceptors.' I fancy though that your great triumph will be with 'The Inspirer.'

I saw some most delightful shades at Selfridge's. I ordered some pink ones—as I think you said that was the shade you wanted. They are sending them on to you but if they do not do please send them back—or to me— as they have promised to change them if not suitable.

They seemed rather expensive so I only ordered ten—but if you want a dozen they can send you two more.

While I was re-reading 'The Maid' last night I was again impressed by the vivid & picturesque descriptions of Cornish Scenery.

If I can be of any use to you next week-end I will gladly come on Friday next. If not I will remain here—working at your MS. until it is finished.

Everyone at home thinks that I look so much better for my holiday. Thank you again dear Mrs Hardy, so very much.

Yours very sincerely
Florence E. Dugdale

Text MS. DCM. *Date* Year from internal evidence.

107 pages: presumably in ELH's MS.; FEH's typescript (the only version extant) has 87 pages.   '*a robe . . . shoulders.*': perhaps not an actual quotation; the corresponding passage in the typescript (p. 47) reads differently but seems no less archaic.   '*The Inspirer.*': Clodd's diary for 27 Apr. 1913 (Alan Clodd) records TH's telling him that this was a 'novel' about a wife who inspired her husband's novels.   *shades*: i.e. candle-shades.

To Emma Hardy

5, RIVER FRONT, | ENFIELD.
4th October '10.

Dear Mrs Hardy,

I am rapidly progressing with the typewriting. I find, however, that I have no other copy of 'The Acceptors.' I remember—quite clearly—that I only did three. One was sent to a publisher—that was the first, & un-corrected. Then I sent you one which you corrected, & then I did another —the one you have now. An earlier copy would be of no use since you have added that last part about 'The Trumpet Call.' It is that copy—the one you sent to your friend at Cambridge—that ought to be retyped for the publisher. I remember I was going to do another copy but something went wrong with the typewriter & I had to sent it to be repaired. If you will send me the MS at once I will type it here. I think I can do it better here than at Max Gate—but I will do just as you wish. I find I have about fifty different things to do this week, & a publisher has just written, asking me for some more little stories about birds.

I think you will find that 'The Inspirer' will be quite the most successful of your works, but I can quite understand that it was impossible for Mr McIlvaine to publish it, since he was Mr Hardy's publisher. He now publishes in America only. There are other—& better—publishers for your purpose. We must make *that* a success, for it will be a big thing.

Yours very sincerely,

F. E. Dugdale

Text MS. DCM.
'The Trumpet Call.': presumably related to 'The New Element of Fire' in *Spaces* (see letter of 18 Aug. 1910). *friend at Cambridge*: Alfred Pretor; see ELH letter of 19 Feb. 1897. *'The Inspirer'*: see letter of 30 Sept. 1910. *McIlvaine*: Clarence W. McIlvaine (1865–1912), currently London representative of Harper & Brothers, TH's American publishers.

[Though trivial in itself, FED's postcard to TH's sister Katharine—like later cards to Mary and Henry Hardy that also survive—is suggestive of the complexity of the relationships in which she had become involved. She had not only accompanied TH on visits to Clodd's at which a good many other people were present, but she was on friendly terms with TH's siblings and a welcome visitor to the Higher Bockhampton cottage (TH's birthplace) where they still lived. Deeply sorry for ELH though she clearly remained, she was increasingly exposed to those who saw the situation from a 'Hardy' point of view. At the same time, her openness and indeed indiscretion when writing to Clodd—an available confidant who was at once sympathetic, intensely curious, and thoroughly well informed—seem to suggest that to a considerable extent she stood emotionally outside the marital tragi-comedy of which Max Gate was then the scene, capable of seeing TH as well as ELH in a sharply critical light.]

To Katharine Hardy

[20 October 1910]

This is Enfield. It is not so pretty as Dorchester—& of course not nearly so sweet as Bockhampton—but still it might be worse. I wish I were back in Dorset. Hope I shall soon see you all again

F.E.D.

Text MS. (picture postcard of The Town, Enfield) Eton. *Date* From postmark.
Katharine Hardy: the younger of TH's sisters (1856–1940).

To Edward Clodd

5, RIVER FRONT, | ENFIELD.
8th November '10.

Dear Mr Clodd,

I am ashamed to worry you when I know you must be very busy, but I hope you won't mind.

Do you remember my speaking to you, as we were on our way to Aldeburgh in August, about a very good reliable boy, an old pupil of mine? He called to see me last night & asked me whether I thought he might apply for a post as clerk in your bank. I said that he had better do so, & that I would write to you as well. His name is Quinton & I think you will have his letter on Friday morning. If there is any chance of his finding a post I am sure he would prove himself most able & reliable. He has brains, & a sterling character.

I am going back to Max Gate on Monday for a week or two. Mr TH. has been in the depths of despair at the death of a pet cat. 'Providence' he wrote, 'has dealt me an entirely gratuitous & unlooked for blow.' But his last letter shows that he is very pleasurably excited over the forthcoming play: 'Mellstock Choir' & he is also finding a melancholy pleasure in writing an appropriate inscription for 'Kitsey's' headstone, so that Providence has not done all the harm it intended, this time.

I was so very sorry to hear, while I was last at Max Gate, that you had been ill. I hope that you are much better & that the cold weather will not affect you.

With kind regards,

Yours very sincerely
F. E. Dugdale

Text MS. Leeds.

Quinton: perhaps one of the sons of Arthur Charles Quinton of Enfield, income-tax collector and a director (like FED's father) of the Enfield Building Society.   *able and reliable*: FED thanked Clodd 24 Feb. 1911 (Leeds) for giving Quinton a position, but later wrote to apologize for recommending someone who had not, in fact, turned out well.   *back to Max Gate*: on 15 Nov. TH himself wrote to Clodd, 'Miss D.—my handyman, as I call her—appeared yesterday with her typewriter, & we are going to be amazingly industrious—in intention, at least: though fine days tempt one out of doors' (*CL*, iv. 128).   *'Mellstock Choir'*: *The Mellstock Quire*, an adaptation by A. H. Evans (see ELH letter of 21 Nov. 1909) of TH's novel *Under the Greenwood Tree*, was presented by the Dorchester Debating and Dramatic Society on 16 and 17 Nov. 1910.   *'Kitsey's' headstone*: still legible in the pets' cemetery at Max Gate but bearing no inscription other than Kitsey's name.

To Edward Clodd

5, RIVER FRONT, | ENFIELD.

11: 11: 10.

My dear Mr Clodd/

Thank you again & again for your kindness. I feel I have no right to bother you so much, especially about a complete stranger.

I shall be delighted to spend that week-end at Aldeburgh—but I am very much afraid that Mr T.H. will refuse to stir from Max Gate. He seems quite planted there for the winter, & as I go there now so often I don't expect he will be in London at all until the spring. It is a pity, for Mr Whale is so nice a man, & I am sure Mr Hardy would like Miss Stephens. Indeed, he was wondering whether you would have liked Mr Whale to visit Max Gate at the same time as yourself.

Now, if you wanted to give Mr TH. a really happy time, you should ask Miss Sinclair, & I could gently intimate to him that Miss Sinclair was so anxious to be there with him, . . . etc etc. Poor Mrs H. says she *won't* have her at Max Gate, & so what is poor Mr T.H to do? I wouldn't at all mind staying with Mrs Hardy, during the time.

But all this is most ridiculous joking, as indeed you will understand. The 'Max Gate menage' always does wear an aspect of comedy to me. Mrs Hardy is good to me, beyond words, & instead of cooling towards me she grows more & more affectionate. I am *intensely* sorry for her, sorry indeed for both.

I am ashamed to burden you too much with my confidences, but your sympathy—the most kindly I have ever known—always encourages me to go on.

I have told you of my kind & good friend in Dublin. His collections, etc are all being sold this & part of next week. At this time of stress & anxiety he has had another—a more crushing blow. His wife, Lady Stoker, died last night. In the face of such calamity I cannot write & sympathise very deeply with T.H. upon the death of 'Kitsey', although he writes, poor man, to ask: 'Was there ever so sad a life as mine?'

Forgive me, dear Mr Clodd, for inflicting this long long letter upon you.

Yours very sincerely & gratefully

Florence E. Dugdale.

Text MS. Leeds.

refuse to stir: TH did indeed decline to go to Aldeburgh on this occasion (*CL*, iv. 128). *Mr Whale*: Clodd's friend George Whale (1849–1925), solicitor and prominent rationalist. *Miss Stephens*: Winifred Stephens (d. 1944), writer on French literature and history; she married George Whale in 1923, a year after the death of his first wife. *Miss Sinclair*: Mary (May)

Amelia St Clair Sinclair (1863–1946), novelist and women's suffrage campaigner, who had gone cycling with TH during a visit to Dorset in Oct. 1908.   *was . . . with him*: FED's above-the-line insertion.   *friend in Dublin*: Bram Stoker's brother Sir [William] Thornley Stoker, Bt. (1845–1912), a distinguished surgeon; FED seems to have spent some months in Dublin during the winter of 1906/7 as a companion to the invalid Lady Stoker whose death is here reported. See Robert Gittings and Jo Manton, *The Second Mrs Hardy* (London: Heinemann, 1979), 38–45.   *collections . . . being sold*: reports of the sale of Stoker's collections of furniture, medals, lacquer work, etc., appear in the *Irish Times* for 16 and 17 Nov. 1910.   *& part of next*: this phrase originally followed 'week' but was arrowed into its present location by FED.

To Emma Hardy

5, RIVER FRONT, | ENFIELD.
Friday. [11 November 1910]

My dear Mrs Hardy,

Please forgive me for not acknowledging, before this, the paper, 'The Author', & the leaflets you so kindly sent me. We have had much anxiety at home. Today we have had to have a specialist, Dr Norman Meachin, down to see her. However, his report is cheering, & gives hope of complete cure, if we are very very careful.

Today a telegram came from Ireland to say that a dear dear friend, Lady Stoker, had died of pneumonia. It is so great a shock to me, & altogether I am so confused that I find difficulty in writing.

I fancy that all has been settled quite satisfactorily with regard to 'The Maid on the Shore', so far so good. I have had an unpleasant rebuff concerning 'The Acceptors.' With regard to the poems if you have others— enough to make up a slender volume—I think we can manage to get that published. My publisher says that it is impossible to mix prose & verse unless the one has a connection with the other. In the case of Kipling he *does* make his stories & his verses accord. We can discuss all this on Monday, however, when I hope to be with you. I will travel by the usual train 12.30 from Waterloo. I am glad to know that you are getting on with the writing. We *must* accomplish something.

Thank you again, so much.

Yours very sincerely.
F E Dugdale.

Text MS. DCM.   *Date* From internal evidence.
'*The Author*': the organ of the Incorporated Society of Authors, Playwrights, and Composers, of which TH had recently become president.   *much anxiety at home*: on account of the illness of FED's mother.   *Meachin*: presumably George Norman Meachen (1876–1955), a

specialist in dermatology.   *Lady Stoker*: see letter to Clodd of 11 Nov. 1910.   *slender volume*: a booklet of her poems, *Alleys*, was pub. from Max Gate in 1912; see ELH letter of 1 Aug. 1912.   *his stories . . . accord*: e.g. in Rudyard Kipling's *Puck of Pook's Hill* (1906) and *Rewards and Fairies* (1910).

To Edward Clodd

MAX GATE, | DORCHESTER.
Saturday morn [19 November 1910]

My dear Mr Clodd/

Thank you very much for your kind letter & post-card. I am not quite sure how matters stand at present—whether you are expecting me at Aldeburgh next weekend or whether you have decided to wait until Mr T.H. is able to come. with me. At all events I shall understand—if I do not hear from you in the meanwhile, that the proposed weekend is 'off' for the present.

I am leaving here today. The ceremony on Wednesday was most delightful, & I quite enjoyed it—far more so than the play.

I went into Mr Hardy's study yesterday & found him working at a pathetic little poem describing the melancholy burial of the white cat. I looked over his shoulder & read this line:

'That little white cat was his only friend.'

That was too much for even my sweet temper, & I ramped round the study exclaiming: 'This *is* hideous ingratitude.' But the culprit seemed highly delighted with himself, & said, smilingly, that he was not exactly writing about himself but about some imaginary man in a similar situation.

Mrs Hardy seems to be queerer than ever. She has just asked me whether I have noticed how extremely like *Crippen* Mr TH. is, in personal appearance. She added darkly that she would not be surprised to find herself in the cellar one morning. All this in deadly seriousness. I thought it was time to depart or she would be asking me if I didn't think I resembled Miss Le Neve. Her latest idea is to go abroad for some months, because that would 'have a good effect on T.H.' I thought it might be an experiment worth trying until she told me that she wanted me to go with her.

I am scribbling this in haste, so please will you excuse the horrid writing & the incoherencies.

Yours very sincerely,
F E Dugdale.

Text MS. Leeds. *Date* From internal evidence.
come. with me: FED added 'with me' but failed to delete the original period. *ceremony on Wednesday*: when TH was presented with the Freedom of the Borough of Dorchester. *the play*: *The Mellstock Quire*, first performed that same day; see letter of 8 Nov. 1910. *'That . . . friend.'*: see stanza 5, line 2, of TH's poem, 'The Roman Gravemounds', first pub., as 'Among the Roman Gravemounds', in the *English Review*, Dec. 1911. *Crippen . . . Miss Le Neve*: Hawley Harvey Crippen, executed 23 Nov. 1910 for the murder of his wife, whose body was found buried in the basement of their house; his mistress, Ethel Clare Le Neve, was acquitted on a charge of assisting him in his attempted escape across the Atlantic. *go abroad*: see letter of 11 Dec. 1910.

To Emma Hardy

River Front, | Enfield.
1st. Dec: 1910

My dear Mr Hardy,

I have, according to your instructions, withdrawn that poem 'A Ballad of A Boy'. On reflection I see that you are both wise & kind in withdrawing it, if you think it would cause any annoyance. Nevertheless it is so good a poem, & so full of life & originality that I am sorry it cannot be published. Personally I cannot see in it one line that would identify the boy with Mr Hardy. But of course you know best.

Since I last wrote we have had a very anxious time with my mother. She has been ill again, worse than she was before, & I have to spend a great deal of time bandaging & dressing her legs, cooking invalid dishes & running up & down stairs with trays. The servant we have now is almost useless & we are going to send her away. However I manage to do an hour or two's writing in the afternoons.

My cousins' flat is in Hampstead, near St John's Wood. However, they tell me they have let it at a nominal rent to some friends of Mr Fletcher, the Conservative Candidate for Hampstead, until after the elections. They said—when I asked them why they had not kept it for me—that they had to keep fires there twice a week, & pay a woman to go in & out, & so they thought they would let these people do the airing. At all events I could not have gone there for a week or two as Mother cannot be left at present. I feel, however, that I would be able to write more freely away from home, either in a London flat or better still at the seaside, away from all interruption.

I am sure that what I am writing now is quite the best work I have done yet, & I expect when you have gone over it—adding & revising—that it will be greatly improved.

The publishers are doing nothing until they have all their Christmas books out. They are keeping back four books of mine, also, until the spring, & they had those in the early summer.

Thank you again, so much, for your kind letter.

Yours very sincerely,
Florence E Dugdale.

Text MS. DCM.
Mr Hardy: sic.   *of A Boy':* the poem has not survived.   *My cousins' flat:* FED's mother's brother John Taylor was a London chemist who had prospered through the production and sale of a skin powder called Cimalite; his daughters, FED's cousins, lived in Adelaide Road, on the southern fringes of Hampstead.   *Mr Fletcher:* Sir John Samuel Fletcher, Bt., Unionist MP for Hampstead 1905–18.   *four books of mine:* not confidently identified, given the absence of publication dates from so many of FED's books, but probably including the Blackie's annual referred to in her letter of 11 Dec. 1910 and perhaps *The Book of Baby Beasts* and its two successors (see letter of 20 Mar. 1914).

To Emma Hardy

5, RIVER FRONT, | ENFIELD.
11: 12: 10.

My dear Mrs Hardy./

Thank you so much for your last kind letter & for sending those papers. I was able to forward a small donation—a very small one—but it may help in the good cause.

It must have been most delightful to meet the American sailors, & visit the Fleet.

We have been quite anxious at Enfield over the election. The Roman Catholic priests all over the country have given orders to their followers to vote *Liberal*—for the aim of this election is to get Home Rule for Ireland so that the R.C. religion may be firmly established there, & then they can work from there. It will then be the stronghold of Roman Catholicism & a menace to this country. I hear that operations will commence there. Mr Asquith is fully aware of all this for the matter has been laid before him, but he is in league with the R.C's.

I think that Boulogne will be delightful later on, when the weather is warmer & more settled. My mother is somewhat better. I am glad to say we have a servant coming on Wednesday so that the most toilsome part of my work will then be over.

I can quite understand what difficulties you have been having. I shall call again on my publisher this week, & try to stir him up about the MSS. but I feel sure it is no good to expect anything until after Christmas. They are so slow. As a proof Blackies have just brought out a story of mine they have kept for *3 years*. Mr Shorter spoke nicely of it in the last number of The Sphere. I hope that you are keeping well, in spite of the dreadful weather. I am doing some writing, every day & will let you have it soon. With kindest regards & very many thanks.

FED.

Text MS. DCM.

the good cause: presumably the anti-Catholic cause; in a letter to ELH of [20 Nov. 1910?] (DCM) FED said she had been addressing her Protestant Bible Class in Enfield 'on the current danger'. *American . . . Fleet*: TH and ELH went aboard the flagship of an American fleet which visited Portland in late Nov. 1910 and subsequently entertained some senior American officers at Max Gate. *the election*: following the General Election of Dec. 1910 the Liberals remained in power, with Herbert Henry Asquith again as Prime Minister. *Boulogne*: in her [20 Nov.?] letter FED, demurring to this suggestion of ELH's, had cited her father as authority for the coldness of the town and the risks of contracting pneumonia there. *this week*: FED first wrote 'next week'. *story of mine*: 'The Silver Bell', in *Blackie's Children's Annual 1911* (London, [1910]). *Mr Shorter*: Clement King Shorter (see ELH letter of 15 Sept. 1904) was always supportive of FED's literary aspirations, in part because of her friendship with his wife, the Irish poet Dora Sigerson (see ELH letter of 23 Apr. 1908). His brief notice of the Blackie volume in the *Sphere*, 10 Dec. 1910, picked out FED's 'very pretty story' for special mention.

[FED seems to have left Max Gate shortly after witnessing the furious argument between TH and ELH on Christmas Day 1910 which she was to describe to Sydney Cockerell many Christmases later (see letter of 25 December 1925). Exhausted and confused by the tensions at Max Gate, she was unwilling to become an occasion of contention between two people for each of whom, if in different ways and to different degrees, she felt affection, gratitude, and respect. If she chose to stay away from Max Gate itself, however, she still kept in touch both with ELH—even holi-daying with her at the seaside resort of Worthing in July 1911—and with TH and his siblings, all firmly in the anti-ELH camp. In April 1911 she and TH went on a tour of some English cathedrals in company with her sister Constance and TH's brother Henry—whom TH seems to have hoped to pair in marriage—and in June the same party, supplemented by FED's father, made a week-long trip to the Lake District, TH having chosen to avoid the commotion and disruption occasioned in London by the Coronation of George V. The autumn of 1911, when TH was beginning work on the revisions for the Wessex Edition of his works, FED seems to have spent mostly in Enfield—typing there in early September the revised preface to *Jude the Obscure*—but shortly before Christmas she accompanied TH and his sister Kate on another brief expedition, this time to Bath, Gloucester, and Bristol.]

To Emma Hardy

River Front. | Enfield.
13: 1: 11.

My dear Mrs Hardy:

I am sorry that you should have the added trouble of Jane leaving just now—although, since her health is failing, I suppose it is as well.

I have interviewed three cooks. One—a highly woman—demanded £30, & fare: the other two, who were ready to take £20, did not want to go so far away. Since I had your postcard I have not pursued the search, but should you need one, later on, I believe there would be little difficulty in finding one. I think that Daisy has the 'makings' of a good cook—as they say, & perhaps would manage better with her sister than with a stranger.

I suppose you have heard nothing further from the publishers. I have not had a word, but I know their dilatory ways, too well.

I hope that you have quite recovered from the shock of Marky's death. Poor little creature. I often speak of her. You should write one of your delightful poems to her memory, just as Matthew Arnold did to his canary, & Mrs Browning to Flush. I have just enrolled five new members to my Bible Class.

Again thanking you for all your kindness.

Ever affectionately.
F. E. Dugdale.

Text MS. DCM.
Jane . . . Daisy: Max Gate servants.   *a highly woman*: 'a highly recommended woman' presumably intended.   *Marky's*: one of the Max Gate cats; see ELH letter of 6 Sept. 1905. *his canary*: Arnold's 'Poor Matthias'.   *to Flush*: presumably Elizabeth Barrett Browning's 'To Flush, My Dog', although it is not in fact an obituary.

To Mary Hardy

5 New Parade. | Worthing.
[9 August 1911]

I hope you are well. I have had a delightful fortnight here bathing once & sometimes twice a day. This card shows the house where I have been staying, & the road I cross daily in my bathing dress!!

F.E.D

Text MS. (picture postcard of the New Parade, East Worthing) Eton.   *Date* From postmark.
delightful fortnight: apparently in the company of ELH; a photograph of FED and ELH together on the beach at Worthing 'circa 1911' is reproduced in Robert Gittings, *The Older*

Hardy (London: Heinemann, 1978), following 148.   *house . . . road*: FED has inked a cross, a dotted line, and an arrow on the photograph of the New Parade, the line annotated 'The way I go to bathe' and the arrow 'The wall I have to jump over'.

To Henry Hardy

[24 November 1911]

Many thanks for kind letter. I will write after Monday. I do wish you were coming to London on Monday to the play. Am a *little* sorry to hear of the auction. Two centuries is a long time. Hope all are well. Love to all.

F.E.D.

Text   MS. (picture postcard of 5 River Front, Enfield) Eton.   *Date*   From postmark. *Hardy*: Henry Hardy (1851–1928), TH's younger brother, was about to retire from the family building business and move with his sisters from the Higher Bockhampton cottage to 'Talbothays', the house he had built (to TH's designs) several years previously.   *the play*: the London performance, 27 Nov. 1911, of the Dorchester production of *The Three Wayfarers* and *The Distracted Preacher*; see ELH letter of 18 Oct. 1911.   *the auction*: H. Hardy had perhaps sent FED the *Dorset County Chronicle* announcement (23 Nov. 1911) of the forthcoming auction of the Hardy firm's entire stock of plant, machinery, and building supplies.   *Two centuries*: the period (presumably as reckoned in H. Hardy's letter) during which successive Hardy generations had been working as building craftsmen.

To Edward Clodd

River Front, | Enfield.
11: 12: '11.

My dear Mr Clodd:

I feel that it is immensely selfish of me to have asked you to lecture here. Of course you must not dream of giving up a week-end to it. I know how very essential to your health those little rests are. Perhaps, if you could give a short address or lecture at the end of January, we might have the pleasure then. I will find out from the committee what dates they have vacant—but I am not sure that it is right to ask you. I ought never to have allowed myself to be persuaded.

Mr T.H, his sister & I had a pleasant little trip last week to Bath, Gloucester & Bristol. He is very well, & seemed quite gay. Mrs Henniker told me yesterday that she had never known him in better spirits than when she was in Dorset, so his passing moods of depression do not signify much perhaps.

That poor young writer—of whom I wrote to you—died yesterday. I had not expected so speedy an end or I should not have bothered my kind friends about him, but I think his last days were brightened by the hope that something *might* be done for him. Thank you again very *very* much.

Yours sincerely

Florence E Dugdale.

P.S—to letter.

I forgot to enclose this. On re-reading it through I do not think it so good as I did at first. This morning I hear from Mr T.H. that he is 'most miserable', so I do not know what has happened. However, I shall see him on Friday. The poem about poor Kitsey—his white cat—comes out in the next English Review, but in deference to my feelings he has altered it a little. Nevertheless, he has retained the line:—

'That little white cat was his only friend.'

I tell him that it is *monstrous* ingratitude on his part. F.E.D.

Text MS. Leeds.

asked you to lecture: on 29 Nov. 1911 (Leeds) FED had asked Clodd if he would speak at one of the 'Men's Meetings', officially 'non-sectarian & non-political', held every Sunday afternoon in an Enfield school.   *dates . . . vacant*: Clodd did not in fact give his lecture until more than a year later; see letter of 30 Jan. 1913.   *Mrs Henniker*: Florence Henniker, née Milnes (1855–1923), novelist, with whom TH had once been in love and for whom FED had for some time been working as an occasional typist; her husband, Major-General Arthur Henniker, died in 1912.   *poor young writer*: Alfred H. Hyatt, journalist, to whom FED seems to have been quite deeply attached, had for many years been struggling against illness and poverty; see letter of 1 Dec. 1914 and Gittings and Manton, *Second Mrs Hardy*, 25–9, 64.   *enclose this*: presumably something FED had herself written and published.   *poem about poor Kitsey*: see letters of 8 and 19 Nov. 1910.

[Because no letters of FED's from the year 1912 have as yet been discovered, it is difficult to be at all specific about her movements prior to the sudden death of ELH on 27 November 1912. FED and TH were certainly together at Clodd's Aldeburgh house for four days in May 1912, and they would apparently have been there again in October had TH not felt obliged to keep working at the proofs of the revised Wessex Edition volumes, currently being published at the rate of two a month. It is also clear from TH's few surviving letters to FED not only that they were maintaining an active correspondence but that he was writing to her about himself and his work with quite exceptional directness and intimacy. There is no sign of FED's having visited Max Gate during the period in question, but at the time of ELH's death she was on her way to Weymouth for a short visit, intending to come into Dorchester for one of the two scheduled performances of the Debating and Dramatic Society's dramatization of *The Trumpet-Major*—performances that Hardy was much criticized, locally, for allowing to go ahead in spite of his bereavement. After a brief trip back to Enfield, FED returned to Max Gate for the first of a series of extended visits that provoked a good deal of Dorchester gossip but evidently ministered very significantly to Hardy's emotional, practical, and creative needs. At the same time the continuing freedom and indiscretion of her letters to Clodd— who had taken it for granted that Hardy would greet his wife's death with relief— seem reflective of a need to find release for her own complex and even confused responses to a situation she had probably never envisaged.]

To Edward Clodd

MAX GATE, | DORCHESTER.

16th Jan. '13.

Dear Mr Clodd:

I do hope that if you feel at all tired or over-worked you will have no compunction in giving up the lecture at Enfield—much as I & others are looking forward to it. It is so extremely good of you to be willing to give it.

I am going home on Tuesday next. Mr Hardy looks very well & seems cheerful. Indeed his youngest sister tells me that he has regained the same happy laugh that he had when he was a young man. But, all the same, his life here is *lonely* beyond words, & he spends his evenings in reading & re-reading voluminous diaries that Mrs H. has kept from the time of their marriage. Nothing could be worse for him. He reads the comments upon himself—bitter denunciations, beginning about 1891 & continuing until within a day or two of her death—& I think he will end by *believing* them. I would give almost anything for you to be able to run in & see him. It is a thousand pities that Max Gate is so far from his mental companions. There is no mental kinship here at all, & he has no visitors & goes no-where, except with me to Stinsford Churchyard, & to see his sisters & brothers at Talbothays—& of course they talk of 'Emma'. The tragedy of twenty years is not ended yet. In spite of this I need hardly say that I am absolutely happy in being here, & able to look after Mr Hardy, to the best of my ability. I read aloud to him every evening after dinner, until eleven o'clock & take as much care of him as I possibly can. The niece came, & then rushed up to London for a week, to sell Mrs Hardy's clothes. She has just come back. I think you must remember meeting her here, years ago. I don't think she will be a great success for she, too, is imbued with ideas of the grandeur of the Gifford family, & the great Archdeacon, & the vulgarity of Mr Hardy's relatives, & she insists, too, that Mr Hardy would *never* have been a great writer had it not been for 'dear aun't influence.' She is Mrs Hardy in little.

I am very much looking forward to seeing you on the 29th, & am most disappointed that Mr Hardy cannot go to Enfield. Please do not trouble to reply. I do not expect any answer to this.

With kindest regards.

Yours very sincerely,
Florence E. Dugdale.

P.S. Reading this over I wonder whether I have exaggerated Mr Hardy's loneliness. Of course nothing could be more lonely than the life he used to lead—long evenings spent alone in his study, insult & abuse his only enlivenment. It sounds cruel to write like that, & in atrocious taste, but truth is truth, after all. F. D.

Text MS. Leeds.

lecture: see letters of 11 Dec. 1911 and 30 Jan. 1913.   *youngest sister*: i.e. Katharine Hardy, the younger of TH's sisters and youngest of his siblings.   *diaries*: discovered by TH following ELH's death and subsequently destroyed; he kept her travel diaries, however, together with the reminiscences of her early life later extracted in *Life and Work*, 69–75, and separately published as *Some Recollections*.   *sisters & brothers*: Henry Hardy was TH's only brother. *the niece*: Lilian Gifford.   *Archdeacon*: ELH's uncle, the Revd Edwin Hamilton Gifford (1820–1905), Archdeacon of London.

To Edward Clodd

Enfield.
Thursday evening. [30 January 1913]

Dear Mr Clodd:

Thank you again & again for so kindly coming down to Enfield & giving us that very interesting lecture. My conscience smote me many times, & now I wonder how I dared ask you to come down, particularly after the busy day you had had.

Ever since last night I have been wondering how I managed to write that silly & clumsy sentence that amused you so. If only I had had an opportunity for a longer talk with you I could have gone into that very complicated subject with enlightenment to you & much ease & relief to myself. You know, of course, what the majority of people are like at a small town like Dorchester, & how they talk. Mr H. is, at present, extremely sensitive & says that if I am seen walking about in Dorchester with him, or even if it is known that I am staying at Max Gate, they will comment unpleasantly. He said that, after a year had passed, they would take no notice. However that may be, that is really all I meant when I wrote.

I hope you will never breathe a word of this to anyone, not even to Mr

H. & least of all to Mr Shorter. Mr Hardy seems more afraid of his curiosity than anything & when letters come from him asking all sorts of questions Mr H. becomes nearly frantic.

I hope that Mr Hardy's regard for appearances will not lead him to decide that I mustn't go to Aldeburgh with him for a twelvemonth or so, but I expect that is what he will do.

His inscription on Mrs Hardy's wreath was 'From her lonely husband, with the old affection.' I must say that the good lady's virtues are beginning to weigh heavily on my shoulders. I had three pages of them this morning. Chief among the virtues now seems to rank her strict Evangelical views— her religious tendencies, her *humanitarianism* (to cats I suppose he means).

In today's letter he says:—'I am getting through E's papers' . . . & speaking of her abuse of him—'It was, of course, sheer hallucination in her, poor thing, & not wilfulness.' I feel as if I can hardly keep back my true opinion much longer. I shall go down about the middle of next week & suppose I shall be there some time, for he ends his letter, 'If I once get you here again won't I clutch you tight: you shall stay still spring. I felt very sad & lonely yesterday: not quite so much today.'

I ought not to write all this I know but it is a most tremendous relief to do so, & I know you won't ever breathe a word to anyone.

Again thanking you very much.

Yours very sincerely,
Florence E Dugdale.

P.S. I hope you will go & see 'Twelfth Night'. It is delightful, & I had a pleasant time behind, with Mrs Granville Barker. I shall try to see it again before it is off. Please don't on any account trouble to reply to this.

Text MS. Leeds.   *Date* Supplied on MS. in Clodd's hand.

lecture: at the Presbyterian Church Lecture Hall, Enfield, 29 Jan. 1913; Clodd's diary (Alan Clodd) shows that he in fact read out, under the title 'The Origins of Right and Wrong', the article on ethical evolution he had recently contributed to vol. v of the *Encyclopaedia of Religion and Ethics*, ed. James Hastings (Edinburgh, 1908–26). Prior to the lecture Clodd and FED both dined with FED's friend John McEwan (see letter of 20 Nov. 1906).   *clumsy sentence*: Clodd's diary for 11 Dec. 1912 records FED as reporting in a recent letter (unlocated) the wagging of 'Mrs Grundy's tongue' over her presence at Max Gate.   *Mr Shorter*: Shorter was in fact an intimate of Clodd's—he and his wife had also been at Aldeburgh when TH and FED stayed there in May 1912—and, as TH later discovered, they routinely shared whatever they had directly or indirectly learned of life at Max Gate.   *to Aldeburgh*: see letter of 20 Apr. 1913.   *Mrs Hardy's wreath*: at her funeral, on 30 Nov. 1912.   *keep back*: FED first wrote 'restrain'.   *still spring*: 'till spring' clearly intended.   *'Twelfth Night'*: Harley Granville-Barker's production, with his wife, Lillah McCarthy, as Viola, currently at the Savoy Theatre.

To Edward Clodd

MAX GATE, | DORCHESTER.
7: 3: '13.

My dear Mr Clodd:

I daresay you have been wondering how TH. is, & I thought you might like a line to tell you. He has been extremely well in health, & quite cheerful, although there have been domestic worries—no servant for a fortnight, & so forth. But now we have two excellent maids & all seems to promise well. On Thursday he started for Plymouth to find the grave of Mrs H's father (—that aimable gentleman who wrote to him as "a low-born churl who has presumed to marry into *my* family.") Today he goes to Cornwall, to St Juliot's Rectory, where he first met his 'late, espousèd saint,' forty-three years ago, this very week.

However, as his youngest sister sensibly observes, 'so long as he doesn't pick up another Gifford down there, no harm will be done'.

His brother is with him, fortunately. It cannot, I think, be good for him to luxuriate in misery to this extent.

He says that he is going down for the sake of the girl he married, & who died more than twenty years ago. His family say *that* girl never existed, but she did exist to him, no doubt.

The strange thing is that this goes on side by side with the reading of those diabolical diaries. I had hoped they were destroyed, but only the other night he produced one from his pocket & read me a passage—written about six weeks before her death—in which she says that her father & *Mr Putnam* (?) were right in their estimate of TH's character: he is . . . . (. . . various oft' repeated adjectives of abuse . . .), & "*utterly worthless.*" Of course Mr Putnam, if she means the publisher, could *never* have belittled Mr Hardy to her. It is in this sort of way that the diaries are so poisonous.

Fortunately TH. seems not to mind them so much now, & I have never before realized the depth of his affection, & his goodness & unselfishness as I have done these last three months. All I trust is that I may not, for the rest of his life, have to sit & listen humbly to an account of her virtues & graces.

It is very quiet & lonely here, but Mr H. returns on Monday, & I keep a loaded revolver in my bedroom.

I hope you are quite well & Mrs Graham & her children. I expect you will have them with you at Easter. How I wish we were going to be at Aldeburgh then! How many changes have happened since then. It was at Aldeburgh, last Easter that I had a letter from my dear, kind friend in

Dublin—saying he was rather ill, but I was not to worry as he would soon be better. He lost consciousness almost directly after, & died in a few days. By next Easter—ie in 1914—I wonder how things will stand. Fortunately I have no anxiety concerning TH's health—he seems more vigorous & well than I have known him for some years.

In April I am going to Southwold, to stay for a while with Mrs Henniker. She wrote to me today to say that she hears that Professor Bury goes to Church & she cannot understand it.

I am afraid that you will *loathe* these cards I send, but they may interest you as being of Mellstock Church & church-yard,—(Under the G.T) & many poems—'Friends Beyond', 'I need not go'—'The Vanished Choir' etc. The flower-covered grave is, of course, Mrs Hardy's, the flat tomb beyond, of his father & mother, the two upright stones beyond that, of his grand-parents & great-grandparents. There *he* will lie, when the time comes, & a corner, I am told, will be reserved for me. How you will *hate* these, or rather *one* of these, cards. The church is quite old & beautiful.

Please don't trouble to answer this letter. Having no one here to talk to it is a relief to be able to write.

With kind regards,

> Yours very sincerely,
> Florence E. Dugdale.

Text   MS. Leeds.

Mrs H's father: see ELH letter of 9 Dec. 1907.   *'late . . . saint,'*: from Milton's Sonnet XIX. For TH's visit to Cornwall see *CL*, iv. 260.   *forty-three*: FED first wrote 'thirty-four'.   *Mr Putnam*: George Haven Putnam (1844–1930), American publisher and author; he apparently visited Max Gate with his wife in June 1911 (*CL*, iv. 156).   *his life*: FED first wrote 'my life'.   *Mrs Graham*: Edith Graham (née Clodd), Clodd's younger daughter.   *friend in Dublin*: Sir Thornley Stoker; see letter of 11 Nov. 1910.   *how things will stand*: FED was perhaps already anticipating a possible marriage to TH.   *Southwold*: a small town on the Suffolk coast where Florence Henniker was renting a house; FED first wrote 'Aldeburgh'. *Professor Bury*: John Bagnell Bury (1861–1927), Regius Professor of Modern History at Cambridge, had a cottage at Southwold and was a frequent visitor to Clodd's Aldeburgh house.   *these cards*: two picture postcards still accompany the MS., one of Stinsford ('Mellstock') church, the other of ELH's grave heaped with flowers immediately after her funeral and interment.   *(Under the G.T)*: *Under the Greenwood Tree*, TH's second published novel.   *one of these, cards*: i.e. the photograph of ELH's grave.

To Edward Clodd

MAX GATE, | DORCHESTER.
Tuesday. II. 3. 13

My dear Mr Clodd:

Just a postscript to my last letter. Yesterday there arrived—together with your kind letter—one from T.H. in which he writes:—

'The visit to this neighbourhood (i.e Boscastle) has been a very painful one to me, & I have said a dozen times I wish I had not come—What possessed me to do it!'

I knew it was an unwise thing to do, & I expect he will come back this afternoon, very miserable. However he meant to go some time & it is over now, & done with, I hope.

With regard to your visit—I *know* he is looking forward to it, & it will do him more good than anything I can think of. He is, however, (& this is strictly between ourselves) very anxious to get the house in a little better condition before you come. It was really in a bad state & the walls have great patches of discolouration & damp. Things will get right by degrees & one bedroom is to be done immediately.

Mrs Hardy's nephew—another Gifford—is coming here for Easter. Although so highly born & related to an Archdeacon, the family is quite impecunious & seems determined to live on Mr Hardy's bounty. They just tolerate his 'low-born' relatives.

Yours very sincerely,
Florence E. Dugdale.

Text. MS. Leeds.

one from T.H.: see *CL*, iv. 260; FED has inserted '(i.e Boscastle)' but otherwise quoted TH accurately.   *your visit*: see letter of 28 June 1913.   *another Gifford*: Gordon Gifford (see ELH letter of 14 Feb. 1899), currently employed as an architect by the London County Council.

To Edward Clodd

Max Gate,
Sunday. [20 April 1913]

My dear Mr Clodd:

Thank you so much for your kind invitation. I am so hoping I may go to see you—but it is in the hands of 'One above me,' & He will write & tell you what has been decided.

Perhaps, all things considered, Mr Hardy would be able to unburden himself more freely were I not there. You will be glad to know that he seems in most excellent spirits, & has said to me once or twice, with the zest of a school-boy 'I *do* feel I like the idea of going to see Clodd at Aldeburgh. I am quite up to it—now.'

Of course I am very worried about his leg, & if I am not there *do please* insist on his resting it on a high footstool or something. He does forget so, to do this, unless constantly reminded. The great danger—Sir Clifford Allbut says—is that a *clot* may form & be carried to the brain or heart, but please *don't* mention it, for he is soon alarmed.

The remarkable change in his spirits has seemed to coincide with the departure of Mrs Hardy's niece. There were several breezes—all about household matters—& she went off—saying it upset her to be here with painting going on, & now Mr H. tells me he has written to tell her she is not to come back at all, but he will pay her a salary all the same, & he has bought her an annuity. But she will come back *eventually*, of course. It is a great relief to hear no more of the Archdeacon—but a rival has risen, in the person of *another* clergyman the Rev: C. Holder. Mrs Hardy's sister was governess to some children & married their grandfather—this same Mr Holder—& it was at his house that Mr Hardy met Mrs Hardy. He is putting up a large tablet in a church in Cornwall, to put on record the fact that Mrs Hardy was sister-in-law to the Rev: C. H. This extreme veneration for the Church is very puzzling, for neither of these clergymen (the Archdeacon or Holder) was ever friendly to him, but Mrs Hardy was always so alive to the magnificence of these connections, that the tablet may be appropriate. Please know nothing of this when it is told you. The whole affair is a most curious psychological study.

I hope that you are well. I was so extremely sorry to hear that you have had trouble with the estate in Jamaica, & that you have rheumatic twinges. I am anxious to know what you think of Mr Hardy's health, so far as you can judge. His doctor says the state of things here, before Mrs Hardy's death—was quite alarming, so far as T.H. was concerned. He said that the lack of attention & general discomfort must have had a serious effect sooner or later. He told this to the sisters & brother.

With kind regards,

Yours very sincerely
Florence E. Dugdale.

P.S. Mr Hardy wouldn't *at all* have minded meeting anyone at Aldeburgh, I am sure, but possibly he will be able to talk more freely to you if you are alone. FD.

Text MS. Leeds.   *Date* Supplied on MS. in Clodd's hand.

invitation: to Aldeburgh; TH finally went alone, 25–8 Apr., after spending several days in the company of FED and Florence Henniker at the latter's rented house in Southwold. See *CL*, iv. 270.   *his leg*: TH was suffering from varicose veins.   *Allbut*: TH's friend Sir Thomas Clifford Allbutt (1836–1925), Regius Professor of Physic at Cambridge.   *Holder*: the Revd Caddell Holder; see ELH letter of late Oct. 1870. After TH's death the tablet to ELH's memory on the wall of St Juliot church was joined by a similar memorial to TH; both were designed by TH himself.   *in Jamaica*: the Clodd family plantation in Jamaica, managed by Clodd's son Arthur, had eventually to be abandoned.   *alone*: Clodd's diary (Alan Clodd) indicates that while at Aldeburgh TH did indeed speak freely of his relationship with ELH.

To Edward Clodd

MAX GATE, | DORCHESTER.
[29 June 1913?]

My dear Mr Clodd:

Very many happy returns of your birthday. You know how sincerely I wish you happiness & prosperity.

It is delightful to think that you will really be here in less than a fortnight. I wish we could have accepted Mr Shorter's invitation, but I think it would have been rather too much for Mr Hardy. He & I went to lunch with the Admiral of the First Battle Squadron on board the St Vincent on Saturday last—& although there was very little exertion—& we enjoyed ourselves most tremendously—yet he has seemed very fatigued ever since. However, he is not really used up. We had a delightful week end here with the Cockerells, & Mr Strang—although we were continually wishing you were with us. They said they had enjoyed every moment of the time. Capt. Fisher, too, an old friend, who called on Friday last said he had never enjoyed any visit so much as that one. If you bring your walking legs down with you I can trot you about when T.H. gives up, & rests. We will go to Talbothays—if you care to—& to Bockhampton—but please don't mention the former visit to Mr Shorter—as T.H. doesn't want anyone but you to go there.

I do hope that Mr Shorter will not try to draw Mr Hardy about Mrs H. for if so it will be horribly upsetting. There is always, I know, a great temptation to get 'copy', or a piquant story for one's friends—but it is quite bad for him, I assure you. Could you just drop a hint, do you think? Mr & Mrs Cockerell & Mr Strang were so very good in steering him away from 'St Juliot' & 'Beeny Cliff', that he forgot to lament, & was in excellent spirits afterwards. He has had cart-loads of sympathy (mostly insincere)—& I cannot see that anyone—dead or alive—is the better off for him being miserable.

I was very interested in hearing from Mr Hardy about your grandson—whom I have always liked ever so much. He told me about the smart new uniform etc. I hope he will be very happy. I thought of him several times on Saturday when we were taken round the Fleet at Portland.

I am a little worried now about this constant 'tiredness' of Mr Hardy's. He seems knocked up by the least exertion, & as for trotting around to Cathedrals etc—as he did a year ago that seems out of the question. However you will be able to tell me what you think, when you have been here a little while. Mr Strang thought he looked much better—that his face had lost some of the lines it used to have—but the fact remains that he went for one short walk with them, while they were here—& that tired him.

Again with very very many good wishes,

Yours sincerely
F.E.D.

P.S. If you answer this I shall *not* write again to you. I don't want an answer, please.

Text   MS. Leeds.   *Date*   From internal evidence.
birthday: see letter of 2 July 1910.   *really be here*: Clodd stayed at Max Gate 11–14 July 1913, when Clement Shorter was also a guest.   *Mr Shorter's invitation*: apparently to a dinner in honour of Clodd's birthday; see *CL*, iv. 282.   *Admiral . . . St Vincent*: the First Battle Squadron, at Portland in advance of naval manœuvres, was commanded by Vice-Admiral the Hon. Sir Stanley Colville aboard the battleship *St Vincent*.   *Cockerells*: Sydney Carlyle Cockerell (see letter of 30 Nov. 1913 and headnote) and his wife Kate (see letter of 13 Feb. 1914) stayed at Max Gate 20–3 June 1913.   *Strang*: William Strang (1859–1921), painter and etcher, produced numerous portraits of TH over the years; he was also at Max Gate 20–3 June.   *Capt. Fisher*: Captain William Wordsworth Fisher (1875–1937), later admiral, currently commander of the battleship *St Vincent*.   *Talbothays*: both Clodd and Shorter appear, in fact, to have visited TH's sisters and brother at Talbothays.   *your grandson*: Derrick Graham, who had recently joined the Royal Navy as a midshipman.

To Edward Clodd

MAX GATE, | DORCHESTER.
21: 8: '13.

My dear Mr Clodd:

I was about to write to you yesterday—concerning that paragraph, for I thought you might feel some uneasiness.

TH, I am glad to say, is in good health, & *wonderfully cheerful*. He has had no fit of depression for quite a long time. The letter was meant to be a private one. Really he did not want to go to be stared at by three hundred American teachers. He need not have written so pathetically but he has paid the penalty by having to answer a batch of letters from acquaintances—Eden Phillpotts, Sir Rider Haggard, etc. His friends all guessed the meaning.

The niece has just returned. She wrote imploringly to her uncle-by-marriage, but she is still what she was before she went. I am reminded by her, a dozen times a day at least, that 'dear Aunt' was a very great lady, & that I am—so she implies—quite a low sort of person. Yesterday we had a visit from a bishop's daughter, & Miss Gifford said afterwards: "How much she reminded me of dearest Aunt! People connected with the aristocracy of the Church have such perfect manners."

I do not know whether she will stay on after the end of this year—but if she does I don't.

I hope that you will have a good time at Aldeburgh. I think there is no doubt of that, if you have your grandchildren with you. Will you please give them my love.

Yours very sincerely.
Florence E. Dugdale.

P.S. Mr Hardy thanks you very much for your kind invitation but he fears he cannot accept it yet awhile. He is very busy just now preparing a volume of short stories—written years ago, of course. 'The Duke's Reappearance', of which you have the MS., will appear in the volume.

He asks me to tell you that he feels he would much like to be with you again. We are looking forward to that visit you promised to pay in the autumn: as soon as Lotus II is laid up.

F.D.

Really he is wonderfully well & in unusually high spirits. Mr John Lane, who came down a week or two ago & paid a flying visit said he had not seen him look so well & so bright, for years.

Text MS. Leeds.

that paragraph: 'Mr. Hardy's Health', *The Times*, 16 Aug. 1913, 6; it quoted from a letter in which TH had excused himself from meeting a party of Canadian teachers on the grounds that 'the strain and stress of one thing and another of late' had rendered him 'quite unable to attend such functions'.   *Phillpotts*: Eden Phillpotts (1862–1960), prolific novelist, playwright, and miscellaneous writer.   *Haggard*: Henry Rider Haggard (1856–1925), novelist.   *a bishop's daughter*: Mary McDowall (see letter of 2 Feb. 1918), daughter of Mandell Creighton, bishop of London until his death in 1901.   *yet awhile*: TH never in fact returned to Aldeburgh, although Clodd stayed at Max Gate again 27 Feb.–2 Mar. 1914, shortly after TH and FED were married.   *volume of short stories*: A Changed Man, The Waiting Supper and Other Tales (London, 1913); the MS. of 'The Duke's Reappearance' (now at Texas) was given to Clodd in Mar. 1912.   *Lotus II*: Clodd's sail-boat.   *Lane*: the publisher; see ELH letter of 20 Sept. 1910. For Lane's recent visit, see *CL*, iv. 288–90.

[Sydney Carlyle Cockerell, formerly secretary to the Kelmscott Press, was from 1908 to 1937 director of the Fitzwilliam Museum, Cambridge. He first visited Max Gate in September 1911, when he persuaded TH to permit the distribution of his manuscripts by gift to a number of libraries and other institutions—the Fitzwilliam itself naturally among them. Grateful to Cockerell for resolving what he had himself regarded as a troublesome problem, TH increasingly depended upon his attentive friendship and his knowledge of printing, publishing, and the literary world, and named him, in due course, as one of his literary executors. Although Cockerell's relationship with the other literary executor, TH's widow, was to become extremely fraught, his early encounters with her as FED seem to have been mutually agreeable. Following their first meeting in June 1913, when Cockerell and his wife spent a weekend at Max Gate, the correspondence between them rapidly developed into one of exceptional intensity and continuity, revelatory of life at Max Gate to an extent of which TH, had he been fully apprised of it, could scarcely have approved. The letter of 30 November 1913 not only reflects an early (though not the earliest) stage in that correspondence but provides a glimpse of FED's devoting herself to Hardy's comfort and career even while struggling to maintain some degree of personal and professional independence.]

To Sydney Cockerell

MAX GATE, | DORCHESTER.
30: 11: '13.

Dear Mr Cockerell:

Thank you so very much for that delightful 'Life of Morris'. It is a book I am extremely glad to possess, & more particularly as a gift from yourself. I have read little bits of it aloud to Mr Hardy—& he thinks he would like me to read all of it to him—which I shall do.

At present I am rather busy book-reviewing, & such-like unimportant little jobs of my own, but as soon as ever I have time—I hope before Christmas—I am going to type out a longish manuscript which Mr Hardy wants to send you—an account of Mrs Hardy's early life, together with extracts from Mr Hardy's own diary note-books.

Mr Hardy's cold is quite well now. He is, in every way, much better than he was.

Again thanking you very much,

Yours sincerely,
Florence E. Dugdale.

Text   MS. Beinecke.
Cockerell: Sydney Carlyle Cockerell (1867–1962), museum director and bibliophile.   *'Life of Morris'*: J. W. Mackail's *The Life of William Morris* (1899), as reissued in 1912 in Longman's Pocket Library; the two vols. are listed in William P. Wreden's cat. no. 11, devoted to books

from the Max Gate library. FEH appears not to have read it aloud to TH in its entirety until 1917 (*CL*, v. 203).   *book-reviewing*: FED reviewed new novels for the *Sphere* with some frequency both before and after her marriage, but always anonymously.   *account . . . early life*: this presumably corresponded to the material selectively included in *Life and Work*, 69–75, and later more comprehensively edited as *Some Recollections*.   *Mr Hardy's own*: FED seems first to have written 'Mrs' and then clumsily erased the 's'; the excerpts presumably included TH's diary entries now in *Life and Work*, 77–8.

To Edward Clodd

MAX GATE, | DORCHESTER.
3rd. December 1913.

My dear Mr Clodd:

Please excuse a typewritten letter, but I want to ramble on, and say ever so much.

I hope that you will enjoy the play. You cannot imagine how much I wish I were going to see it, sitting next to you, as in former years. Giles Winterborne is such a nice man; in fact you would like all the players.

Things here go on pretty much the same. I dreaded the anniversary of Mrs Hardy's death, but T.H. took it very, very quietly, and seemed his normal self: if anything a little more cheerful I thought. We made a pilgrimage to the grave carrying flowers, wearing black, and so forth. After wearing colours for some months I suddenly had to go back into black—buying all new black things. In fact I am still in mourning, but really since it is more than I would have done, even for a beloved parent or sister, I think I can break out into colours again soon. Mr Hardy, though, suggested that I should *always* wear half mourning in future, as a mark of devotion to *her* memory. Sometimes I wonder if there is not something in the air of Max Gate that makes us all a little crazy.

Upon the whole I think that T.H. is more cheerful than I have ever know him to be, but at times he gets upset at trifles, and gives way most alarmingly. And there is always this extraordinary idealization of Mrs Hardy—whom now he says, and I think *believes*, was the sweetest, most gifted, most beautiful woman who ever existed.

The niece is still here. Mr Hardy says she is to go after Christmas, to live with her mother for a little time, and then come back here. He will, of course, pay for her board etc. most generously. I cannot tell you what she is like. I have spoken about her to nobody else, but I think everyone who comes here sees what she is like, for they say things to me that I pretend not to notice. I have told you how very good Mr Hardy has always been to my family, to my mother and sisters particularly. One of my sisters, a most harmless hardworking girl—a teacher—came this August to stay near here, and Mr Hardy asked her over to tea, to go and see Mrs Hardy's grave first and then come on. We had an awful scene. I have only seen a similar one when Mrs Hardy was alive. My poor sister could hardly keep from bursting into tears. This woman insulted her, behaved in fact like a mad-woman. Mr Hardy tried to make things right after, by taking her to his study and giving her (my sister of course) a book, writing an affectionate inscription in it, and so on, but she says she refuses ever to meet Miss Gifford again. I don't think a day ever passes but I get some gibe or sneer. To Mr Hardy she is effusive, because she was frightened by his not letting her come back for three months the last time she went off. She knows that if she begins to talk in a senti-mental way about dear Aunt, and St Juliot, and Archdeacon Gifford (whom she never saw) he is bowled over completely. Today she has been telling me how much better her aunt looked after him than I do. I don't mind that so much, for he says himself he was never so well looked after in his life as he is now, and his brother says the same, very emphatically.

This is a specimen of what is always going on. A little time ago when we were out in Mr Lea's motor she saw a small butcher's shop with the name Dugdale over it. I, stupidly, pointed it out, and said, trying to be funny, "Another of my illustrious family."

For days and days after that I was always hearing how dreadfully vulgar it was to be connected with tradespeople, and finally she said pointedly: "A person must be *very low down indeed to* have a butcher in the family." By the way I had never heard of this butcher before—& don't in the least know who he is.

I feel it a great and undeserved humiliation to have to put up with that. A more broad-minded person would laugh—and I can do that sometimes, but not always. Please don't tell anyone, for I should not like anyone but yourself to know I stayed here and tamely submitted to it. I don't tell my own people.

Mr Hardy could, I believe, stop it, if he chose. As it is he says she is an "innocent childlike creature"—like her aunt—and says these things without meaning it. She is thirty-four years old, and by no means childlike, although she puts on the air of a child of ten when talking to him. She runs about Dorchester telling tales to all the idle gossiping women in the place, and then tells me how much they sympathise with her. She does *nothing* in the house. If I ask her to help me ever so little she says she is 'not a servant' "I" (very proudly) "was never brought up to earn *my* living".

Frederick Harrison, who came here a couple of months ago, saw how matters stood, although I never uttered one word to him. He spoke to her rather severely, and said that she was much stronger than I, and that I had far too much to do. He said the same to Mr Hardy, and repeated it emphatically before he left—but it had no effect.

Henry Hardy—the brother—absolutely *swears* when he talks about it. The sisters merely say that they went through it all.

Of course, her brother is an imbecile—one of them at least—and an uncle died in an asylum, and her grandfather was mad at times, so I ought to be profoundly sorry for her—but I *can't* be that. There is so much malice, and no apparent mental weakness. She says the Giffords all have tongues that "cut to the bone", and she seems to be proud of that gift.

After this tirade—and I am so ashamed of letting out like this,—you need not be very astonished to hear in January that I have left Max Gate. I always lived very happily and peacefully at home, and I have very devoted parents and sisters, with whom I have never quarrelled. Mr Hardy had more than twenty years of insults, and apparently enjoyed them very much—according to what he says now. I don't enjoy them.

He still sees very few people. The County people have begun to look him up and ask him out again—but he puts them off if he possibly can—even his old friends. Mrs Sheridan, for instance, has tried three times to come and see him, but he makes excuses. Workmen have been in the house for a couple of months, painting etc. and a little conservatory is being put up outside the drawing-room. All this amuses him tremendously.

He talks very often of "next year" and things that he will do then, of the people he will have here to stay, and the visits we will make to Cathedrals —but I think he will just go on now, very quietly, writing poems about Mrs Hardy, and so forth. It is rather funny when I remember those he used to write to me—one of which is shortly going to appear in "The Sphere".

I do wish you knew Mr Cockerell—of the Fitzwilliam, Cambridge. He was almost everything to William Morris during the last years of his life, and he is very good to Mr Hardy—absolutely like a son, in somewhat the same way.

Of course Mr Hardy is as kind to me, and as affectionate as ever he was. It is only for his sake that I manage to rub on from day to day. It would be too dreadful if, at his time of life, he were to be upset and distracted by two women quarrelling, in his house.

I hope that Mrs Graham and your grandchildren are well. I suppose you are looking forward to having them about you at Christmas. I hope, too, that you keep well.

Yours affectionately,
Florence E. Dugdale.

Text MS. (typed) Leeds.
the play: the London performance, 8 Dec. 1913, of the Dorchester Debating and Dramatic Society's production of *The Woodlanders*; the part of Giles Winterborne was played by Henry Charles Austin Martin, a clerk with a Dorchester auctioneering firm. *devotion to*: FEH typed 'devotion the'. *One of my sisters*: apparently Constance Dugdale, five years younger than FED, who taught at Enfield throughout her career. *Mr Lea's motor*: Hermann Lea (1869–1952), Dorset photographer and topographer, author of *Thomas Hardy's Wessex* (1913); he owned and chauffeured a car which TH liked to hire for trips into the countryside and sometimes further afield. *butcher*: probably the Wareham butcher William Dugdale (1867–1925). *By . . . he is.*: ink insertion by FED. *Harrison*: Frederic Harrison (1831–1923), positivist thinker and publicist, had been friendly with TH for many years. *came here*: FEH typed 'came her'. *her brother . . . an uncle . . . her grandfather.* FEH refers—with some exaggeration—to ELH's nephew Randolph Gifford, her brother Richard Ireland Gifford, and her father John Attersoll Gifford. *no . . . mental weakness*: for Lilian Gifford's subsequent admission to a mental hospital see letter of 10 Aug. 1919. *Mrs Sheridan*: see ELH letter of 27 Dec. 1899. *poems about Mrs Hardy*: subsequently pub., as 'Poems of 1912–13', in *Satires of Circumstance* (1914). *in "The Sphere"*: 'To Meet or Otherwise', *Sphere*, 20 Dec. 1913. *Morris*: William Morris (1834–96), influential as poet and artist and especially as printer, designer, and socialist; as secretary to the Kelmscott Press Cockerell had worked closely with Morris during his last years. *Mrs Graham . . . grandchildren*: see letters of 7 Mar. and 29 June 1913.

[TH's persistent American admirer Rebekah Owen, still living in the Lake District with her sister Catharine, had not allowed the death of ELH to become the occasion of her losing touch with TH himself. In November 1913 she travelled south to see one of the Dorchester performances of *The Woodlanders*, that year's 'Hardy play', and to pay a call at Max Gate, characteristically following up that visit with an ostentatious gift of rose-bushes. FED's first letter to her of 10 December 1913 received a rapid response, at least two more letters being extorted from her before the end of 1913, and during the early years of her marriage she remained trapped, as a necessarily unsatisfactory surrogate for TH himself, in a time-consuming and sometimes difficult correspondence with a woman she scarcely knew.]

To Rebekah Owen

MAX GATE, | DORCHESTER.
10th Dec: 1913.

Dear Miss Owen:

Thank you so much for your extremely kind gift. We are looking forward with great anticipations to a feast of creamy-white roses. The two trees are to be planted against a little conservatory that is now being built— & we will re-christen them, & call them by your name, which will mean so much more to us than François Guillot.

Mr Hardy wishes you had told us how your return journey prospered—

how long you stayed at Bath, & so on. He says he could & would gladly find you house, but he knows you wouldn't live in it, if he did. He is, I see, quite inclined to 'sniff' a little at your pirated copy of the 'Milkmaid', which he doesn't love, rare & valuable though it may be.

We have had a great excitement this week—great to us, who live so soberly & remotely. Sir Hubert Herkomer's son has been down, arranging with Mr Hardy for the production of a film of 'Far from the Madding Crowd,' & he hired the local 'picturedrome', & gave a little private entertainment of Herkomer films to ourselves & Mr Hermann Lea, who was invaluable in finding scenes, properties, etc, for the film. Mr Herkomer hopes to induce our excellent Mr Pouncy to be the Joseph Poorgrass on the film.

An extraordinary case of witchcraft has occured in Higher Bockhampton—in the next cottage to Mr Hardy's birthplace. Everyone in the village believes firmly in witchcraft—including, I believe, Mr Lea himself.

It must be exceedingly difficult to practice Catholicism at Ambleside. If one has need of a religion, that, I am sure, is the only one.

With kind regards from Mr Hardy & all of us.

Yours very sincerely
Florence E. Dugdale

P.S. Wessex sends his love. He grows dearer every day, & is to have his photograph taken this week.

Text   MS. Adams.

you house: 'you a house' clearly intended.   *the 'Milkmaid'*: R. Owen owned an American pirated edition of 'The Romantic Adventures of a Milkmaid', one of the stories collected in TH's recently published *A Changed Man*.   *Herkomer's son*: the Herkomer Film Company, formed by Sir Hubert von Herkomer, the painter, and his son Siegfried, had recently purchased the film rights to *Far from the Madding Crowd*; Sir Hubert died in 1914, however, and the film was never completed.   *Pouncy*: Thomas Pouncy, Dorchester saddler, had played Robert Creedle in the recent Dorchester dramatization of *The Woodlanders*.   *witchcraft*: a case of 'overlooking' reported in the *Dorset County Chronicle*, 4 Dec. 1913, under the heading 'Higher Bockhampton. Witchcraft To-Day in Wessex'.   *Mr Lea himself*: Lea (see letter of 3 Dec. 1913), currently living in the cottage in which TH was born, had pub. an article on witchcraft in 1903 (*CL*, iii. 47).   *Wessex*: FED's troublesome, locally notorious, and ultimately famous dog was at this date only a few months old.

[FED had confided to Edward Clodd in July 1913 'a great secret', though one which Clodd himself, according to his diary, had long suspected. Other visitors to Max Gate had also foreseen the possibility of TH's marrying FED once a decent period of time had passed since ELH's death, and most of them, as old friends of TH's, seem to have looked forward to the event as guaranteeing him company, care, and even comfort in his final years. From FED's point of view, the advantages of such a marriage, though very considerable in social and economic terms, were in other respects far less clear-cut: at thirty-five years old (as of 12 January 1914) she might be thought to have few alternative 'prospects', and yet it was no light matter to accept responsibility, as she would in effect be doing, for the management of Max Gate, the secretarial needs of an immensely famous writer, and the physical well-being and eventual nursing of a man already well into his eighth decade. The continuing presence at Max Gate of ELH's niece, Lilian Gifford, was a particular irritant and deterrent, and FED, her devotion to TH tempered by at least a limited instinct for self-preservation, was evidently prepared to threaten termination of the entire marriage arrangement if her exclusive command of the household could not be guaranteed. It is not clear whether, at the time of this crisis, the marriage had already been planned for 10 February 1914, or whether the crisis itself and its resolution in FED's favour served to accelerate the course of events. In any case, the wedding took place in Enfield Parish Church at 8 a.m. that day in the conditions of exceptional privacy demanded by Hardy's public fame, only TH's brother and FED's father and youngest sister being in attendance at the ceremony itself, and only the closest family members having been notified in advance.]

To Edward Clodd

MAX GATE, | DORCHESTER.
1 : 1 : '14.

My dear Mr Clodd:

I am deeply grieved that your kindness to me, & to that worthless lad, has been so ill-requited. I can hardly say how very sorry I am that you should have had the annoyance & trouble. It is a lesson to me—a bitter one. Of my pupils, the two to whom I was perhaps more kind than any, came to grief. There is *no* excuse for this lad. I am sure he has a good home—although I have no personal knowledge of that—but his father takes a leading part in local politics, as a Liberal, & in charitable affairs—is on the Hospital Committee, etc. I have seen practically nothing of this lad since he was in my class at school, when he was a very good boy, but meeting him in the street some time back I had an unpleasant feeling that he had deteriorated very much, & my sister told me then that she thought I had made a great mistake in recommending him, as she continually saw him about the streets with loafing companions.

His father can afford to send him abroad, anyway, & I have determined never to try to find another berth for any of my old boys. Others, however, have done well. One, a young man who is going to be a Roman Catholic priest, wrote me a deligtful New Year's letter today, from his college at Ware. I am sorry that you had the black sheep.

Mr Hardy seems very well. We had a quiet Christmas—the only excitement being a visit to the grave on Christmas Eve—& another yesterday.

Katie Hardy who saw us there yesterday said she never saw two such dismal 'critters' in her life, as 'Tom' & myself.

It was so kind of you to write me such a friendly & helpful letter, & it very much cheered me.

With regard to the future, the situation stands thus, at present. If the niece is to remain here *permanently*, as one of the family, then I will not enter into that compact of which I spoke to you last summer. This must be decided in a week, & if it is settled that she stays I return to my own home, & *remain* there. Henry Hardy approves of this decision, & says it is the only way to avoid a life of misery, & Katie agrees that the 'ménage à trois' is an impossible situation. Anyhow, the matter must be settled *now*, one way or the other. T.H. has told her that she is to go home to her mother for a time—but she will never go, & he is not the man to make her go.

I hope that this year will bring you much happiness & prosperity.

Yours very sincerely,
Florence E. Dugdale

Text MS. Leeds.
worthless lad: see FED's letter of 8 Nov. 1910. *my sister*: Constance; see FED's letter of 3 Dec. 1913. *young man . . . priest*: unidentified. *last summer*: the entry in Clodd's diary (Alan Clodd) is dated 13 July 1913, while he was visiting Max Gate.

To Ethel Richardson

River Front. | Enfield.
Monday. [9 February 1914]

My dearest Ethel:

The ceremony takes place tomorrow at 8. o'clock. I wish you had come over tonight old girl. However, as things are it may be as well. Don't send any telegram as Mr Hardy wants to get into Max Gate quietly before the townspeople know. He was mortally afraid of a deputation meeting him, at the station.

If it had been possible I should have been so glad for you to have been at the wedding. However, Mr Hardy seemed quite determined that *no one* outside the house should be asked, & he wanted Connie & father both to go to school, as usual, at *the usual time*!

You *must* & *shall* come to Max Gate, my dear Ethel, & in years to come, if I am still there, I hope you & your children will spend many hours there.

Tell your husband why it is that everything has been kept so quiet. It was merely the fear of reporters & horrible snap-shotters.

With love to you & the children & kind regards to your husband:

Your affec: sister,

Florence E. Dugdale

Text MS. (with envelope) Daphne Wood.
Richardson: Ethel Richardson, wife of Henry William Richardson, a London headmaster, was the eldest of the five Dugdale sisters and a schoolteacher herself.   *go to school*: FED's father and her sister Constance both taught at local Enfield schools.

To Ethel Richardson

[10 February 1914]

Business completed all well

Florence

Text Telegraph form (in hand of postal clerk) Daphne Wood.   *Date* As stamped. *completed*: the message was handed in at Enfield at 9.58 a.m., perhaps by someone other than FEH herself; cf. *CL*, v. 9.

To Sydney and Kate Cockerell

MAX GATE, | DORCHESTER.
13 : 2 : '14.

Dear Mr & Mrs Cockerell:

I can hardly find words to express my gratitude for your kind letter & telegram. My one fear in marrying Mr Hardy was that the friends for whom he has the greatest affection might disapprove of the marriage. I knew that he had a few friends the loss of whom would make him very miserable, & myself far more so.

However, your very kind letter puts my mind at rest upon that score, & I am infinitely grateful.

Thank you too, so much, for the beautiful book you so kindly sent. It will always be one of my treasured possessions.

The reason of my marriage with Mr Hardy is so happily expressed in your letter. I did indeed marry him that I might have the right to express my devotion—& to endeavour to add to his comfort & happiness. Had I not married him I realized that I should not be able to remain at Max Gate, & I dreaded that, when the time came that he most needed my care, I should not be able to be with him.

I am hoping that, when the weather is a little more inviting, you will give us the great pleasure of seeing you both at Max Gate.

Yours very sincerely,
Florence Hardy.

Text MS. Beinecke.
Kate Cockerell: Cockerell's invalid wife, Florence Kate Cockerell, née Kingsford (d. 1949), artist and illustrator; see Wilfrid Blunt, *Cockerell* (London: Hamish Hamilton, 1964), 165–8.   *beautiful book*: a photographic reproduction, introduced by Cockerell, of the 14th-century *Book of Hours of Yolande of Flanders* (Chiswick Press, 1905), later Lot 57 in the 1938 Hodgson sale of the Max Gate library.

To Rebekah Owen

MAX GATE, | DORCHESTER.
20th March 1914

My dear Miss Owen:

We hardly know how to express our warm thanks for your kind, & really beautiful gift. The spoons are absolutely lovely. We had nothing of the kind, before they came, & they will be treasured at Max Gate—as being the gift of you & your sister. My husband admires them so much. Thank you again & again.

The flowers were charming & now adorn our drawing-room, being shown with great pride to all callers. I had never seen those wonderful little daffodils before. My husband prefers Scoticus Plenus.

I have quite delightful gardening letters from Eden Phillpotts, who also sends books of his—'My Garden', 'The Joy of Youth' etc—with delightful bits about his garden. Our own garden, alas, is nothing to speak of, nor our little conservatory. We will try to grow Sparmannia, & we should much treasure one that you had grown, but would be sorry to give you much trouble about it.

We have been to Town for a couple of days—to two dinners, one of which was given for us by my husband's publishers. We tried to do too much, & to see too many people, & he is rather done up, & caught a slight cold through being caught in a drenching rain.

I have been prevented from writing before, through an unfortunate family catastrophe. My husband's brother has had a slight stroke & we have had to spend a great part of our time there. He was unconscious for hours & is now slowly recovering. He is one of the best friends I have ever had—true, strong & generous in every thought & deed—Giles Winterborn in the flesh— or perhaps Gabriel Oak. I have always looked upon him as a dear brother.

I was interested to know that you had been reading Mrs Chadwick's book on the Brontës. She is an old friend of mine, & lived almost next door to my people, for years. She has *no* literary gift, I think, but is so painstaking & thorough that she manages to *make* a fairly interesting book. Her mind, though, is commonplace to a degree.

To my great grief I am just obliged to refuse to write, for my publisher, a book about dogs—to be illustrated by that splendid artist—Detmold. I have a pile of books, too, to review, but I suppose that it is unfair to my husband to take up so much outside work.

I have only met Mr Reginald Smith once, but I always think of him with gratitude, for he wrote me a delightful letter about a little story of mine that appeared—years ago—in "The Cornhill".

This is a bad letter but I am so busy today, & we are going over to lunch with Mrs Sheridan. I will try to atone for this by writing a better one next week. My husband *loves* your letters. He listens to them with a look of keen interest, & now & then a smile of appreciation. I am sure *he* wishes much that you lived nearer.

With kindest regards to you both, from both, & again *many*, many thanks

Yours very sincerely

F. H.

Text   MS. (with envelope) Colby.

Phillpotts: see letter of 21 Aug. 1913; TH and FEH later made several visits to his home in Torquay.   *'My . . . Youth'*: pub. in 1906 and 1913 respectively.   *Sparmannia*: a shrub, native to southern Africa, with heart-shaped leaves and clusters of white flowers.   *publishers*: i.e. Sir Frederick Macmillan and other members of the Macmillan firm.   *slowly recovering*: though often ill, Henry Hardy lived until Dec. 1928.   *Winterborn*: spelled Winterborne in *The Woodlanders*.   *Mrs Chadwick's . . . Brontës*: Esther Alice Chadwick once lived with her husband at 3 River Front, Enfield; her *In the Footsteps of the Brontës* (London, 1914) was reissued in 1971.   *Detmold*: Edward Julius Detmold, noted etcher and illustrator, had illustrated three of the books FEH wrote before her marriage, *The Book of Baby Beasts* (1911), *The Book of Baby Birds* (1912), and *The Book of Baby Pets* (1913).   *to review*: for the *Sphere*.   *Smith*: Reginald John Smith (1857–1916), barrister, publisher, and editor of the *Cornhill Magazine*; FEH (as FED) pub. two stories in the *Cornhill*, 'The Apotheosis of the Minx', May 1908, and 'Blue Jimmy: the Horse-Stealer', Feb. 1911.

To Rebekah Owen

MAX GATE, | DORCHESTER.

April 5th. [1914]

My dear Miss Owen:

We have been hoping to hear that you were in Dorset. I wonder if we really are to have the pleasure of seeing you this spring? It would be so delightful if we could. It would be difficult, though, I am sure to leave your daffodils—we have a little army standing in a bed behind the hedge at the end of the lawn, but they are very ordinary ones that I bought in Dorchester from that nice young woman who played the part of Mrs Charmond's lady's maid, Ellis, in 'The Woodlanders."

Wessex grows most interesting. He sends his love to your dear Pietro.

T.H. has just written a poem I like so much. It will appear in the Fortnightly Review in May or June. The buried people at Stinsford hear the guns being fired at Portland. I hope you will see it. In last week's 'New Weekly'— a new paper—he has a charming pathetic little poem about hopes in February that become regrets in October. But it is not nearly so fine as the one that is to go in the Fortnightly.

We try to keep abreast with the young poets—the "Georgians" as they call themselves—but we have great disappointments, & have to fall back on the Old Testament—Malachi—etc. There *is* poetry there.

Masefield wants very much to come & see my husband, & I hope he will come, later, for a weekend. In some of his poetry I think him great. At present we are having a bedroom enlarged so that, if T.H. feels equal to it, we may have two or three people together, to amuse one another. The dust & noise is terrific, as they are knocking down a wall, but I think *he* enjoys it.

I am so sorry that your servants have been tiresome. Our little housemaid is dreadful, but T.H is far too kind ever to dismiss anyone, & so we have to suffer her, & an idle, dishonest, drinking gardener. "Robert Creedle" is anxious to get us better servants, but we cannot get rid of these we have.

Henry Hardy is better—but really a broken man. I am sure you would like his sisters, but for the twenty years preceding Nov: 1912 they had not been allowed inside Max Gate, so I am not surprised that you never met them. It was a tragedy & the wounds are not yet healed.

I take out our beautiful spoons every now & then & absolutely gloat over them.

With kindest regards from both to both:

Yours very sincerely:
Florence Hardy.

Text MS. (with envelope) Colby. *Date* Year from internal evidence.
Ellis: played in the 1913 Dorchester production by Miss M. F. Rogers, of Rogers, the Dorchester florists. *Pietro*: R. Owen's dog. *a poem*: TH's 'Channel Firing', *Fortnightly Review*, May 1914. *little poem*: 'Before and After Summer', *New Weekly*, 4 Apr. 1914. *Masefield*: John Edward Masefield (1878–1967), poet and author, later poet laureate. *bedroom enlarged*: the one TH had used as his writing-room in the 1890s. *Creedle"*: Thomas Pouncy (see letter of 10 Dec. 1913).

[Lady Hoare was, like Rebekah Owen, an enthusiast for TH's work and a demanding correspondent whom FEH inherited from ELH. Visits were occasionally exchanged between Max Gate and Stourhead and TH himself wrote briefly to Lady Hoare from time to time, but it was FEH who sustained the main burden of the correspondence, writing as if on a basis of genuine friendship—with both Lady Hoare and Rebekah Owen she was soon on first name terms—but with a persistent fulsomeness that was in part responsive to the extravagance of Lady Hoare's own epistolary style but may be chiefly indicative of social anxiety, a constant awareness that she was writing to *Lady* Hoare of Stourhead. FEH seems also to have been somewhat in awe of her aristocratic friend's sheer personality and presence. On 19 December 1914 (Wiltshire R.O.), in a letter highly critical of women in general ('the meanest of created beings'), she told Lady Hoare: 'I love, in you, what your son so rightly recognises as *masculine*—the *breadth* of view, the large-minded generosity & downrightness (my husband says you are the ONE broad-minded woman he knows). And I adore the feminity. How well I remember that afternoon when I first met you. My first sensation was of the open-air—almost a sea-breeze—only that doesn't quite convey it. Then, in a flash, there was that wonderful tenderness & feminity, & intuition. And all that has *lasted*—thank Heaven.']

To Lady Hoare

UNIVERSITY ARMS HOTEL, | CAMBRIDGE.
7th April [May] 1914.

My dear Lady Hoare:

Thank you so much for your two letters. That which you wrote to my husband was so beautiful & poetic that I sincerely wished that you could be persuaded to rewrite it in the form of a poem or story. *He* was very much impressed by it—& the weird idea of the spirits in the wood. You have excellent material there—for poem or story.

Cambridge is so extremely kind to us (with the exception of the hotel pen) that I begin to think people can be too hospitable. But I am full of joy to see how my husband finds himself in his, true environment here. He went off just now in his cap & gown—very, *very* pleased with his adornments—to dine in his college (Magdalene)—& he loves being Dr Hardy. He is really just like a boy—or a nice child. He hates wearing his Order of Merit—but he is tremendously proud of his cap & gown—& longing for the day when I can see him—either in his scarlet gown—or sitting in his stall in chapel in a surplice.

I often wonder how many people realize the simplicity of his nature. He told me the other day that he thought he had never grown up.

I hope you won't think me very foolish in writing like this—but he said only today that he thought 'Lady Hoare' was 'different from any one else in Wessex." "She"—he said, "has spiritual insight."

And he was amused—& really quite pleased—to hear about the naming of the mares.

If you will let Mr Lea know what day you are going to Bockhampton I will do my best to take him there—on that day. But he says he feels he is the *last* person who ought to show you his old home.

Thank you again so much for your kind letters & message.

Yours very sincerely,
Florence Hardy.

Text MS. (with envelope) Wiltshire R.O.   *Date* Corrected from postmark (7 May 14) and internal evidence.

your two letters: neither has survived.   *Cambridge*: TH received an honorary Litt. D. degree from Cambridge in June 1913 and was installed as an Honorary Fellow of Magdalene College in Nov. 1913; for the May 1914 visit see *Life and Work*, 392.   *hotel pen*: a reference to the series of blots on the MS. above 'Cambridge'.   *his, true*: *sic*, but possibly another unintended product of the hotel pen.   *naming of the mares*: perhaps after some of the heroines of TH's novels.   *take him there*: TH did not in fact accompany Lady Hoare and FEH to the birthplace—and tea with Hermann Lea—on 19 May.

To Lady Hoare

MAX GATE, | DORCHESTER.
Wednesday. [22 July 1914]

My dear Lady Hoare:

I am so pleased that you like the photograph. It was very kind of you to want one of me. The same photographer—Miss Edis—took some when we were in Town—but she has not yet sent me any copies, & I have no other photographs. When they arrive I should like you to have one, immensely, but I don't make a good photograph—at all. There is someone who is now living at Lower Bockhampton—a Emily Whittaker—daughter of the old sexton at Stinsford—who *might* suit you admirably as a upper housemaid. She has been that in a large house somewhere, & is said to be extremely reliable & excellent in her work. I don't know whether she wants to go to service again though—but I might just ask—without mentioning your name, & let you know. My husband's family wanted him to have her here, as working-housekeeper, when things were going rather awry with the niece— before he married me. But he felt he didn't want anybody quite of that sort. He wanted a housekeeper who could be a companion & read to him— etc—& so I came in. I am so delighted & proud to know that you are fond of him. I think he really needs affection & tenderness more than anyone I know—for life has dealt him some cruel blows. I remember, some years ago, he said to me most pathetically:—"I do not ask for much—I only want a *little* affection."

I enclose a rough statement of expenditure for June. I try to make £20 cover everything—food—servants' wages—cleaning materials, lighting (oil— candles)—postage of parcels—etc. But *not* wine, spirits (of which we hardly drink any) or coal.

I am sure my husband's sisters would be *very very* delighted to see you— but should like, if you don't mind, to mention it to them first, as they are so nervous & shy. We showed these delightful photographs to my hus- band's brother yesterday—& he was so interested & admired them so much.

This is really a poor letter & so hurriedly written, but a magazine editor has sent me back a little story & asked me to make it a thousand words longer—& it is *so* difficult to add to anything, once completed. And he says he *must* have it by the end of the week. That is a question upon which I should so like to ask your advice someday—if you would be so very kind. Ought I—in fairness to my husband—to give up my scribbling? It really amounts to so little. Some day *perhaps* I might be allowed to talk it over with you, & explain the position.

We were so sorry we missed that ghost of a chance of seeing you on Monday. *How* we would have rejoiced. Perhaps you may be able to come *some day* & spend a *long* time. *He* is so pleased to see you. I think more pleased to see you than anyone else in the world.

We both feel that what you say about poor people is so true & so just. Charity *may* be made the most degrading thing.

My husband's great-grandfather played in the choir at Puddletown Church, & is buried in the church-yard—& my husband's grandfather was born at Puddletown.

With warmest thoughts from us both.

Florence Hardy.

Text MS. (with envelope) Wiltshire R.O. *Date* From postmark and note on MS. by Lady Hoare.

Miss Edis: Olive Edis (1876–1955), photographer, later married to a cousin of John Galsworthy's; she photographed TH at Max Gate in Dec. 1913. *Whittaker*: Emily Whittaker (d. 1928, aged 58), daughter of Stephen Whittaker, bootmaker and for many years sexton of Stinsford church. *editor . . . story*: unidentified. *great-grandfather . . . grandfather*: John Hardy (1755–1821) and Thomas Hardy (1778–1837); see *Biography*, 5, 8. *Puddletown*: 5 miles NE of Dorchester; associated with *Far from the Madding Crowd* and evidently visited by Lady Hoare during her Monday excursion.

[The unexpected outbreak of war in early August 1914 had little direct impact on everyday life at Max Gate. Psychologically, however, its horror was a pervasive presence, extorting comment or reflection of some kind in many of FEH's letters, especially those to Lady Hoare, whose son had immediately volunteered. Although FEH's thoroughly conventional views of the war are consistently represented as shared by her husband, she had perhaps not entirely registered the complex reservations underlying his quasi-patriotic belief in the justice of the British position and the desirability of an Allied victory.]

To Rebekah Owen

MAX GATE, | DORCHESTER.
5th September. [1914]

My dear Miss Owen:

Thank you so very much for that box of most delicious fruit. They were lovely peaches, & we have much enjoyed them. It really was most kind of you to send them to us—we both think so.

My husband was called hurriedly to Town on Wednesday—on war business. But he, dear heart, is not able to do much. The horror of this is making a great change in him—I can see. To me he seems ten years older. The thought of it all obsesses him. That is why, I think, he writes no poem about it. He cannot about the things he feels most deeply. Kipling's poem I thought good—he feels very despondent, that is clear. My husband met Henry Newbolt in Town, & he, too seems in the depths of despondency. A Cabinet Minister told my husband that the rumour about the Russian troops sent through Scotland & England has not a grain of truth in it. Russia could not spare the men. And yet quite a dozen people have told us that they knew someone who had seen the trains, counted them, etc. etc. I had three letters in one morning to tell me this tale. We had hoped it would be found true. The same minister told my husband that things were just about as bad as they could be.

Recruiting is going on better here now. I meant the working-class men & boys when I said how backward they were. The others, I think, are doing nobly. I hope that your sister will much stronger, & better in health. I am so very sorry not to have a better account of her. Your garden sounds too lovely for words. I had two lovely rows of sweet peas, but, alas, they had to be pulled up a week ago to make room for leeks. It was a tremendous sacrifice & I felt quite heroic when it was done. We have, alas, so little space. But I have had one superb gladiolus—Elfin—the loveliest I have ever seen.

I sympathise with your trouble about the gardener's nephew. I have the same trouble here, in a way. Our very quick, capable house-parlourmaid beguiled me into having her deaf & dumb sister here, as between maid. I pay this deaf & dumb girl £16, & she does very little, while her sister, who is deeply attached to her, does the work of both. I meant it kindly, but I think I did a foolish thing in having here—& it was just a few days before the war broke out. I find her sitting in the kitchen like a little doll (she is really pretty, poor girl) or else ironing her own & her sister's embroidered petticoats. And it so hard to reprove a deaf & dumb girl. Now, of course, it seems impossible to send her away.

We see next to nothing of Mrs Hayne. I was out when she called, & have only met her once since, when I thought I liked her rather better than I did when I met her at Mrs Leslie's. I will write again very soon.

Yours affectionately,

F.H.

Text   MS. (with envelope) Colby.   Date   Year from internal evidence.
war business: following the outbreak of the war against Germany and Austro-Hungary in early Aug. 1914, C. F. G. Masterman, the cabinet minister assigned responsibility for propaganda, had summoned TH and other leading writers to a discussion of the role that might be played by literary figures in formulating and disseminating British war aims.   *Kipling's poem*: 'For All We Have and Are', The Times, 2 Sept. 1914 (and in other newspapers on the same day).   *Newbolt*: Henry John Newbolt (1862–1938), poet and author.   *Cabinet Minister*: probably Masterman himself.   *Recruiting*: writing to R. Owen 30 Aug. 1918 (Colby), FEH had said that the slowness of 'the young men' to volunteer made her 'feel that it is almost time England ceased to exist as a nation'.   *your sister*: see letter of 1 Dec. 1914.   *will much stronger*: 'will soon be much stronger' presumably intended. *having here*: 'having her here' presumably intended.   *it so hard*: 'it is so hard' clearly intended.   *Mrs Hayne*: wife of Henry Hayne, of Dorchester, and a daughter of Walter William Ouless, the painter.   *Mrs Leslie's*: Margaret Elizabeth Leslie, daughter of TH's deceased friend Henry Joseph Moule, was the wife of the Revd Edward Charles Leslie and a friend and correspondent of the Owen sisters (Weber, 74–5, etc.); she and her husband had just left William Barnes's old parish of Winterborne Came.

To Rebekah Owen

Max Gate, | Dorchester.

1st Dec: '14

My dear Betty:

Because I have not written to you before that does not mean than I have not thought of you constantly—& *spoken* of you both here & at Talbothays. I hope, *with all my heart*, that you are well, & happier—though I feel it is almost useless to wish that. Life is altogether so sad—so infinitely sad. I cannot attempt to comfort you, for I *know* how futile that is. Some three years ago I lost a friend who was more to me than anything else in the world—for whom I know I would *gladly* have died. Nay, even now, I think could I give up the rest of my life for just one brief half-hour with that one, I would give it cheerfully. As I write I feel the old dull ache spring into life again—& so I know your pain. I think I lost, then, the only person who ever loved me—for I am not loveable. But for you—God grant—(if there be a God—some one who will fill the place of your dear gentle white-souled sister.

I wish (how often I must have said this & far more often thought it) I *wish* that you were nearer. I think we might do a little to help you to forget. Not that you want to forget—really. You would hardly believe—but sometimes I, too, feel that awful loneliness—the feeling that there is no one much in the world who cares whether I be happy or sad. It is of all feelings the worst.

Your housekeeping worries are indeed bad—but I am glad you got rid of that horrible woman. I don't believe there are many Tesses. Indeed I doubt if there ever was one.

The clergyman who has come to Came Rectory tells us that he found some very good lodgings in Dorchester, where he stayed before he went to the Rectory. I could ask about them if you liked. He said—I think—that the wife had been a cook & the husband a butler to the Herringstone Williamses. I think I am right. But he said they looked after him *well*.

Of course—were my husband less nervous & any visitors—old & dear friends included—I should love—absolutely *love* you to come here to stay for a long, *long* time. But at all events let us know, far ahead, when you are coming to Dorchester, & we may be able to arrange something.

I rushed up to see "The Dynasts" last Wednesday. My husband did not go as he had a cold—but really he didn't mean to go in any case. It was received enthusiastically, but I don't think it will run for long. Some of the scenes were too harrowing. But I enjoyed my brief trip to Town, although I returned early next morning. I sat next to John Masefield & his wife (I like him so much), & I had a brief & lively conversation with H. G. Wells, & I renewed acquaintance with William Archer, & Mr & Mrs Clement Shorter sat in front of me & they are very genial & very kind *always*. People say he has a motive always in what he does, but, after all, kindness is rare enough Heaven knows, & one had better accept it thankfully, with looking too closely. At all events *she* is genuine enough, & a sweet woman.

How is your dear Pietro? He must be a great comfort to you. Mrs Henniker wanted me to have the daughter of her two dogs—Milner & Empire—named Brittania. I must confess I was weak enough to feel that I wanted to have little Brittania, as a playmate for Wessex. But my husband objected—quite wisely I am sure.

I regret to say that Henry Hardy is seriously unwell & has to see a specialist this week. Mary has been ill with asthma but is now better.

With all my love, my dear Betty

Yours affectionately
Florence Hardy.

Text MS. (with envelope) Colby.
mean than: 'mean that' clearly intended.   *comfort you*: Catharine Owen had died 15 Sept. 1914. TH sent a telegram when the news first reached Max Gate (Weber, 178–9) and FEH wrote next day.   *a friend*: evidently Alfred Hyatt; see letter of 11 Dec. 1911.   *horrible woman*: apparently a dishonest cook who had profited from the household disorder following C. Owen's death.   *clergyman*: the Revd Thomas Hardy Newby, rector of William Barnes's old parish of Winterborne Came.   *the wife*: Mary Jane Green, a distant relative of TH's (as FEH was perhaps not aware).   *Williamses*: the family of Edward Wilmot Williams, a former High Sheriff of Dorset, living at Herringston House, near Dorchester.   *nervous & any*: 'nervous of any' clearly intended.   *"The Dynasts"*: as staged by Harley Granville-Barker at the Kingsway Theatre.   *Wells*: the novelist; see letter of 18 Oct. 1918.   *Archer*: William Archer (1856–1924), theatre critic; FEH had met him at Clodd's house in August 1909.   *with looking*: 'without looking' clearly intended.

[Although most of FEH's many letters to Lady Hoare during the winter of 1914–15 seem self-conscious and somewhat lacking in substance, a few of them show her writing with genuine intimacy in response to some of her correspondent's characteristically direct questions. The letters of 6 and 9 December 1914 are especially notable for their open expression of FEH's pain at what she saw as TH's public celebration of his first wife's virtues in the 'Poems of 1912–13' section of the newly published *Satires of Circumstance*. Not included here (but see *CL*, v. 74) is FEH's 7 January 1915 transcription of TH's response to Lady Hoare's enquiry as to his opinion of the novels of Charles Dickens.

To Lady Hoare

MAX GATE, | DORCHESTER.
6th December. [1914]

My dearest Alda:

You have indeed given us a great pleasure to look forward to. When we heard that you were really coming to Max Gate before Christmas we were overjoyed, & now that you say Sir Henry is coming with you—well, I can only say we are as glad as it is possible for anyone to be these times. My husband *beamed* when I told him. But he wonders whether, as the days are so short, whether it would not be possible for you to come to lunch—at any time you chose to fix—to go where you want to afterwards & then have tea here before returning home. We should be so truly delighted &

honoured if you would. We have no engagement at all in prospect, & if we know the day beforehand we will be at home & alone, for I *know* my husband won't share you with anyone. It is so delightful to have your visit to look forward to: the *one* bright spot in the future.

I feel so much what you say about the spirits from the woods. There are such spirits I feel sure—& there are sad spirits often that haunt this house, & stand by the little graves in the garden.

My husband was so pleased with the list of poems you liked best. When I read "Wessex Heights" it wrung my beart. It made me miserable to think that he had ever suffered so much. It was written, in '96, before I knew him—but the four people mentioned are actual women. One was dead & three living when it was written—now only one is living.

But I must confess to you—& I would confess this to noone else—the book pains me horribly, & yet I read it with a terrible fascination. It seems to me that I am an utter failure if my husband can publish such a *sad sad* book. He tells me that he has written *no* despondent poem for the last eighteen months, & yet I cannot get rid of the feeling that the man who wrote some of those poems is utterly weary of life—& cares for nothing in this world. If I had been a different sort of woman, & better fitted to be his wife—would he, I wonder, have published that volume? Well———.

I ought to have said at the beginning of the letter that his cold is well now, I *trust*, but we are very careful, & he has not gone out yet.

With love from both,

Florence Hardy.

Text   MS. (with envelope) Wiltshire R.O.   *Date*   Envelope postmarked 5 December 1914.
graves in the garden: i.e. in the pets' cemetery at Max Gate.   *liked best*: of those collected in *Satires of Circumstance*, pub. by Macmillan 17 Nov. 1914.   *in '96*: FEH first wrote 'of course'.   *actual women*: usually identified as TH's cousin Tryphena Sparks (already dead in 1896), TH's mother (d. 1904), ELH (d. 1912), and Florence Henniker (still alive in 1914).

To Lady Hoare

MAX GATE, | DORCHESTER.
9th December '14.

My dearest Alda:

Many, many thanks for the kind gift of game that came today. It is so good of you and Sir Henry to think of us, & send us such a useful present. I am sure we shall enjoy them very much.

Your letter fully accomplished what must have been its object. It put things straight in my mind in an incredibly short time, & I hope I see them now in the true perspective. You must have a quite magical insight for I am sure you saw right into my mind & heart. Moreover—and it seems as if this cannot have been a mere accident—you chose from the poems the two *very* examples that could convince me that your argument was right.

You mentioned "The Death of Regret." As it stands in that volume it is a lament for a friend—a man. 'to forget *him*'—'*his* last departure' etc. The poem was, in the first place, written about a cat—a little cat who was strangled in a rabbit wire on the barrow in sight of this house, & she is buried by a sycamore in our garden here. My husband thought the poem too good for a cat, & so made it apply to a person.

Again, in "Wessex Heights" there is one woman "one rare fair woman' of whom he says 'now I can let her go'.

She has always been a sincere & affectionate friend to him, staunch & unaltering—&, I am glad to say she is my friend too. There was never any idea of his letting her go—for he, too, is true & faithful to his friends but the *poet* wrote that.

It is quite wonderful that you should have chosen these two passages as an illustration of your argument—that one must not make the man responsible for what the poet writes, since I really knew the actual fact behind the poem.

But, as I said before, "Wessex Heights" will *always* wring my heart, for I know when it was written, a little while after the publication of "Jude", when he was so cruelly treated. Oddly enough, as if to show me how right & just your letter was, he has been particularly bright & cheerful the last day or so. And of course I do know he has a tender protective affection for me—as a father for a child—as he has always had—a feeling quite apart from passion. And I feel towards him, sometimes, as a mother towards a child with whom things have somehow gone wrong—a child who needs comforting—to be treated gently & with all the love possible.

Your letter was—I could almost say inspired, & I shall always feel most grateful for it.

Your promised visit sheds a sort of sunshine over all the days here. He is looking forward to it ever so much. I suggested—rather to tease him than of serious intent—that we should invite some friends to lunch to meet you. His face fell. 'O, that won't be the same thing at all", he said dolefully.

He (& I too) were so interested to hear that your son had been moved nearer the coast. I wonder does that mean an expected invasion? A friend who had been at Sheerness wrote to tell us that his men had had to sleep in their boots one night, after a heavy day's marching, as they expected a raid.

The people at Bockhampton & Stinsford declare that Mr Hermann Lea is a German spy. He is erratic & desultory, but one of the most harmless of men. His mother was a German woman—unfortunately.

With our love, & many lookings-forward,

Florence Hardy.

Text   MS. (with envelope) Wiltshire R.O.

about a cat: evidently Kitsey, also the original subject of 'The Roman Gravemounds'; see letters of 8 and 19 Nov. 1910.   *one woman*: Florence Henniker.   *your son*: Henry Colt Hoare, the Hoares' only son, currently an army officer.

[FEH, up until the time of her marriage, had been obliged to make her own way in the world as schoolteacher, journalist, companion, secretarial assistant, and writer of children's stories, and she evidently felt, and with some justice, that she had experienced exploitation in pursuing each of these directions. Once married, she continued to complain with some frequency and freedom about the problems of running Max Gate and about some of the tasks imposed upon her as a literary wife. Unlike ELH, however, she responded to male dominance not with resentment and open protest but rather with apparent acceptance and even celebration of male strength: in a letter of 27 March 1915 (Wiltshire R.O.), for example, she agreed with Lady Hoare that women—geniuses such as George Eliot and Charlotte Brontë apart— were 'only strong when they realize their weakness & dependence on men'. The articles she contributed from time to time to mass-circulation newspapers such as the *Sunday Pictorial* also projected a thoroughly conservative view of the role of women, not least in wartime. Her emphasis on child-bearing as a woman's supreme purpose and achievement clearly had personal as well as social implications, and comments appearing as if incidentally in several letters speak to an acute and indeed painful self-consciousness about her personal appearance and especially about her position as a childless woman likely, given her husband's age, to remain so.]

To Sydney Cockerell

MAX GATE, | DORCHESTER.

Sunday. [20 June 1915]

Dear Mr Cockerell:

How very good of you to send me that delightful picture of your three dear children. I am so pleased to have it, although it fills me with envy. What would I not give to have *one*—any one of the three—for my own. I have been trying to make up my mind as to which I would choose were you to offer me one as a gift—& I am quite unable to decide, for I know that any one of those children would make me as proud & happy as any woman on earth. And you & Mrs Cockerell are so fortunate as to have *three*.

We have been expecting to hear from you as to that visit you promised to pay us in June, & this perfect weather may soon be over. We have no engagements in prospect except a couple of days in Town, the date as yet undecided. Nothing would take us there except necessity & I don't think we shall go up again for a long *long* time, once we have this business over, & that will make your visit all the more delightful to us since our Dorchester friends—and kinder folk there could not be—are not *very* enlivening.

The small operation I had was wonderfully successful & quite painless. I hope it has rid me for ever of a tiresome nasal catarrh that had bothered me for years. I expect now to be better in health than I have ever been.

I hope that both Mrs Cockerell & yourself & children are all very well. My husband is very well indeed. I try to tempt him into the open air as much as possible & we have had several little trips lately in Mr Hermann Lea's motor-car which he has thoroughly enjoyed—& I think he has been much better for them.

With kind regards from us both

Yours very sincerely,
Florence Hardy.

Text MS. Beinecke.   *Date* Supplied on MS. by Cockerell.
children: Cockerell and his wife had two daughters, Margaret (later Minns) and Katharine (later Laughton), and one son, Christopher (knighted 1969), the inventor of the hovercraft.
operation: on her nose, performed in London in late May 1915 by Macleod Yearsley (see letter of 16 May 1920). See *CL*, v. 101–10, for TH's letters to her while she was in the nursing-home and then convalescing at the home of his old friend Lady St Helier (1845–1931), formerly, as Mrs and then Lady Jeune, a leading London hostess but currently a London County Council alderman.

To Caleb Williams Saleeby

MAX GATE, | DORCHESTER.
8th July '15.

Dear Dr Saleeby:

Many thanks for both your kind letters. I ought to have replied to one of them before this, but I was really waiting until my husband had found time to copy out the verses for you. He always takes rather a long time to do such things—putting them off sometimes for months—& I find that it is of no use to urge him as that is the way to prevent it being done at all. However, I hope to be able to send it to you in time. I want him also to copy out for me some verses—but there is nothing for it but to wait.

Thank you so much for the delightful article you enclose—"Saving the

Future". I have read & reread it with interest. To me it is wonderful that everyone does not realize the fact that out first duty is to protect the infancy of the nation. It seems to me that a great work might be done by the hosts of women who, like myself, are unhappily childless.

The Miss Dugdale whose letter you sent to me is not a sister or relative of mine, although I have a sister whose initials are the same.

It is so very good of you to say that you liked the article I wrote for the Sunday Pictorial. As a matter of fact I felt rather ashamed of it. It seemed so sentimental—almost treacle-y. I think I could do better, & I must have another try.

We will look, with great interest, for your article in the Suday Pictorial.

I think that my nose is quite healed up & well, although there is a little soreness there, at times, if I motor rapidly but I am most intensely thankful to have had it done.

I have one more visit to pay to Mr Yearsley but we have not been able to go up to Town since I left Lady St Helier's.

With kind regards from us both,

Yours very sincerely,
Florence Hardy.

P.S. We have now the music-rolls you chose for us. They are so excellent. My husband particularly likes the waltz from "Der Rosenkavalier." I am entraced with that rather horrible Danse Macabre—Saint-Saens. One hears the rattle of bones & the gnashing of teeth in the fleshless skulls all through.

Text   MS. Adams.

Saleeby: Caleb Williams Saleeby (1878–1940), doctor, eugenist, and miscellaneous reformer; he had called on the Hardys at Max Gate in late April 1915 and on FEH while she was in the London nursing-home.   *the verses*: TH's 'The Pity of It' (*Fortnightly Review*, Apr. 1915) had been suggested by an article of Saleeby's; after many delays, TH did eventually send him a fair-copy MS. of the poem. See Purdy, 189.   *delightful article*: Saleeby's 'Saving the Future', *Child-Study*, 9 (1916), 21–9; it was first delivered as a lecture and Saleeby had perhaps sent FEH a copy of it in that form.   *The Miss Dugdale*: unidentified; 'The' clumsily corrected from 'This'.   *article I wrote*: ' "Greater Love Hath No Man . . ." The Story of a Village Ne'er-Do-Well', *Sunday Pictorial*, 13 June 1915, 7. FEH's own judgement of this story—in which a mother's worthless son wins the Victoria Cross—seems correct, though perhaps understated. Saleeby's promised article has not been traced.   *music-rolls*: for the Max Gate pianola.   *"Der Rosenkavalier."*: opera (1911) by Richard Strauss (1864–1949).   *Danse Macabre*: tone poem (1875) by Camille Saint–Saëns (1835–1921).

To Lady Hoare

Monday. [30 August 1915]

Dearest Alda:

Thank heaven it is only a sprained knee. I was thinking so much of your son this morning, & hoping, oh so much, that he was well. Do you know I have an inward feeling that he *will* be protected & I have a hope too—which I can tell *you* & you alone—that he is to do some *very* gallant deed, & win renown. I feel that is very *very* likely.

Just before your kind letter—how good it was of you to write it—a telegram came to say that our dear young cousin Frank George was killed on the 22nd. He was already dead when the letters arrived of which I told you but, of course, we did not know.

If you had known him, dear Alda, I am sure you would have liked him. We were both *very* fond of him. Some day, if I may, I will show you his portrait.

We had hoped that, when we were gone, he would live here after us, & that in my husband's last days he (T.H) would have had that strong arm to lean upon. What his mother & sisters will do without him I cannot think. But it will be our duty & our pleasure to try to make life easier & happier for them, if they will let us. He was, as my husband says, *"our one"*.

With my love & *constant, constant* thought of you & yours. And my husband sends you his love—

Florence

Text MS. (with envelope) Wiltshire R.O. *Date* From postmark.
your son: see letter of 9 Dec. 1914. *Frank George*: Frank William George (1880–1915), killed in action at Gallipoli, was in fact a distant cousin of TH's, his great-grandfather having been a younger brother of TH's grandfather. TH's interest in him, though not of long standing, appears to have been genuine: he wrote a short obituary of him for *The Times* and a poem, 'Before Marching, and After (In Memoriam F.W.G.)' for the Oct. 1915 *Fortnightly Review*.

[Mary Hardy, born the year after TH, had always been far closer to him in age, temperament, and interests than either of his other siblings, and he was deeply affected by her death on 24 November 1915, a month short of her seventy-fourth birthday. Although she was always delicate, her emphysema had taken a dangerous turn only in the last two or three weeks and TH, not expecting so rapid a conclusion, was not present when she died. For FEH the rituals of death as observed in the Hardy family seemed horrifyingly primitive, and she was also disturbed by what seemed a jarring preoccupation with the disposition of Mary Hardy's money—much of it, of course, given to her by TH over the years.]

To Rebekah Owen

MAX GATE, | DORCHESTER.
Friday morn. Dec. 3rd [1915]

My dearest Betty:

I am so very delighted that you were able to have that brief interval of change and rest—way from Belmount Hall—and in such delightful and luxurious surroundings. It sounded most delightful and must have toned you up.

You will, I hope, have received the Dorset Chronicle before this and have seen their account of the funeral. Part of the obituary notice T. wrote. You may recognise his hand. The funeral was a most depressing affair—the day was wet and Katie seemed in a state of suppressed temper the whole while. But I suppose, poor thing, it was her way of showing her grief. I shall miss Mary very, very much for she had a much more aimable and placid disposition than the others, and also she rather held them in check. Henry and Katie nearly quarrelled with Tom the night before the funeral because he (Tom) said he would rather not go back to Talbothays after the funeral. He rather, I think, dreaded the relatives who would be there. Henry was so rude to Tom—and of course it ended by our going back there. It was my first experience of a funeral and I had no idea of the attendant horrors of death. I suppose country people are rather like that. Poor Mary died early on Wednesday morning and she was buried on Monday. They kept on worrying and worrying us to go up to see her, even to the last moment—and wanted us to keep on kissing her. I got a horrible sore throat the last two times I went up. All this seems so needless. Mary of course died intestate—she has left a good bit of money—Katie is in terror lest anybody but herself should have any of it. I have heard of this sort of thing happening after death but, so far, have had no experience of it. Of course neither Tom nor I want a penny of Mary's money—or indeed anything that was hers.

I write so freely to you because I know how safe everything is that I tell you. I would not tell that to my own sisters even.

Tom is wonderfully calm and composed. I think he felt that her death was a release from pain to her and hence not to be much lamented—but of course he was fond of her.

Melbury and our visit there seems to have receded into the dim past. Of course it is very beautiful—not so full of treasures as Holland House, of course, but I like it better. It is a *home*. I did not think it much more luxurious than Mrs Henniker's or Lady St Helier's or Lady Hoare's or even my friends house at Dublin where I used to stay before the husband and wife both died. Perhaps the war is making them live simply. Lady Ilchester is sweet and I call her beautiful—she is a tall big handsome woman and has a cordial charming manner—absolutely friendly. She is most unceremonious and by no means 'dressy'. She wore all day an ordinary walking skirt and silk sports coats over shirt blouses. Her evening dresses were quite simple—black and black and white. But she wore her famous pearl necklace and lovely diamond ear-rings. She spent all the time with us—showing us the house the park and the villages and motoring us about. There was nobody there of much importance—some of the Digbys, her relatives—a Miss Sonia Keppell—very young—a French lady of title—which title I have now forgotten.

Tomorrow Rogers, the florist, is coming to dig up and pack for you some delphiniums and paeonies. I have had a touch of sciatica and the weather is so wet that I cannot get out and do it myself.

I most sincerely hope that your chauffeur is not going to turn out a failure. I did hope that you would have been able to get a really good man after your long waiting. I wish there were someone very good indeed who would take the place of Dickinson. It seems almost tragic that you are obliged to go without early morning tea—I wish I could bring you some every morning.

Tom—to my great dismay—says he feels that he never wants to go anywhere or to see anyone again. He wants to live on here, quite quietly, shut up in his study. He says that if any of his men friends from Town want to see him they must come and put up at an hotel here and come out to tea. Of course they won't do that. I do wish that some of my own people or some of the friends I had before my marriage lived nearer—say at Bournemouth.

I was so unused to buying mourning that I made a great muddle of it. I sent up to my London dressmaker and she sent me a satin blouse a really nice skirt—and a coat—black velour cloth trimmed with black fox cuffs and collar, and a black hat. They all fitted very well. But I think I might have saved a great deal had I been able to go up to London and choose.

How long ought I to stay in mourning do you think? Lady Ilchester has not worn at all deep mourning for her father—and Mrs Hanbury—daughter-in-law of Lady Hanbury who owns La Mortola—hardly wore mourning at all for her mother. She wore nearly all white during the first few months—and now she is 'out' and it cannot be much more than six months since Mrs Jeune died. I hope I won't horrify you by not using a black-edged envelope—but I haven't one to fit this paper. I have so many letters to answer. I am afraid this is a very poor letter. There are several other things that I want to say to you and perhaps I will write them later. I hope that I have not been hard upon Katie. Of course I realize her point of view.

With all my love,

Yours ever affectionately,
Florence Hardy.

Text   MS. (typed, with envelope) Colby.   *Date*   Year from internal evidence. *obituary notice*: *Dorset County Chronicle*, 2 Dec. 1915.   *aimable*: though typed, this habitual misspelling of FEH's has been left uncorrected.   *because*: FEH typed 'becase'.   *Melbury*: Melbury House, in NW Dorset, the seat of Giles Stephen Holland Fox-Strangways, 6th Earl of Ilchester, and his wife Helen, daughter of the 6th Marquess of Londonderry.   *Holland House*: the Ilchesters' London house.   *There was*: FEH typed 'The was'.   *Digbys*: the eldest daughter of the 3rd Earl of Ilchester married the 9th Lord Digby (of Sherborne Castle) in 1837.   *Keppell*: Sonia Rosemary Keppel (1900–86), later Cubitt; she was the daughter of George and Alice Keppel (King Edward VII's mistress) and the younger sister of Violet Trefusis, the lover of Vita Sackville-West.   *Dickinson*: R. Owen's former chauffeur and manservant.   *I think*: FEH typed 'I thnk'.   *Mrs Hanbury*: Effield Dorothy Hanbury (née Jeune), wife of Cecil Hanbury of Kingston Maurward House, near Dorchester.   *La Mortola*: villa and gardens owned by the Hanbury family in Ventimiglia, Italy.   *Mrs Jeune*: Dorothy Hanbury's mother; her father, John Frederic Symons Jeune (see letter of 3 Jan. 1922), was a connection of ELH's by marriage.

[While FEH fully supported her husband in his desire for personal privacy and his resistance to intruding journalists, interviewers, and biographers, his increasing reclusiveness undoubtedly intensified her own sense of isolation at Max Gate, where she felt cut off from friends and family, from important neighbours and interesting visitors, and even from TH himself during the long hours he spent working in his study. Driven by that loneliness, reinforced by an element of grievance, FEH continued to write with her customary lack of discretion to such correspondents as Lady Hoare and Rebekah Owen. There was little risk, in fact, in writing freely to Lady Hoare, whom TH seems also to have admired: FEH's letter of 6 February 1916 (Wiltshire R.O.), for example, reports his acceptance of Lady Hoare's judgement that he had been wrong to omit the final stanza of 'The Dead and the Living One' from its first printing in the *Sphere*—FEH herself having thought that 'it quite spoilt the poem' (letter of 7 January 1916, Wiltshire R.O.). But Rebekah Owen was known to gossip, and when she shared some of her Max Gate information with her sardonic Lake District neighbour Albert Fleming, he not unnaturally passed it on to his friend Sydney Cockerell, who was disturbed to learn that his private discussions with TH about the literary executorship and other such delicate issues had so rapidly become public.]

To Rebekah Owen

Max Gate, | Dorchester.
Tuesday. [18 January 1916]

My dearest Betty:

I have not been well & I still feel rather dizzy & confused. Tomorrow, I think must be spent in bed & so I am scribbling you a line tonight. I hope you are well & that you have less trouble with the chauffeur & all the other tiresome servants who treat you so badly. It will be so delightful to have you here. Would it were actually *here*—at Max Gate. My husband went out today for a walk for the first time, but not very far. He gets soon tired but is much better. My father has been very ill but I have not been able to get to him. It seems impossible to leave. People may safely shower invitations on me for they may be certain I shall not be avail myself of them. Already this year I have had most cordial invitations to stay from Lady St Helier— Mrs Henniker & others.

Mr Cockerell wanted to come this vacation, but my husband felt unequal to the effort of entertaining anyone.

Mr Cockerell is really a wonderfully fine man—at least he seems so to me. He has such a different way of looking at things from most people— he has such high ideals & lives up to them. He & Clement Shorter (whom I cannot help liking) are miles apart. Of course Mr Cockerell does rather take great men in hand, but he does not exploit them for his own benefit. I don't suppose that he has ever asked for so much as an autograph from T. But he does like to set people on what he thinks (& what probably is) the right path. Morris, I think, loved him. He has a way of behaving like a son to elder men. In his own way he is really unique. He is so splendid in the way he gets things done. I may, of course, be mistaken in my estimate of him, but I really do admire his Zeal. It is a little disconcerting to know that he has been a great friend of G. B. Shaw, & knew Tolstoi—Ouida & a host of other folk of like renown. But he seems to keep his friends.

My husband has been horrified at learning that one of his friends is going to publish a volume of reminiscences—you will probably guess whom I mean. He (T.) thought this friend was a man who would be perfectly safe— a man whom he trusted implicitly. Now he finds that he has been keeping a record of all conversations etc—& they will probably be published. Two other men of his acquaintance (friends I might say) also keep diaries & it is generally supposed that they will publish their reminiscences too.

I had to write a very decided letter to the first man & say that if he published anything about my husband—he (T.H) would write to the papers about it. He has such a dread of the person who comes here & goes away to write down things, so I dared not mention to him your diary, although I know quite well that you are so entirely different from these men—particularly the first man—that you would not ever dream of doing what they have done & intend doing. I keep a diary—probably like yours—with incidents recorded—no personalities. A dull affair no doubt—but when I remember the *awful* diary the first Mrs T.H. kept (which he burned) full of venom, hatred & abuse of him & his family I am afraid to do more than chronicle facts. I *hope* you burn my letters. Some are, I fear, most horribly indiscreet. I wouldn't write as I do to any woman in the world but you, for you have always seemed to me the truest & most high-minded woman I ever know. That is why one regrets so the domestic troubles that seem to dog you in such a fiendish way.

Wessie sends his love. He is really a good dog—but all of his kind are fighters—more or less. My husband actually kisses him every night before he is carried off to bed. Perhaps he won't always fight. Today he met a curly brown water spaniel & had a great frolic with him. But he hates smooth haired fox terriers because one attacked him once—one with a black face. And he hates black faces.

Much love—post in two minutes.

F.H.

Text MS. (with envelope) Colby.   *Date* Pencilled on MS. (by R. Owen?), confirmed by postmark and internal evidence.

be avail: 'be able to avail' evidently intended.   *this vacation*: the Cambridge Christmas vacation.   *Morris*: see letter of 3 Dec. 1913.   *Shaw*: George Bernard Shaw (1856–1950), the playwright, whom Cockerell had known since 1891.   *Tolstoi*: for Cockerell's visit to Count Leo Tolstoy, the novelist, see Meynell, ed., *Friends of a Lifetime*, 78–86.   *Ouida*: pseudonym of Marie Louise de la Ramée (1839–1908), novelist and essayist; see *Friends of a Lifetime*, 144–52, and Blunt, *Cockerell*, 73–4.   *one of his friends*: Edward Clodd; see letter of 23 Sept. 1916.   *your diary*: that R. Owen responded angrily to the implication of 'Cloddishness' on her part is clear from FEH's letter to her of 22 Jan. 1916 (Colby).   *ever know*: 'have ever known' or 'ever knew' clearly intended.

To Sydney Cockerell

Max Gate | Dorchester
3rd March 1916

Dear Mr Cockerell:

I ought to have replied to your kind letter before, but I have been very busy.

My husband is very well now, & most cheerful, but he stays upstairs in his study & we have meals there. He has not been downstairs since

Monday. But this, I imagine, does him no harm as the weather is so cold & trying. I have, for a long time tried to persuade him to wear a skull-cap & a night-cap. I suggested that a year ago, but he says that he has known certain men who have worn skull-caps & he has always disliked those particular men.

Perhaps, a little later, when the weather is warmer, it would be an excellent thing if you would be so very kind as to run down again & finally settle the questions he was discussing with you.

You ask me whether the matter of the literary executorship has been mentioned to anyone. My husband's sister Mary knew, & was keenly interested. Now that she is dead no other member of the family takes any interest in my husband's literary work, & if your name was ever mentioned it has probably been forgotten.

A week or two after our marriage Mr Clodd came down to see us. At that time my husband used to confide in him freely & the question of the literary executorship was then discussed. Mr Reed—the solicitor—was asked to dinner & when he had gone Mr Clodd said to me that he thought "that man" was "worse than nobody as a literary executor". I think that my husband told Mr Clodd that he intended to ask if you would be so good as to act for him. I was not present at the conversation, but I know from certain of Mr Clodd's questions Did I like you? etc. that this was so. And he said he would like to meet you some day.

Sometime after this I discovered, to my amazement, that Mr Clodd must have mentioned many details of this conversation to a friend of his in London. At one time my husband trusted Mr Clodd entirely, but that is now at an end.

So far as I know noone else has been told anything about the matter, & Mr Clodd does not know now how it was finally settled.

The friend in the Lake District has been told nothing except that you were a great friend of my husband's. She seems to have formed the idea that you are writing a biography of my husband. I judge so, at least, from her persistent questioning. I have neither denied this or said anything to encourage her belief. She has known my husband for thirty years, & I believe poses as his greatest friend. She was very much in the confidence of the late Mrs Hardy, & she has a number of friends here with whom she carries on a voluminous correspondence, & I think she asks them questions about us—what we are doing—who are our friends here, & so forth. She seems to have tried to investigate Ruskin's private life in the same manner.

Mr Shorter's rival at Hove is a stranger to us—his name is Williams, &, from the heading of some business-paper upon which he wrote he seems to be an house agent. He did not ask for permission to reprint "The Oxen", but it was not necessary.

I do hope that Mrs Cockerell is feeling better. Will you please give our love to her.

With kind regards from us both,

Yours very sincerely,
Florence Hardy.

P.S. It has suddenly occured to me that my husband *may* have mentioned the matter of the literary executorship to Mr Gosse. He says he cannot remember doing so—but his memory is not quite so good now as it was, & he forgets things. I think he would have told me if he had discussed the matter with Mr Gosse. F.H.

Text   MS. (mourning stationery—following Mary Hardy's death) Beinecke.
the questions: related to TH's will, his choice of literary executors, etc.   *Mr Reed*: William Wilton Reed (1856–1923), Dorchester solicitor.   *friend of his in London*: probably Clement Shorter.   *my husband trusted*: FEH first wrote 'my husband used to confide'.   *& Mr . . . settled*: a late insertion.   *friend . . . District*: Rebekah Owen; from FEH's letters to her of 21 Feb. and 8 Mar. 1916 (Colby) it appears she had shared gossip from earlier letters with Cockerell's (and Ruskin's) friend Albert Fleming (see Blunt, *Cockerell*, 49–50) who had re-layed it to Cockerell himself.   *his greatest*: FEH first wrote 'my greatest'.   *the late*: FEH began to write 'the last'.   *Ruskin's private life*: see ELH letters of 14 Feb. and 24 Apr. 1899. *Williams*: Edward Williams, of New Town Road, Hove, was Shorter's rival in that in 1914 both had issued TH's uncopyrighted poem, 'Song of the Soldiers', in pamphlet form; 'The Oxen', similarly reprinted by Williams in 1915, was also uncopyrighted (see Purdy, 157–8, 175).   *Mr Gosse*: Edmund William Gosse (1849–1928), man of letters and one of TH's oldest friends; he was named in TH's final will as alternative literary executor had Cockerell declined to serve.

To Caleb Williams Saleeby

MAX GATE, | DORCHESTER.
Easter Sunday. [23 April 1916]

Dear Dr Saleeby:

I hope that you do not object to a typed letter. I am confronted by a pile of unanswered letters and this is the only possible way I have of clearing them off. You asked me about the word which my husband had altered in the copy he made for you of his sonnet. He often does alter words, and even lines, after he has had poems printed in periodicals. Sometimes I think that the second reading is not so good as the first—as in the case you quoted—but he generally has some reason for the change of word.

Thank you so much for the interesting articles you send us, which we read with interest.

So far as we can judge here the war news of the moment seems rather bad. We had a depressing letter this morning from a friend who professes to have special information. My husband fortunately keeps a very calm mind about the whole. At the beginning he faced the worst possibilities of the war and since then, I think, has not been unduly cast down.

Monday.

I was called away at that point and was unable to continue until today. I wish there were a gleam of hope somewhere; the papers and our letters bring us none.

We are interested to know that you are still vigorously continuing your campaign against ignorance and extravagance—the producers of disease and poverty. I wonder if there will be one shred of self-respect left to us, as a nation, after the war? I feel that I ought not to be writing at all just now, being in so pessimistic a mood. If one *must* write letters when one is in such a frame of mind the only reasonable thing to do is to burn them instead of posting them, but with a threatened shortage of paper I suppose even that is a course that is not to be strictly commended.

My husband—one bright spot in the general gloom—is now very well I am glad to say. We stay at home and live very quietly—there is no extravagance here, unless it be of language when we discuss newspapers and politics.

With kind regards from us both,

Yours very sincerely,
Florence Hardy.

Text MS. (typed) Adams.   *Date* Year from internal evidence.
his sonnet: 'The Pity of It'; see letter of 8 July 1915. The alteration was apparently of 'by-talk' (or 'bye-talk') in line 5 to 'small talk'; in a letter to Saleeby of 10 Nov. 1916 (Adams) FEH reported TH as agreeing with Saleeby that it was not an improvement.   *interesting articles*: unidentified; Saleeby wrote prolifically on numerous current issues.   *a friend*: unidentified. *continuing*: FEH typed 'cintinuing'.   *and extravagance*: FEH typed 'and extragavance'.

To Sydney Cockerell

MAX GATE, | DORCHESTER.
August 12th 1916.

Dear Mr Cockerell:

Very many thanks for your letter & enclosure. There is so much to say about different matters that I am appalled at the prospective length of this letter, & if I were not afraid of seeming casual I would type it, for your greater ease in reading.

I hope that Mrs Cockerell & you all will have much happiness in your new home, & that the benefits of the holidays may be lasting.

What a delightful letter from Miss Mackail! My husband, said when I read it to him, "What a nice girl to write like that now!" He so much appreciated Professor & Mrs Mackail's visit, & it is quite pathetic to me to think he gets so very little opportunity of meeting anyone so sympathetic to him as Professor Mackail. After they had gone he (T.H.) said "What it would have meant to me to meet that man years ago." Then, at dinner-time, he suddenly said "I *hope* I shall meet him again." Later on while walking out he said:—"I wish I could have had a longer talk with him." Two days after he was delighted to have an interesting letter & pamphlet from him. He is shut off here, almost entirely, from the society he appreciates & falls so easily into the hands of Clodds & Shorters whose one idea is to exploit him & advertise themselves. A propos of that, I have a not very agreeable story to tell you when we meet.

Thank you ever so much for all the trouble you have taken about the Shakespeare poem. I must admit that I feel rather "Shorterish" about the matter.

I am sending off to your friend the MS. of "The Poor Man & the Lady," since you so kindly wish to have it bound. We have been looking at "Under the Greenwood Tree" (which belongs to me now) & my husband says that it really ought to do in its present binding, unlovely as it is, for if at any future day we have to sell it the buyer would profit by your generosity— & if it goes to a museum they themselves ought to have it rebound. Were it not war-time we might think otherwise. Thank you again & again for so kindly suggesting the re-binding.

I am also sending you a Mr Blunt's poem which has greatly interested my husband.

He is *very* hard at work now—rather too hard I think—but he says that 'when the wheels are going round it is a mistake to stop them, for they may not be able to start again.' He is working practically all the day until after dinner when I read to him until 10.30—& yesterday feeling very much inclined for work he did not even go for the daily walk. I am going to make a tremendous fight for a few days holiday in September—probably in North Cornwall, for I believe he would rather go there than anywhere else.

My sister Margaret had hoped to be married at the end of this month, believing that the young man was going to France in September. To the dismay of both he was sent off to France last Tuesday with only two days notice. She was at the seaside with his sister & he had only time to rush to say 'Goodbye' to her.

With kindest regards to you both & my warmest thanks for sending that delightful letter which I return herewith,

Yours very sincerely,

Florence Hardy.

P. S. I did not say how very much *I* liked the Mackails. They are charming people I think. F.H.

Text MS. Beinecke.

Miss Mackail: Clare, younger daughter of John William Mackail (1859–1945), scholar and critic, and his wife Margaret, daughter of Edward Burne-Jones, the painter. *pamphlet*: Mackail sent a copy of his British Academy lecture, *Shakespeare After Three Hundred Years*. *Shakespeare poem*: see letter of 9 Sept. 1916. *your friend*: Katharine Adams, later Webb (1862–1952), the bookbinder. *"The Poor . . . Lady,"*: TH's never-published first novel; although much of the original MS. had been absorbed into later works a substantial portion of it still survived at this date (see letter of 16 Feb. 1917). *they themselves*: 'themselves' arrowed in by FEH from its original position following 'rebound'. *a Mr Blunt's poem*: Wilfrid Scawen Blunt (1840–1922), traveller, poet, and politician; the specific poem has not been identified. FEH perhaps meant 'a poem of Mr Blunt's', although it is not clear that she was as yet aware of Cockerell's friendship with Blunt. *My sister . . . young man*: Margaret Alicia Dugdale (1893–1979), youngest of the Dugdale sisters; she married Reginald Soundy (1894–1943), currently an officer in the Royal Flying Corps, in Feb. 1917.

To Sydney Cockerell

KING ARTHUR'S CASTLE HOTEL, | TINTAGEL, CORNWALL.

9th September. [1916]

Dear Mr Cockerell:

I am most exceedingly obliged to you for the trouble you have taken about the reprints, & the sale of the ten copies. I was really amazed to receive the cheque, as I could never actually believe in their money value— in spite of Mr Shorter's assertions. However, the cheque is solid testimony. It's arrival was most opportune for the afternoon before, Lady Ilchester horrified me by saying that, since funds were low, each member of our committee (of which she is President) must subscribe an additional £5. You have no idea how very uncomfortable it is to be on a committee where every other member is a wealthy person.

My husband looks much better for this short holiday—although once or twice he has been rather tired. Yesterday we had tea at St Juliot Rectory with the very nice Rector & his sister, & we walked back to Boscastle along the Valency Valley. This morning we explored King Arthur's Castle here, & lay for a hour or so, on the grass, in the sunshine, with sheep nibbling around us, & no other living thing—while cliffs & greenyblue sea & white surf seemed hundreds of feet below. When we came down & saw where we had been my husband declared that it was the last time in his life that he was going up there—in such a dangerous place. But we had both enjoyed it, & I hope he has found the germ of an Iseult poem.

I am afraid that our holiday is not likely to extend beyond Monday, but it has been quite a success so far—& the weather perfect. This hotel looks—on this paper—vulgar & noisy. But really it is most quiet & comfortable & we have a room overlooking the sea & King Arthur's Castle.

We both hope that Mrs Cockerell is still improving in health. Will you give her our affectionate good wishes.

We are looking forward to your visit later,

Yours very sincerely

Florence Hardy.

Text MS. (hotel stationery) Beinecke.   *Date* Year supplied on MS. by Cockerell.
reprints: Cockerell had actively assisted FEH in the production (at the Chiswick Press) of her privately printed pamphlet of TH's poem 'To Shakespeare After Three Hundred Years' (Purdy, 177–8, and, for FEH's pamphlets generally, 349–50).   *our committee*: the Dorset county committee of the Red Cross.   *Rector*: the Revd John Harold Dickinson, rector of St Juliot 1906–25; his sister, L. M. Dickinson, was also living at the Rectory.   *Castle*: Tintagel castle.   *Iseult poem*: subsequently completed and pub. (1923) as *The Famous Tragedy of the Queen of Cornwall*.

To Sydney Cockerell

MAX GATE, | DORCHESTER.

17th September. [1916]

My dear Mr Cockerell:

We are looking forward to seeing you at the end of this week. I think you said about the 22nd so conclude that you will be here about Friday or Saturday. Do let us know your train & I will ask Mr Lea to meet you with his car.

When I last wrote to you I had not seen the mob of fashionable people who filled the dining-room at the hotel at Tintagel. My husband found old friends among them—but he was eager to return here on the Monday & so we came back without prolonging the holiday. The journey back was tiring: we left Tintagel at 10. o'clock & reached here at 5.30. & my husband was rather knocked up. But he says he has got over it now. Yesterday we went to look at the heath from a point which I did not know & stood on the old coach road to London—now overgrown with bracken & heather—& my husband had visions of coaches rolling along, bearing George III—& the Princesses, & Pitt & Nelson, & Captain Hardy—& then his mother, as a child. Material for a lovely poem—which, I fear, Kipling has already done. If he feels up to it we think of going to Stinsford Church tonight. I had a nice letter from the Librarian at Edinburgh—& formal acknowledgements from other libraries—except Aberdeen—which has not replied at all. I want to send one to Shakespeare's house as you suggested. To whom should I address it?

Yours very sincerely,
Florence Hardy.

P.S. Our kindest regards to Mrs Cockerell. We hope she is getting on. F.H.

Text MS. Beinecke. *Date* Year supplied on MS. by Cockerell.
old friends: Charles Beilby Stuart-Wortley, MP (created 1st Baron Stuart of Wortley in 1917), and his wife Alice, daughter of Sir John Everett Millais, the painter; see *Life and Work*, 404. *Pitt*: William Pitt (1759–1806), Prime Minister 1783–1801, 1804–6. *Nelson*: Horatio Nelson, Viscount Nelson (1758–1805), British admiral victorious at the battle of Trafalgar. *Captain Hardy*: the Dorset-born Sir Thomas Masterman Hardy, Bt., Nelson's flag-captain at Trafalgar. *poem . . . Kipling*: the reference is to his 'The Road Through the Woods'. *Church tonight*: i.e. for Sunday evening service. *Librarian . . . other libraries*: FEH had been sending out presentation copies of *To Shakespeare After Three Hundred Years*.

To Edward Clodd

MAX GATE, | DORCHESTER.
23rd September. [1916]

My dear Mr Clodd:

Many many thanks for your most delightful & valued "Memories". It will provide for my husband & myself many pleasant hours of after-dinner reading. I am ashamed to say that I have already skimmed through its pages— an act of great unfairness to the author, my husband tells me—but I can never resist that temptation, when a book interests me. Close, serious reading follows. You know, of course, my husband's strong feeling against the majority of books of reminiscence but this holds nothing that the most ultrasensitive person could object to. Mrs Sheridan & her sister were with us yesterday, & Mrs Sheridan is eager to read it also. I do not say this to suggest that you should send her a copy, for, if I know her, she has ordered one by this time, as she ought.

I am a little perplexed by the liking you evidently had for Lang—whom of all men, living or dead, I think my husband most detested,—& others I have heard speak in the same way. But doubtless you were happy in finding a more loveable side to his nature. My husband so endores Meredith's criticism "Lang had no heart."

What strikes me forcibly is the Meredith shines out as the brightest star in your galaxy. If I were Mrs Lynn Linton's ghost I would squeal pitifully at that *awful* portrait of herself being given. The fragment of autobiography I have already read to my husband & we both think it delightful & wish there were more of it.

I hope that you have good news of your son, & that Derrick is enjoying his new life. And I hope that Mrs Graham's knee is better.

With our very kindest regards to you & Mrs Clodd—who, I hope, is very well,—& ever so many thanks.

Yours very sincerely,
Florence Hardy.

Text MS. Beinecke. *Date* Year supplied on MS. by Clodd.
"Memories": Clodd's *Memories* (London: Chapman & Hall, 1916); the Max Gate copy (Beinecke) is inscribed by Clodd to FEH. TH's forebodings (see letter of 18 Jan. 1916) had proved to be so far unjustified that FEH could tell R. Owen (19 Nov. 1916, Colby) that the book was 'so dull'. *Lang*: Andrew Lang (1844–1912), man of letters. *endores*: 'endorses' clearly intended; the criticism was perhaps spoken rather than written. *the Meredith*: 'that' or 'the way that' presumably intended. *Linton's*: Eliza Lynn Linton (see ELH letter of 27 Dec. 1899); her photograph faces p. 264 of *Memories*. *son . . . Derrick . . . Mrs Graham's*: see, respectively, letters of 20 Apr., 29 June, and 7 Mar. 1913. *Mrs Clodd*: Clodd's estranged first wife died in 1911 and in Dec. 1914 he married Phyllis Rope, formerly his secretary.

[As the Hardys became increasingly dependent upon Sydney Cockerell for advice and practical assistance of many different kinds, so the latent tensions between Cockerell and FEH came nearer to the surface. In commenting on Cockerell in her letter to Rebekah Owen of 3 November 1916, FEH was only following up the confession, in her letter of 26 October (Colby), that she was 'beginning to be quite afraid of Mr Cockerell. . . . Last time he was here I felt once or twice that I loathed him. I caught an expression of his face—a hateful expression once—that dwells in my memory and has destroyed any liking I have had for him. . . . Of course Mr Cockerell does certain things for us, and perhaps I am a mean beast to write this. But I have that uncomfortable feeling. How I wish we could talk it over. I have found that he takes notes of his conversations here.']

To Rebekah Owen

MAX GATE, | DORCHESTER.
3rd. November 1916.

My dearest Betty:

Many thanks for your letter. I am hurriedly answering it so that I can catch the morning post—11.30—and I will send a longer letter later.

I had arranged, provisionally, to go to London next week, possibly on Monday, to have the portrait begun. But yesterday morning we had a visit from Police Constable Paine (a great personage in Dorchester). My heart went into my boots when I heard who it was for I thought "Wessie again". But fortunately it was not. He had come to know how many soldiers he could billet on us. Being a nice man he promised that it would be two officers (if any), and possibly we might escape altogether. Of course I should not mind privates, poor men, but people say they bring such awful things into the house with them. Even officers do, I am told, who come from a camp. However that knocks on the head any project I may have had, and I wrote off at once rather gladly, to tell Miss Ouless that I could not possibly leave home while this was hanging over our heads. The servants, although excellent in every other respect, are very inexperienced outside their ordinary work and would not know how to manage at all in an emergency. The cook, who is so faithful and honest and economical that we would not part with her for worlds quite loses her head if anything unusual happens. Besides my husband would be so dreadfully worried. I have had many invitations to stay with friends in Town, while having the portrait done. Lady Ilchester has been so sweet and kind and helpful. She is so human and warm hearted. Mrs Henniker too, has offered her house as hotel or restaurant. But cousins who have a large house in St John's Wood, with three or four spare bedrooms, and four servants and a boy, put me off when I suggested going to them—on the score of *war economy*. That is just because I could not let them make this a sort of second home, as they intended. And their house is quite near the studio.

It is so nice to think that you are coming here. Oddly enough I had two letters this morning from Brighton. I have a sister there, the most attractive member of the family, who is nursing in a Red Cross Convalescent Home for Officers on the King's Cliff—Lady Anchester's Home. She wrote to me today. I should love to go there and see her but I cannot leave. My youngest sister is going to marry her airman on his next leave—in December or January. And I shall try to go up to Town for that, and we have promised that they can spend their honey-moon here, while we both go away somewhere, probably to Cornwall.

I am so glad that poor dear Pietro is rather better. How very anxious you must have been. I hope he will soon be quite all right.

I find I have lost the post and it is pouring with rain so I had better go on and finish this letter properly.

I hardly know what to say about your little L.G. I have no doubt that she is very nice or you could not have liked her so. But I do candidly think she is not quite playing the game with you. After all if one takes a situation, or post, one must stick to it for a reasonable time unless there is some serious fault with the employer. To take up a post and then want to leave for family reasons is hardly fair. I remember when I first took up work on The Sphere there were reasons soon after that made it desirable that I should resign, give notice, or whatever you call it. I remember Mr Shorter spoke very plainly and very sensibly about it. He said he had done his best to give me what I had wanted—work that other literary women would have jumped to get—and it was not fair to him or to the paper to throw it up after a month or two, when I had just become of use etc, and they had had the trouble of initiating me and showing me what to do. The consequence is that I still work for them, although not going up to the office of course. I had a cheque from them this morning, and a fresh supply of work. Of course I do admit the cases are not the same, exactly, but there is even more reason for your Miss P. to stay with you for a while. However, I know full well how trying home ties can be.

I don't know what to think about your leaving Belmount Hall. Of course from some points of view it seems a most splendid thing to do. But I wonder whether you will be heart-broken at leaving your garden. At all events I do hope you will settle within easy reach of us. You will find, I fear, that T. is more and more of a recluse, and cannot talk long with anybody without fatigue. But it would be a great joy to me to have you near.

With regard to Mr Cockerell I feel a beast to hint that he is not perfection, since he does I think try to be so kind and helpful. But he is so arrogant and masterful. He tries to take the whole household in hand, and rule my husband entirely. I think sometimes that he considers he has charge of us. Of course it is his manner partly, but he *does* interfere. There is, at present, a quite perceptible feeling between us, but we are both pretending there isn't. I will tell you a lot more when I see you. The difficulty is, of course, that my husband does really depend upon him in a great many ways. He has such tremendous energy and he is the sort of man who can do things or get things done. An open breach with him would be rather disastrous. But again there is the fact that he has benefitted very considerably from his friendship with my husband—in a money sense, besides the great uplift he gets in literary circles, through being known as my husband's greatest friend and confidante. I now realize that he had made hundreds of pounds—or at least has got that value—from him. It is so strange for my husband's chief grievance against Clement Shorter is that he (C.S.) has always been trying to get autographs out of him, in his books, for the sake of enhancing their value.

However, all this is very petty.

With love,

Your affectionate,
Florence Hardy.

Text MS. (typed, with envelope) Colby.
the portrait: by Catherine Ouless (1879–1961), landscape and portrait painter; if completed, it has not been located. A portrait of TH by Walter William Ouless, RA, Catherine's father, is in the National Portrait Gallery. *Paine*: correctly Payne (cf. *CL*, iv. 113 n.). *great . . . although . . .finish . . . course . . . fresh . . . whether*: FEH typed 'geat', 'althought', 'finsih', 'couse', 'frest', 'hether'. *cousins*: see letter of 1 Dec. 1910. *sister*: Eva Anne Dugdale, eight years FEH's junior. *Lady Anchester's*: unidentified; FEH perhaps meant Lady Ancaster (widow of the 1st earl), although *Kelly's Directory of Brighton* for 1914 shows the house as occupied by the Marchioness of Sligo. *her airman*: see letter of 12 Aug. 1916. *L.G.*: i.e. lady gardener, a Miss Pallin. *reasons soon after*: i.e. her marriage to TH.

To Sydney Cockerell

MAX GATE, | DORCHESTER.
10th November. [1916]

Dear Mr Cockerell:

I feel quite overwhelmed. Of course I never dreamed, nor did T.H., of such a munificent cheque, & we both thank you most heartily for all the trouble you have taken, & for your kind thought in promoting & carrying through the scheme. I quite realize that it will not do to produce too many reprints & agree that some time must elapse before we produce another— if at all. Two are already among the missing. I sent a copy of each to our friend the Edinburgh barrister who has been in the trenches the last few weeks. He did not receive them, & I hear a mail-boat was sunk about that time. But it doesn't matter—I believe some of them ought to be destroyed or lost, to add to the value of the others.

Also I return the two books you so kindly lent us. I think that James Stephen's book is heart-breaking—especially the description of the men who were executed—particularly Connolly. My husband however is ada- mant so far as Ireland is concerned. Thank you so much for lending us the books.

The play, so far as we know, is fixed now for Dec: 6th & 7th. I hope you will be able to come then. We find our zest for it has already evaporated. There is a possibility of two officers being billeted on us, but we may escape that. However we are not letting it worry us.

Yesterday my husband paid a visit to the Commandant of the Prison Camp here who took him to see the German prisoners. T.H's kind heart melted at the sight of the wounded & he expressed his sympathy with them by eloquent gestures to which they responded in a most friendly manner— & also he wished many of the *well* prisoners 'Good-day' to which they replied with alacrity, & now he is sending them some of his books in German— for their library.

The Commandant—who is absolutely beloved by them all—explained to some of them who T.H. was, but I am not sure whether they had heard of him. At all events they seemed, he says, to appreciate his visit. He came home very moved by the experience, & glad that he had gone, although he went most unwillingly. I wanted him to get some of the prisoners here to cut down a few trees. But we are waiting now until the Kaiser's head forester has got over an operation for appendicitis—for he will come & advise, & possibly superintend operations.

We hope that Mrs Cockerell is getting on nicely & we send her our love. We are *very* sorry to hear that Mrs McTaggart has not been well. I am afraid that T.H. is not very much inclined, at present, to leave home for any visit even to Cambridge.

With our kind regards & ever so many thanks,

Yours sincerely,
Florence Hardy.

Text   MS. Beinecke.   *Date*   Year supplied on MS. by Cockerell.
the scheme: the private reprinting of TH's poem 'When I Weekly Knew' (Purdy, 188–9); Cockerell's note on MS. indicates that 10 copies had been sold to Maggs, the London booksellers, for £42.   *Edinburgh barrister*: Lieutenant Stair Agnew Gillon, a correspondent of TH's during the war years, subsequently solicitor in Scotland to the Board of Inland Revenue.   *two books*: James Stephens's *The Insurrection in Dublin* (Dublin, 1916) and, as appears from FEH's letter to Cockerell of 31 Oct. 1916 (Beinecke), a vol. of Wilfrid Blunt's poems.   *The play*: the Dorchester Debating and Dramatic Society production of *Wessex Scenes from The Dynasts*.   *The Commandant*: Lt.-Col. Henry Charles Bulkeley, DSO; he wrote, 16 Nov. 1916 (DCM), to thank TH for the books in German he had sent.   *Mrs McTaggart*: Margaret M'Taggart, née Bird, wife of John M'Taggart Ellis M'Taggart, the Cambridge philosopher, with whom TH had occasionally talked and corresponded.

[Gertrude Bugler, one of the youngest members of the Dorchester Debating and Dramatic Society, had first attracted TH's attention in 1913 when—sixteen years of age, growing into beauty, and possessed of both histrionic talent and theatrical ambition—she played Marty South in a dramatization of *The Woodlanders*. The outbreak of war put an end to any plans there might have been for 'Hardy plays' in Dorchester in 1914 and 1915, but in 1916 the gap was filled by a production, for wartime charities, of TH's own adaptation of the Wessex scenes from *The Dynasts*, into which he had written a small but significant part for Gertrude Bugler. FEH, already jealous of the younger woman, was nevertheless obliged to deal with her on TH's behalf, her letters striving for civility and even fairness but often revealing an edge of animosity in the very structure and sequence of the sentences.]

To Gertrude Bugler

Max Gate.
Wednesday. [13 December 1916]

Dear Miss Bugler:

I have been waiting ever since Sir James Barrie left—last Thursday morning—thinking that perhaps he might write to me, but I have not heard. From that, & from what he said after the performance on Wednesday I can only conclude that he feels he can do nothing towards helping you on to a career on the stage.

I explained to him, & so did the friend who was with us, & who had seen you in "The Woodlanders", that you really did infinitely better in that play. Sir James said, however, that it was better to judge an actress from a poor part, to see how she could struggle against difficulties, & *make* a poor part good through her own powers.

Personally I *do* consider that you acted well, & as an amateur I am sure you will always give pleasure. But I am afraid that, now I have heard all this, that there is really next to no chance for you as a professional—even if you parents were able to pay a large sum of money, & willing to do so, about which of course I do not know. Sir James said the chance was not one in a hundred. I am so sorry because I feel that you may be disappointed, but one never knows what there may be in the future. When one is greatly disappointed at missing anything something very much better often turns up.

Sir James is so extremely kind to so many people that I feel sure he would have done his best to help you had it been possible. I asked him to stay on to the matinée & go to the tea where he would have seen you, but he preferred not to do so.

We showed him your portraits which are very charming & & tried as well as we could—both my husband & I—to impress him in your favour.

Of course it is harder now to get on the stage than ever it was, & as the war goes on it will get worse & worse. I am told that in London there are hundreds of young actresses on the verge of starvation.

Of course you might easily, I think, recite at Concerts & so forth, & give little dualogues. Probably you will find many opportunities of using your talent.

I do sincerely hope that anything I may have said or done has had the effect of unsettling you. If I could have been of any·real use to you I would have been very delighted,

Yours sincerely,
Florence Hardy.

Text MS. Bugler.   *Date* From internal evidence.

Bugler: Gertrude Adelia Bugler (1897–1992); she married her cousin, Ernest Frank Bugler, MC, in 1921.   *Barrie*: TH's old friend Sir James Matthew Barrie, Bt. (1860–1937), playwright and novelist, on whose advice and friendship FEH was to become increasingly dependent.   *performance on Wednesday*: the first of the two Dorchester performances of *Wessex Scenes from The Dynasts* was on Wednesday, 6 Dec.   *friend who was with us*: Cockerell.   *you parents*: 'your' clearly intended.   *& & tried*: FEH's duplication. *anything I may have said*: 'nothing I may have said' presumably intended.

To Rebekah Owen

Max Gate. Dorchester
Thursday. [14 December 1916]

My dear Betty:

Do let us have a line to say how you are & whether you got home safely. My husband is better, but we are worried by hearing that the promised soldiers are coming in on Saturday next. I wish I had shown you the rooms I have got ready for them. Your visit seemed so short & I had so much to tell you. I wish it were going to begin again, but I fear you will not be again tempted hitherward in winter. How is your cold?

I am afraid that Barrie was not pleased with his visit. I felt it was rather a mistake to send him off to Kingston House. He has not written since.

As to Mr Cockerell I want to retract anything I may have said against him. Do please, dear Betty, destroy anything I may have written concerning him. I felt this time that he was a good & honourable man & anxious to be of service. All badness must have been in myself to have thought anything to his discredit. We did not have long enough to be able to talk together, but my husband's illness & one thing & another hindered.

I had wanted to have a little luncheon party on the Thursday before the performance, & have asked you & others, but as things were of course it was impossible & both Barrie & Mr Cockerell departed early that morning —before lunch.

Barrie said he did not want to know people who were only anxious to meet him because of his work. He wanted friends to care for him for himself etc. etc. But of course that is very limiting. Some of the best people

we know have been attracted to my husband merely because of his work.
F.

Is Miss Pallin with you still? I hope so. And how did you find Pietro?
With love,

Yours affectionately.

Florence Hardy.

Text MS. (with black-edged envelope) Colby.   *Date* Supplied (by R. Owen?) on MS.
and confirmed by postmark.

got home safely: R. Owen had been in Dorset to see *Wessex Scenes* and visit friends.   *husband
is better:* TH, missing *Wessex Scenes* because of a cold, had evidently missed (or avoided) R.
Owen also.   *promised soldiers:* see letter of 3 Nov. 16.   *Kingston House:* TH and FEH
were to have accompanied Barrie to dinner with the Hanburys at Kingston Maurward, but
TH's illness had evidently obliged Barrie to go alone.   *said against him:* see letter of 3
Nov. 1916; writing to R. Owen, 19 Nov. 1916 (Colby), FEH said that Cockerell had expected
to patronize and control her, and TH through her, but now knew her to be less pliable than
he had thought.   *Some . . . his work.* F.: late insertion, begun at this point but completed
(and initialled) at foot of page below signature.   *Miss Pallin:* see letter of 3 Nov. 1916.

To Sydney Cockerell

MAX GATE, | DORCHESTER.

16th. February 1917

Dear Mr Cockerell:

I am not returning the proof as my husband thinks that it is not necessary
as it is quite all right. He says that he prefers the sonnet divided in the way
it is, as it does not present a solid block of lines, and is easier to read. Where
the rhyme allows, he says, he always prefers that way of dividing a sonnet.
But thankyou for drawing his attention to it. The title-page, too, he thinks
is quite satisfactory.

He says he is going to write to you to thank you for having the manuscript bound so beautifully for him. I am sure we both feel most immensely
grateful to you, and it will be a great treasure here—treasured by us both—
and if any of these manuscripts ever leave Max Gate, as I suppose they must
some day, I hope that the destination will be a museum.

I return the letter from Mrs Webb. I think she must be a delightful
friend, and her work is exquisite. The other manuscript you speak about
must certainly wait until after the war, when the matter can be reconsid-
ered if need be.

We hear this morning that some of the German prisoners are to be sent
here to do some digging for us—we intend to grow more potatoes next
year, and I think that some of the trees are coming down. But I notice that

T.H. is wistfully regarding certain pines from his study window, and of course if he wishes them to remain they must. The house will be much less damp if some come down though—especially those that touch the north-east walls of the house.

I am hourly waiting a telegram which is to summon me to my sister Margaret's wedding, which was to take place this week-end, if the young man can get home from France. As it has already been postponed four times I shall not be astonished if no telegram comes. My husband's sister, Katie, astonished me by saying that she would go up with me, but she has not been to London for fifteen years and her courage may fail her, although I hope not, at the last moment. The honeymoon is to be spent here, and with great self-abnegation my sister says she hopes we shall all travel home together in the same carriage. Poor pathetic children!

We are deeply interested in Mr Mackail's Life of Morris and have just reached an account of the journey to Iceland. When I read it before I think I began in the second volume, by my husband's instructions, which is certainly not a fair way to treat a book.

You were to keep, of course, the copies of the letters about "Jude". You shall have one of the pamphlets if they ever come, if you care about it.

With kindest regards and love from us both to Mrs Cockerell and the children.

Yours very sincerely,
Florence Hardy.

Text   MS. (typed) Beinecke.

the proof: of FEH's privately printed *England to Germany* pamphlet; it included TH's sonnet 'The Pity of It'.   *the manuscript*: of *The Poor Man and the Lady* (see letter of 12 Aug. 1916); TH later destroyed it.   *Mrs Webb*: see letter of 12 Aug. 1916.   *go up with me*: Katharine Hardy did attend the 24 Feb. wedding, in Enfield, of Margaret Dugdale, FEH's youngest sister, and Reginald Soundy (see letter of 12 Aug. 1916).   *Mackail's . . . Morris*: see letter of 30 Nov. 1913.   *letters about "Jude"*: the pamphlet, *Jude the Obscure, A Letter and a Foreword*, pub. later in 1917 by the American collector Paul Lemperly (see letter of 7 Mar. 1919).

To Sydney Cockerell

MAX GATE, | DORCHESTER.
Friday. [27 April 1917]

Dear Mr Cockerell:

I return this book with very many thanks. We have so much enjoyed reading it. My husband is going to jot down for me to send you his opinion of the book—which is, of course, brilliantly written.

If you can spare the unsigned ticket for the Private View, if you get it, I shall be so very glad to have it as then I can take my sister with me. I do not care to use the one with T.H's name on, as they are not transferable.

We were most delighted to see you here last week, & hope it will not be long before you come again. Meanwhile I suppose that we shall have to go through a period of strict abstinence. The ultimate fate of Wessex hangs heavy on our hearts. My husband wonders whether we could feed him (& ourselves) on the Cow's parsley which grows profusely in our garden. I will write again.

Yours very sincerely,
Florence Hardy.

Text MS. (typed) Beinecke.   *Date* Supplied on MS. by Cockerell.
this book: Edmund Gosse's *The Life of Algernon Charles Swinburne* (London, 1917); FEH had requested the loan, on TH's behalf, in her postcard to Cockerell of 12 Apr. 1917 (Beinecke), and TH wrote to congratulate Gosse 26 Apr. 1917 (*CL*, v. 211).   *Private View*: of the Royal Academy's Summer Exhibition.   *strict abstinence*: because of the threat to food supplies posed by Germany's recent resumption of unrestricted submarine warfare.

[Prompted by increasing age, the death of his sister Mary, and the encouragement of Cockerell and FEH, TH embarked during the early months of 1917 upon a narrative of his own life. Originally envisaged as a collaborative project in which FEH would write up and organize the 'notes' which TH had dictated or drafted, it seems quickly to have developed into an arrangement by which a manuscript entirely written by TH would be typed up by FEH and then returned to him for correction and reconsideration. It was always TH's intention, however, that the resulting book should be posthumously published as an official biography authored by his wife, and indeed FEH made both additions to and deletions from her husband's text before bringing it out in two volumes, *The Early Life of Thomas Hardy* (1928) and *The Later Years of Thomas Hardy* (1930)—often referred to collectively as the 'Life'.]

To Sydney Cockerell

MAX GATE, | DORCHESTER.
23rd. July 1917

Dear Mr Cockerell:

Many thanks for your kind letter received this afternoon. I must apologize for my last hurried note, but our friends stayed longer than I thought and the post goes early.

My husband is not surprised at what you tell us about Russia. He feels that there is great danger in that direction.

I have forwarded your message to Mrs Inglis. I am sure she should be, and is, most grateful to you.

I have to go to Town tomorrow to see the surgeon and the bacteriologist who have my nose in hand. My husband has decided to come with me as he wishes to see his publishers and also his stockbrokers if there is time. We have also promised to go and see Lady St Helier and Mrs Henniker, so that our time will be fully occupied as we return on Thursday and so have only one clear day. He thinks that there is little use in making any arrangement to see you (pleasant as that would be)—should you be in Town, as you will very likely be as occupied as ourselves, and as you promise to come to see us shortly, which we shall like very much. The heath is looking lovely now. T.H. and I cycled there last week and walked about on it and picked heather. It was delightful and he was not overtired. He can cycle five or six miles with ease, if he takes his time, and finds it far less fatiguing than walking two miles. We have a great treat in prospect, if things can be arranged. Eden Phillpotts thinks that he may be able to get for us a permit to have a certain quantity of petrol, and if so Mr Lea is going to hire a car from a friend, for us, and drive us to Torquay and Plymouth. We should be away two nights if we go, but we may not be able to get the petrol. I think that T. is longing for this, and we shall have no more motoring this year. I suppose we really ought not to be thinking of such things now, but he says if we have to wait until after the war he may be too old to enjoy it.

To my great regret our very nice housemaid is going to leave to become a nurse at the County Asylum. We are going to manage with our faithful old cook and her young niece until after the war. This will mean, I am afraid, that we shall only be able to have one friend here to stay at a time, but I know you will not mind that. My youngest sister Margaret and her husband want to come here for three days before he returns to France, but he does not yet know the date. It is not likely, though, that that would clash with your visit. He rather hopes that he won't go back until the end of September. He is now training pilots near Harrow.

You will be amused when I tell you that my nervousness of air-raids is such that I have today made my will and had it duly witnessed. It occurred to me that if T.H. & I were killed and I died before him, all that I had would go to his brother and sister, and it seemed better to leave what little I had before my marriage to my own people, who could do with it very well. I have ventured to put you down as sole executor, thinking you would not mind, and both my will and instructions from T.H. will be left on the study table. We shall always do this in future when we go away together. The study door is always locked, of course.

I hope you don't think this very ridiculous.

I have been taking notes but find them very difficult to do without constantly appealing to T.H. for verification, and he is now almost at the end of his present job—revising his note-books (they are practically diaries)—and we are going to work together. At least that is what we propose doing. Man proposes—.

If you have not bought the little book of Russian stories please wait until you come here and you can have ours if you like.

With kind regards from us both,

Yours sincerely,
Florence Hardy.

P.S. We are staying with Barrie while we are in Town. I am looking forward to that very much. But we shall really have very little time with him.

Text   MS. (typed) Beinecke.
grateful to you: Cockerell had been instrumental in finding a governess for FEH's close friend Ethel Inglis, wife of Colonel Henry Alves Inglis, commander of artillery at Weymouth. *surgeon . . . bacteriologist*: respectively, Macleod Yearsley (see letter of 16 May 1920) and a London specialist named Harry Greenwood Butterfield; in a letter to R. Owen (fragment [early Feb. 1917?], Colby) FEH described her condition as 'chronic rhinitis'.   *our time*: FEH typed 'out time'.   (*pleasant . . . be*): inserted in FEH's hand.   *sole executor*: Cockerell does not so figure in FEH's final will, made after the collapse of their friendship.   *note-books*: these were subsequently destroyed, some by TH himself, the remainder following his death.   *Russian stories*: presumably the 1917 collection of stories by Anton Tchehov (*sic*), *The Lady with the Dog*; a copy signed by FEH appears as no. 189 in William P. Wreden's cat. II (1939).   *But . . . with him.*: added in FEH's hand.

To Sydney Cockerell

Max Gate. | Dorchester.
Wednesday. [24 October 1917]

Dear Mr Cockerell:

I am so sorry to hear that Katherine has had that trouble with her tonsils. I hope that this slight operation has removed all chance of trouble later. And I am sorry that Christopher is not quite up to the mark either, & also that he finds school somewhat tiresome. My husband says he did not like going to school as a boy—& he remembers being sent when he was really ill—could hardly walk in to Dorchester, but of course Christopher has not to undergo hardships like that. It has been a trying summer & is a trying autumn for children.

I send 12 copies of the poems, two of which are for you if you will accept them. If for any reason you think it inadvisable to sell any of these to

Messrs Maggs please do not trouble about them—perhaps there has been enough money-making on my part, & I do not want to appear horribly avaricious. You will know about that better than I do.

We had a delightful time at Torquay as we stayed from Thursday evening until Saturday morning with Mr & Mrs Phillpotts who are two of the kindest & most warm-hearted people I know. We arrived in Plymouth about mid-day on Saturday & had a tiring & rather depressing time there. To me there is nothing more dismal than visiting wretched decayed houses, with the plaster falling from the walls, where people, now dead, were born & lived more than seventy-years ago, & graves with broken coping & weeds,—a thick crop of groundsel growing over one—& half-obliterated names. How much better to have no neglected little plot of ground to testify to the indifference of grand-children to their grand-parents' memory. In one case where my husband had sent money for a grave to be kept in order the relative—a great-niece—had obviously never been near it. Our journey back on Monday was rather long—from 12 to 8 o'clock—& my husband has caught a slight cold, not enough to send him to bed, but sufficient to prevent his going out for a day or two. Otherwise he is very well. This afternoon—since I began this letter—we have had a very pleasant visit from Colonel Inglis & a camouflage (?) officer, a Mr Mills, a *Punch* artist, who was most entertaining. I think T.H. enjoyed talking to them, for he was very bright & lively & forgot his cold. I hope that for both Mrs Cockerell's sake & his, that the winter will not be very severe, especially as coal is so difficult to get. I wish you could write & tell us that Mrs Cockerell was *not* using the chair, but able to go about quite well without. Will you give her warmest greetings from T.H. & myself.

Yours very sincerely,
Florence Hardy.

Text MS. Beinecke. *Date* Supplied on MS. by Cockerell.
Katherine . . . Christopher: see letter of 20 June 1915. *the poems*: FEH's pamphlet of 1917 containing TH's 'The Fiddler's Story' and 'A Jingle on the Times', privately printed in 25 copies (Purdy, 192–3). *people, now dead*: specifically ELH's parents and grandparents, buried in the churchyard of Christ Church, Plymouth. *a great-niece*: two of ELH's cousins appear to have been still living in Plymouth at this date (*CL*, iv. 311). *Mr Mills*: A. Wallis Mills (1878–1940), artist on the staff of *Punch* for many years, currently serving in the Camouflage Corps. *the chair*: a bath-chair, originally purchased for ELH (see ELH letter of 24 Feb. 1907), which TH had recently sent to Cambridge for Kate Cockerell's use.

November 1917

To Thomas J. Wise

MAX GATE, | DORCHESTER.
25th Nov: '17.

Dear Mr Wise:

I am so glad that you like the pamphlet. Thank you so much for the interesting photographs of your splendid library. What a delightful room! How I wish my husband had a study like it. But perhaps he is happier in his own shabby little den where every article of furniture is a very old friend. We do both admire your room exceedingly & are pleased to have the photographs of that & yourself.

With kind regards from us both,

Yours sincerely,
Florence Hardy.

Text   MS. BL.
Wise: Thomas James Wise (1859–1937), book-collector and bibliographer, later revealed as a forger; he 'cultivated' TH, at least to the extent of sending him the volumes of the *Ashley Library* catalogue as they appeared, and purchased some items from FEH following TH's death.   *the pamphlet*: see letter of 24 Oct. 1917.

To Rebekah Owen

Max Gate. Dorchester.
Thursday. [13 December 1917]

My dear Betty:

I am ashamed—& aghast—when I realize how long it is since I wrote to you. I was not certain even whether you or I had written last. *Certainly* you have never offended or bored me, nor had I any desire to let the correspondence lapse. I have for months been under medical treatment. I had to go to London last week to see two specialists, & tomorrow I go to our doctor here to begin *yet another* course of inoculations. In addition to this I have had home worries, of a kind sufficient to break down any woman's nerve I think. I know mine broke down utterly last week. I went to see "Dear Brutus" & wept between the acts from sheer misery (although it was a delightful play) & after the matinée when I went to tea with an old friend of my husband, I made a fool of myself, & burst into tears & sobbing when a few sympathetic questions were asked. Anyhow we two were alone, & I think no harm was done, as my position seemed realized. I am more myself now.

And, in addition, I have been making strenuous efforts to pick up again

135

my literary work—but I found that all the energy & time that ought to have been given to my own work & making some sort of career for myself, was given to letter-writing. I have come to the conclusion that many people (not you, of course or I wouldn't write this), try to inveigle me into a correspondence so that they can boast of being in constant touch with Max Gate & my husband, Clement Shorter, for one, does, I know. And I was horrified not long ago to see in one of Lady Hoare's books—a 1st edition of T.H's—a carelessly scribbled letter of mine, pasted in & preserved because I had said something about him & his poems. My dear Betty, if anything should happen to me I *entreat* you to burn every scrap of my writing. I do write so carelessly & injudiciously that I fear there are letters of mine preserved that I should hate to have seen.

My youngest sister's mar[*two and a half lines excised*]

You saw in The Times, I expect that Mrs Mansel is dead.

How nice for you to have those invitations from Lady Crossley & Miss Pallin. You ought to go. I am sure it would do you good. I wish that I could go away for a fortnight somewhere. Going away for a couple of nights to see doctors & to grapple with family difficulties, or try to is no holiday & no rest for me. I come back more exhausted that when I went.

It is very kind of you to bother about that rose for me, but *please* don't give yourself any trouble about it. Ethel Inglis has ordered one for me which she much admired at Hampton Court—or Kew—& my husband's brother gave me three ramblers—so really I have hardly any room in the garden for any more, although of course, if *your* rose came to hand without any trouble to yourself, it would receive a warm welcome. But I don't want you to buy it or trouble about ordering it.

Wessie is well—boisterous & dirty. He sends his love to you, & respects to Pietro.

We are reading Lord Morley's Recollections, with great interest. Have you read it? I rather like "An Autumn Sowing" by E. F. Benson. I hope you are well.

With love.
F.H.

Text   MS. (with envelope) Colby.   *Date*   Supplied (by R. Owen?) on MS., confirmed by postmark.
"Dear Brutus": J. M. Barrie's new play, first performed at Wyndham's Theatre 17 Oct. 1917. *old friend of my husband*: possibly Barrie himself, more probably Florence Henniker.   *Lady Hoare's books*: FEH and TH letters were pasted into several of the vols. in the Stourhead library.   *sister's mar.* truncated word obviously 'marriage'; the excision, presumably of hostile hence potentially hurtful comments on Reginald Soundy, was probably made in the early 1940s by R. Owen's neighbour Mrs Heelis (i.e. Beatrix Potter; see note to ELH letter

of Dec. 1899), through whose hands the Owen books and papers passed on their way to Colby College (Weber, 229–30). *Mrs Mansel*: Clara Henrietta Mansell, widow of Captain Arthur E. Mansell, died in Dorchester on 10 Nov. 1917, aged 81. *Lady Crossley*: Florence Josephine, wife of Sir Kenneth Crossley, Bt., of Pull Woods, Ambleside. *Miss Pallin*: see note to letter of 3 Nov. 1916. *exhausted that*: 'exhausted than' clearly intended. *Inglis*: see letter of 23 July 1917. *Morley's Recollections*: John Viscount Morley, *Recollections* (2 vols., London, 1917). *Benson*: Edward Frederic Benson's *An Autumn Sowing* (London, 1917) seems not to have been among the novels FEH reviewed for the *Sphere*.

[Throughout the winter of 1917–18 Hardy was intensely engaged in writing the essentially autobiographical narrative that was to become the 'Life', and FEH was correspondingly occupied in making a typescript in three copies (a ribbon copy and two carbons) from the successive pages of her husband's manuscript—which would then be destroyed. Cockerell seems to have been the only person outside Max Gate who knew about the project, at least in general terms, and even he may never have realized how much of the initial text was being generated by TH himself. Although in her letters to Cockerell FEH generally referred only briefly to the progress of 'the notes', she did from time to time evince exasperation at the laboriousness of the work and the extensiveness of her husband's revisions. On 20 January 1918 (Beinecke), for example, she reported that she and TH were 'still hard at work at the notes—but I am really dismayed at the labour T.H. insists upon expending on them. He now thinks they ought to be re-written from another standpoint, & all the original copy destroyed.']

To Sydney Cockerell

Max Gate, | Dorchester.
Saturday. [2 February 1918]

Dear Mr Cockerell:

Thank you so much for your & Mrs Cockerell's most kind invitation to Cambridge. There is nothing I should love better than to hear the lecture, but it is so obviously my duty to stay here. I am in the midst of reading Colvins 'Keats' to *Him*, & working hard at notes, which he corrects & adds to daily, as I go along, & moreover our 15 year-old house-parlourmaid wants so much help from me that the day is quite filled up—& I should feel such a truant if I deserted my post in the midst of all this. I should *love* to see a report of the lecture.

About the end of the month or the beginning of March I *must* go to Town to see my bacteriologist—as I hope to leave off inoculations soon, & I shall then see the 'Madding Crowd" MS, which is being bound by Rivière & promised for Feb. 12th. I have given back to T.H. the beautifully bound "Poor Man & the Lady" as he says he wants to feel himself at liberty to do what he likes with it. I am *quite sure* that it is the exquisite binding alone when prevents him from burning it—as he feels now his early MSS. had been better destroyed. You know he burned my precious MS of "Domicilium", his first poem. However, he *must* do as he likes. He thinks there will be altogether too much of him in the Red X. Sale & so wishes me to send no more than the two little 1st editions. I would be glad & proud to send the set. The play was a wonderful success. Crowds turned away from the doors so that they had to give an extra performance last night. I gave the players tea after, & T.H. spoke to them—a sort of speech—which delighted them. Mrs Vaughan—the daughter of John Addington Symonds—came & charmed them all—a most delightful woman. And the McDowalls. *He* wrote the article in the Times. No one stayed here—altho' there were so many I would gladly have invited—but no one would have been more welcome than yourself. And *if only* Mrs Cockerell could have come—*how* she could have helped by suggestions etc. Still, one day that may be. I hope so.

Ethel Inglis was so pleased with the players' manner to T.H., mingled affection & reverence. It has always struck me particularly. He is very well. I am sending you the promised programmes—but they are not very good. I have been so busy the last 2 days or should have sent them before. Thank you again so much for inviting me. I wish I could. Our love to Mrs Cockerell.

Yours very sincerely,

Florence Hardy

Text   MS. Beinecke.

the lecture: 'The Poetry of Thomas Hardy', given 20 Feb. 1918 by Sir Arthur Quiller-Couch (1863–1944), man of letters, King Edward VII Professor of English Literature at Cambridge since 1912.   *Colvins 'Keats'*: *John Keats: His Life and Poetry, His Friends, Critics, and After-Fame* by Sir Sidney Colvin (London, 1917); see letter of 24 Feb. 1918.   *Him*: FEH first wrote 'him'.   *'Madding Crowd' MS*: this MS., thought to have been destroyed, had just been discovered (*CL*, v. 243–4) and sent to be sold at auction on behalf of the Red Cross, 22 Apr. 1918.   *Rivière*: the famous bookbindery.   *when prevents*: 'which prevents' clearly intended.   *little 1st editions*: FEH's privately printed pamphlets.   *The play*: a revival, for charitable purposes (see *Life and Work*, 414–15), of the Dorchester Debating and Dramatic Society production of *The Mellstock Quire*; see FED letter of 8 Nov. 1910.   *Mrs Vaughan*: Eleanor Mary Vaughan of Tarrant Hinton, Dorset, daughter of John Addington Symonds (1840–93), the author.   *McDowalls. . . . Times*: Arthur Sydney McDowall (1877–1933), critic, and his wife Mary (see letter of 21 Aug. 1913); McDowall's review of *The Mellstock Quire* appeared in *The Times*, 2 Feb. 1918.

To Sydney Cockerell

MAX GATE, | DORCHESTER.
7th February. [1918]

Dear Mr Cockerell:

I am greatly tempted to try for Feb: 20th. You said, I think, that I could catch an early train—8.31 from Liverpool St & be back in London the same day. I should love to go to hear the lecture, & to see Mrs Cockerell again & the two children you have at home. But I fancy that T.H. looks coldly on the project. However, I am waiting to hear from the bacteriologist & if he fixes a possible date say the 19th or 21st, I will sound T.H. again.

I could send you 2 more programmes if you care to have them. I bought a dozen, meaning to send you 9, & left them upstairs in the room where I gave the tea. They were under a basket of mine & I thought they were safe, but when I took them, after the performance I found that half had disappeared, leaving only six. And when I inquired for more next morning I found they had sold out, owing to the large audience, & had to print cheap ones on a single sheet for the extra performance. But I managed to get 2 more from the Secretary which I can send you—or keep for you when you come. No—we have not seen the interesting account, you mention, of the trial of Joan of Arc. Perhaps you would keep that, though, until you come, & then only lend it to us.

It would be very nice if we could both go to see the 'Madding Crowd' MS. I think Rivière promised it for Feb. 12th.

With regard to the notes, I realize that *on no account* must we mention the word 'autobiography' or call them 'autobiographical'. If they are regarded as being of that nature I am perfectly convinced that they will be promptly destroyed which would be a great pity as they have taken many hours of hard work. T.H. declares that he would never write an autobiography the mere idea—or suggestion—annoys him. It would be a thousand pities if the MS were burned now. The safest plan is to say as little as possible about it until the thing is completed—as far as we are able to complete it. Perhaps I have said too much about it already—but I would not breathe a word about it to anyone except yourself.

I am glad that Katherine is so well & hope that Margaret will return from Bognor also strong & well. With kindest regards from us both to you both

Yours sincerely,
Florence Hardy.

Text MS. Beinecke. *Date* Year supplied on MS. by Cockerell.
for Feb: 20th: i.e. the Quiller-Couch lecture; see letter of 2 Feb. 1918. *programmes*: for *The Mellstock Quire* (see letter of 2 Feb. 1918). *account . . . Arc*: unidentified.

To Sydney Cockerell

MAX GATE, | DORCHESTER.

24th Feb: [1918]

Dear Mr Cockerell:

Thank you so much for the cheque, & for all your kindness. We have been reading this morning, in the Cambridge Review the account of Q's lecture which I wish I could have heard. But I still hope to be London on the 7th March, & to see the MS.

My husband has been saying that he thinks we might reprint "Domicilium" —as he would like to have a few copies to give to his friends. It will not be for sale—unless, of course, Maggs or someone offers to buy a copy later. T.H. thought that we might give a prefatory note, explaining how it came to be written. He wonders whether it would add to the interest if it were to be printed in Dorchester. Personally I think I would rather it were well done, as the others have been. What do you think of the idea?

I have the other programmes for you when you come, if you would care to have them.

By the way—on looking through Colvin's 'Keats' again, before sending it back, T.H. came to the conclusion that the critical chapters were worthless— & that a poet may be much injured by over-criticism, that too much commenting & prying into motives etc, rubs the bloom off the poetry.

We feel very depressed about the war—although of course T.H. is wonderful—with that inner radiance of his: a true sun-shine giver. But, from the very beginning of the war, neither of us has ever expected that we should defeat Germany. S. Sassoon's poem in this week's Cambridge Review is excellent.

I hope all is well with your family.

Yours very sincerely

Florence Hardy.

Text MS. Beinecke. *Date* Year supplied on MS. by Cockerell.
Cambridge Review: as in her later reference to Sassoon, FEH must mean the *Cambridge Magazine*, which reported the Quiller-Couch lecture (see letter of 2 Feb. 1918) in its issue of 23 Feb. 1918 (cf. *CL*, v. 256); the *Cambridge Review* report did not appear until 28 Feb. *the MS.*: of *Far from the Madding Crowd*; see letter of 2 Feb. 1918. *"Domicilium"*: said to have been TH's first poem, it was privately printed by Clement Shorter in 1916 (Purdy, 176–7) and again by FEH in July 1918 (Purdy, 208). *others have been*: the 1918 printing was indeed done at

the Chiswick Press.   *Colvin's 'Keats'*: see letter of 2 Feb. 1918.   *Sassoon's poem*: 'Suicide in the Trenches', *Cambridge Magazine*, 23 Feb. 1918; see letter of 27 July 1918.

To Lady Hoare

MAX GATE, | DORCHESTER.
Sunday. [21 April 1918]

My dearest Alda:

Many many thanks for your kind & most interesting letter which de-lighted my husband. He cannot help being proud of your appreciation of his poems, & your brilliant, & just criticism. I read your letter to him twice, & then left it on his study table, so that he could re-read it, & ponder on it. He was greatly interested in the extract from the French critique. He met the writer once at Edmund Gosse's.

I am glad you like so much 'Before Marching & After". To me it will now have a double significance—it applies to *two* who lie out in the East—two, through whose loss the whole world is the poorer, in the eyes of those who loved them. Apart from the sentiment of the poems I think that the Shake-speare one is the finest—T. had certain Dorchester folk in his mind when he wrote—many of whom would say—if Shakespeare had lived here to-day—"We did not know him." I liked, too, so much "In time of 'The Break-ing of Nations'." Most of the critics look upon that as one of his masterpieces. But you appreciate & understand as well as the finest professional critic.

In reading a little volume of poems by the soldier-poet Robert Nichols we were so struck by this verse:—

"Was there love once? I have forgotten her.
Was there grief once? grief yet is mine.
O loved, living, dying, heroic soldier,
All, all my joy, my grief, my love, are thine!"

I must thank you over & over again for your kind & most helpful words about my sister. I realize now that having her here in a nursing-home was a *mad* scheme, for it would have been quite impossible to have her & the baby here afterwards, & if I had her here immediately before the infant might arrive rather early (as my eldest sister's babies *always* did) & there would be a fine fuss & trouble for my poor husband. He is genuinely afraid of babies—& why, after all, should he be bothered with all this fuss for another man's wife & child.

She (my sister) is most reasonable & thinks it will be far better for her to start her own home somewhere near my own people where they can keep an eye on her. She reminds me of a little robin gathering together straws & scraps for the nest. Babies seem to choose to come where there is little room for them, & to carefully avoid going where their presence would be most eagerly welcomed. A man who worked for my husband's father was told by his parson that

"God sent babies, but he also sent bread."

"Aye" replied the man, "But he sends the babies to one house & the bread to another."

How eagerly a baby would have been welcomed in *this* house—Max Gate—years ago!

I hope that you are really feeling stronger, & that the cold winds are not too trying for your throat.

With regard to the war I feel it almost impossible to write anything. Every nerve must be stretched now to utmost pitch of endurance. The news the last day or two has been more hopeful however.

My husband sends you his *best* love & his constant thought. He thinks, & speaks, of you both so often.

Ever yours affectionately,
Florence Hardy.

Text MS. (with envelope) Wiltshire R.O. *Date* From postmark.
his poems: TH's *Moments of Vision*, pub. 30 Nov. 1917. *French critique*: by Henry-D. Davray (1873–1944) in his 'Lettres anglaises' column, *Mercure de France*, 16 Mar. 1918; for Davray's friendship with Gosse see Ann Thwaite, *Edmund Gosse: A Literary Landscape, 1849–1928* (London: Secker & Warburg, 1984), 415–16. *two . . . East*: TH's distant cousin Frank George, killed at Gallipoli (see letter of 30 Aug. 1915), and Henry Hoare, the Hoares' only child (see letter of 9 Dec. 1914), who died of wounds in Alexandria in Dec. 1917. *"We . . . him."*: from stanza 5 of 'To Shakespeare', collected in *Moments of Vision*; previously pub. as 'To Shakespeare After Three Hundred Years' (see letter of 9 Sept. 1916). *Nichols*: Robert Malise Bowyer Nichols (1893–1944), poet; FEH quotes, accurately, the final stanza of 'Fulfilment', from his *Ardours and Endurances* (London: Chatto & Windus, 1917), 44. *my sister*: Margaret Soundy.

To Sydney Cockerell

Max Gate, | Dorchester.
Saturday. [22 June 1918]

Dear Mr Cockerell:

Thank you so much for that beautiful poster. I do like it so much, and have had it fastened up in my little attic—where I type etc. Now I am sending it to a tiny niece who will be glad to have it I know. Thank you also so much for the book of poems by Charlotte Mew. I have read most of them to my husband. He thinks they are rather too obscure. I think them very good, and he says I can read some again to him tonight. The first one, "The Farmer's Bride", is certainly very good, and others too. I can see that they are the sort of poems that improve on a second, or third reading. I am sorry that the poetess is one of that large army of daughters who have their life blood drained by a vampire of a parent. And the vampires always think they are such perfect parents—sharing in the joys and the sorrows of their children.

We have had four delightful visits from H. M. Hyndman and his wife. My husband had not met him before and liked him so much. He brought a cleaner and fresher atmosphere with him. I am sure he is a very good old man. We knew his wife before she was married and like her too immensely. She is a perfect wife and companion to him. I hope that his quarrel with Morris was not a very bitter one and that he was not much to blame. He has a beautiful smile, and my husband says one can always judge a man by his smile. He is so different from those people who come here on the hunt for copy, autographs, etc. I wish he lived near us.

Mrs Allhusen, Lady St Helier's daughter, is coming here for the next week-end and I think that my husband will like that as he has always been very fond of her. She calls him "Uncle Tom", which sounds so strange, but it is nice of her and I like it. The cook is so terrified that she begs me to send for my sister to help with the cooking. She cannot find a flat or house within her means. I don't know what she will do if one does not turn up.

My husband is busy revising the notes. It seems a great labour, more difficult than actually writing them. I almost wish he would not do it, but the thing is so nearly completed that it would be a pity to stop now.

I hope that the children are well now and that Mrs Cockerell is feeling better. I hope too that you have managed to find good servants. Fortunately the new one we have is a great improvement on that child, and so I am very glad that she left. I shall never try a house-parlourmaid aged fifteen again if I can help it.

With kindest regards from us both to Mrs Cockerell and yourself,

Yours very sincerely,
Florence Hardy

Text MS. (typed) Beinecke. *Date* Supplied on MS. by Cockerell.
tiny niece: Monica Richardson, daughter of FEH's sister Ethel. *Mew*: Charlotte Mary Mew (1869–1928), poet, whose work Cockerell was seeking to make better known; the book was *The Farmer's Bride* (London, 1916). *Hyndman*: Henry Mayers Hyndman (1842–1921), socialist leader and publicist; his (second) wife Rosalind (née Travers) had written verse and is referred to in *Life and Work* (417) as 'a charming woman'. *quarrel with Morris*: William

Morris had led the group within the Social Democratic Federation which rebelled against Hyndman's leadership and broke away to form a new organization, the Socialist League, in Dec. 1884.   *Mrs Allhusen*: Osma Mary Dorothy Allhusen (1877–1965), wife of Augustus Henry Eden Allhusen, MP, was a daughter of Lady St Helier's by her first husband, John Constantine Stanley, and had known TH since her childhood.   *She cannot find*: ink insertion of '(my sister)' following 'She' not in FEH's hand.

To Sydney Cockerell

MAX GATE, | DORCHESTER.
27th. July 1918.

Dear Mr Cockerell:

Many thanks for your kind letter. Of course you must keep the third Domicilium. It is very good of you to suggest that Maggs might be willing to take one or more copies. Of course I cannot pretend that I should not be glad of the money, as my sister thinks she has found a suitable little flat and I want to help her furnish it. For a young couple without a penny of private means to have to start furnishing and providing for the advent of a baby in these times is no light matter, and I think that people like my husband and myself, with no children and no anxiety about money, ought to be made to help, if we are not willing to do so. It is so obviously our, or at least my, war-work. At the same time I should not like Maggs to think that I am a greedy commercial person, an imitator of Wise and Shorter. And I am in no real need of money, for I could easily sell some of my rubber shares, and indeed I would do so if they were not rather low at the present moment. Do just what you think best.

We were very sorry to hear that Siegfried Sassoon was again wounded. Surely they ought not to let him go out again. I do wish that my husband would go to see him. He thought the review in the Nation was most unjust.

He has been carefully studying Charlotte Mew's poems again, and still prefers "In Nunhead Cemetery". I read him "Madeleine in Church" again twice. He says it would be a fine poem if there were more clearness of thought. As it is it requires half a day's careful study. To me it seems fairly clear, but I cannot understand who Monty is, in the second verse. Is he the husband or the lover for whom she was divorced. And who is Stuart? Is he her lover, and was he divorced by his wife because of Madeleine, or was he Madeleine's husband? In "Fame" it is difficult to know whether the speaker is an actress or a society woman. Why does she speak of "my stair"? There is an extraordinarily pathetic wail in most of the lines. My husband says he would like to know her.

A very attractive little poetess came to us the other day from the old Vicarage where the Moules used to live. She is only twenty one but has had one poem published in the Times Literary Supplement. Her name is May O'Rourke, and she is deeply interested in the Moule family and seems to have found out a great deal about them from the old people living near. She tells me she visited Horace's grave in May, on his birthday. We only heard of her the other day through a friend who lives at Newquay. She has had a little volume of verse printed, distinctly better than the average that is sent here, but not nearly so fine and original as Miss Charlotte Mew's.

Thank you for sending Clare Mackail's letter which we were glad to see. What a delightful holiday she must be having. When T.H. heard of the adventures in the boat he remarked that he thought it was time her father and mother went down. It sounded very dangerous.

Three American soldiers came over to us from Bovington Camp the other day, and T.H. was very pleased with them. They were a distinct fine type.

With kind regards from us both,

Yours very sincerely,

Florence Hardy.

P.S. Of course I will gladly write an inscription in one of your 'Domicilium's.

Text   MS. (typed) Beinecke.

Domicilium: see letter of 24 Feb. 1918.   *Sassoon*: Siegfried Loraine Sassoon (1886–1967), poet and prose-writer; he had been wounded on 13 July.   *review*: the unsigned review of *Counter-Attack and Other Poems* in the *Nation*, 13 July 1918, spoke of Sassoon's 'verses' as expressing 'nothing, save in so far as a cry expresses pain'.   *Mew's poems*: see letter of 22 June 1918.   *more clearness*: undeleted following 'more' at the very foot of first page are the words 'clearness of thought, but as it i', which FEH typed, abandoned because of paper slippage, but did not actually strike through.   *Monty is, in*: FEH typed 'Monty is, is in'.   *old Vicarage*: of Fordington St George, formerly the home of the Revd Henry Moule and his family.   *Moules*: FEH typed 'Moule's'.   *Supplement*: FEH typed 'Suppliment'.   *O'Rourke*: May O'Rourke (1897–1978), later employed as an occasional secretary at Max Gate. Her poem, 'To England', appeared in *The Times Literary Supplement*, 29 Mar. 1917, and her vol., *West Wind Days*, was pub. by Erskine Macdonald in 1918.   *Horace's grave*: TH's friend Horace Moule (1832–73) is buried in Fordington churchyard.   *friend . . . Newquay*: Sir Robert Pearce Edgcumbe, formerly a Dorchester banker and politician; see *CL*, i. 180 n.   *Bovington Camp*: an army training establishment in south Dorset.   *With . . . 'Domicilium's.*: added by FEH in ink.

[TH, as his wife testified, was always on the look-out for new poets, and he was especially alert, during and immediately following the years of the First World War, to the emergence of such figures as Siegfried Sassoon, Robert Nichols, Robert

Graves, and Edmund Blunden. But the writer whose acquaintance he most actively pursued at this time was Charlotte Mew, a very different figure possessed of a highly individual voice with which he sometimes found difficulty in coming to terms. It would appear that Mew was initially taken up by Cockerell, that Cockerell sang her praises to FEH, and that FEH then became Cockerell's ally in arousing and maintaining TH's interest first in Mew's verse and then in Mew herself. Once she had met Mew FEH became genuinely attached to her, and the two met and corresponded on a number of occasions over the next several years.]

To Charlotte Mew

MAX GATE, | DORCHESTER.
24th September '18.

Dear Miss Mew:

I believe that you have heard from our friend Mr Sydney Cockerell of the immense pleasure your poems have given my husband. It is long since I have known him so engrossed by a book, as by 'The Farmer's Bride'. It now lies by him on his study table & I have read all the poems to him— some of them *many* times—& shall probably read them to him many more times.

He is, as you know, not a young man & he cares to see but few people nowadays, but he has expressed a wish to meet you if that should be possible.

It is a tedious journey to Dorchester from London, & not the time of year when one cares to go into the country—but if you should ever be near us—or indeed if you thought it worth while to come that distance to see him, we should be most delighted to put you up for the night.

Yours very truly,
Florence Hardy

Text MS. (with envelope) Berg.
Bride': see letter of 22 June 1918.   *put you up*: Mew accepted the invitation but FEH was twice obliged to change the date, so that the visit did not take place until Dec. 1918.

To H. G. Wells

Max Gate, | Dorchester.
18th Oct: '18.

Dear Mr Wells:

My husband wrote too hurriedly to thank you for 'Joan & Peter' for we had not read further than about page 60, & though he liked it, he did not know how much. He has listened to it all with delight—& several chapters have been read over to him twice. A Cambridge don came to see us & we read aloud to him passages that we thought would have a good effect on him—particularly those about Cambridge. It became a usual sight here—my husband coming down to dinner with your book under his arm, to have it read aloud to him.

But we don't know anything really of the young life in this book—the people we come into contact here mostly—our most frequent visitors—are clergymen's wives.

I loved Dolly—but I am afraid I did not like or understand Joan. I expect I was rather jealous of her. In the death of Dolly I felt I had lost a friend with whom I might have spent many delightful hours.

I think your novels are really the only ones that my husband can read with any enjoyment nowadays. I read him a few pages of the wonderful Leonard Merrick—& he said he didn't want to hear any more—although on the authority of the greatest writers of the day he ought to have been overcome with admiration. I hope that you are well, & Mrs Wells & your boys. I wish we were in London where everything must be very exciting just now.

Yours sincerely,
Florence Hardy.

My husband sends his kindest regards.

Text   MS. Univ. of Illinois, Urbana.
Wells: Herbert George Wells (1866–1946), novelist and author; FEH told Lady Hoare, 11 June 1917 (Wiltshire R.O.), that her husband thought *Love and Mr Lewisham* Wells's best work and admired *Mr Britling Sees It Through* because 'it gave such a vivid picture of how things were in England at the beginning of the war'.   *'Joan & Peter'*: Wells's *Joan and Peter: The Story of an Education* (London, 1918); see *CL*, v. 280.   *Cambridge don*: unidentified, but perhaps J. B. Bury (see letter of 7 Mar. 1913).   *contact here*: 'contact with here' evidently intended. *Merrick . . . greatest writers*: Leonard Merrick (1864–1939), popular novelist, whose works had just been reissued in a collected edition with introductions by Barrie, Pinero, G. K. Chesterton, and other notable contemporaries; FEH seems not to have realized that one such introduction was by Wells himself.   *exciting just now*: as the end of the war approached.

To Sydney Cockerell

Max Gate, | Dorchester.
25th. Oct. '18

Dear Mr Cockerell:

I sent off a very meagre note today in reply to your kind letter, & so am following it up with another. First of all I must relieve your anxiety with regard to the drawing-room pictures. We think they look delightful—they have never looked so well. I am most grateful to you for re-arranging them. All that has happened (with regard to alteration) is that T.H. has hung that picture by Sir Arthur Blomfield, over the mirror by the clock—where there was a space. It came back with a nice new glass, looking much better, & affection for his old chief made him feel it must go up.

Grandmother Gifford & the great ARCHDEACON have not returned, & I can well dispense with them.

T.H. is very well. He did not feel up to much, & for a fortnight I kept off everyone—except Mrs McDowell who asked herself to tea. He seems to like her exceedingly & is always bright when she is here, so I thought that would not hurt him. Yesterday a Mr Elliott Felkin called—he is an officer of the German prisoner's guard here, & was at Kings, & knows the Burys well. He is rather a brilliant young man, & exceedingly pleasant. He had an introduction from Lowes Dickinson & came in the spring from Blandford to see us. Now he is living in Dorchester. He talked so well that T.H. enjoyed his visit—& as he is living in Dorchester he will probably come again. These two have been our only visitors in 3 weeks so I think I have been successful in keeping folk off.

As for poor Miss Mew I hardly know what to do, for T.H. says that owing to the scarcity of coal we cannot entertain any visitors until next spring—when fires are over. He ought to have said that before I wrote to her. I made a bungling excuse—he really was not feeling well at the time—& I will try to make it all right & have her a little later. *Of course* we can manage. Mr Felkin says he can send us 3 *nice* German prisoners in about a fortnight to cut down trees, & if we cut down two or three ash trees they burn green beautifully & will give us fuel for some time.

Lord Northcliffe wrote to tell me he & a friend had hunted all through the Perth bookshops to find a copy of one of my husband's books, & couldn't get it. He said should he write to Macmillans. I said perhaps it would do good if he did, whereupon he sent the enclosed letter to Sir F. Macmillan. Would you mind returning it, please. I thought it exceedingly kind of him to take so much trouble.

I meant to say, in writing of Mr Felkin—that he knew Rupert Brooke well, & yesterday he told us that the Memoir of him published lately, which you lent us, did not show one side of him—that there was a *hardness* in his character. I rather felt that, myself, while reading his letters & poems. He knew, also, your other friend, Archie Don.

Thursday morn.

148

This ought to have been sent off last night, but there was not time to catch the post. If the weather holds up we (T.H. & I) are going to cycle to the heath at Bockhampton—taking sandwiches. It is so beautiful there now with dead bracken.

Yours very sincerely,
Florence Hardy.

Text MS. Beinecke.   *Date* FEH first wrote '21st'.
Blomfield: Sir Arthur William Blomfield (1829–99), the London architect for whom TH worked between 1862 and 1867; the subject of the picture is unknown.   *ARCHDEACON*: FEH wrote this very large and underlined it once; for Archdeacon Gifford himself see letter of 16 Jan. 1913.   *dispense with them*: i.e. with their portraits.   *Mrs McDowell*: i.e. McDowall; see letter of 21 Aug. 1913.   *Felkin*: Elliott Felkin (d. 1968), later an international civil servant with the League of Nations and the United Nations.   *the Burys*: Professor John Bagnell Bury (see letter of 7 Mar. 1913) and his wife Jane.   *Dickinson*: Goldsworthy Lowes Dickinson (1862–1932), historian, philosophical writer, and fellow of King's College, Cambridge, where Felkin had recently been an undergraduate.   *come again*: Felkin kept a record of his conversations with TH; see *Encounter*, 18 (Apr. 1962), 27–33.   *Lord Northcliffe . . . Macmillan*: Alfred Harmsworth, Viscount Northcliffe (1865–1922), journalist and newspaper proprietor; for his letter to Sir Frederick Macmillan, see *CL*, v. 282.   *Brooke*: Rupert Chawner Brooke (1887–1915), poet, subject of Edward Marsh, *Rupert Brooke: A Memoir* (London, 1918).   *Don*: Archibald Don (1890–1916), of Trinity College Cambridge, killed in action; see David Newsome, *On the Edge of Paradise. A. C. Benson: The Diarist* (London: John Murray, 1980), 247, etc.

[TH had been a Justice of the Peace for the Borough of Dorchester since 1884, qualified to sit as a magistrate at the Borough Petty Sessions, and from 1894 onwards he had the additional responsibilities of a Justice of the Peace for the County of Dorset, sitting at the County Petty Sessions and the Quarter Sessions and as a member of the Grand Juries that determined whether cases should go forward for trial at the Assizes. Although he attended the Borough Petty Sessions with some regularity in the 1880s, his performance of such duties later became more sporadic, eventually narrowing down to once-a-year attendances at the Grand Jury. Beginning in December 1917, however, he made several appearances on the Borough Petty Sessions bench when it was dealing with infringements of wartime regulations fixing the price of food—this being, so *Life and Work* quotes him as saying, 'the only War-work I was capable of'. FEH, anxious in a time of scarcity to maintain good relations with the local tradesmen, had grounds for regretting her husband's zealous performance of his magisterial role, but she was herself to accept appointment as a JP for the Borough of Dorchester just six years later.]

To Louise Yearsley

Max Gate. | Dorchester.
10th Nov: '18.

My dear Louise:

I meant to have written, long before this, to tell you that my sister Margaret has a dear little son (following your excellent example) who is to be named Thomas after my husband—whom I hope he may resemble in as many ways as possible—besides in name. He evidently knew that he was not going to be born into a very welcoming world—so he delayed his appearance three weeks—& was not born until Oct. 24th. That was a nuisance as the nurse my sister had engaged was obliged to leave on Nov. 2nd—& though she was able to get another for a fortnight it has not been *very* satisfactory. How my sister will manage without one I do not know, for she insists that she will not have a little servant—& the poor girl is still very weak. However I hope some arrangement will be made.

I have only been in Town for *one* day since your boy arrived, & then I was sneezing furiously & would hardly have dared to go & see you—for fear of giving you cold—even if I had had time. I was frightfully rushed. But I hope to come later.

I hope that you are quite well & strong now, & Mr Yearsley well too. My husband is splendid, & says that he has not felt so strong & able to *do* things for years. (My pen-holder *is* wood—or I should be afraid to write that). The only interesting thing that has happened here for some while is a visit we have just had from my husband's *adored* young friend Siegfried Sassoon— one of the most brilliant, & handsome & likeable young men I know. He is on leave after his *third* wound a head one, this time. But he has the Military Cross. He tells me he has been asked to stand as *Labour* member for a certain constituency, but has declined. The humour of that does appeal to me, & will I expect to Mr Yearsley. Imagine—a son of the Sassoon family & cousin of the Rothschilds, a *Labour* member. I have been roped in by the Conservative party, & have promised one of our best friends here to support her at a meeting in favour of the present member—Robert Williams—*also* a friend & neighbour. Now that I consider the matter I am dismayed for I cannot think of *any* of our friends—except your kind husband—who would not execrate me for doing this. My *father* always abused me for being a Radical. I tell my husband I am going to back out—but he says I *must* do what I have promised to do—& having had a remarkably cordial letter & invitation, to go & see him, from Lloyd George—I suppose I *must*. But I'm so vague, that I don't know if our member represents Lloyd George. And then Lord Northcliffe has been very kind & civil to both of us. My head spins—& I wish heartily that women had never been given the vote.

How splendid the news is; An officer from the Prison Guard was here to tea today & told us that one of the Germans told him that the abdication of the Kaiser has spoilt all the joy of anticipating a speedy return to Germany. I am afraid I cannot sufficiently sympathise with the poor man. We were hoping to have two Bavarians here to cut down trees, but expect that will be "off" now.

My husband & Major Cosens have been fining all the local tradesmen for profiteering & soon I shall be unable to enter a shop in Dorchester. The last was our own grocer!!

With love to yourself & the boy & kind regards to Mr Yearsley.

Yours affectionately,
Florence Hardy.

Text MS. (with envelope) Eton.
Yearsley: Louise Yearsley, whom FEH had met as the spouse of the surgeon Macleod Yearsley (see letters of 16 May 1920 and 4 Nov. 1922); several of FEH's friendly letters to her, written over a number of years, are at Eton.   *Thomas*: Thomas Soundy (1918–88), later radio operator on the *Queen Elizabeth* and other ocean liners.   *Williams*: Colonel Sir Robert Williams, Bt., MP for West Dorset 1895–1922; he lived at Bridehead, Dorset.   *Lloyd George*: David Lloyd George, later Earl Lloyd-George (1863–1945), Prime Minister; though himself a Liberal, Lloyd George was the leader of a coalition, including Conservatives, which continued in power following the 1918 general election.   *Northcliffe*: see letter of 25 Oct. 1918.   *Major Cosens . . . grocer!!*: at the Sept. 1918 Borough Petty Sessions the two sitting JPs, TH and William Burrough Cosens (a local doctor who had recently served with the Royal Army Medical Corps), imposed a fine of £15 upon the proprietor of the County Stores, Dorchester, for selling rice at more than the controlled price.

To Sydney Cockerell

Max Gate, | Dorchester.
6th Dec: '18

Dear Mr Cockerell:

Miss Mew has just left us. I think I never met anyone who was so different from the picture my fancy had made. What a pathetic little creature! One longed to be kind to her & look after her. And she was not silent— talked all the time. We never have had anyone here who talked so much, from the moment I met her at the station. She was immensely relieved I think to find she had not to walk out here with her bag—for I had a fly to bring her along. She had been dreading the walk.

T.H. did not dislike her & felt very sorry for her, & talked very kindly to her, & read her some of his poems. But she is not his type of woman at all. He prefers women like Mrs Inglis—whom he declares he likes best of all my friends, & whose departure he is always lamenting (as do I). "She *fitted* me so well" he says "I always liked seeing her. I wish she would come & live near us." Mrs Snaith, too, who is about the same age & very bright & attractive he likes. But poor Miss Mew is *so* pathetic. I made her stay two nights instead of one when I found how she liked being here—& would gladly have kept her a month had it been possible. She has genius, I think.

Thank you so much—from T.H.—for your letter which he will answer, so he says. I remember how he & I went together to see Swinburne's tomb & how vexed he was with the cross on top of it. I remember he [*remainder of letter absent*]

Text   MS. Beinecke.
Mrs Snaith: Madeleine Ruth Snaith, née Armstrong, wife of John Collis Snaith, novelist.
genius, I think: as printed in *Friends of a Lifetime*, 300, the letter ends at this point, apart from the valedictory 'Yours sincerely | Florence Hardy' supplied on the MS. in Cockerell's hand.
he & I: FEH first wrote 'we'.   *Swinburne's tomb*: at Bonchurch, Isle of Wight; the visit, the occasion of TH's poem 'The Singer Asleep', was made in Mar. 1910, four years before their marriage.

To Sydney Cockerell

MAX GATE, | DORCHESTER.
22nd Dec. '18.

Dear Mr Cockerell:

Many thanks for your kind letter & good wishes, which we were delighted to have. We send Mrs Cockerell, yourself & family our very best wishes for Christmas & the New Year.

T.H. was much interested in the cuttings you enclosed, & is just pasting two of them in his Dowden's 'Shelley'. He is very well & most cheerful, & working steadily. The whole of the MS. will have to be re-copied very shortly as so many additions have been made. We were much interested in hearing of your sight-seeing in London—I wish I could be there to see Wilson. It must have been a delightful experience taking Margaret to her first 'grown-up' play. I remember taking my sister Eva—eight years younger than myself—to see 'The Only Way". She sobbed, & tears ran down her cheeks, & I felt so remorseful at having brought her—when she turned to me, & mopping her eyes said 'Oh how lovely! I *am* enjoying myself."

I have been reading to T.H 'Eminent Victorians'. He was much interested & did not think any of the essays unfair, except that about Gordon.

He (T.H) admires him more than the other 'Victorians' because he was so disinterested. He thought it 'sinister' of Lytton Strachey to harp on the B & S. We have also read Mrs Ward's 'Recollections' which he found rather interesting.

We have been wondering could anything be done for Miss Mew. I asked T.H. if he could write a very short appreciation of her poems, but he will not do that. He said if she had written more he could perhaps have got her a Civil List Pension that the few poems she has published are hardly sufficient. I am begging everyone to read her poems, & have given away several copies. She has had friends though—Mrs Crackanthorpe for one—who would have helped her if it had been possible. She (Mrs Crackenthorpe) has great influence, I know, with several editors—Courtney & others. The only help one can give I think is to encourage her—& urge her—to write more poems. I could easily get a little article about her poems published if I wrote it, in the Boston Transcript or elsewhere. I wonder whether that would be any help. Have you read one that was printed in 'The Englishwoman' 'On the Road to the Sea'? It is one of her best I think. I read the first verse to T.H. without telling him who had written it, & he sat up alert & interested at once. "That's *good*" he said "Who wrote it?" Miss Mew had previously recited it to us but he had forgotten, or not followed.

There is a packet here of nearly all the photographs of T.H that have been taken.

The 'Hardy' players were thinking of getting up a little Mumming play to be performed here about Jan. 9th, but they find they are unable to carry it through, & it is to be given, all being well, next autumn. They had also a plan of coming here to give the play in our hall, & sing carols to T. but that, also, has fallen through as they are all so occupied. Later, I suppose, when men are released from the army there will be more leisure.

We shall be delighted to have another of those little Bains books. I lent the second one 'Digit of the Moon' to Eden Phillpotts & he has not returned it, so I must remind him that he has it.

With many thanks & every good wish,

Yours very sincerely,
Florence Hardy—

Text   MS. Beinecke.
Dowden's 'Shelley': TH's copy of Edward Dowden, *The Life of Percy Bysshe Shelley* (2 vols., London, 1886), is now in the Adams collection.   *Wilson*: President Woodrow Wilson of the United States and his wife made a state visit to Britain, 26–31 Dec. 1918.   '*The Only Way*": an adaptation, by the Revd Freeman Wills and Frederick Langbridge, of Dickens's *A Tale of Two Cities*; it was produced in London on several occasions between 1900 and 1908.

'Eminent Victorians': by Giles Lytton Strachey, first pub. 1918; General Charles George Gordon, killed at Khartoum in 1885, was the subject of one of the essays.   *harp on the B & S*: Strachey's several references to Gordon's drinking brandy and soda serve to suggest, though not to assert, that he took refuge in alcohol at times of stress.   *'Recollections'*: *A Writer's Recollections* (London, 1918) by Mary Augusta Ward, usually known as Mrs Humphry Ward.   *Civil List Pension*: eventually obtained.   *Pension that*: 'Pension but' (or 'but that') presumably intended.   *Mrs Crackanthorpe*: Blanche Alethea Crackanthorpe (1848–1928), literary hostess, widow of Montague Hughes Crackanthorpe, barrister and writer. *Courtney*: William Leonard Courtney, editor of the *Fortnightly Review*.   *Boston Transcript*: the nature of FEH's connection with this newspaper is unknown.   *'On . . . Sea'*: in *The Englishwoman*, 22 (June 1914), 300–2.   *Mumming play*: presumably *The Play of St George*; TH's own version was performed publicly by the 'Hardy Players' in Nov. 1920 and privately, at Max Gate, on 20 Dec. 1920.   *Bains books*: Cockerell gave TH three or four humorous books by Francis William Bain at different dates; *A Digit of the Moon* was first pub. 1899 and often reprinted.

[The composition of the 'Life' continued into the early months of 1919—on 18 April FEH reported to Cockerell that she was 'working hard at the "Notes" for several hours daily'—and TH also began sorting through, and copiously throwing out, the accumulated papers of a literary lifetime. A particular problem was presented by the thousands of incoming letters that he had received over the years and for the most part kept, often accompanied by drafts of his replies. The bulk of this material was simply destroyed, and while FEH might regret the disappearance of particular letters or of entire correspondences she had learned by this time that TH was immovable once his mind had been made up. She felt that her husband had grown much older of late, forgetful of things that had happened within the last few days and of people whom he had recently seen or heard from, even though his memory of his early life remained 'miraculous'. When they first met, she recalled in a letter to Cockerell of 18 February 1919 (Beinecke), TH 'was so wonderful—he was writing "The Dynasts" and his mind was luminous. Not but that he isn't far beyond the average young man even now.']

To Sydney Cockerell

Max Gate | Dorchester.

30th January. [1919]

Dear Mr Cockerell:

Thank you so much for the two tickets for the Ruskin lecture. How I wish I could use one of them! However, I have sent them to my eldest sister who will keenly appreciate your kindness.

All goes here very well. We were *very* sorry to hear about your eyes, & we *do* hope that you will rest them as much as possible, for they are of so much importance to so many people as well as yourself—a nice selfish remark. But really we *are* sorry.

T.H. is still busy with his letter-sorting, having reached 1893. Quite four-fifths or more have to be destroyed—some I rather regret, but when he wants to burn he will burn, & not all the King's Horses nor all the King's Men could prevent him. And I expect he is right. We are reading that new Life of Meredith by our little friend "Paul Pry"—of whom we may have told you. Rather a cruel book, but quite well done in its way.

I have written to the R.S.L. to send Miss Mew a card of admission to their lectures. Rebekah West has called here & she was very keen on Miss Mew's poems. My husband thinks Miss West a wonderful critic. She is young & pretty—not the middle-aged spinster I imagined. We hope that Mrs Cockerell is better & the children well. With grateful thanks.

Yours very sincerely,
F.H.

Text MS. Beinecke. *Date* Year supplied on MS. by Cockerell.
Ruskin lecture: by J. W. Mackail, part of the Ruskin centenary celebrations, Royal Society of Arts, 8 Feb. 1919. *eldest sister*: Ethel Richardson; see letter of 6 Feb. 1919. *Life of Meredith*: *George Meredith: His Life and Friends in Relation to His Work* (London, 1919) by Stewart Marsh Ellis (d. 1933), who had called at Max Gate on several occasions. *R.S.L.*: Royal Society of Literature. *West*: adopted name of Cicily Isabel Fairfield (1892–1983), author; she came to Max Gate with H. G. Wells, 29 Jan. 1919 (*CL*, v. 293).

To Sydney Cockerell

MAX GATE, | DORCHESTER.
6th. February 1919.

Dear Mr Cockerell:

First, in reply to your query, my husband has dictated this answer—not however to be quoted as his.

"There is a fragment of truth in what Mr Shorter is reported as having said —though it is not all true. Crabbe was not the *most* potent influence, but was *one* of the influences that led him towards his method—in his novels not in his poetry. The report probably arose from T.H.'s saying that he owed more of his realistic style to Crabbe than to Zola. The knowing English reviewers asserted that all English realism came from Zola, but it existed in Crabbe fifty years before Zola's time. But in his other sort of writing he was influenced far more by Shakespeare, Shelley, Browning &c. than by Crabbe."

We are glad to hear that your eyes are rather better, but do beg you to be careful.

I was most interested in hearing that you had been talking to two school-mistresses who were fellow students with my sister Ethel at college. She is the sister to whom I gave the "Ruskin" tickets, as she does so appreciate anything of the kind. She has a passion for good pictures, music, and so forth, which I am always so glad to be able to gratify as she had the misfortune to lose the sight of one eye when her second child was born, and the remaining eye is very inflamed, she tells me, and gives her much anxiety. My husband calls her "the pick of the family" and is, I think, very fond of her. She has (even with three children) managed to save money out of her small private income and buy houses etc. of which he highly approves, and says she is like his mother in her economy and devotion to her children. She writes me most interesting accounts of all the good concerts she goes to, and the picture galleries she visits, so I enjoy them at second-hand. She will probably send me a far more interesting account of Professor Mackail's lecture than I shall get from any paper.

We are still reading Mr Ellis's book on George Meredith with the greatest interest. It is not so very well done, a lot of padding which probably he was obliged to put in to make the book the required length, but he has certainly been clever in getting every possible scrap of information. I doubt though whether a man ought to write the life of anyone against whom he has a grudge. It was obvious, when speaking to him of Meredith, that he did not like him. Mr Clodd is quoted freely as saying that Meredith told him this, that, and the other. I doubt if statements of that kind ought to be admitted. In reading Mr Clodd's highly coloured version of events that happened at Aldeburgh when I was there I am inclined to take with caution all that he relates about Meredith. He poses now as one of Meredith's oldest and dearest friends, whereas Barrie told me (and I believe him implicitly) that Meredith warned him against Clodd and advised him not to go to Clodd's house, which he called a trap.

The letter sorting is still going on—nineteen years more to do. When they are all sorted I am going to rearrange them under initials, instead of dates. A most interesting letter of Swinburne's has come to light—in praise of "Jude the Obscure" which ought to have been included in Swinburne's Letters.

I think I saw once in an editor's office an exceedingly useful piece of furniture, with drawers for storing letters—each drawer marked with an initial—and I think a wire spring inside each drawer to hold the papers. There is no hurry about this but I should like to get something similar, and if you know of anything of the kind would you tell me. It ought to something which will lock, I think, and I should like it to be a good piece of furniture, such as would not be unsightly in any room. If I knew of the right place to go to I would get it when I am next in London. There is a good shop I believe at the end of Chancery Lane (in the Strand). I do not know whether they would have that sort of thing there.

The notes will have to be completely re-typed when the letter sorting is finished as much fresh material is being inserted.

T.H. is very well and very cheerful. He had a visit yesterday from Lady Ilchester and her daughter and we were quite a noisy party—shouts of laughter, such as I had not heard here for many months. He insisted upon telling that awful story of the burning of Mary Channing, with all its gruesome details. I tried in vain to stop him, for the daughter turned quite white—she is only fifteen.

We had another tea-party, of a kind you would *not* appreciate. The Rector of West Stafford and his wife, the Vicar of Stinsford and his wife, an elderly and religious peer, Lord Ellenborough, and our neighbours at Syward Lodge—all good Conservatives and staunch Anglicans. T.H. declares that he understands that type of person better than any other, and he prefers to know the rather narrow, churchy, conservative country person to the brilliant young writer who is always popping in and out of the divorce court. An interesting statement from the author of "Jude" and "The Dark-Eyed Gentleman". I am ashamed to begin another sheet of paper so will end here.

Yours very sincerely.

Florence Hardy.

Text   MS. (typed) Beinecke.
Shorter . . . said: perhaps a reference to Clement Shorter's 'Literary Letter', *Sphere*, 24 Oct. 1903, which reports TH as identifying Crabbe as 'his earliest influence in the direction of realism'.   *before Zola's time*: cf. *Life and Work*, 351.   *at college*: St Katharine's College, a training college for teachers.   *"Ruskin" tickets*: see letter of 30 Jan. 1919.   *had the misfortune*: FEH typed 'has the misfortune'.   *letter of Swinburne's*: dated 5 Nov. 1895; TH made and kept a copy (DCM) and gave the original to the Fitzwilliam Museum.   *an exceedingly*: FEH typed 'and exceedingly'.   *get something similar*: Cockerell suggested that large envelopes would be preferable to pigeonholes and TH agreed; in practice the preserved letters seem to have remained tied up in bundles year-by-year.   *to something*: 'to be something' clearly intended.   *finished*: FEH typed 'finsihed'.   *her daughter*: for Lady Ilchester, see letter of 3 Dec. 1915; her daughter was Lady Mary Theresa Fox-Strangways.   *Channing*: an 18-year-old woman burned to death in early 18th-century Dorchester for the murder of her husband; TH was fond of narrating the episode and did so in print in his 'Maumbury Ring', *The Times*, 9 Oct. 1908.   *Rector*: the Revd Edmund Henry Corbett-Winder.   *Vicar*: the Revd Henry Guise Beatson Cowley; he and his wife Ethel, at Stinsford 1911–33, were frequent callers at Max Gate.   *Ellenborough*: Cecil Henry Law, 6th Baron Ellenborough, a former professional soldier; he was nine years younger than T.H.   *Syward Lodge*: a large house close to Max Gate, then occupied by Thomas Henry Ricketts Winwood but since pulled down.   *"The Dark-Eyed Gentleman"*: a poem first pub. in *Time's Laughingstocks* and evidently regarded by FEH as somewhat *risqué*.   *I am . . . Hardy.*: added by FEH in ink holograph.

To Paul Lemperly

MAX GATE, | DORCHESTER.
March 7th. 1919

Dear Mr Lemperly:

Your second gift of a box of delicious candy has arrived, & I thank you for it most sincerely. It is exceedingly kind of you to send it. Soon, I hope, I shall be able to post to you another pamphlet—there has been a delay in the printing as my husband changed his mind about one of the poems, & decided that he would not have it printed. But in a few days I hope to be able to send it off.

We were so delighted with that charming portrait of your little grand son. What a darling little boy—& what a typical young American. There is no mistaking his nationality. I expect he is very intelligent. I wish I had just such a grandson.

I hope that you will find your new home, if you buy it, quite to your satisfaction. My husband had this house built for him five & thirty years ago, & has lived here ever since, & will, I am sure, never move from it. But we are not modern. We fear no frosts as there are no water pipes, practically, in the house. All our water has to be pumped up directly from a well, & heated in kettles & saucepans over the kitchen fire. We have no boilers, no gas, we use oil-lamps & candles for lighting, & have no bathroom even. I expect this is the only house of this size in Dorchester without. And we are not connected with the main drainage either. Nevertheless there has not been a case of infectious illness in the house since it was built, & only one death, that of the late Mrs Hardy, & she died of heart complaint, suddenly. Our books I am afraid, are kept very badly & you will doubtless be horrified if ever you see them, as I hope you may some day.

I quite thought you had often been in England as a friend told us that he could remember your going to buy some of William Morris's books at the Kelmscott press—evidently a mistake.

Please *do let me know* if you are unable to get the first editions you require of Capt. S. Sassoon's poems, for if you bookseller cannot procure them I will write to him directly (Siegfried Sassoon) & ask him if he has a spare copy. He is one of the most attractive young men it is possible to imagine, & a fearless, true-hearted man.

With our kindest regards

Yours sincerely,
Florence Hardy.

Text MS. (with envelope) Colby.
Lemperly: Paul Lemperly (1858–1939), of Lakewood, Ohio, American businessman and book-collector.   *candy*: Lemperly had earlier sent to Max Gate several gifts of items in short supply in wartime England.   *another pamphlet*: apparently the privately printed pamphlet containing TH's 'Jezreel' and 'The Master and the Leaves', although it did not appear until Sept. 1919 (Purdy, 209–10).   *a friend*: evidently Cockerell, who had been secretary to the Kelmscott Press.   *you bookseller*: 'your' clearly intended.

[When FEH in her widowhood spoke and wrote about her late husband and answered questions about his life and writings, she of course drew heavily upon her memories of what he had himself told her on various occasions in the past. When, however, such questions touched upon matters in which she was herself directly interested—for example, TH's relationship with his first wife—her recorded responses have necessarily to be examined for traces of personal bias. There has proved to be no substance to Robert Gittings's suggestion, in *Young Thomas Hardy*, that FEH deliberately lied in asserting that ELH's niece Lilian Gifford had been in an asylum; on the other hand, it is clear that she deplored her husband's obsessive devotion to ELH's memory and his continuing cultivation of the Gifford family and that she resolutely (and successfully) opposed any suggestion that the deeply troubled Lilian might return to Max Gate.]

To Louise Yearsley

MAX GATE, | DORCHESTER.
Sunday. [10 August ·1919]

My dear Louise:

So many thanks for those delightful snap-shots of the little family. I am so glad to have them. 'Himself' looks more of a darling than ever, especially where he is shown with you—on the rug. What a dear little face it is! I hope you are all still feeling the good results of the holiday.

It is most kind of you to say that my sister Eva may call to see you. I am sure she will be delighted.

I hear that you *most kindly* suggest going to see my other sister, Marjorie, this week. How nice it would be if it happened to be Wednesday afternoon, as I am likely to be going to have tea with her then, about 5. I have to go to Town to see a Miss Gifford—niece of the first Mrs T.H. She has gone off her head, poor thing, & been put in an asylum, & I am going to see her as my husband is really not fit for the journey this weather. He is rather attached to her as she lived here as a child for some years—& she has stayed with us from time to time since we were married. She was always a *most* difficult person to live with—but now I understand that the poor woman could not really help her trying ways & temper. At first T.H. said that she was to come here directly she comes out of the asylum, to live permanently, but now I think he is beginning to feel a trifle nervous at the prospect.

We had a flying visit from Granville Barker & his new American wife on Thursday—they came to lunch as they were motoring through Dorchester trying to find a house near here. There are several to be let, but none seems to suit. His wife is enormously rich, & very charming. I feel rather a traitress in liking her so much, as the first wife, poor Lillah, is by way of being a friend, too. It is rather awkward being on *kissing* terms with a man's two wifes.

We are going to have another mild excitement in the shape of a visit from my husband's adored young friend—Siegfried Sassoon—who is to bring a "Tribute", from all the English contemporary poets, to T.H. Kipling—the Poet-Laureate—practically everyone has contributed I am told, but it is a *sort* of secret. The last affair of the kind was when W B Yeats & Newbolt brought him his gold medal. I am not sure whether the occasion demands a new dress, but the prices are so *appalling* I really daren't. How delightful you look in that white frock in the snap-shot.

With love

Yours affecly
F.H.

Text MS. Eton. *Date* Supplied on MS., apparently by L. Yearsley.
'Himself': L. Yearsley's infant son. *Miss Gifford*: ELH's niece Lilian Gifford had been committed, as 'of unsound mind', to the London County Council asylum at Claybury, Essex. She seems to have been released within less than six months, TH and some of L. Gifford's relatives having provided financial and other guarantees (*Biography*, 527–8). *nervous at the prospect*: writing to Cockerell 7 Aug. 1919 (Beinecke) FEH quoted TH as saying that he had had thirty years of living with someone like L. Gifford (i.e. ELH) and felt 'unable to go through it again'. *Barker*: Harley Granville-Barker (1877–1946), producer, dramatist, and critic; recently divorced from Lillah McCarthy, the actress (later Lady Keeble), he had now married, as his second wife, Helen Huntington (née Gates), herself just divorced from Archer Huntington, one of Barker's theatrical backers. *"Tribute"*: the 'Poets' Tribute' (DCM), a gathering of autograph poems by 43 poets on the occasion of TH's 79th birthday, 2 June 1919—although Sassoon did not take it to Max Gate until Oct. 1919 (*CL*, v. 326). *the Poet-Laureate*: Robert Bridges (*CL*, v. 327). *his gold medal*: of the Royal Society of Literature, presented by William Butler Yeats and Henry Newbolt on the occasion of TH's 72nd birthday; see *Life and Work*, 385.

To Sydney Cockerell

MAX GATE, | DORCHESTER.
19th. August '19.

Dear Mr Cockerell:

You must have thought me rather cool in proposing that we should pay you a visit, but really I did not understand that you would be staying with a friend. I thought that you were having a house lent to you, no-one else being there. As it is I know we ought not to descend upon you, and in addition it would hardly be possible as some part of Mr Lea's car is broken and he may have to wait for weeks for a new part, and T.H. feels that he could not do any calling just now. But I wonder if there is any chance of your coming here by car? Sir Henry and Lady Hoare and Mr and Mrs Whibley motored over from Stourhead the other day, and that, I think, is quite near you. I need hardly say how delighted we should be. Could Mrs Cockerell come do you think? How much we should like to see her again.

I went to London last week and saw poor Lilian Gifford. I did not perceive any particular symptom of insanity, but the doctor and the medical superintendent assured me that she *was* insane. I had a long interview with them, but of course I could not take her out without their consent, though she implored me to do so. It was very painful. The next day I saw her brother and he told me that he and his wife had had a dreadful time with her the last few years, all in the same old Gifford style, my husband says. The brother's wife, being a dressmaker, was not fit to associate with Lilian, and so on, continual scenes and unkindness just as in the old days, and that absurd obsession about the grandeur of the Gifford family. My husband is not so much upset about it as I should have thought, but what seems to annoy him more than anything is that she has sold the good gilt-edged securities he bought for her and invested in such things as Bovril, Associated Newspapers, etc. without telling him. Her annuity, of course, is intact. He provided for her far more liberally than I imagined, so there is nothing he can reproach himself with on that score. The Medical Superintendent told me that from what he knew of the case she can never have been quite sane. Her one idea seems to be to come here to live, but I agree with you that would never do.

I am so sorry that your little ones have this spell of wet weather for their holidays but I hope that it will soon improve. Our love to Mrs Cockerell and the children,

Yours very sincerely,
Florence Hardy.

Text   MS. (typed) Beinecke.

with a friend: Cockerell's diary (BL) shows that he and his family stayed with Sir Richard
Paget, Bt., at Cranmore Hall, near Shepton Mallet, Somerset, from 18 Aug. to 5 Sept. 1919.
Whibley: FEH typed 'Whibly'; Charles Whibley (1859–1930), man of letters, and Ethel Whibley,
his first wife (née Philip), who died the following year.   *her brother*: Gordon Gifford.
Gifford style: FEH typed 'Girrofd style'.   *brother's*: FEH typed 'brrother's'.   *never do*:
she feared, however, that TH might still 'give way' on this point (FEH to Cockerell, 27 Aug.
1919, Beinecke).

To Sydney Cockerell

MAX GATE, | DORCHESTER.
25th. September '19.

Dear Mr Cockerell:

My husband asks me to write to ask you to do something for him—if
you really do not object to doing it. You know, I expect, that Herbert
Trench has written a play "Napoleon" which he says, I think, is based on an
old tradition, viz. that Napoleon came over to England to reconnoitre. My
husband says he invented this himself, and it is to be found in "A Tradition
of 1804" Published Christmas 1882. He says he heard of no tradition when
he wrote it, and until this play it has never been suggested that there was
one. He would be interested to know if there really was one, and perhaps
you could find out by writing to some paper to inquire. He does not like
to write himself, naturally. What do you think?

We are much looking forward to Siegfried Sassoon's visit tomorrow. I
hope that the weather will be fine.

Thank you so much for offering to see me while I am in Town. I think
I had better make no arrangements as I am not yet certain whether I can
go. If I do go I shall have almost every moment filled with necessary shopping etc. If I do not go to Town I may go to Seatown for three days, before
my sister starts work at her hospital. Anyhow I feel all right now. It is most
kind of you to offer to dispose of the pamphlets to pay for the holiday, but
as a matter of fact I can very well afford the holiday. I have enough for a
couple of months away, did I choose, or were I able, to go. My cousin is
a well-to-do woman and would not let me pay for her, as she was left by
her father (my mother's uncle) over a thousand a year. She is most generous and was very kind to me when I was a young girl.

With regard to our own finances here, there ought to be no difficulty in
my having a holiday, as our income is well over two thousand a year, and
last year we spent about £600—rates, taxes, etc. The Surveyor of Taxes told
me so when I went to see if I could get back any of the income tax that had

been deducted from my dividends. I found I could not get any back. Of course my husband is exceedingly generous in many ways—he gave his sister another large sum a few months ago—£250—to invest. His economy is quite a matter of principle, not of greed—for no-one cares less for money than he does. But I think it has become now something not very far short of an obsession, and I do not know how it will be possible to get along in the future. He has just paid £10 for altering the tomb of the first Mrs T.H. and yet he will not buy himself a thread of clothing and he upsets himself about trifles of household expenditure involving only a few pence. Our new cook—one of the nicest women we have ever had here—says she cannot stay unless some alteration is made in the kitchen arrangements. She says the heavy pumping is not fit work for a woman, and the lack of hot water doubles her work. It was almost by a miracle that I got this cook—quite a dozen people were after her, and if she goes I do not know who I can get, or who will stay. I suppose this sort of thing is natural when people get on in years, and the newspapers make it worse. If we were badly off, or had a large family to provide for, of course I should say nothing.

The new little pamphlets look delightful. I have not had time to number them yet. With very many thanks,

Yours sincerely,
F.E.H

Text   MS. (typed) Beinecke.

"Napoleon": Napoleon (London, 1919) by Frederic Herbert Trench (1865–1923), poet and playwright.   *of 1804"*: TH's story, 'A Tradition of Eighteen Hundred and Four', first pub. in *Harper's Christmas*, Dec. 1882, and later collected in *Life's Little Ironies*.   *find out*: Cockerell reported to TH, 9 Oct. 1919 (DCM), that he could find no trace of any such event; for TH's response see *CL*, v. 326.   *Seatown*: FEH's doctor had diagnosed a nervous breakdown (FEH to Cockerell, 14 Sept. 1919, Beinecke) and insisted that she must go away for a holiday; her current plan was to go briefly to the Dorset seaside hamlet of Seatown.   *my sister . . . hospital*: FEH means that once Eva Dugdale had taken up her position at the new Swanage Children's Hospital she would be unavailable to stay with TH at Max Gate during FEH's absence.   *the pamphlets*: possibly those mentioned at the end of this letter but more probably the remaining copies of 'Domicilium' (see letter of 27 Dec. 1919).   *My cousin*: Edith Taylor; see letter of 1 Dec. 1910 and *CL*, iv. 174–5.   *new little pamphlets*: see letter of 7 Mar. 1919.

To Sir Frederick Macmillan

MAX GATE, | DORCHESTER.
30th. Nov: '19.

Dear Sir Frederick:

You may perhaps remember that when I last called to see you I told you of a manuscript I had which you kindly promised to keep for me, in a safe. My husband thinks that an excellent idea, but before we send it he wishes to go through it carefully once again when perhaps we may be able to add a little more material to it. He has been very busy the last few weeks or we should have finished it by now.

My reason for wishing to get this all settled is perhaps a rather morbid one, but I think I had better explain it to you to prevent misunderstanding. I have not been very well for the last few months & a specialist I see in London, from time to time, does not seem very encouraging. I thought that if anything did happen to me there was just a chance that if the three copies of this manuscript were in this house they might possibly be destroyed & as they represent nearly four years of hard work that would be a pity— particularly as the material could never be regained, once lost. At present my husband is taking care of them, but I hope to send you a copy shortly.

Please do not trouble to reply, as I am only writing to explain the delay.

Yours sincerely,
Florence Hardy.

Text MS. BL.
Macmillan: Sir Frederick Orridge Macmillan (1851–1936), publisher; TH in old age relied heavily upon his advice.   *manuscript*: evidently the 'Life', as is confirmed by FEH's reference to 'the three copies', although it is not clear that any copy was in fact sent to London prior to TH's death.

To Sydney Cockerell

MAX GATE, | DORCHESTER.
Saturday. [27 December 1919]

Dear Mr Cockerell:

I really think it would be better *not* to offer all those copies of 'Domicilium' for sale, as I might want a spare copy some day. It was kind of you to think of that. Perhaps 3 or 4 would be enough to sell—& of course there is *no* hurry. We had a very quiet Christmas, we too, alone, with Wessie—our only diversion being that T.H. *would* give Wessie goose & plum-pudding, & the result was what might have been expected—& he (T.H) didn't even

clean up the result, as he ought. He saw a ghost in Stinsford Churchyard
on Christmas Eve, & his sister Kate says it must have been their grandfather
upon whose grave T.H had just placed a sprig of holly—the first time he
had ever done so. The ghost said: 'A green Christmas'—T.H replied 'I like
a green Christmas'. Then the ghost went into the church, &, being full of
curiosity, T. followed, to see who this strange man in 18th century dress
might be—& found—no-one. That is quite true—a real Christmas ghost
story.

We went to Talbothays on Christmas day in the afternoon.

All being well here I go to Town next Saturday, & hope to see Miss Mew
on Monday evening. I hope that you all had a very happy Christmas,—I am
sure you did. With best wishes for the New year from us both—

Yours very sincerely,
Florence Hardy.

P.S We have finished the biography of S. Butler, which is depressing at the
end as all biographies must be—decay, disillusion, death. Now we are reading Dean Inge's "Outspoken Essays" which T. thinks good. F.H.

Text   MS. Beinecke.   *Date*   Supplied on MS. by Cockerell.
'Domicilium': see letter of 24 Feb. 1918; it is not clear why 'all those' copies still remained to
be disposed of.   *we too, alone*: 'we two, alone' possibly but not necessarily intended.
grandfather: Thomas Hardy (1778–1837).   *Talbothays*: see letter of 24 Nov. 1911.   *from us*
both: FEH first wrote 'from us all'.   *biography of S. Butler*: Henry Festing Jones, *Samuel*
Butler, Author of Erewhon, 1835–1902: A Memoir (2 vols., London, 1919).   *Essays"*: *Outspoken*
Essays [first series], by the Revd William Ralph Inge, Dean of St Paul's (London, 1919); TH
subsequently judged Inge to be 'something of a trimmer' (*CL*, vi. 36).

To Macleod Yearsley

MAX GATE, | DORCHESTER.
16th May '20.

Dear Mr Yearsley:

Thank you so much for your most kind invitation for Sunday, May 30th.
We should be delighted to go to Weymouth to see you all, but I am sorry
to say that my husband has been obliged, partly through his age & declin-
ing strength, & partly through pressure of work, to give up going out to
lunch. He finds that doing so disorganizes, for him, the whole day. He is
now correcting proofs of The Dynasts for the new edition, & there are five
volumes of poetry to follow & this is, for him, an exceedingly heavy task.
He allows nothing to interfere with his morning's work (he is hard at it
now) & by lunch time he is always tired & unfit for conversation, but after

a rest in the afternoon he is generally quite fresh again, & glad to see friends then. It is a frightfully disappointing rule—so far as I am concerned, especially when such delightful invitations as yours come—but I suppose it is only by steeling himself against such temptations that he is able to be working now—at the age of 80—& with a tremendous bulk of work behind him. He says he hopes to be able to go over to see you at Weymouth soon after your arrival & will also look forward to seeing you here. On Sundays we nearly always go to see his brother & sister—& that particular Sunday, being the one just before his birthday, they will certainly demand our attendance. On the Monday afternoon I (& perhaps my husband, if he is equal to it) will go over to Weymouth to see you—unless you would be able to come here. But perhaps you may have an engagement for that afternoon. His birthday is going to be, I am afraid, rather a trying day but fortunately the Society of Authors has chosen the three best possible representatives to bring the address—all old friends, to see whom again will be a joy to him. Others have written for London & Cambridge—asking if they can come "just to shake hands with him"—"to see him for a few minutes" —"to spend an hour with him" etc—& to these I have been reluctantly & ungraciously obliged to say "Please don't". Wiser ones are coming before— we are looking for a brief visit from Lord Grey (or is it Gray?) one afternoon this week, & as I missed him last time he came I am anxious to meet him as the man whom—some say—could have stopped the war had he chosen. But I doubt it.

I hear from my sister Marjorie that Louise has written her a sweet letter— how very good of her—I am sure she must be very busy preparing for the flitting to Weymouth. You won't have any mishap with a motor & a perambulator this time I hope. If there is anything I can do for you before your arrival please let me know—I may even find myself, by accident, at Weymouth that afternoon—& near Mrs Vickery's. But no—on second thoughts you'll all be very tired, & only desirous of settling in comfortably. Let me have a card later as to Monday afternoon—will you be here to tea or shall I (or we) go to you.

All affectionate messages to Louise

Yours very sincerely,
Florence Hardy.

Text MS. Eton.
Yearsley: Percival Macleod Yearsley (d. 1951), surgeon and author; see letter of 10 Nov. 1918 for FEH's friendship with Louise Yearsley.   *old friends*: John Galsworthy, Sir Anthony Hope Hawkins ('Anthony Hope', the novelist), and Augustine Birrell, author and statesman; for the address see *Life and Work*, 436–7.   *written for*: 'written from' clearly intended.

Lord Grey: Edward Grey, Viscount Grey (1862–1933), British Foreign Secretary 1905–16; he stayed with the McDowalls (see letter of 2 Feb. 1918) at Warmwell Mill and TH and FEH met him there.   *Mrs Vickery's*: Mrs Bessie Adelaide Vickery rented apartments at 14 Royal Crescent, Weymouth.

To Sydney Cockerell

MAX GATE, | DORCHESTER.
Sunday. [8 August 1920]

Dear Mr Cockerell:

We were glad to have your letter. T.H. says *another* case of thought transference, as I had been saying to him the two or three days before: 'I wonder what has happened to Mr Cockerell?' I was not sure *who* wrote last.

We are so sorry to hear that the children have not been well. I think that Cambridge cannot agree with them. I hope this holiday will do them, & Mrs Cockerell, worlds of good.

Of course we shall be delighted to see your friend here. Would you like to send me the address of her friends so that I could call on them—or would it be better for you to tell her that she may call to see us. If she sent a card to say *when* we would be in. We shall like to meet her.

The scarlet gown & bonnet have been returned unharmed, by Miss Doughty with an exceedingly graceful note of thanks. Also her papa sends his long poem 'Mansoul'. T.H. has looked in it but is not tempted to read it I regret to say—but I am sure Dr Doughty is a delightful man.

T.H. is very well. We walked to Stinsford Church this morning—a delightful walk, as you know. The friendly Vicar, seeing T.H there, read his favourite lesson, when he generally goes to hear on the evening of the 11th Sunday after Trinity—which we call "Small-Voice Sunday"—because of the lesson. Last year when we went Mr Cowley made a mistake & read the wrong lesson, but this time he read it a week beforehand so that we should not miss it. And by a lucky chance they had also an old chant T.H. liked as a boy, & one of his favourite hymns—the old morning hymn—so it was a successful venture, particularly as we did not go in the Hanbury's to lunch.

We are reading Jane Austen. We have read "Persuasion" & "Northanger Abbey", & now are in the midst of "Emma". T.H. is much amused at finding he has *many* characteristics in common with Mr Woodhouse.

My mother is better, thank you so much, better than I thought she would ever be again. She has been at Weymouth for a fortnight, & I have been to see her every other day. My eldest sister—Ethel Richardson—is with her, & takes her home on Tuesday or Wednesday. My father was there with her for a week. Instead of entertaining my family here I know a place at Weymouth, with a most delightful & kindhearted landlady, where they are well looked after, & so they can stay there. This arrangement suits everyone best, & T.H. is not bothered. I wish I could get away for a week but I am afraid there is no chance this year. I wonder if you are likely to be coming to see us again before the winter. You must be delighted to see your brother again after so long an interval.

Yours very sincerely,
Florence Hardy.

P.S. Mrs Henniker has been staying for three weeks at Weymouth. We enjoyed her visit greatly. FH.

Text MS. Beinecke. *Date* Supplied on MS. by Cockerell.
your friend: Katharine Adams, the bookbinder (see letter of 12 Aug. 1916); for her report on the visit see Viola Meynell, ed., *The Best of Friends: Further Letters to Sydney Carlyle Cockerell* (London: Rupert Hart-Davis, 1956), 24–5. *Miss Doughty*: Dorothy, daughter of Charles Montagu Doughty (1843–1926), traveller and poet; Doughty, recipient of an honorary Litt.D. from Cambridge, had borrowed TH's doctoral robes for the occasion. *'Mansoul'*: Doughty's poem *Mansoul, or The Riddle of the World* (London, 1920). *Vicar*: Cowley; see letter of 6 Feb. 1919. *favourite lesson*: from 1 Kings 19, including 'and after the fire a still small voice' (v. 12). *when he*: 'which he' clearly intended. *morning hymn*: Bishop Ken's 'Awake, my soul, and with the sun'; see *Life and Work*, 290–1. *go in the Hanbury's*: 'go into the Hanburys' presumably meant; the Hanburys (see letter of 3 Dec. 1915) lived at Kingston Maurward House, close to Stinsford Church. *landlady*: Mrs Vickery; see letter of 16 May 1920. *your brother*: presumably his elder brother, Theodore, a distinguished biologist.

To Rebekah Owen

MAX GATE, | DORCHESTER.
15th. October 1920.

My dear Betty:

I ought to have written to you before but you have no idea what a nightmare letters have become to me. Whenever I have a spare moment there seems to be an avalanche of unanswered letters descending upon me to prevent my resting or reading or doing anything in the garden. However I really ought to have answered yours before. I am glad that you will be able to come to the play—although I have an uncomfortable feeling that you may be disappointed. It is such a long journey to take, but I hope you will be repaid. I must warn you, however, that my husband has altered very much of late with regard to seeing people. He cannot stand a long conversation—it seems to exhaust him so, and then too he behaves so oddly to visitors that I hardly know what to do. Only the other day some old friends whom he really likes very much, called to see him, and by appointment. He was a long time coming down to them, and I could see that they were very much surprised. We had tea—he did not appear—and as we were talking I saw the husband (an eminent academician) looking out of the window. I looked too and there was my husband in the garden. He had only been to post a letter, it is true, but his friend looked very confused and annoyed. The wife had her back to the window and went on talking pleasantly—but I felt very unhappy for a few minutes until at last my husband came in. However you have known him so long that I am sure you will understand. The fact is—in plain English—that there are times when he doesn't care about seeing anyone, and these times tend to become more frequent. A relative of his called the other day—a man with whom he had always been on good terms. He firmly refused to come down, and the relatives—father and daughter—had to leave looking none too well pleased.

We had, though, a most pleasant visit the other day from Miss Sheila Kaye-Smith. He was feeling fairly well that afternoon I think and all went off well—especially as she didn't ask for an autograph—which I was dreading, knowing what the result would be if she did. Lord Blyth sent him, about three weeks ago, a most useful and costly present—and he hasn't acknowledged it, and I do not expect he is going to do so. He never, now, acknowledges presents or books. A man wrote to him the other day

"Dear Sir:

I am wondering why the devil you don't answer letters."

There is no muzzling here—if there were poor Wessex would have to be put to sleep as he gets into a frantic state of rage when he is muzzled and no-one dare go near him. The difficulty is, I believe, getting dogs through areas where the muzzling order is in force. An American lady who has taken Osmington House told me that she took her dog north in her car and when she arrived at her destination—a hotel where she had reserved rooms—she was not allowed to stay there because of the dog, and she had to motor on miles further to a Town where she was allowed to have the dog.

You are lucky in having someone who can look after Pietro when you go away. We have a man and his wife who live on the premises, and, unfortunately, their child, a spoiled girl of 13. Now they have introduced a cousin, who is really very good, as house-parlour-maid—but four in the kitchen is too many these times.

I hope that the coal strike will not spread to the railways and prevent your coming. I see the papers say that the miners can hold out for six weeks. If the railwaymen strike too I think it quite possible that the Government will have to give in to them.

I think I must not continue this letter as my brain seems not to be working properly.

With love,

Yours affectionately,
Florence Hardy.

Text   MS. (typed, with envelope) Colby.
the play: the forthcoming Dorchester production of *The Return of the Native*.   *long*: FEH typed 'llng'.   *old friends*: unidentified, but 'academician' suggests Sir Hamo Thornycroft, RA, the sculptor, and his wife Agatha.   *father and daughter*: perhaps TH's cousin John Antell and his daughter Gertrude.   *Kaye-Smith*: Sheila Kaye-Smith (1887–1956), author of regional novels.   *Lord Blyth*: James Blyth, 1st Baron Blyth; the gift is unidentified, but he had sent TH onions a year before (*CL*, v. 339).   *"Dear . . . letters."*: this document (DCM), a correspondence card more accurately quoted in *Life and Work* (437), was written by Alun H. Jones of Letchworth.   *muzzling*: muzzling of dogs had been made compulsory in areas affected by rabies.   *American lady*: unidentified; the house belonged to Major Hew Crichton.   *coal strike*: it ended 4 Nov. 1920 without involving the railway workers.

[The post-war resumption of activities by the Dorchester Debating and Dramatic Society had led almost inevitably to the staging of another of TH's novels by the 'Hardy Players', as they now liked to term themselves. A. H. Evans, the adaptor of pre-war days, having left the area, the task of dramatizing *The Return of the Native* fell to the Society's producer Thomas Tilley, a prominent citizen and former mayor of Dorchester. TH himself was much entertained, as always, by theatrical business, and involved himself in the production to the extent of providing an abbreviated reconstruction of the Dorset mumming play of St George. For FEH, however, the chief concern was her husband's obvious attraction to the increasingly beautiful Gertrude Bugler in the central role of Eustacia Vye.]

To Sydney Cockerell

MAX GATE, | DORCHESTER.
26th Dec: '20.

Dear Mr Cockerell:

We hope that your children are now quite well & lively again & that Mrs Cockerell is feeling stronger. And we hope that you all spent a happy Christmas & that 1921 will be for you all a most prosperous & happy year.

I return, with most grateful thanks for the trouble you have taken, the proof of the poem, which T.H. has corrected. Thank you also for that most amusing little book. I have been reading it aloud to my husband & we think it very good. Because I appeared yesterday in a very skimpy & up-to-date tea frock he christened me 'Madge Asking-for-it.' Anyone more unlike, I flatter myself . . . . or perhaps regret!!

We, contrary to our usual custom, have spent a most exciting Christmas. Yesterday the Mummers (under our beloved Mr Tilley) came & performed in the drawing room here, to the intense joy of T.H. his brother & sister (whom I had here) & the rest of the household. And friends who accompanied them fiddled to us & sang carols outside—the *real* old Bockhampton carols. Then they came in had refreshments in the dining room & we had a very delightful time with them—Miss Bugler looking prettier than ever in her mumming dress. T.H. has lost his heart to her entirely, but as she is soon getting married I don't let that cast me down *too* much. But the other members of the company are being a *little* upset by *all* the applause being given to her, & Mrs Tilley says "We'd better send Miss Bugler to London *alone* on the 27th, (of Jan—when they perform there) as the rest of us are not wanted." So you see it *is* possible to have *too* good a leading lady. Will you be able to see it there do you think or will you come down *here* to see it with T.H. at Weymouth? We shall be delighted to see you here *whenever you are able to come.* T. is very well. At the party (of the Mummers etc) last night he was so gay—& one of them said to me that he had never seen him so young & happy & excited. He is now—this afternoon—writing a poem with great spirit: always a sign of well-being with him. Needless to say it is an intensely dismal poem.

Our very best wishes to you all,

Yours very sincerely,
Florence Hardy.

P.S. I do not yet know the date of the Weymouth performance—I have your programme—waiting here until you come. F.H.

Text   MS. Beinecke.
poem: FEH's privately printed pamphlet of TH's Armistice Day poem, 'And there was a great calm' (Purdy, 211).   *little book*: unidentified.   *Mr Tilley*: Thomas Henry Tilley (1864–1944).   *getting married*: to her cousin, Captain Ernest Frank Bugler of Beaminster.   *Mrs Tilley*: Emma Edith Tilley (1864–1956).   *to London*: for a single performance of *The Return of the Native* at the Guildhall School of Music.   *at Weymouth*: this performance appears not to have materialized.

To Louise Yearsley

Max Gate. | Dorchester
30th Dec. [1920]

My dear Louise:

So many thanks for your kind & interesting Xmas letter. I am now writing to wish you all three a very happy & prosperous New Year. I trust that it will bring you all good luck, & no disappointments of any kind—& the best of health.

We have had a rather lively Christmas in one way & another—so many people having desired to pay their 'respex' to T.H. I estimate that between 50 & 60 people have been in this house, as guests, since Christmas day— but that includes the mummers & two little tea-parties. I tell T.H that next week I will keep everyone rigorously at bay—but at present he seems well enough & *most* cheerful.

I am sure you will admire Miss Bugler in 'The Return of the Native'. She is a beautiful creature, only 24, & really nice & refined. She tells everyone that she is taking my advice *not* to go on the stage, & I am puzzled as to *when* I did give that advice—but I think *T.H* did—he is quite crazy about her, & also much admires the photograph of the new Mrs Clement Shorter— sent us by the proud husband. I say there's safety in numbers.

I want to go up to Town *soon* but really it is difficult to get away. I haven't even time to get to Weymouth or Bournemouth. By the way our telephone no is 43 Dorchester if ever you wanted to ring us up. We have had several calls from London lately, all wonderfully clear. Tommy grows the sweetest little fellow, but it is tragic to think of his going to Canada to that father. However Marjorie knows what he is like, & if she insists upon going no one can prevent her. Over there I foresee that she'll have to work to support not only the boy & herself but the husband. And *yet* she seems fond of him, now he is at a distance.

With love to you all & every good wish.

Always yours affectionately,
Florence Hardy—

Text   MS. Eton.   Date   Year from internal evidence.
proud husband: Shorter had recently married, as his second wife, Annie Doris Banfield.
Tommy: her nephew Thomas Soundy; see letter of 10 Nov. 1918.   *to Canada*: specifically to Windsor, Ontario; FEH, always protective of Margaret (familiarly Marjorie) Soundy, her youngest sister, had little sympathy with Reginald Soundy's difficulties in finding post-war employment.

To Sydney Cockerell

MAX GATE, | DORCHESTER.
31st. January 1921.

Dear Mr Cockerell:

I wrote off last night rather too hurriedly, after writing orders for cyder, meat and other mundane things—and after typing several letters for T.H.

and I feel that I did not say half that I should like to have said—or meant to say.

Anyhow, I am not troubling you about that—on the very day of your departure for a well-earned but too-brief rest. I enclose a letter with a question from T.H. Is it a genuine letter from the right John Burns? He wondered rather whether it might be a trick played by some spurious John Burns to obtain an autograph. But the writing and the tone of the letter seems genuine to me. Do not trouble to reply until you have leisure.

By the way I went to see the painting of T.H. at the Grafton Galleries, exhibited by the National Portrait Society. It is by Jaques Blanche, and I expect you know it. What do you think of it? Mr Debenham intends to purchase it, I believe. It gave me a shock when I saw it—the colouring is so unpleasant, almost cancerous, and he looks such a feeble old man. I came away quite unhappy, as I had fondly thought that it was the one perfect portrait of T.H. I suppose the truth is that I am no judge, and that no portrait would really satisfy me. I should be curious to know your impression of it if you have seen it.

I hope that you will be able to throw off depression—the almost inevitable result of influenza I believe. I know, as well as anyone, I think, what depression is. Night after night I lie awake and face gloom unutterable. I try to think that it is merely physical and that it will pass off some time or other. When I get away from here it vanishes almost entirely—in fact *quite* entirely, and also almost intolerable pains that I suffer from here—which proves that it is a matter of nerves and nothing else.

I hope that the change of a few days will set you right, although I wish you were going away for a longer time.

I hope that Mrs Cockerell is beginning to feel benefit from her dental operation.

With our very best wishes,

Yours sincerely,
Florence Hardy.

P.S. I did not tell you I think that my sister Margaret & her little boy are going to Canada to join that husband of hers—in April. I think it almost suicidal—but she is very determined to go. FH—

Text MS. (typed) Beinecke.

Burns: John Elliot Burns (1858–1943), labour leader, politician, and collector of antiquarian books; his brief letter to TH of 27 Jan. 1921, forwarding an article on TH from a New York newspaper or magazine, is in DCM.   *Blanche*: Jacques-Émile Blanche (1862–1942), French portrait painter; he painted TH in 1906. FEH formed a more favourable impression of the portrait after seeing it a second time (FEH to Cockerell, 28 July 1921, Beinecke).   *Debenham*:

Ernest Ridley Debenham (1865–1952), businessman and farmer.   *P.S. . . . FH—*: added in ink holograph.

To Gertrude Bugler

Max Gate, | Dorchester.
Tuesday. [1 February 1921]

Dear Miss Bugler:

I am so sorry that I did not reply to your letter yesterday but I was absolutely overwhelmed with correspondence.

I am sure you need not apologize for not having seen my sister. *She* ought to apologise to Mr Tilley for having gone behind at all. I am writing to her today to tell her how vexed I am about it. She had no business there at all, but I expect she got very excited and hardly knew what she was doing.

I am afraid that you did have a very trying time—but no doubt there were agreeable moments.

With regard to what you ask me about writing your impressions I can only answer your question straightforwardly. You say "Would I write them?" Frankly I would not. I do not want to seem unfriendly to the Dorset Year Book as I have already refused to answer some silly questions, "Confessions" they are called, and Mr Galpin also asked me to write—which I am not able to do. I do honestly think that if anyone wrote Impressions of the London Audience it ought to be Mr Tilley. I think all this booming and trying to make it a one star play will be the downfall of the Hardy plays. I must be frank, as you asked me to be—and I may not be right of course. I am afraid Mr Flower's article will vex many of the caste, and I am sorry for that, as I have a great regard for Mr Flower whom I look upon as one of the most honest and downright men of my acquaintance. He is a valued friend of mine and I do not really think he wrote that article in any spirit of vindictiveness. Both Mr Hardy and I think he was really actuated by a great—perhaps exaggerated—admiration for my husband's work—especially "The Return of the Native". Both he and Mr Baughan were annoyed, I expect, by the ridiculous and utterly dishonest booming that the Daily Mail started. I know, as well as they do, how such things are started, and they did well to call it a journalistic stunt, for that was precisely what it was. In the long run these things do far more harm than good, and are apt to bring ridicule upon what would otherwise have justly been acknowledged to be a very good amateur performance. However the Times and other papers gave a more just appreciation. I remember so well what Sir J. M. Barrie said to me, when he came to see the "Country Scenes from the Dynasts" and he is as good a judge of acting and plays as any man in England—in fact in the world. He saw much to admire and a few things to criticise, but there was none of the excessive laudation.

I am afraid that you felt very tired after it all. It must have been a great strain on you. I am so glad that you had those pretty bouquets.

Yours sincerely,
F. E. Hardy.

Text MS. (typed) Bugler.   *Date* From internal evidence.

my sister: G. Bugler's note on the MS. indicates that it was Eva Dugdale who went backstage following the London performance of *The Return of the Native*.   *Mr Tilley*: see letter of 26 Dec. 1920 and headnote.   *Mr Galpin*: Stanley Galpin, London paper merchant and editor of the 1921 *Year-Book* of the Society of Dorset Men; although the *Year-Book*'s report of the London performance featured G. Bugler in accompanying photographs there was no article by G. Bugler herself.   *Mr Flower's article*: Newman Flower (1879–1964), Dorset-born London publisher; his review in the *Evening Standard*, 28 Jan. 1921, criticized both the incoherence of the play itself and the 'affectation' of G. Bugler's acting.   *Mr Baughan*: Edward Algernon Baughan, drama critic; his *Daily News* review, 28 Jan. 1921, referred dismissively to the 'much-boomed Gertrude Bugler, the victim of "stunt" journalists'.   *the Times*: the reviewer (29 Jan. 1921) judged G. Bugler's acting 'extremely good for an amateur' though not 'on the same level as her personal appearance'.   *"Country . . . Dynasts"*: i.e. *Wessex Scenes from The Dynasts*; see letter of 13 Dec. 1916 and headnote.   *excessive laudation*: writing to Cockerell, 30 Jan. 1921 (Beinecke), FEH privately agreed with Flower's and Baughan's criticisms of G. Bugler and recalled Barrie's having 'refused to see in her the material for a great actress'.   *bouquets*: FEH typed 'bouquests'.

To Howard Bliss

MAX GATE, | DORCHESTER.
3rd April '21.

Dear Mr Bliss:

It is quite unpardonable of me not to have written before to thank you for your most generous—*far too* generous—& greatly prized gift. But if it leaves a gap in *your* collection, then I must not take it from you. Have you, or are you likely to obtain, another copy? If not I think I must keep this 'Pair of Blue Eyes' for a few weeks, to read in the 1st edition, & then return it. I have always wanted to see it. I have never even seen a 1st edition of it before. And this is indeed an interesting copy, having belonged to Coventry Patmore—who wrote to my husband so kindly about it.

He (T.H) was very interested to hear about the page of MS. in the first Mrs Hardy's writing. She did indeed frequently copy for him any pages that had many alterations. She liked doing it. There are some pages of her handwriting in the MS. of several of the novels. I can find none though in my MS. of 'The Woodlanders'. The mystery to my husband is how that page came into anyone's possession. I imagine that when the bundle of MS. was sent to be bound this extra page was found by someone & kept.

But my husband says he will try to find you another page of manuscript, upon the authenticity of which there can be no doubt.

We have no doubt that Mr Shorter's collection is a fine one—though neither of us has ever seen it—nor indeed his house at Missenden, nor the present Mrs Shorter. I hope to find for you a rare little pamphlet which is not in his collection, nor, so far as I know, in anyone else's, except my own—a genuine 1st edition—the first of my husband's writings which was printed in pamphlet form. I am going to Town tomorrow but will look for it & send it to you immediately on my return.

We shall be delighted to see you whenever you are in this neighbourhood again.

Yours sincerely,
Florence Hardy—

Text   MS. (with envelope) Princeton.

Bliss: Howard Bliss (1894–1977), musician, art collector, and one of the earliest and most successful collectors of Hardy's books and MSS.   *return it*: when Bliss insisted that he had another copy, FEH accepted the three vols. as a gift (now in DCM); the first vol. has Coventry Patmore's bookplate, the signature of Patmore's wife, and, tipped in, Patmore's letter to TH of 29 Mar. 1875.   *none . . . Woodlanders'*: in fact, as Bliss later discovered (see letter of 14 Dec. 1924) and has noted on this MS., numerous pages of *The Woodlanders* MS. are in ELH's hand.   *Missenden*: i.e. Great Missenden, Bucks.; for Shorter's marriage see letter of 30 Dec. 1920.   *in pamphlet form*: 'To Shakespeare After Three Hundred Years' was the first of FEH's privately printed pamphlets, but she perhaps refers here to the never-issued preliminary broadside, of which Bliss owned a signed copy (Purdy, 177–8).   *to Town*: to have six of her teeth removed, although the operation was in fact postponed until ten days later (*CL*, vi. 81–2).

[One of the most attractive features of life at Max Gate during the 1920s was the warmth of the welcome extended to younger writers who had excited Hardy's notice by their writings or brought themselves to his attention by calling, pilgrim-fashion, at his door. Forster, already a well-established figure by this date, also had the recommendation of his connections with Siegfried Sassoon and with many of TH's Cambridge friends. In later years his friendship with T. E. Lawrence was a greater recommendation still.]

To E. M. Forster

MAX GATE, | DORCHESTER.
17th June. '21.

Dear Mr Forster:

We were exceedingly pleased to hear from you, & my husband thanks you much for your kind messages.

We have often thought of you & spoken of you, but had no idea that you were in India. You must be having a romantic & interesting time. But you did not tell us in your letter how long you were staying in India, which is what we are anxious to know. I hope that you do not intend to remain there for several years—interesting & delightful though it may be.

The Keats first edition is a wonderful little volume. I hope that you will be able to see it some day. The address is not yet presented so it is possible your signature may yet be on it—which would add to its value for T.H.

We (both T.H. & myself) have received several indignant letters from authors demanding of us *why* they had not been asked to join in the address. Dear old Mrs W. K. Clifford wrote me a very grieved letter. I could hardly point out to her that it was a presentation from 'younger authors.'

T.H. is wonderfully well. Even I, knowing the splendid soundness of his constitution, have been surprised the last week or two, to see how well he bore the heat, & how well he can walk & cycle. I think that cycling at his age is marvellous.

We have not seen Siegfried Sassoon for a long time. I wish we had. He promised to come to stay with us in June, but we have not heard from him since he wrote to us from Wales, in May, when he went to investigate the coal strike. John Masefield has been to see us, & is making a large model of a ship for T.H. as an ornament for his study. It is what T.H. always longed to possess as a boy, but now he rather wonders what he shall do with it.

We have lately made the acquaintance of Walter de la Mare in the flesh—in the spirit we seem to have known him long & well. He is, as friends had reported to us, one of the most utterly delightful of beings; & T.H. was happy in his visit. He stayed with us for a couple of days.

I hope very much that when you are in England again we may see you. Your letter has given us both much pleasure. It was kind of you to write. With our cordial good wishes,

Yours sincerely,
Florence Hardy.

Text MS. King's College, Cambridge.
Forster: Edward Morgan Forster (1879–1970), novelist, currently serving as private secretary to the Maharajah of Dewas State Senior. *Keats first edition*: a first edition of *Lamia, Isabella, The Eve of St. Agnes, and Other Poems* (now DCM) had been presented to TH on his birthday by more than a hundred 'younger comrades in the craft of letters' (*Life and Work*, 445), although their signed address did not arrive until early Sept. 1921. *Clifford*: Sophia Lucy Clifford (d. 1929), novelist; the widow of W. K. Clifford, the philosopher, she continued to write as Mrs W. K. Clifford. *coal strike*: a national miners' strike had begun at the end of Mar. 1921. *Masefield*: see letter of 5 Apr. 1914; the ship is now in DCM. *de la Mare*: Walter de la Mare (1873–1956), poet and novelist, stayed at Max Gate in mid-June 1921.

To Charlotte Mew

MAX GATE, | DORCHESTER.

2nd October 1921.

My dear Miss Mew:

I have meant some time to write to thank you for your kindness in having my sister to tea with you. She wrote me such a glowing account of it, & really it was good of you to have her—for she is not in the least literary—& her life has been exceedingly narrowing, besides being most frightfully hard—& full of painful & unpleasant experiences.

We hope that you are well, & that you are writing more poems. Lines from 'On the road to the sea' are continually echoing in my mind. In our little conservatory for two years I have grown white geraniums because of two lines in 'Madeleine in Church'. I had never seen "the dreams upon the eyes of white geraniums in the dusk." before.

I hope that your sister is well. Will you please give her a greeting from me.

I hope to be in London in a week or two but fear I can hardly be away more than a couple of nights. I should so like it if I could see you then. I will write again as soon as I really know if I can get away—& when—& then perhaps you could let me know if you could spare me an hour or so— to have lunch or tea with me.

Mr Cockerell was here for one night last week. I thought he did not look well. I think it is a pity that he pursues people so ardently as it seems to be wearing him out. He is going to see Conrad this week I think.

T.H. sends you his kindest regards, & I my love—

Yours very sincerely,

Florence Hardy—

Text MS. (with envelope) Berg.
my sister: evidently Eva Dugdale. *"the dreams . . . dusk."*: accurately quoted from C. Mew's 'Madeleine in Church'. *your sister*: her younger sister, Anne, with whom she lived and

whose death from cancer in 1927 seems to have contributed to her own suicide in Mar. 1928.   *see Conrad*: Cockerell's diary (BL) shows that he stayed with the Conrads near Canterbury over the night of 6 Oct. 1921.

To Sydney Cockerell

MAX GATE, | DORCHESTER.

3rd Jan. '22.

Dear Mr Cockerell:

I feel the most ungrateful wretch in the universe for not having written before, to thank you for your most kind gift, also for your suggestion that we should lunch together in Town & go to a matinee—which would have been a great treat to me.

You did—since you really wish to know—send me that same book last January. So I will return it to you, as no doubt someone else will be delighted to have the copy. Please do not send anything in its place, as receiving the kind gift did, indeed, give me great pleasure.

As for London, I had arranged to go up today, lunch with the McDowalls, & go home for one night. But T.H. seemed so strongly opposed to it that I gave up the plan. To begin with he said he could not have my sister—or *anyone* here. He said he could not bear the strain of having to talk or listen to her, or to anyone. Then he said he felt very ill, & years older than six months ago—& *really* he began to look very unwell, & I was alarmed at what seemed to be a marked change. He began to put his papers in order & told me he was doing it lest he should die suddenly, & also gave me minute directions as to what I should do if he did die. By this time I began to think it would be wrong to leave him & so I sent off & cancelled all my engagements—at least the three I had made—whereupon he suddenly became quite well, which was a tremendous relief. Today he is full of vigour & quite cheerful.

Perhaps it is that the prospect of being left does really alarm him & makes him feel ill. It may be as well, too, that I did not go to London as I feel I could hardly have stood the journey. We are a cheerful pair—T.H. & I.

You must have had a pleasant Christmas. We were quite alone, the only caller during the week being Mr Jeune (Mrs Hanbury's father) [*remainder of letter absent*]

Text   MS. Beinecke.

same book: unidentified.   *Mr Jeune*: John Frederic Symons Jeune (1849–1925), formerly Examiner of Standing Orders for the Houses of Lords and Commons; he was the father of

Dorothy Hanbury of Kingston Maurward (see letter of 3 Dec. 1915) and related by marriage to ELH's uncle, Archdeacon E. H. Gifford.

To Siegfried Sassoon

MAX GATE, | DORCHESTER.
February 9th. [1922]

Dear Siegfried Sassoon:

It was so kind of you to write, & at just the right moment for T.H. was very hurt, I think, about that article, & he is only just recovering from a severe illness, & is not yet out of the doctor's hands. If I had read the article myself first I would not have let him see it, but as it was in the Mercury I naturally thought it would be at least a just estimate. Three weeks ago, for just a couple of days, I was much alarmed for him as two doctors thought there was something *terribly* wrong, for which nothing could be done—no operation on account of his age. But I am thankful (*how* thankful you will understand) that they were utterly wrong & now he is rapidly gaining strength & will, I trust, be quite himself very soon.

One night he was talking to himself, & I heard a few sentences about critics—of what nature you may guess—when suddenly he said in a loud & clear voice: "I wrote my poems for men like Siegfried Sassoon." I have meant, ever since, to let you know, & your note gives me the opportunity.

He said once or twice during his illness that he so much wished you lived somewhere near—at Weymouth or somewhere like that.

The volume of poems in in the hands of the printers—I do wish you could have helped him with the final selection—for there was only me, & if I think a poem ought to be left out I cannot bear to tell him so. He is now hard at work on a preface—he is able to be in his study & working —& I think too that would be better submitted to someone other than myself—although of course I appreciate it & love reading it, & listening to it.

How delightful that Dr Head is writing a preface. Did I tell you how much we liked them both.

Thank you again so much for writing, & for all you do for T.H.

Yours very sincerely.
Florence Hardy.

P.S. I have had printed a little 1st edition of "Haunting Fingers" & there are alterations which T.H. thinks may interest you. I am sending you a copy. F.H.

Text MS. Eton. *Date* Year supplied on MS. by Sassoon.
that article: Joseph M. Hone's 'The Poetry of Mr. Hardy', *London Mercury*, 5 (Feb. 1922), 396–405; though ostensibly respectful, Hone's article was essentially destructive, observing, e.g., that 'Mr. Hardy has qualified more than once for inclusion in an anthology of the Hundred Worst Poems by famous writers' (396).   *volume of poems*: *Late Lyrics and Earlier*, pub. by Macmillan in May 1922; TH's 'preface' appeared as 'Apology'.   *in in the hands*: 'is in the hands' obviously intended.   *Dr Head . . . both*: the anthology, *Pages from the Works of Thomas Hardy* (London, 1922), by Ruth Head (née Mayhew), included an introduction by her husband Henry Head (1861–1940); the latter, a distinguished neurologist, had been a colleague of William Halse Rivers, who treated Sassoon at Craiglockhart Hospital in 1917.   *"Haunting Fingers"*: included with 'Voices from Things Growing' in another of FEH's privately printed pamphlets (Purdy, 213–14).

To Sydney Cockerell

MAX GATE, | DORCHESTER.
April 2nd. [1922]

Dear Mr Cockerell:

T.H. thanks you so much for sending back the proofs so carefully read. Your help has been most valuable to him. Personally I think the preface a mistake, although undoubtedly a fine bit of writing. He has managed to catch a bad cold through going to Stinsford last Tuesday in unsuitable weather—it rained while he was going. Before that he seemed to have quite regained his normal good health & had just finished with the doctor. I hope that your little Katherine is now well, & that she had not chicken-pox—& I hope the others are all well now, & Mrs Cockerell stronger.

We are hoping to see you during the Easter holidays, as you promised. I expect you will be coming after the 17th, as I know you like to be at the Museum about Bank Holiday time—& that will suit us well, as I expect our servants will expect to have Easter Monday off. But if you would rather come then it will make no difference. I am afraid you thought me very extravagant when you read in T.H's letter that we had *three* new servants coming in—but one is a child of 15, who has to wait on the cook. I found I could only get a cook by having a between-maid. One housemaid left saying that the place was "so awful quiet" it got on her nerves—the next, after a few days here, said being here was "like living in a dungeon", & the present one, who came a fortnight ago, says it is so dull here she thinks she will try to get a place at Weymouth. I have not been anywhere since Christmas—not even once to tea with a clergyman's wife, which is the dullest form of entertainment I think exists—but they do not seem inclined to follow my good example.

Today has been enlivened by the reading of J. C. Squire's article in the Observer upon Mrs Watts-Dunton's book on Swinburne. T.H. read it at first quite seriously, thinking that Squire admired the book. "He thinks *well of it*," he said, "He says that he wishes other great poets had been so fortunate in their biographers." It is the most amusing thing I have read for a long time.

I am grateful for your perception that the new volume of poems is quite incomplete in having no poem on Wessie. In vain have I long pointed out this defect—a grave one. T.H. says that he could write one if Wessie were *dead*—but why should the poor little animal have to *die* before a poem is written to him? How about Mrs Browning's Flush? However I must admit that Wessie bears up well, & continues to snarl & growl & fly at people with all his accustomed spirit & sweetness. Other people's dogs are dying all round—Mrs Henniker's nice dog has died of cancer in the throat, Granville-Barker's delightful Irish terrier of gastric influenza, & my own good old dog at home of the same complaint a day or two ago—but Wessex flourishes, although a poem awaits him if he only had the thoughtfulness to pop off.

Yours sincerely

F.E.H

Text MS. Beinecke. Date Year supplied on MS. by Cockerell.
proofs: of *Late Lyrics and Earlier*. T.H's letter: of 22 Mar. 1922 (*CL*, vi. 124). book on Swinburne: Clara Watts-Dunton's *The Home Life of Swinburne*, ironically reviewed in the Observer, 2 Apr. 1922, by John Collings Squire (1884–1958), poet and man of letters. if Wessie were dead: TH did later write 'A Popular Personage at Home' during Wessex's lifetime; see letter of 10 Dec. 1925. Mrs Browning's Flush: see FED letter of 13 Jan. 1911.

[The extent to which FEH felt threatened by Gertrude Bugler's youth and beauty emerges painfully from her extreme sensitivity—and, indeed, hostility—to the younger woman's having committed the social *faux-pas* of calling at Max Gate and asking to see Mr Hardy instead of observing the formality of first addressing herself to Mrs Hardy, as mistress of the house. In the long and difficult relationship between the two women this was by no means the only instance of FEH's seeking to take her stand upon the high ground of manners, ethics, or concern for TH's health and reputation.]

To Gertrude Bugler

Max Gate, | Dorchester.

June 13th 1922.

Dear Mrs Bugler

I am afraid I seemed very astonished yesterday when you told me that Mr Watkins had said that you might call—not on me, but on Mr Hardy. As you must know this is a most extraordinary thing to do. In the first place all invitations to Max Gate, naturally come from me, as is the custom, & again it is not usual in our station of life for any lady to call upon a gentleman. It is simply "not done". Since my marriage all calls at this house have been made on me—it is also the custom for the husband's friends, when calling, to ask for the wife, as their call is supposed to be upon her—unless of course it is upon business. In that case they do not call in the ordinary visiting hours. A lady who wished to see my husband on business wrote & asked me if she might call, & I of course arranged a meeting, since I understood her business. I think this is the only time a lady has called expressly to see my husband, though many have been brought here for that purpose in which case I am regarded & treated as the hostess. I am explaining all this as it seemed so very extraordinary to be told that Mr Watkins had said you might call to see Mr Hardy as you had "much to tell him". I am not a great stickler for etiquette, but there is a certain amount of courtesy due to myself, which I must insist upon from all who visit my house. But I still think there must be some misunderstanding. I shall always be pleased to see you if you call upon me, & if you have any *business* matter to talk of with Mr Hardy I shall be glad to arrange for that, too.

Yours very truly,
Florence Hardy.

Text   Transcript (in G. Bugler's hand) Bugler; original MS. apparently donated to the National Library of Iceland, although as yet unlocated there.

Mr Watkins: William Watkins, Dorset-born businessman, founder and first secretary of the Society of Dorset Men in London.   *misunderstanding*: both G. Bugler's notes on the transcript and the typed draft (Bugler) of her reply to FEH insist that she knew 'that a lady does not call on a gentleman' and did not think of herself as being on visiting terms at Max Gate 'in the ordinary way', but that TH had invited her to 'come over' whenever she needed help or advice.

To Gertrude Bugler

MAX GATE, | DORCHESTER.
June 17th. [1922]

Dear Mrs Bugler:

I am very glad to have your letter as there have been I expect, misunderstanding upon misunderstandings—which are now in so hopeless a tangle that it seems hopeless to remove them by a letter. Now that we have reached the point of discussing them frankly it is just possible that we may be able to clear them away—only I fear that it is impossible to explain in a letter what has really started all the trouble. It has nothing, I assure you, to do with those horrible reporters, and I readily accept your assurance that the Barrie story did not come through you. I see in another paper his name is again mentioned in reference to us—the fact that he comes and stays here (which we particularly wished never to have mentioned in print) and that my husband liked his speech, which no-one in the world but Mr Watkins knew—and also that we had motored to Bournemouth and the North of Dorset with Mr Watkins. Anyhow that is evidently nothing to do with you. Although Barrie is my greatest friend I don't know how long that will survive if he thinks I gossip or brag about him to reporters, as the paragraphs lead one to imagine. Still this is outside the letter and I am sorry I mentioned it.

The main thing that I wish to explain here is that I deeply regret you should have thought I treated you as a stranger and an unwelcome intruder. I did try to tell you, only at the moment it was difficult, that my distrait and worried manner was due to the fact that a sister, whom I shall not see again for months, was just leaving me under trying circumstances, I had only that afternoon heard most upsetting news about my sister in Canada—my youngest and favourite sister—who is in terrible trouble, and also my other sister here had just told me of a discovery she had made about one of my servants. I was frightfully upset at the moment you called, and really meant to have been "out" to callers, only the wretched dog rushed barking at the door and I went to try and keep him from flying at the postman, as I thought it was he at the door. Beyond being worried I think my greeting to you was normal, for I really did feel pleased to see you, though sorry things were in such an awkward state at that moment. What you said was this—if you remember—I think I quote your exact words:

"Mr Watkins told me I might call to see *Mr Hardy*. I have much—much to tell him". I remember you twice repeated the word "much". I must, to be perfectly honest, confess that I should have been surprised at any young lady saying that to me, though I quite see now how it came about, and you did not mean what it implied to me. I am afraid I have been rather spoiled by our friends so identifying me with my husband, that they always address their conversation to me jointly, not to him alone, and his friends almost without exception address their letters to me, as to both, and I answer in his name, and in discussing business matters he always says "we". We are, in fact, almost one person. It seems impossible to get things right in a letter, and if I were only nearer Beaminster I would call and see you, for I feel certain that now we have reached this point of frankness things could be soon cleared up—only there are some things that one cannot write.

I would say that I am sorry I wrote, but if it helps to clear matters up only a little I cannot regret it, except in so far as it may have hurt your feelings.

As for Mr Watkins—I still have my own opinion about the way he conveyed the message, if you have an accurate recollection of what he said. And I do not think my husband would have sent a message through Mr Watkins, although I may be wrong. That wasn't quite the right way to do it, if he did,—at least in my opinion. Several times both before your marriage and after it, I have been on the point of writing to you, and explaining certain things, but something—perhaps it was pride—prevented.

With regard to your not being on "visiting terms" at Max Gate I can only say again that there is no-one in Dorchester would more cordially and gladly receive you, did I understand your visit was to me. In fact I shall always be glad to see you.

I most sincerely hope that your forebodings about having played your last part in the Hardy plays is not true—except that I have a feeling that this next play—"Desperate Remedies" will be the last, but from reasons entirely unconnected with yourself. But I may be, and hope I am, wrong, and that you will another year be quite well and strong and able to enter into them.

Yours sincerely,
Florence Hardy.

Text MS. (typed) Bugler. *Date* Year from internal evidence.
horrible reporters . . . Barrie story: apparent references to the 'booming' of *The Return of the Native* by the London press; see letter of 1 Feb. 1921. *stays here*: most recently in May 1922. *his speech*: Barrie's Rectorial Address ('Courage') to St Andrews University, 3 May 1922; a copy of the printed text inscribed to FEH by Barrie, June 1922, was in the Max Gate library. *have thought*: FEH typed 'have though'. *a sister*: evidently Eva Dugdale, summoned to assist in nursing T.H. during an acute episode of diarrhoea. *to me jointly*: FEH typed 'to be jointly'. *I answer*: FEH typed 'I amswer'. *Beaminster*: in north-west Dorset, where G. Bugler lived. *In fact . . . you*: holograph insertion. *"Desperate Remedies"*: produced, as *A Desperate Remedy*, in Dec. 1922, although G. Bugler's pregnancy prevented her from participating. *but from*: FEH typed 'bu from'.

To Siegfried Sassoon

MAX GATE, | DORCHESTER.
21st July '22.

Dear Siegfried Sassoon:

At the risk of being a nuisance I must write a line to say how much we liked Edmund Blunden. His visit was an immense pleasure to us both. Isn't he a *real* poet—every inch of him—T.H. was saying only an hour ago that if we had had Keats here he would have been like that. I feel now *most* thankful that he gained that prize, & I only wish it were £1,000. instead of £100.

The funniest thing though was Wessie's adoration of him. He thought him the most perfect being that had ever entered Max Gate, & he lavished blandishments on him. The moped & fretted for two days after E. Blunden went.

I do trust he will have a fortunate career—(E.B.).

E. M. Forster's visits were delightful too. T.H. a little bit difficult to know at first, but before he went had discovered how much he liked him, & said he reminded him of someone he knew—& adored—when he was a boy at school.

We hope you are well. Don't answer this please or I'll be ashamed of having bothered you with a letter.

Yours sincerely,
Florence Hardy.

Text   MS. Eton.
Blunden: Edmund Charles Blunden (1896–1974), poet and prose-writer; his visit had been arranged by Sassoon.   *that prize*: the Hawthornden Prize (for writers under 40) for *The Shepherd, and Other Poems of Peace and War*; Blunden had earlier sent a copy to T.H. (*CL*, vi. 136).   *The moped*: 'He moped' or perhaps 'The dog moped' presumably intended.   *T.H. a little*: 'found him' evidently omitted by FEH in turning the page.

To Sydney Cockerell

MAX GATE, | DORCHESTER.
August 3rd. 1922

Dear Mr Cockerell—

I hope that you will excuse a typed letter. It is the only way I have of getting through my letters. I have been meaning to write to you for a very long time and we were delighted to have your letter. I hope that you are keeping well and that Mrs Cockerell and the children are well and having a good time. I wish that we were fortunate enough to possess a beautiful old farm-house that we could lend you for your holidays. It must be very nice for Mr Blunt to be able to see something of them all, and you for the week-ends.

T.H. is really wonderfully well. Yesterday he cycled to Talbothays and did it well, not even feeling tired afterwards. This is his first ride this summer— cycle-ride I mean of course. He has got rid of all minor ailments for the time being, and is very busy. We shall be exceedingly pleased to see you in September, as you promise. I expect that Dorothy Allhusen—Lady St. Helier's younger daughter, will be with us for two nights—Aug. 31st and Sept. 1st. or thereabouts. After that we shall be quite alone. Sassoon has been down, staying at the Kings Arms. Mrs Henniker and her old German maid came the week after and stayed at the King's Arms too. But this so exceedingly unpleasant to me that I feel I had rather they did not come. It is quite painful to feel that friends, such as these, are in Dorchester and not staying here. Mrs Henniker has been dangerously ill since her return, with two nurses, and had to be moved in an ambulance from the house she had taken for the summer, at Highgate, to her own home in Hyde Park Square. I hope it was not the bad cooking at the King's Arms that made her ill. E. M. Forster stayed there a few days later for a couple of nights and he said that it was pretty bad.

I should love to see the Queen's dolls' house. Do you think there would be any chance of my having a private view of it? I shall be in Town early in September for a day, if not before. Princess Marie Louise has written two or three letters to T.H. about it. A tiny volume of some of his poems is to be in the library, but he is not copying them out, merely signing them. I asked Sassoon if I could see the Dolls' House, and he said he thought it could easily be managed, but he didn't say how. He is, as I expect you know, in Germany.

We have been looking over T.H.'s will, and really it is an appalling document. If anything should happen to you the literary executorship falls into the hands of either Gosse or Shorter. I cannot imagine what he was doing when he arranged that. Even he was rather appalled when he read it, for he had forgotten what was in the will. He realizes the necessity of making a fresh one and suggests going to London in October for that purpose. But I think it a pity to put that off for a single week, although of course it is not likely that all of us are going to die suddenly. It is a pity that a good will was not made years ago, under proper advice. I don't think that anyone of eighty-two can make a really good will, except under expert guidance. And the solicitor who drew it up has now gone rather queer in his head and is suffering from melancholia.

I could not help being amused at the two names—Gosse and Shorter—both hating each other, and neither, to my mind, in the least degree suitable for a literary executor. However it all the more incumbent upon you to keep strong and well to prevent such an awful situation being possible.

I rather envy you your holiday at home without servants. I should like to be in a house without any for a fortnight. We have hardly been motoring at all this summer, but the Granville-Barkers sent for us and took us to an afternoon service at Exeter Cathedral and then sent us home again in their car. How nice to be rich enough to do things like that. They brought John Drinkwater to see us one day last week.

Yours very sincerely,

F.E.H.

Text MS. (typed) Beinecke.

Mr Blunt: Wilfrid Scawen Blunt; see letter of 12 Aug. 1916.   *Allhusen*: see letter of 22 June 1918.   *German maid*: Anna Hirschmann.   *But this so*: 'But this is so' clearly intended. *to be moved*: FEH typed 'to me moved'.   *Queen's dolls' house*: this elaborately furnished model (now at Windsor Castle) seems not to have been finally completed and presented to Queen Mary until 1924.   *Marie Louise*: Princess Marie Louise of Schleswig-Holstein (1872–1956), a granddaughter of Queen Victoria; see *CL*, vi. 136.   *for that purpose*: TH's new (and final) will was in fact drawn up by H. O. Lock, of the Dorchester firm of Lock Reed and Lock, and dated 24 Aug. 1922.   *the solicitor*: see letter of 3 Mar. 1916.   *However it all*: 'However it is all' clearly intended.   *Drinkwater*: John Drinkwater (1882–1937), poet and playwright.

To Gertrude Bugler

MAX GATE, | DORCHESTER.

19th Oct. [1922]

My dear Mrs Bugler:

It was very kind of you to send the enclosed & I look upon it as an act of true friendship. But I took your word implicitly upon the matter, & out of the different stories of the affair that were told me I believed yours. I must say, though, that the letter you sent for me to see *staggered* me. However I feel I must not say what I think as Mr W. has just done me a great kindness by going to see my youngest & favourite sister in Canada, & thus relieved my mind greatly, as I have had terrible anxiety about her. He is certainly kind, & I think he is your friend, in fact I am sure he is, but I am amazed that a man who has travelled, & knows the world, should ignore one of the most elementary rules of social etiquette. It is the only time, during the ten years of my married life, that any man has behaved with such discourtesy to me. However it is all over now—& I quite understand your point of view. The amusing thing is that it is only through *me* that Mr Watkins has ever been invited here, as my husband does not care much for him, & does not altogether trust him. (I know this is quite between ourselves.)

I have asked my husband about the book. I asked him, in fact, some time ago, & he will look one out for you—I hope—& I will send it to you as soon as I get it.

I am very sorry that you are not taking part in the play. Mr Granville-Barker will not, I think, do much in the way of coaching as he has now no connection with the stage as his wife objects. I doubt if he will say one word to the performers about their acting, but I hope he will.

I am glad that you are feeling better & hope that all will be well. I hope that we shall see you again some time soon.

With kind regards

Yours very sincerely
Florence Hardy.

P.S. I really think no more now of that bygone affair. In fact we must both look upon it as an amusing instance of what errors may arise through men's blunders. FH

Text MS. Bugler.   *Date* Year from internal evidence.
the enclosed: evidently a letter to G. Bugler from William Watkins ('Mr W.'); see letter of 13 June 1922.   *the book*: T.H. seems not to have presented any of his books to G. Bugler until Dec. 1924 (*CL*, vi. 290).   *the play*: see letter of 17 June 1922.

To Ernest Rhys

MAX GATE, | DORCHESTER.
October 30th. 1922.

Dear Mr Rhys:

I owe you a hundred apologies for not replying before this to your kind letter. As a matter of fact I have been able to get a direct answer from my husband, who has been very busy and preoccupied with worrying business—cinema rights, a new edition, etc.

He admitted, when I asked him, that "The Fiddler of the Reels" was one of the best of his short stories, better than "The Three Strangers", which so many people think the best because R. L. Stevenson praised it so highly. Another that ranks very highly in his estimation—and my own—is "A Tragedy of Two Ambitions". For quite a long time "On the Western Circuit" was my own favourite, though I am not quite sure whether it would be so suitable for your purpose as the other two. Anyhow you couldn't go far wrong with "A Fiddler of the Reels".

I may be in Town next month, but I am very tied here as we have no secretary or housekeeper, and every moment of my time is occupied. By the way I did not quite understand from your letter whether your intention was to pay for publishing the story, or whether you wished permission to print it without fee. I think Macmillans would have to be consulted about that if it were the latter case, as they were rather vexed once when permission was given to publish something else without payment. You will excuse this mercenary query. As to my own articles, I must admit I am a little ashamed of them. They wanted me to write on on "Worthless Wives" and my husband so disliked that subject that I have not written another since. He thought that such an invidious subject, which it was. But I know I could write some far better ones if only I had the time.

With kind regards,

Yours sincerely,
Florence Hardy.

Text   MS. (typed) BL.

Rhys: Ernest Percival Rhys (1859–1946), author, and editor of Dent's Everyman's Library; TH's 'The Three Strangers' had been included in the Everyman *English Short Stories* of 1921 after TH himself (*CL*, vi. 97, 99) had declined to make his own choice, and the object of Rhys's renewed enquiry is unclear.   *that if it were*: FEH typed 'that is it were'.   *my own articles*: the most recent—and possibly the last—of FEH's occasional contributions to the Sunday tabloids was 'No Superfluous Women', *Weekly Dispatch*, 17 Sept. 1922, 8.   *write on on*: FEH's duplication, perhaps an error for 'write one on'.

To Sydney Cockerell

MAX GATE, | DORCHESTER.
4th. November '22.

My dear Mr Cockerell:

It was indeed most kind of you to go to see Sir Clifford Allbutt on my behalf. It was a true act of friendship and such as noone else that I know, living, would have done for me. It is certainly a great help to know what he thinks. However I shall do nothing further until I have had a chance of going to London and seeing Mr Macleod Yearsley, a personal friend of mine, who operated on my nose six or seven years ago. He is a very good surgeon and a specialist for the throat nose and ear, recommended highly by many doctors, but he harmed himself professionally some years ago by leaving his wife to live with another woman. He behaved most honourably I thought, and his wife disgracefully, but that has nothing to do, of course, with his professional skill. Anyhow I trust him most implicitly, as much as I distrust Dr Gowring, whom I have invariably found wrong in his diagnoses. You remember his saying that my husband had cancer, and then some other horrible complaint, when it was probably merely influenza. I think my sister Eva can form a more correct opinion of a case than Gowring. Every specialist I have consulted after him has declared him to be utterly wrong. I have been using some iodex ointment that Mr Yearsley prescribed two years ago, but which I foolishly did not keep on with, and there is already a remarkable improvement. I shall use that carefully for a few weeks and then go up to see Mr Yearsley. Of course Mr Yearsley told me long ago that I would never be really well until I had a good holiday and he told my sister so a short time ago, but my husband says the air here is as good as anywhere in England, and that the modern craze for holidays is absurd, and that his mother for the last twenty years of her life never had a holiday at all etc. etc. I must say that I am reluctant to leave him as he seems to depend so much upon me for every little thing and letters are far more numerous now than they have ever been. Then a very little illness pulls him down. He has a slight cold at present and I would not be away for anything, as he so obviously wants looking after.

We are very sorry that you are not coming to see us but the play is very poor this year. It is certainly not worth coming a long way to see and T.H. says he would rather you came at some other time when he could talk quietly to you.

Dorothy Allhusen has been staying at the King's Arms with her daughter Elizabeth. She is Lady St. Helier's younger daughter and one of the sweetest dearest women I know, and very very pretty. Her daughter, too, is just as nice, and T.H. loved seeing her. She asked me if I know anyone who knew G. B. Shaw very well, and I, without thinking much, gave her your name. You may have a letter from her that will explain what she wants. I hope it won't be troublesome. I hope you will meet her some day. T.H. used to carry her in his arms when she was a tiny child. Her home is at Stoke Court, part of which used to be the poet Gray's home. She is, in a way, much more simple than Mrs Henniker in her way of life and she is, all the time, doing things for other people. She had a boy and two girls, but the boy died early this year. I think she is trying to deaden her sorrow by hard work, for she is opening a home in France next year, for consumptive and neglected children from the devastated area. She is in no sense a society lady, and does not mind working with her own hands.

Your photograph has been framed and installed on our drawing-room mantlepiece and she looked at it and decided that she need not fear a very sharp rebuff from you.

I had a card yesterday from Sassoon. He says he will be home in about a week and suggests running down for a night very soon which we shall like.

I have just finished reading aloud to T.H. "The Way of All Flesh", and I cannot think how it is I have never read it before. It is a remarkable book, only T.H. thinks he spoils it by touches of spitefulness, especially about his parents and the clergy generally. He has not T.H.'s respect for the Church of England. Did you once lend us the Life of Samuel Butler? If you have it I should be so pleased if you would be kind enough to lend it to us again some day. I feel so much more interested in him now I have read that book. I have just begun to read to T.H. the new essays by Dr Inge; always thoughtful and good, but very prejudiced.

T.H. has decided that he cannot support Labour and would rather vote for the Lloyd-Georgians than anyone else, but we have only a Tory candidate here opposed to Labour. We both went and voted against Labour in the Municipal election last Wednesday, but I must admit that I felt mean in doing so. I must end this letter now or you'll never be able to read it.

Always yours sincerely,
Florence Hardy.

P.S. We were so glad to hear about Mr Doughty's pension.

Text   MS. (typed) Beinecke.
Allbutt: Sir Thomas Clifford Allbutt (1836–1925), Regius Professor of Physic at Cambridge, whom TH had known for many years; FEH had evidently sought his medical advice. *another woman*: i.e. Louise Yearsley.   *Gowring*: Benjamin William Nettlefold Gowring, the Max Gate doctor at this date.   *the play*: A Desperate Remedy.   *Her daughter*: D. Allhusen's younger daughter, Dorothea Elizabeth Allhusen (1903–26).   *Shaw*: George Bernard Shaw; D. Allhusen perhaps hoped to gain his support for one of her many 'causes'.   *Gray's home*: adjacent to Stoke Poges churchyard.   *the boy*: Henry Christian Stanley Allhusen (1899–1922).   *consumptive*: FEH typed, abandoned, but failed to delete 'consu' at the foot of the previous page.   *"The Way . . . Flesh"*: Samuel Butler's novel The Way of All Flesh, pub. posthumously in 1903.   *Life . . . Butler*: by Henry Festing Jones; see letter of 27 Dec. 1919.   *Inge*: see letter of 27 Dec. 1919; D. Allhusen had given TH a copy (DCM) of the second series of Inge's *Outspoken Essays* (London, 1922).   *support Labour*: in the General Election of 15 Nov. 1922.   *Doughty's pension*: Cockerell had been active in securing a Civil List pension for Charles M. Doughty (see letter of 8 Aug. 1920) in Oct. 1922.

To Sydney Cockerell

MAX GATE, | DORCHESTER.
26th Nov: 1922.

My dear Mr Cockerell:

All being well I should greatly enjoy seeing a performance of the Puppets, on Dec. 13th—at 5.30 o'clock. It will be a great treat. I have been asked to act as judge at a literary competition here, arranged by our Debating & Dramatic Society, on the evening of Dec. 12th. & the earlier hour—5.30.—

might be better for you. I hope T.H. will be well enough to be left. The last week has been a little depressing as the 24th was the anniversary of his sister Mary's death, & his first wife's birthday—always forgotten during her lifetime. She told me once I was the only living person who ever remembered it—now always a painful memory. "What a revenge did you but know it." And tomorrow is the 10th anniversary of her death. Looking back I seem to see a clear division in my life, for on that day I seemed suddenly to leap from youth into dreary middle-age. I suppose because I had no responsibility before.

But, to a more cheerful topic. T.H. is immensely gratified at the bestowal of the honorary fellowship of Queen's. It is long since I have seen him so genuinely pleased at anything, & he quite intends visiting Oxford in the spring, he says, probably by motor, when he will stop to see his grandmother's birthplace, Fawley, on the way.

I think I perceive your kind hand in this new honour for T.H. In fact I feel firmly convinced that it is so, & I tell him you have arranged it, in the wonderful way you have of bringing things off.

If I go to London, as I hope to be able to do, on the 13th, I shall see Mr Yearsley. I think that for once I shall not endeavour to see any of my relatives, but take a rest from them.

We sent to see my husband's people a few days ago & we found the brother in a pitiful state, groaning, & apparently hardly able to speak, & declaring in painful gasps that he would be dead in a few weeks. But I rather think all this was because we had not been to see him for a fortnight, as he cheered up soon, &, growing excited about some news we brought, spoke loudly & cheerfully in his natural voice. Nevertheless he is in bad health.

The performance of "A Desperate Remedy" was farcical in the more serious parts, & the audience was convulsed with laughter when they should have been aghast. Poor Gertrude Bugler seems to have suffered agonies at being cut out by a rival leading lady, Ethel Fare, & the tragic climax is that she had a still-born son on the day of the performance.

What a gossip I am, but I don't expect that you want a letter on literary matters. Thank you so much.

Yours very sincerely
Florence Hardy.

The critique in The Times was written by Charles Morgan—who was Secretary of the O.U.D.S. when they produced 'The Dynasts" at Oxford. I have a programme for you. F.H.

Text MS. Beinecke.

the Puppets: a programme presented in London by the sculptor William Simmonds.   *literary competition*: for original contributions of not more than 750 words; the occasion was reported in the *Dorset County Chronicle*, 14 Dec. 1922.   *"What . . . know it."*: from the final stanza of TH's poem 'The Torn Letter'.   *visiting Oxford . . . Fawley*: for TH's visit to Queen's College, Oxford, and to Fawley in June 1923, see *Life and Work*, 453–5.   *sent to see*: 'went to see' evidently intended.   *dead . . . weeks*: Henry Hardy lived until Dec. 1928.   *Fare*: Ethel Fare, a former schoolmate of G. Bugler's, took the part of Cytherea.   *Morgan*: Charles Langbridge Morgan (1894–1958), novelist and playwright, currently dramatic critic for *The Times*; his notice there, 17 Nov. 1922, was more favourable than most of the other reviews.   *O.U.D.S.*: Oxford University Dramatic Society; the production was in Feb. 1920.

To Sydney Cockerell

MAX GATE, | DORCHESTER.

17th December. [1922]

My dear Mr Cockerell:

The accounts I have been reading in the papers about the puppets have been making me almost dance with rage, at myself, in having lost such a beautiful treat. If they come again I MUST see them 'Let or wet' as the Dorset folk say. But, as things turned out it was well I didn't go, as T.H. has a mild attack of 'flu. caught from me no doubt, & this was followed by the same feeling of extreme lack of energy. He said he had never felt so despondent in his life. And he told me that if anything happened to me he would go out & drown himself, which, considered rightly is a compliment, isn't it. However he is well now—though he doesn't seem to want to do much.

I told the doctor that I didn't think the illness was serious, but he said, at his age influenza is *always* serious. It was wonderful how quickly he got over it, & I think that was the result of taking two bottles of champagne— not all at one go, but two glasses twice a day. That seems always to do him more good than anything.

It must be a delightful time for you & Mrs Cockerell now, expecting the children home for Christmas. I hope that it will be a joyous festival for you all. I know it will.

Ghostly strains just now reach me from the drawing room (I am in the dining room) T.H. playing a Christmas hymn—on that most pathetic old piano.

With best wishes from us both to you all—

Always yours sincerely

F.E.H.

Text MS. Beinecke. *Date* Year supplied on MS. by Cockerell.
about the puppets: e.g. the enthusiastic review by A. B. Walkley in *The Times*, 13 Dec.
1922. *old piano*: see letter of 15 Jan. 1929.

To Sydney Cockerell

MAX GATE, | DORCHESTER.
23rd Jan. '23.

My dear Mr Cockerell:

Thank you so much for 'Marie Chapdelaine' which arrived this morning. I know that I shall have great pleasure in reading it, & I think it was most kind of you to send it.

I hope that by now you have quite recovered from your attack of influenza. I hope that you have not got about too quickly.

T.H. is in bed with a chill. Yesterday he complained of a pain in his chest, but today he seems fairly well, apart from the cold, & quite cheerful, so I hope he'll be well in a day or two. John Galsworthy has written to ask him if he can be present at that dinner I told you about, to foreign writers, in May. T.H. has asked me to reply that he is now quite beyond going to London, & has long given up dining out, even in Dorchester.

He tells me that he is just thinking out a poem he means to write so the time in bed will not be wasted. We have managed to give his study a partial clean—without touching the books—while he is in bed, & I have had a man sent out from Dorchester to put up brackets, curtain-rod & curtains at the window so that that it will be more comfortable for him when he gets up. He doesn't know that it has been done. I hope he won't mind.

A day or two ago the following conversation took place—

F.H.   It's twelve days since you spoke to anyone outside the house.

T.H.   (triumphantly). I have spoken to some one.

F.H   (surprised.) Who was it?

T.H.   The man who drove the manure cart.

F.H   (much impressed.) What did you say?

T.H.   'Good-morning'.

I suppose you have seen that Mr Pocock is retiring from the Zoological Gardens in March. I suppose they will come to live at their little house near Chideock. He is one of the nicest men I know.

Again thanking you,

Yours very sincerely.
Florence Hardy.

Text   MS. Beinecke.
'Marie Chapdelaine': correctly *Maria Chapdelaine*, by Louis Hémon, trans. W. H. Blake (London, 1922); the copy Cockerell sent FEH is now at Texas.   *dinner . . . writers*: the first international congress of the P.E.N. Club; see *CL*, vi. 192.   *so that that*: FEH's repetition.
Pocock: Reginald Innes Pocock, superintendent of the Zoological Society's Gardens, Regent's Park, 1904–23; he and his wife had been friendly with the Hardys for several years.
Chideock: Dorset village SW of Bridport.

[FEH had long known of her husband's feelings for Florence Henniker, with whom he had fallen profoundly though unrequitedly in love during the 1890s, and she herself, in the years prior to her marriage, became deeply attached to Mrs Henniker while working for her as an occasional secretary. FEH had spent a weekend with Mrs Henniker in January 1923 and was well aware of her poor health and spirits, especially following the loss of Anna Hirschmann, her maid and companion of many years; the news of her death was none the less received at Max Gate with a shocked regret suggested, if hardly articulated, by the laconic expressiveness of Hardy's exclamation, 'After a friendship of 30 years!']

To Louise Yearsley

MAX GATE, | DORCHESTER.
10th April. [1923]

My dear Louise:

It was so good of you to write such a nice long letter. I know how very busy you are. With regard to the little suits I enclose cheque for £2–10–0. It is very good of you to spare them. If you change your mind don't mind telling me. Do just what suits you best.

The cottage at Angmering sounds absolutely perfect, & I should *love* to go & stay with you there. Thank you so much for asking me. But, alas, I see no chance whatever of getting away, except for hurried rushes to Town. My husband is miserable if left, & he doesn't like anyone brought here to stay with him. He says he would rather be alone. And I feel a brute every time I leave him, if only for two days. If I do take a holiday it will be in a nursing home, having this gland removed.

We feel very sad today as our dearest friend—Mrs Arthur Henniker—has been laid in her grave this afternoon. She has been T.H's closest friend for 30 years, & my dear friend for 13. I knew her before I was married. When I went to stay with her at Epsom in Jan. she seemed utterly broken by grief, & the serious illness of Lord Crewe—her only brother—was the last blow, & she sank under it. I told her every detail of my life & she entered into it as a sister. She used to come to Dorset yearly to stay near us, & I went to see her frequently, & could use her house as a hotel practically, when-ever I liked. She was beautiful & gifted & the kindest woman that one could conceive. My last letter reached her on the morning of the day she died, & her last message was one asking me to go to London to see her. We have lost friend after friend this last six months. But I must not con-tinue in this dismal strain. Moreover it is post time—

With my love & many thanks,

Yours very sincerely,
Florence Hardy

P.S. I enclose cheque.

Text MS. Eton. *Date* Year from internal evidence.

little suits: L. Yearsley had offered to send FEH (for forwarding to Thomas Soundy in Canada) some of the suits she had knitted for her own son. *Lord Crewe*: Robert Offley Ashburton Crewe-Milnes, 2nd Baron Houghton and Marquess of Crewe (1858–1945), statesman, cur-rently British ambassador in Paris; he and F. Henniker were the children of Richard Monckton Milnes, 1st Baron Houghton, politician and man of letters. *My last letter*: it seems not to have survived.

[Thomas Edward Lawrence (1888–1935), famous as 'Lawrence of Arabia', had been serving in the Royal Air Force as Aircraftsman J. H. Ross until discharged following the revelation of his true identity. He had since obtained a transfer to the Tank Corps under the alias of Private T. E. Shaw, and his current posting to Bovington Camp, near the Dorset village of Wool, was enabling him to become a frequent and much cherished visitor to Max Gate—to be mentioned, however, only to those, such as Cockerell, who were privy to the secret of his whereabouts. Lawrence's admiration for TH's work and for TH himself was almost unqualified, but he also developed a sympathetic relationship with FEH that became especially important to her in the years following her husband's death. A more troublesome visitor to Max Gate in the summer of 1923 was Edward, Prince of Wales, the heir to the throne. On 30 June FEH wrote to Cockerell (Beinecke) to complain that her head was aching all day 'with the worry of it', a particular source of anxiety being the rather limited indoor plumbing at Max Gate: 'And he will want to wash his hands—etc—here which is terrible. You know what our house is like.' But TH himself, she added in some bemusement, 'is *pleased*'.]

To Sydney Cockerell

MAX GATE, | DORCHESTER.
13th. May 1923.

Dear Mr Cockerell:

I was sorry that we were not able to go to the Private View and have a few minutes talk with you, but I quite agree that it was better for us not to go. I had a heavy cold at the time and I think T.H. really never meant to go. His programme was quite appalling. I am sure that he could never have done all that he intended and returned here the same day. Just at present he is as well as I have ever known him, and working at full speed, finishing some work that he has enjoyed doing. But now that Macmillans have printed the thin paper edition with an index of first lines I think they would not welcome any fresh volume just at present. In fact it would not be fair to them to publish anything much just yet. But I shall have a most interesting little volume privately printed I think, if you agree. This of course later on.

The letters from T.H. to Mrs Henniker arrived two days ago. I opened the parcel before T.H., thinking it was an autograph album from some tiresome stranger, and it was a most painful moment when I saw what I had. I think the most painful experience one can have is to receive a legacy from someone one has loved. I have put them away just for the present, but later on shall carefully type them. Naturally T.H. wanted to begin taking out passages. For instance in the letter he wrote about his first wife's death he says "It would be idle to pretend that we did not have differences." He thought he would ink that out. However it will be better to do nothing just at present. I know perfectly well what Mrs Henniker wished done with them, for we discussed that the last evening we spent together, and my last sight of her was as she turned into her bedroom, carrying these letters in her hands. I wish had not died. I miss her letters and the feeling that she was there.

I hope that Mrs Cockerell and you are well. I suppose the children have gone back to school. You must miss them.

The Granville-Barkers were here last Thursday, both looking so well and much younger than when they went abroad. They are very kind in wishing us to go to see them. They beg us to let them send the car, and have made two or three attempts, by telephone, to get us there, but T.H. has been so busy with his poem, which he is now copying.

When Walter de la Mare wrote last he said that his wife was going with him for the holiday in Wales, or Cornwall, and I thought perhaps he felt that we should have asked her to come with him, so I wrote off at once, of course, to ask if she would come too, though I fear it will make the visit far more tiring for T.H. I feel sure that she is exceedingly pleasant and I should like to know her, but I am afraid it will spoil the visit for T.H.

That Mrs Ffooks, the Dorchester lady who spends her time in hunting celebrities, has very cleverly extracted a long and very nice letter from Conrad. She told me of it with triumph when I met her the other day. She has a hundred ways of getting into touch with well-known people, and merely to extract autographs etc. It is a mania with her. I wonder that Conrad fell such an easy prey.

We have heard no more of Colonel Lawrence. I do not know even whether he is at Bovington still. I hope that he will come over again, but I hardly think he will.

Please do not trouble to reply—at least for some time. I always feel guilty when I write to you as I know how very many letters you have to write in addition to so much other important work. I was very sorry to hear about Miss Mew's mother—or rather, sorry that she could not see you and W. de la Mare. But I really think she does not want to meet people.

Yours very sincerely

F. E. Hardy.

Text   MS. (typed) Beinecke.
Private View: of the Royal Academy's Summer Exhibition.   *thin paper edition*: of TH's *Collected Poems*.   *little volume*: the work TH had just completed was presumably the poem 'Winter Night in Woodland', privately printed in pamphlet form early in 1925 (Purdy, 232–3).   *"It . . . differences."*: FEH's imprecise recollection of a sentence which survives, unobliterated, in TH's letter to F. Henniker of 17 Dec. 1912 (*CL*, iv. 243).   *wish had not*: 'wish she had not' clearly intended.   *to see them*: at their country house in Devon.   *his wife*: Constance Elfrida de la Mare (née Ingpen); for de la Mare himself, see letter of 17 June 1921.   *Mrs Ffooks*: presumably Dorothy Ffooks (née Keep), the wife of Edward Archdall Ffooks, Clerk of the Peace for the County of Dorset.   *Miss Mew's mother*: she was dying but had declined visits from both Cockerell and W. de la Mare (Cockerell diary, 2 and 9 May 1923, BL).

To Sydney Cockerell

MAX GATE, | DORCHESTER.

28th. May 1923.

Dear Mr Cockerell:

Mr and Mrs de la Mare have just left us. We have enjoyed their visit so much, though I fear it has left T.H. rather limp. Mrs de la Mare is a charming woman and I am so very glad that I know her. I feel that we are friends already, and I am thankful for Mr de la Mare's little hint that made me write and ask her to come.

I hope that you are all quite well. I had a letter today from poor Miss Mew, though I begged her not to reply to my letter of condolence. I know exactly how she feels, but in a few weeks I hope she will be able to make a good fresh start in life.

I forget whether I told you that I have been able to nip in the bud

Newman Flower's idea of a lunch to T.H. in Dorchester, or a little gathering of his friends here. I am sure that his friends do not want to be brought here under the leadership of anyone. They can come by themselves, singly, if they wish. Max Beerbohm is coming this week I believe. Colonel Lawrence came to meet the De la Mares. I thought I would ask him in case he wished to meet them and he did very much want to do so and came. It was a success for they seemed to like each other immensely, and there was no nonsense about introducing him as Mr Shaw. I just said "Colonel Lawrence".

Mrs Henniker thought, when we talked about the publication of the letters to her from T.H. that it would be a good plan if they could be published separately in a little volume instead of being printed with a lot of others. They are so very distinct from all other of his letters, that this might be advisable, but that will need careful consideration. They reveal so much that they are rather sad. T.H. thinks (and of course I agree) that it would be quite impossible to print them in his lifetime. All that can be done then is to have them copied carefully and the copy and letters put away for whoever will have, in years to come, the melancholy task of editing them. Mrs Henniker has been through them and cut out a great deal and destroyed many of the letters—many more, I expect, than need have been destroyed. If anyone else has to edit them I think there should be a portrait of her and a little account of her work and her loveable personality. I miss her so much.

Yours very sincerely,
Florence Hardy

Text MS. Beinecke.
condolence: on the death of her mother.   *Beerbohm*: Henry Maximilian Beerbohm (1872–1956), cartoonist and author, knighted 1939; he was at Max Gate on 2 June, TH's 83rd birthday. He and his wife, the American actress Florence Kahn, remained friendly with FEH after TH's death.   *lot of others*: FEH first wrote 'lot of other letters'.   *rather sad*: FEH first wrote 'rather sad letters'.   *edit them*: TH's letters to F. Henniker were first edited by Evelyn Hardy and F. B. Pinion in 1972 and subsequently re-edited for *CL*.

To Sydney Cockerell

MAX GATE, | DORCHESTER.
Monday. [23 July 1923]

My dear Mr Cockerell:

We hope that you are now better from the high temperature & discomfort caused by the inoculation. I return the letter as requested. We think that Mr Gosse is entitled to his opinion—also that the promoters of the memorial are entitled to theirs, & that the shortest & wisest course would be to put Mr Gosse's letter aside, & proceed as if you had not written to him.

My husband says he agrees with Mr Gosse so far as to think that the tone of the recommendation was perhaps a little too strong, but as the point was to get the pension he thought he would pass over that & sign it, with the reservation he denoted. His advice is that "in *the interests of Miss Mew* a drafted form of petition should be drawn up in the usual way, based on Masefield's letter, but slightly softened down, & that he should then be asked to sign it with the rest of us, which I am sure he would do if the reason of the softening were told him—i.e. to get more to sign." (quoted)

Yes, it was a very pleasant day, Friday, in one sense, & there was no strain or flurry of any kind. When I saw that very weary, rather sulky young face looking at me I forgot to be nervous & behaved to him as to any other young man. I tried not to be in either photograph but he said 'Oh yes, you must be photographed too. Come along." So I did. And the second time I tried to back out he said 'Come on." But when I saw the photographs I did feel dismayed at the free & easy appearance of T.H. & myself. I said to T.H. 'I did not appear nervous, did I, for I wasn't,' & he replied, "No, on the contrary I thought you were behaving rather too coolly." I didn't fuss round him, & I think he was grateful. He made himself very much at home. But what a mercy for us that ours is a limited monarchy. Imagine that young man with the power to control the destiny of our empire! In repose I think his face is absolutely miserable. Please do not say one word of this to anyone. He grew rather gay & jocular during lunch.

It is reported in Dorchester that, as he left the house he said he had enjoyed "that" more than anything, but I don't think he can have said it, nor do I know how anyone could have heard him. What an awful life! I had been told he ate nothing. He made an excellent lunch, & asked for a second helping of ham, & finished up with a glass of 40 year old sherry & one of the cigars.

I hope that poor Miss Mew seemed better & happier.

Always yours sincerely
Florence Hardy.

Text MS. Beinecke.   *Date* Supplied on MS. by Cockerell.

the memorial: Cockerell was the orchestrator of this (successful) application to the Prime Minister for the award of a Civil List pension to Charlotte Mew; Gosse refused to sign, and while TH had already added his signature to the original version drawn up by John Mase-field—'saying he could not alter another man's letter, especially as it was signed' (FEH to

Cockerell, 13 July 1923, Beinecke)—he too evidently thought its language a little extravagant. *young face*: that of the Prince of Wales, who visited Max Gate 20 July 1923 (*Life and Work*, 455–6).   *saw the photographs*: as widely reproduced in the national press.

To Dorothy Allhusen

MAX GATE, | DORCHESTER.
28th August. [1923]

My dear Dorothy:

I was so pleased & interested to hear the news of the expected arrival. I trust that all will be well.

T.H. sends his love & says he is much obliged for your explanation & details about the church repairs, & says that he sees nothing to object to in what it is proposed to do. He has asked a friend, who knows the church, what ought to be done, & he is told that a local builder, Mr Hartley, whose grandfather built the spire, could repair it without an architect, for about £600 (irrespective of the land). He suggests that this could be done from local funds, & an appeal could be made to the public for the land only. This would be something definite & people would not be afraid of doing harm by a contribution, as they might if the church were included, so much mischief having already arisen from restorations.

He says that for himself he feels too old to enter into these questions personally, & that you must pass him over for some younger man.

Of course this is what he says, & has nothing to do with me. I *much* wish he would write the letter, but I know that no amount of persuasion will induce him to change his mind. He has been asked many times lately to write to the papers about one thing & another & he always refuses. I am absolutely powerless to make him do any thing he does not wish to do.

It will be so very delightful to see you & Elizabeth here if you can come. I hope you will not be too vexed with T.H. for his obstinacy. He is an old man, & was never very easy to persuade I think.

I hope the last batch of recipes was of use, but I expect that, with so much to think about you have had to lay by the cookery book.

With love from us both.

Yours affectionately,
Florence Hardy.

Text MS. Beinecke.   *Date* Year from internal evidence.
expected arrival: D. Allhusen's elder daughter Madeleine, married to Geoffrey Cecil Congreve, gave birth to her first child 1 Sept. 1923.   *church repairs*: TH had already evaded (*CL*, vi. 206) one request from D. Allhusen that he give public support to an appeal for funds to

repair the spire of Stoke Poges church, setting for Gray's *Elegy in a Country Churchyard*; for her connection with Stoke Poges see letter of 4 Nov. 1922.   *Mr Hartley*: perhaps Edward Hartley, living in Windsor at this date.   *restorations*: TH had confessed his own sins as a restoring architect in his paper of 1906, 'Memories of Church Restoration' (Purdy, 311). *Elizabeth*: see letter of 4 Nov. 1922.   *cookery book*: D. Allhusen's *A Book of Scents & Dishes* (London, 1926) includes a few recipes supplied by FEH.

[Among the many visitors to Max Gate during the late summer and early autumn of 1923 were H. G. Wells and Rebecca West, John Drinkwater and the violinist Daisy Kennedy, the painter Reginald Eves, and the American writer Hamlin Garland. T. E. Lawrence also called, to be promptly recognized by another visitor—causing FEH to wonder, in a 4 September letter to Cockerell (Beinecke), why he came at all 'if he doesn't wish to be known, as people are always dropping in'. No one made a greater impression, however, than Marie Stopes, the scientist and reformer, who had recently purchased the Old Lighthouse on Portland Bill as a summer retreat: 'T.H. was very fascinated!!' FEH told Cockerell, perhaps only half-ironically, in that same 4 September letter. Although both the Hardys were wary of Marie Stopes's personality—and of her somewhat sensational reputation as an outspoken advocate of birth control—they seem none the less to have been prodded by her persistent questioning into quite unaccustomed bursts of personal revelation.]

To Marie Stopes

MAX GATE, | DORCHESTER.

14th Sept. [1923]

Dear Dr Stopes:

Thank you so much for the pamphlets I have received. It was good of you to send them, & I have read them with great interest. I have tried to interest my husband also, but I feel that now he is of an age when interests are few. He is absorbed in his own special work, the writing of poetry, & I think that now he does not give much though to social problems. But certain passages in "Jude the Obscure"—concerning Sue Bridehead & her luckless children might have been written to illustrate the value of your teaching.

I find on talking to him that the idea of my having a child at his age fills him with terror. He is far more nervous & highly strung than appears to anyone outside the household. At present he is very worried & upset about all sorts of little things—proofs, a portrait that has just been painted, a new publisher's agreement, & so forth, & the result is that he does not sleep at night. He said he would have welcomed a child when we married first, ten years ago, but now it would kill him with anxiety to have to father one.

However I shall make use of your kind advice with regard to the alkaline douche, as I think it may be beneficial to health—and I thank you so much for giving me the directions.

How you must miss the wonderful air & scene of Portland, though I expect your own home is equally beautiful in another way. I hope that we shall see something of you when you are there again.

With our kindest regards to you both & my best thanks,

Yours very sincerely,
Florence Hardy.

Text MS. BL. *Date* Year from date of receipt as noted on MS.
Stopes: Marie Charlotte Carmichael Stopes (1880–1958) did significant work as a palaeobotanist before devoting herself to the encouragement of sex education and family planning—evidently the subject-matter of the 'pamphlets' received by FEH. *much though*: 'much thought' clearly intended. *of my having*: 'my' an above-the-line insertion. *have to father one*: 'to father' an above-the-line insertion. *alkaline douche*: Stopes's 1921 pamphlet *Truth About Venereal Disease* recommends potassium permanganate as effective 'against the germs of sex diseases' (38). *your own home*: Stopes and her husband, Humphrey Verdon Roe, lived at Givons Grove, a large house and estate near Leatherhead, Surrey.

To Sydney Cockerell

MAX GATE, | DORCHESTER.
1st Dec. [1923]

My dear Mr Cockerell:

I am much looking forward to next Wednesday's gathering. It is so kind of you to include me. By the way I suppose Miss Mew will turn up?

We are glad that you liked 'The Queen," but I wish you had seen it in greater comfort on Thursday. We greatly enjoyed your short—all too short—visit. It was kind of you to come.

I hope that I will not appear to have Lawrence on the brain if I explain that I did *not* ask him to show me his cottage. I had no idea we were near it nor had I ever dreamed of seeing it, when he slowed down his motor-bicycle & said: 'Would you like to see my cottage?' Naturally I said 'Yes', feeling pleased, & he said "It's just down this turning", & we were within a few yards of it. Just as he was going that afternoon he turned & said, without any prompting from me: 'I'll take you there to see it again when it's finished." I suppose it is a natural pride in a very neat piece of work, for it is being restored beautifully. And I did *not* fish for an invitation for a ride as T.H. suggested. I had asked Russell (the private) in to tea, & I think

Lawrence was pleased at that, & when I said to Russell "You seem to have a good time being carried about the country in that luxurious little side car," Lawrence said at once, "You must have a ride in it. Russell, do you think it is comfortable enough for Mrs Hardy?". So that's all it was. I hate to be pictured as throwing out broad hints, for I had never dreamed of riding in that car. Not that it is of any consequence.

John Drinkwater made himself *very* pleasant on Friday, & that *most* enchanting little violinist quite won our hearts. She is a *very* nice woman, & devoted to her two little girls. I hope they will be happy. T.H. actually went in to the evening performance on Friday, although it was the anniversary of the funeral of E.L.H. When he went behind with Drinkwater they were loudly cheered, to Drinkwater's great embarrassment, so he said. Drinkwater said that Dr Smerdon's second song moved him to tears. They were all so much better on Friday.

T.H. is disinclined to fall in with Barrie's plan of having the company up to the St Martin's Theatre for three afternoons, as Drinkwater promises to do his best to get it produced by London actors. I am inclined to back Barrie's judgement, as he thinks that these players can give it an atmosphere that no professional actors could. Poor Mr Tilley will be greatly disappointed if he is not allowed to produce it at least *once* in London, but I fear that T.H. has quite decided against that.

I wish you could meet Miss Daisy Kennedy (Mrs Drinkwater that is to be). I don't know when I've met a nicer woman & she is *very* nice looking.

Yours very sincerely,

F.E.H.

Text MS. Beinecke. *Date* Year supplied on MS. by Cockerell.
Wednesday's gathering: Cockerell's diary for 5 Dec. 1923 (BL) records as highly successful the lunch he had arranged as an opportunity for Charlotte Mew and Walter de la Mare to meet; also present were Anne Mew, FEH, and Philip Burne-Jones.   'The Queen,'': Cockerell had come to Dorchester to attend the first performance, 28 Nov. 1923, of the local production of TH's new verse-drama *The Famous Tragedy of the Queen of Cornwall*.   *if I explain*: apparently in correction or modification of remarks made by TH during Cockerell's recent visit.
his cottage: at Clouds Hill, east of Max Gate; it is now the property of the National Trust.
Russell: Private Arthur Russell, one of Lawrence's friends in the Tank Corps and later a pallbearer at his funeral.   *violinist*: Daisy Kennedy (1893–1981), Australian-born violinist, married John Drinkwater in 1924; she had two daughters by her first marriage, to Benno Moiseiwitsch.   *evening performance*: of the *Queen of Cornwall*, followed by two 'folk-pieces', *O Jan! O Jan! O Jan!* and *The Play of St George*.   *loudly cheered*: by the audience; according to the *Southern Times*, 8 Dec., TH was recognized at the interval as he crossed in front of the stage on his way backstage.   *Smerdon's*: Edgar Wilmot Smerdon, a Dorchester doctor, played the part of Tristram.   *decided against that*: the Dorchester production was nevertheless performed in London on 21 Feb. 1924.

To E. M. Forster

MAX GATE, | DORCHESTER.
6th. Jan. '24.

Dear Mr Forster:

I hope it is not too late in the year—after all this is old Christmas day—to wish you a very good New Year. Also to thank you for your most kind letter. We wonder very much what you think of T.E.L's book—if you could spare a moment or two to let us know, some time, we should be so interested to know. But I feel I ought not to ask you. It is betraying no secret I hope to tell you that he has the *greatest admiration* for your work, especially for your latest book of Essays 'Pharos'. I have never heard him speak so enthusiastically about any other book. If you are able to come to Dorchester soon, it would be a proud moment for Max Gate if you two could meet here—if you have not met before then.

By the way Wessie has been clipped by the vet: his mouth well tied with tape, & myself gripping his collar & terribly alarmed. He nearly burst with rage, but looks much improved.

I never thanked you for your very kind advice about seeing a specialist with regard to the enlarged gland that was worrying me. I did as you suggested & went to a specialist in Welbeck St. who I knew to be absolutely honest, & a friend of ours. He advised me *not* to have it removed, & now it is much smaller & I hope will soon be normal. He gave advice that sounded odd from a surgeon: "There is danger in all operations, however slight, & it is best always to avoid them if necessary."

Thank you again so much.

We are glad to hear that Siegfried Sassoon is well. I hope is isn't annoyed with us about anything, but I fear he is. T.H. was a little annoyed with him about some trifle the last time he was here. (It was because he wouldn't read the proofs of the Queen of Cornwall), & S.S. was vexed with T.H. I think about something he said about his poems. He thought too, I imagine, that T.H. had not read them all—but he did read them, as soon as the book came. I am sorry because I know they really are very fond of each other, underneath this petty exasperation.

Yours very sincerely,
F. E. Hardy.

Text MS. King's College, Cambridge.

T.E.L's book: Forster had presumably seen one of the early private printings of T. E. Lawrence's *Seven Pillars of Wisdom: A Triumph.* 'Pharos': Forster's *Pharos and Pharillon*, pub. by the Hogarth Press in 1923. *specialist*: Macleod Yearsley. *if necessary*: 'if not necessary' or 'if possible' presumably intended. *hope is isn't*: 'hope he isn't' evidently intended. *his* poems: *Recreations* (privately printed in 75 copies, 1923); TH's copy was inscribed 'Thomas Hardy, with love. S.S.' (Frank Hollings Cat. 212, no. 97). *petty exasperation*: FEH had called Sassoon 'sometimes a little "touchy"' in a letter to Cockerell of 7 Nov. 1922 (Beinecke), adding that it was 'frightfully easy to upset him' unless one 'saw a certain danger signal in time—a quick glint of his eye'.

To John Middleton Murry

MAX GATE, | DORCHESTER.
March 30th. [1924]

Dear Mr Middleton Murry:

I can hardly find words to express my most grateful thanks to you for your splendid reply to George Moore's outrageous attack on my husband. It is very good of you. I can assure you, my husband feels far more that he could show in his letter to you. He said to me that of all his friends you were the only one who had cared to defend him—& that he would never forget it. Neither shall I. Edmund Gosse had his opportunity, but could only say that although Mr Moore might appear to be moved by envy that was not the case—or words to that effect.

I hope that we shall see you soon after your return to England.

Again thanking you *most* sincerely—& with every good wish,

Florence Hardy.

Text MS. Berg. *Date* Year from internal evidence.
Murry: John Middleton Murry (1889–1957), critic and author, currently editor of the *Adelphi*. *reply . . . attack*: Murry's article, 'Wrap me up in my Aubusson carpet', *Adelphi*, Apr. 1924, had defended TH against the attack made by George Moore (1852–1933), the novelist, in his *Conversations in Ebury Street* (London, 1924). *that he could show*: 'than he could show' clearly intended; in her letter to Cockerell of 7 Feb. 1924 (Beinecke) FEH said that Moore's attack had worried TH to the point of making him feel unwell. *his letter to you*: of 28 Mar. 1924 (*CL*, vi. 242–3). *Gosse*: TH was especially irritated that Gosse, one of his oldest friends, should have said (*Sunday Times*, 3 Feb. 1922) that Moore's attacks on TH, James, and Conrad sprang not from jealousy but from his being 'constitutionally unable to conceal anything', including his feelings of 'instinctive repulsion' for the work of other novelists. *return to England*: Murry in fact abandoned his scheme for a round-the-world journey.

To Rutland Boughton

MAX GATE, | DORCHESTER.
June 29th. [1924]

Dear Mr Boughton:

I have told the Hardy Players of your suggestion about the char-a-banc, & they seem very keen, & I hope they will turn up in force. We are greatly looking forward to Glastonbury, but I fear that T.H. will not be able to go to the first performance—though I wish he would. He never sleeps away from home now, if he can get to any place & back in the day.

We enjoyed your visit so much, & loved hearing the music—in spite of the horrible piano. By the way, you promised to send me a communist paper. The magistrates here were being sorted out the other day at a committee meeting—according to their politics, & I, for the first time, declared myself 'Labour', to the amazement of the chairman.

I gave out the circulars to the two booksellers here, & have sent a few round—

Yours very sincerely,
Florence Hardy.

Text MS. BL. *Date* Year from internal evidence.
Boughton: Rutland Boughton (1878–1960), composer, especially of the immensely successful music-drama *The Immortal Hour*; visiting Max Gate earlier in 1924 he had greatly impressed both FEH and TH—who declared, so FEH reported to Cockerell on 7 Feb. (Beinecke), that he liked Boughton better than anyone he had ever met. *to Glastonbury*: TH was not at the first (evening) performance, 21 Aug. 1924, of Boughton's musical setting of *The Queen of Cornwall* at the Glastonbury Festival (of which Boughton had been a co-founder), but did attend a later matinée (see letter of 18 Aug. 1924). *communist paper*: FEH reported to Cockerell, 21 June 1924 (Beinecke), that during his most recent visit Boughton had been 'in a violent mood' and 'talked communism nearly all the while—to T.H.'s discomfort'; see *Life and Work*, 458. *The magistrates*: FEH had recently been appointed a Justice of the Peace for Dorchester. *circulars*: advertising the Glastonbury programme.

To Marie Stopes

MAX GATE, | DORCHESTER.
9th July. [1924]

My dear Dr Stopes:

I always feel so sorry for the recipient when I answer my husband's letters for him, but I know that you will excuse him writing when I tell you that he caught a slight chill sitting out of doors when the Balliol players performed their Greek play in our garden. What with that, & the eye-weakness from which he suffers, I am obliged to do his personal writing & the secretary his business letters.

We are so glad to hear that you are able to get to your lighthouse home with your beautiful baby. You are indeed to be envied in possessing him— the greatest treasure that a woman could have. May he be dowered with every gift of mind & body. We were extremely sorry to hear of the very serious illness you had, & the fractured bone—& we hope you are now feeling really quite strong & well.

As to your kind suggestion that T.H. should be one of the godfathers he asks me to say that he is not only too old for such a function, but has his doubts if he could conscientiously undertake it—the only case of the kind he has agreed to for the last 50 years having been for a family connection of his, & he consented very reluctantly. But he sends every possible good wish to your little son, & to you & your husband.

With our kindest regards.

Yours very sincerely
Florence Hardy.

Text MS. BL.   *Date* Year noted on MS., apparently by M. Stopes.
Balliol Players: this undergraduate company performed *The Oresteia* on the lawn of Max Gate, 1 July 1924 (*Life and Work*, 459).   *the secretary*: May O'Rourke (see letter of 27 July 1918) had been working as an occasional secretary at Max Gate since the spring of 1923; see her pamphlet, *Thomas Hardy: His Secretary Remembers* (Beaminster, 1965).   *lighthouse home*: see headnote to letter of 14 Sept. 1923.   *baby*: her son, Harry, was born 27 Mar. 1924.   *family connection*: in Sept. 1921 (*Life and Work*, 448) TH had acted as godfather to Caroline Fox Hanbury of Kingston Maurward; as a granddaughter of J. F. Symons Jeune she was distantly connected to ELH (see letter of 3 Jan. 1922).

To Sydney Cockerell

MAX GATE, | DORCHESTER.
18th. August. '24.

My dear Mr Cockerell:

We are very sorry to hear of the many calamities you seem to have had. I hope that the deaths of friends did not include that of Mrs Cockerell's sister or mother. I hope they are both well now. We knew that the death of Conrad would be a blow to you as you valued his friendship. I am sorry for Mrs Conrad who seems to have been a most devoted wife.

T.H. is, this morning, in rather a bad state of nerves and vows that nothing will induce him to go to Glastonbury on Friday, and that he must have been mad to have contemplated such a proceeding. Until now I thought he was quite anxious to go. Yesterday we went to lunch with the de Bunsens (Sir Maurice and Lady) and Lady Evelyn Cecil and daughter were there, to meet him. He felt the strain rather as he has not been to lunch anywhere this year, until then, but I really think he did enjoy it, in a way. Perhaps he will feel better tomorrow. Anyhow this places me in rather an awkward position with regard to Mr Watkins, who insists upon coming from London to take us to Glastonbury in his car—which he certainly would not have done had he not been told that T.H. was going. I felt at the time that it would have been much better to hire our own car in Dorchester and go quite independently. However it is possible that T.H. may change his mind. People little know when they see how bright and vigorous he is to outsiders, what a state of frenzy he works himself into when alone here with me. The only remedy is to remain quiet and say nothing, and he calms down after a time.

. . . .

Since typing the above I have been up to the study and he seemed better and was writing a poem. He had forgotten about Glastonbury apparently as he asked me which was the better phrase "tender-eyed" or "meek-eyed". I pointed out that "tender-eyed" is used in the Bible (in reference to Leah) as meaning "sore-eyed"—which was why Jacob didn't want her. So a little biblical knowledge is handy at times: "tender-eyed" was promptly abandoned.

How very nice for Christopher to be going to France. One of my sisters is having a wonderful holiday in Switzerland.

Yours very sincerely,

FEH.

Text   MS. (typed) Beinecke.
Conrad: see letter of 2 Oct. 1921 for a visit of Cockerell's to Joseph Conrad (died 3 Aug. 1924) and his wife Jessie.   *Glastonbury*: see letter of 29 June 1924.   *de Bunsens*: Sir Maurice de Bunsen, Bt. (1852–1932), retired diplomat, and his wife Berta Mary, née Lowry-Corry.   *Cecil*: Alicia Cecil (née Amherst), wife of Sir Evelyn Cecil, was an authority on gardens.   *in the Bible*: Genesis 29: 17.   *"tender-eyed" . . . abandoned*: the poem-in-progress has not been confidently identified.

[On 30 September 1924 FEH was operated on in London for the removal of a potentially cancerous tumour on her parotid gland. Earlier advice from Macleod Yearsley and others had suggested that the suspicious lump on her neck might be merely a swollen gland or a cyst, and her husband's terror of hospitals and surgeons had tended to reinforce her own natural preference for inaction. Yearsley finally recommended an operation, however, and in mid-September 1924 Dr Henry Head introduced her to James Sherren, a leading London surgeon who happened also to have a Dorset background. Sherren declared the operation a success, and the subsequent nine-day period of rest and recuperation in a comfortable London nursing-home not only provided FEH with a welcome respite from the duties and pressures of Max Gate but placed her for once at the centre of attention. The fact that TH remained throughout at Max Gate also gave her the opportunity to form more personal relationships with her two principal visitors, Charlotte Mew and Sydney Cockerell, to both of whom she now began writing on a first-name basis.]

To Charlotte Mew

Fitzroy House
[7 October 1924]

My dear Charlotte:

I have so loved reading the magnificent poems you so kindly sent. I think "Here lies a prisoner" is my favourite. It is so strong & so clear cut—I love "frozen breath of his silenced soul". May I take that home to show T.H. I *will not lose it* I faithfully promise (no I will copy it if you don't object).

Fin de Fête I do not like quite so much as some others of yours—though of course I *do* like it. And the same with "The Rambling Sailor" which, though it is fine, I admit, does not appeal to me so much as "Hurt not the trees". How T.H. would love that. But I fear if he read it never again would one bough be lopped of the trees that hem us round & make some of our rooms so dark & depressing. I have read the poem again since I wrote those last words, & it is more & more wonderful. There is no other living poet—man or woman—who could have written just that poem. Thank you so much for sending them.

It did me so much good to see you again here. It was so good of you to come. I am writing this at 6.30. in the morning—having watched the dawn & listened to the milk carts rattling by. I am ashamed to confess that I am rather enjoying these last few days.

I am so looking forward to seeing your sister.

With love—& please do make me proud by calling me Florence.

Always yours affectionately,
F.E.H.

Text MS. (with envelope for hand-delivery) Berg. *Date* See below.
Fitzroy House: London nursing-home originally established by TH's friend, the Dorset-born surgeon Sir Frederick Treves, Bt. *poems*: later collected in Mew's *The Rambling Sailor* (London, 1929). *kindly sent*: C. Mew's 3 and 5 Oct. 1924 letters to FEH (Berg) indicate that she visited FEH on 5 Oct., sent the poems and some books that evening or the next day, and arranged for her sister Anne to pick them up from FEH on 7 Oct. *"Hurt . . . trees"*: collected as 'The Trees Are Down'.

To Siegfried Sassoon

Fitzroy House Nursing Home, | Fitzroy Square. W.1
[7 October 1924]

Dear Siegfried Sassoon:

Thank you so much for the lovely, *lovely* bunch of violets—my favourite flowers. They have been the greatest joy. And thank you also for your visit, which did me an enormous amount of good. I had never dreamed that you would come, & it was such a joy to see you. But I was so sorry that that poor half-crazy little woman, the wife of an old friend of T.H's should have been there. I thought I would ask her here, as T.H. obstinately refuses to see her now, & hurls her well-meant gifts of provisions, violently away.

I am absolutely well now—& I think I have partly you to thank for it, as it was through you that we knew those splendid people—Dr & Mrs Head—& without their help the whole thing, I *know*, might have been hopelessly bungled.

As it is I feel better—& happier—than I have felt for years & I depart joyfully—at 1. o'clock tomorrow—by car for Max Gate. The surgeon & nurses say there is absolutely no point in my remaining longer. T.H's brother has promised to fetch me in his new car & seems to delight in the job—but T.H. insists upon an experienced chauffeur accompanying him.

It would have been a great treat to see you here tomorrow—& it is so kind of you to suggest coming—but, as I said, I shall be leaving about one. Thank you so much, & for the lovely flowers. The violets I shall carry down with me, in the car.

Always yours sincerely
Florence Hardy.

P.S. I shall feel very happy when I hear you have another horse—a very good one.   F.H.

Text MS. Eton.   *Date* Supplied on MS. by Sassoon.
little woman: not confidently identified.   *Head*: see letter of 9 Feb. 1922.   *fetch me*: see Biography, 554–5.

[In the autumn of 1924 the group of Dorchester amateurs calling themselves the Hardy Players had embarked, with the author's enthusiastic co-operation, upon a production of *Tess of the d'Urbervilles* as dramatized by TH himself in the 1890s. Though FEH at first viewed the proceedings with somewhat sardonic amusement, she soon became distressed and dismayed by her husband's increasingly obvious infatuation with Gertrude Bugler, now seen not just as a beautiful and appealing young woman but as the ideal embodiment of Tess Durbeyfield, the most clearly 'personal' of all his fictional creations. FEH's existing irritation with Mrs Bugler (as she now was) soon flared into an active antagonism that she could not contain at the time but was later to regret and even attempt to remedy.]

To Sydney Cockerell

MAX GATE, | DORCHESTER.
22nd October. [1924]

My dear Sydney:

Many thanks for your letter. All is well here—T.H. cheerful & working hard. For a few days I felt unexpectedly weak, & as if I could hardly crawl about the house—but I did not give in, did not even have breakfast in bed one morning—& now feel almost myself again—but not quite.

The days in the nursing home remain as a happy memory. E. M. Forster has just written reviling Siegfried for having concealed from him the fact that I was in London in a n.h. as he says he would so like to have seen me there & had some long talks—which I too would have enjoyed. I feel inclined to have another little operation so that the friends, who say they would have been to see me, had they known, may have their turn.

T.H. is very anxious that I should rewrite the "materials", adding passages here & there, that he thinks might improve the work. I suppose I had better do it but it is a fairly stiff job. Blacks—the publishers—have just written to ask me to do a book on "Dorset", for which they already have illustrations. I am strongly tempted—but he (T.H.) thinks it would be unwise.

The Hardy Players have been here rehearsing. Both Tess & Angel (Mrs Bugler & Dr Smerdon) are pretty bad to *my* mind—but Alec d'Urberville (a newcomer) & our old friend Tom Pouncy are excellent—also Mrs Major as Tess's mother. Tess twitters affectedly in the tragic parts. She *may* pull up though, but she's so satisfied with her own performance that I'm afraid she not going to be the gigantic success that is anticipated. Dr Smerdon has not got hold of Angel Clare in the least—but he probably will improve as he realizes he cannot yet pull it off. The young man (Mr Atkins—a bank clerk here) who does Alec, would have made a splendid Angel. However they have another five weeks before them & probably all will be well. T.H. is enormously interested, which is very good for him—so long as he is not worried—

Always yours sincerely
Florence Hardy

P.S. I enclose some stamps for those I commandeered at Fitzroy House. FH.

Text MS. Beinecke. *Date* Year supplied on MS. by Cockerell.

Siegfried: Sassoon. *the "materials"*: i.e. the draft of the 'Life'. *book on "Dorset"*: the eventual author of *Dorset* (London: A. C. Black, 1925), illustrated by Walter Tyndale and A. Heaton Cooper, was H. O. Lock, TH's solicitor. *Pouncy*: see letter of 10 Dec. 1913; he played John Durbeyfield in the Dorchester production of *Tess*.   *Mrs Major*: Ethel Homer Major, née Jameson, Dorchester confectioner.   *afraid she not*: 'afraid she is not' obviously intended.   *Mr Atkins*: Norman J. Atkins; he wrote of his theatrical experiences in the pamphlet *Hardy, Tess and Myself* (Beaminster, 1962). See also FEH's 3 Nov. 1924 letter to Ada Galsworthy in H. V. Marrot, *The Life and Letters of John Galsworthy* (London: Heinemann, 1935), 549–50.

[TH's dramatization of *Tess of the d'Urbervilles* dated back to 1895, but his attempts to get it staged at that time were consistently defeated, partly—in that heyday of the actor-manager—by the absence of any strong and 'sympathetic' male role, partly by his own unwillingness to allow any tampering with the play's text or structure, but also by the confusion that resulted from his inability to choose among the several actresses to whom he had offered or half-offered the part of Tess. When talk of a London production was revived by the national publicity surrounding the Dorchester performances of November 1924, much the same difficulties again arose, complicated on this occasion by the praise that had been heaped upon Gertrude Bugler—beautiful and affecting in the Tess role but wholly without professional training or experience—and by the opposition between TH's admiration of her and FEH's dread. To a far greater degree than TH seems ever to have realized—or, indeed, than the circumstances appear to have warranted—FEH came to see the Gertrude Bugler episode as a marital crisis of major proportions, justifying the adoption of extreme measures in the defence of her marriage, her husband's reputation, and her own fragile sense of self-worth.]

To Gertrude Bugler

MAX GATE, | DORCHESTER.
Tuesday morning. [2 December 1924]

Dear Mrs Bugler:

I am glad you have written as it gives me a chance to explain the position clearly (please excuse typed letter as I am terribly busy).

When I read the enclosed notice in yesterday's Times—I understand it was also in other leading papers—I thought I had better look up the letters written by my husband to her about the play. He keeps copies of them all, of course. I found that he had definitely promised her that she should produce "Tess", with herself in the title-role. You see she is producer as well as actress, and therefore is in a position to produce the play, which an actress, who is not also a producer, could not do. My husband had written to her most enthusiastically and said she was the only woman he would care to play "Tess" in London. She would not have put those notices in the papers without authority, as she is a thoroughly nice woman, highly educated, and the daughter of a Dean— or something of that sort. Her father,

214

oddly enough, was a one time curate at the church at Bere Regis. I only mention this to show that she is not the type of woman who would invent a story about a promise— or publish a false statement in papers. Until I read the letters I did not realize that my husband had been so definite.

Moreover, when her husband—Mr Casson—had tea with us on Saturday they were discussing how the play could be altered—as it could never be produced in London in its present form—it would not run a fortnight, so I am told, by a leading producer. My husband was even discussing who should make the alterations as he did not feel competent to do them him-self—and indeed it is obvious that he has no knowledge of stagecraft.

He suggested to Mr Casson that Miss Thorndyke should find you a part— say as one of the milkmaids—to prevent your being disappointed. I looked at him in amazement when he said this, and could hardly believe my ears, and Mr Casson seemed quite embarrassed and murmured something about his wife being pleased to do what she could.

I tried to convey this to you on Saturday evening, but had no chance. When I saw my husband so deep in conversation with you and for so long, during the supper, I did not know he was making wild promises. I thought he was explaining to you how things stood.

What we all forget—owing to his wonderful activity and spirit—is the fact that he is in his eighty-fifth year, and the sole sign of his age, to me, is that he does forget what he says and what he promises. He is easily carried away when talking to any young woman and would promise anything— but verbal promises go for nothing, Miss Thorndyke has hers in writing.

But, putting Miss Thorndyke aside—I do not think that Mr Harrison has any intention of producing a series of matinees of "Tess" in London. He was most evasive when he was here, and I feel convinced that he would not do anything that would seem dishonourable to Miss T. He told us that the play would not be suitable as it is. In spite of all these tales of its having laid aside for thirty years I can assure you that it was offered to Charles Frohman in 1913—when my husband told Miss Lillah MacCarthy (Granville Barker's first wife) that she was the only person he wanted to see as "Tess", and it was rejected, mainly by Barrie's advice—as I happen to know. Lillah MacCarthy, telling me about it at the time, said that when she had read it she did not feel that she wished to play that part. That was just before my marriage and she spoke quite freely.

Years ago my husband arranged to let a certain French writer translate "Tess". Some time after he met a charming French lady—Miss Madeleine Rolland, who attracted him greatly and he gave her permission. She trans-lated the novel, and then the first translator came down on him for damages, and he had to pay a considerable sum to avoid a lawsuit. I don't say that Miss Thorndyke would bring a lawsuit, but I do say this, that no London manager would produce "Tess" while Miss Thorndyke has the written promise that she alone could produce it. And, by these notices, she obviously means to assert her rights.

Sir J. Forbes Robertson has written to ask if he could produce it, with his wife in the title-role. My husband has explained to him about Miss Thorndyke and promised that he could have the rights if Miss Thorndyke backs out.

I have written this long letter and told you all this that you may see clearly how the thing stands at present, and not be misled by ambiguous promises. If we hear anything from Frederick Harrison about a series of matinees I will let you know immediately, but don't build on that. Basil Dean will have nothing to say to the play.

Your chief hope now is in Barrie's finding you a part, which he could do more easily than anyone in London. My husband has not the slightest influence with producers or stage managers.

I am just going into Dorchester to post to you the books he has promised you. Many thanks for letter, and with kindest regards,

Yours very sincerely,
Florence Hardy.

Text   MS. (typed) Bugler.   *Date*   Supplied on MS. by G. Bugler.
enclosed notice: a paragraph in *The Times*, 1 Dec. 1924, quoted Sybil Thorndike (1882–1976), famous for her performance in Shaw's *Saint Joan*, as claiming that TH was 'reserving' for her the 'professional rights' to the *Tess* play, even though she would not be able to produce it in the immediate future.   *definitely promised*: but see note on Robertson below.   *Her father*: the Revd Arthur John Webster Thorndike.   *Casson*: Lewis Casson (1875–1969), actor and producer.   *leading producer*: the opinion was probably Barrie's.   *should find*: FEH typed 'shoul find'.   *during the supper*: preceding the final Dorchester performance of *Tess*, 29 Nov. 1924.   *easily*: FEH typed 'easilly'.   *Harrison*: Frederick Harrison (1854–1926), theatrical manager; for TH's advocacy of G. Bugler's claims, see *CL*, vi. 295–6.   *He told us*: FEH typed 'almost' following 'He' but later deleted it by hand.   *Frohman*: Charles Frohman (1860–1915), American theatrical manager.   *MacCarthy*: correctly, McCarthy; see letter of 10 Aug. 1919.   *Rolland*: Madeleine Rolland (see ELH letter of 30 Aug. 1909) seems to have been given permission to translate *Tess* prior to her first meeting with TH; for the other translator, said by TH to have exceeded the time-limit specified in his permission, see *CL*, ii. 164–5, 170–2.   *down on him*: FEH typed 'down on his'.   *Robertson*: Sir Johnston Forbes-Robertson (1853–1937), actor and manager; he had turned down the play in 1895 but his wife since 1900, the American actress Gertrude Elliott, was now eager to play Tess. In the letter to which FEH presumably refers (*CL*, vi. 288) TH in fact speaks of G. Bugler as having first claim to play Tess in London—ahead even of Sybil Thorndike—if any manager of a professional company offered her the part.   *Dean*: Basil Dean (1888–1978), recently successful as the producer of James Elroy Flecker's *Hassan* (1923).   *the books*: inscribed copies of Osgood, McIlvaine editions of *Tess* and *The Return of the Native*; see *CL*, vi. 290.

December 1924

To Howard Bliss

MAX GATE, | DORCHESTER.
14th Dec. [1924]

Dear Mr Bliss:

I hope you were not too tired after your return from Dorchester. The journey down must have been very trying, but it was good of you to come.

I have been talking to T.H about 'The Woodlanders' MS. & he is appalled to think so many pages were not his. At first he suggested that they could be taken out, & he would write in the passages (I am horrified to find I have started this letter on a half sheet!) but that seems unfair to the one who copied in so many pages with no thought save that of being helpful.

If this defect—for I know it is a defect—in the MS is disappointing do please —as an act of real friendship—let us have it back & the cheque would be returned—& it would really be no more than paying back a penny postage stamp —in our eyes. And then, later, some other MS. might be found for you.

My husband says—apart from all this—that he would like to give you an original MS. of one of his later poems, & he will do so.

I should so much like to see your collection some day during the early part of January when I shall be in Town for a day or two, if you are not too busy—I have never seen a proper Hardy collection & shall be most interested.

T.H. sends his kindest regards.

Yours very sincerely,
Florence Hardy—

Text MS. Princeton.   *Date*   Year supplied on MS. by H. Bliss.
Woodlanders' MS.: which Bliss had recently purchased from TH; it was later repurchased, when Bliss was in financial difficulties, and is now in DCM.   *appalled . . . not his*: but in ELH's hand, as Bliss had pointed out (cf. letter of 3 Apr. 1921); Bliss has asterisked 'appalled' in this MS. and noted, 'On the contrary, these pages in Emma's writing added interest. And it was because of this interest that they were pointed out. H.B.' In typed notes (Beinecke) perhaps sent with this letter FEH relayed TH's insistence that ELH never corrected his MSS. but sometimes took dictation, 'when he was tired', and made fair copies of pages 'that were much deleted and altered'.

To Gertrude Bugler

Max Gate.
Monday. [22 December 1924]

Dear Mrs Bugler:

Everything is going on well, & I am sure the Haymarket production will be an accomplished fact. Sir James Barrie (I want to write merely Barrie only I am told he dislikes that) has taken it in hand. We have just heard from him. He can be the most marvellous friend in the world, as *I* have found, & I should think he would certainly put you in one of his plays—he is now writing a new one I am told—if this one is a success. I enclose a letter which he wrote to Mrs G. B. Shaw. It was given to me, & you might care to have it to keep. The first "Tess" refers to the play & the second Tess to you—but of course I need not explain. I should like to have seen you but I hope to do so later on. It was about nothing of importance, only I thought I would like a quiet talk to explain many things.

Fortunately all seems quite happy now here, & the foolish trouble has blown over—for good I hope. All my happiness lies in that one direction. Unlike you I have no child to promise future happiness, no career before me—everything seems to lie behind. However I could talk this over with you much better, & may do so some day, when there is an opportunity. Of course I know I am very run down, & my nerves all anyhow. But I do hope & trust that everything here is now quite right. Thank you so much for your kind letter, & please excuse this horrible scribble.

Yours sincerely,
Florence Hardy.

Text MS. Bugler. *Date* From internal evidence.
taken it in hand: see *CL*, vi. 298–9. *new one . . . this one*: Barrie's next new play seems to have been *Barbara's Wedding*, staged in Aug. 1927 as a curtain-raiser to Strindberg's *The Father*; by 'this one' FEH apparently means the projected Haymarket production of *Tess*. *letter . . . Shaw*: Barrie told Charlotte Shaw (8 Dec. 1924, Bugler) that the *Tess* play ' "got home" again and again in queer triumphant inexplicable ways', G. Bugler delighting him 'beyond most actresses'. *a quiet talk*: in her letter of 17 Dec. 1924 (Bugler) FEH had suggested they might meet in the Ladies' Club over the Dorset County Museum rather than at Max Gate, 'where there is always the chance of someone coming in'. *one direction.*: FEH struck through the original continuation of this sentence, 'If only I could rid myself of a feeling', but left it entirely legible.

[In a letter to Gertrude Bugler of 2 January 1925 (Bugler) FEH offered to help her in finding suitable accommodation and meeting influential people while she was appearing in the projected matinées of *Tess* at the Haymarket Theatre. As the days passed, however, as TH seemed to grow more distant and short-tempered, and as Gertrude Bugler came again to Max Gate for professional discussions, FEH increasingly surrendered to extravagant fears of what her husband's infatuation might portend for the future of their marriage—and what embarrassing indiscretions he might commit if tempted to go to London to see the play and visit Mrs Bugler's dressing-room. So oppressive did her fears become that at the beginning of February she visited her 'rival' privately in her Beaminster home and proceeded to plead, argue, and browbeat her into withdrawing altogether from the Haymarket scheme.]

To Gertrude Bugler

MAX GATE, | DORCHESTER.
February 7th. [1925]

Dear Mrs Bugler:

Of course it was quite right that you should let my husband know that you had written to Mr Harrison. I do, as a rule, open his letters to save him trouble & keep back applications for autographs from strangers. But I gave him yours unopened, directly I saw your writing, before I had read yours to myself—knowing, of course, that it would be all right.

I do trust that all will go on quietly now, for neither he (at his age) nor I can stand any great emotional disturbances. But I do not see why all should not be well if we just wait a bit & go on in a normal way.

I would give all I possess to be able to believe that all I have been so worried about was the result of overstrained nerves—but I put that question to Dr Head, & he told me very emphatically that I was to put that out of my head at once, & not to be persuaded that my anxieties were a delusion. He has seen so much of the kind. And then Mr Cockerell (who would be my husband's trustee in case of illness—& will manage his affairs, with myself,) used his own judgment—& he is very acute & far-seeing, & when I asked him if it were possible that I was suffering from an hallucination, he said he was afraid it was real enough. You see I know all that has been said here—to myself & other people.

But the main thing now is to try to forget everything & go on in a quiet manner, helping one another as much as possible.

If anyone asks me about the London scheme—of yourself as Tess, I shall merely say that you felt you could not leave your baby, & that it was very good of you to put her & your husband first. But so far no one has mentioned the subject to me. I have not seen Mr Tilley & should not tell him anything about it, if I did see him—nor anyone else.

I should think a recital at the dinner of Dorsetmen in London would be very interesting—but as to reciting T.H's poem I do not know what to think. Might I ask Dr Head? He is a great friend of the surgeon who operated on me—Mr Sherren, who is a Vice-President of the Society & destined to be some day president, & they would know what was best—& Mr Sherren *does* know I am not hysterical or neurotic—having seen so much of me at a trying time. But perhaps you would think it better not to say anything more for a while—nor mention your name.

If you could recite anything from another author it might prove your versatility & disprove what some critics say—that it is merely T.H's name that attracts the attention. A lady—a friend of Mr Watkins—has just recently been giving Hardy recitations under the auspices of the Society of Dorsetmen. However we might think over what is best to be done. My fear is that he would insist upon 'coaching' which is not only ludicrous, but might arouse all the old difficulties that I hope are over. I hope I shall see you soon. So many thanks for your letter.

Yours very sincerely

F.E.H.

Text   MS. Bugler.   Date   Year from internal evidence.
to Mr Harrison: Frederick Harrison replied to G. Bugler 4 Feb. 1925 (Bugler), regretting her decision but not actively questioning its wisdom.   all right: i.e. following her call at G. Bugler's home (see *Biography*, 557). G. Bugler's letter to TH (4 Feb. 1925, DCM) explained her change of plan in terms of her obligations to her husband and young child; for TH's reply see *CL*, vi. 308.   *Dorsetmen in London*: i.e. the Society of Dorset Men in London, of which William Watkins was the secretary and TH himself a past president.   *Hardy recitations*: the *Dorset Year-Book* for 1925 reported a Miss Ena Hay Howe as reciting TH poems both at the Society's Annual General Meeting and at a separate performance.

To Sydney Cockerell

MAX GATE, | DORCHESTER.

10th. March 1925.

My dear Sydney:

I have been meaning to write to you for some time but we have been very busy. I hope that the children are now well and back at school, and that Mrs Cockerell and yourself have kept well, with no influenza. T.H. had a bad cold and was in bed for five days, but I looked after him carefully and he had a fire in his bedroom night and day and had three half bottles of champagne and is now as well as ever. He would not hear of a doctor being called in, and there seemed no need, but I should have sent for one the moment he seemed really ill. We have been for a walk this afternoon and the wind was rather cold so I think he had better keep in till the weather is milder. He is getting on rapidly with his poems and we are sending several out. The volume will be ready for publication this summer. *Are you coming down at Easter.* He says he will be very pleased to see you if you can come. Any time.

All is well and happy here now, since Mrs B. gave up the Haymarket scheme. That had a great effect and saved the situation. I will tell you about it when we meet. If all remains quiet for a few months I think there will be nothing to fear—and if I can manage it the Hardy plays will stop now.

I cannot go through another experience like that, and it would be bad for him also.

On Saturday last I motored over to Beaminster to see Mrs Bugler and took with me her birthday present—an inscribed book. I thought that would be rather what is called, I believe, "un beau geste". I told her that if she liked negociations about the play could be recommenced—but I knew it would be all right, and she said she had no regrets.

I saw Barrie on Thursday last and he told me that Augustus John had observed the situation, to his huge amusement and delight, and was talking about it everywhere—and it came to Barrie's ears that way. I guessed that Barrie had heard from a very affectionate letter he wrote me. Augustus John was behind the scenes with T.H. and myself and the rest for about an hour the last night of the play in Dorchester and I thought he seemed a bit amused. Barrie was *most* kind.

I saw Sybil Thorndike also. She would make a good Tess I feel certain. But she is dubious now about the play. Barrie is very emphatic about the merits of the play and says that he is sure it is a good play, and he is emphatically against anyone but T.H. touching it. Miss Thorndike is calling here the week after Easter, and will talk the matter over. But Mr Golding Bright—Barrie's agent—is anxious that T.H. should let him go on with the arrangements and get someone else for the part of "Tess". T.H. is desperately keen on having it produced in London and seems not to mind Mrs Bugler being out of it. He says he would rather Miss Fay Compton did it than Mrs Bugler. Fortunately the poems he is doing now occupy his mind and he is an entirely different being from what he was when you were last here.

Your friend Miss Bateson is lunching with us on Thursday and we are much looking forward to her visit.

With many thanks for all you have done.

Yours affectionately,
F.E.H.

Text   MS. (typed) Beinecke.

Are . . . Easter: underlining added in ink; ink insertions are 'Any time.' at end of para. 1, 'about the play' in para. 3, and 'Barrie . . . kind.' in para. 4.   *stop now: Tess* was indeed the last production of the 'Hardy Players'.   *amusement*: FEH typed 'amusememt'.   *Augustus John*: the artist (1878–1961); his portrait of TH was presented to the Fitzwilliam Museum in Jan. 1924.   *Bright*: Reginald Golding Bright, theatrical agent recommended to TH by Barrie (20 Dec. 1924, DCM) and in fact previously employed by TH.   *Compton*: Fay Compton (1894–1978) had played leading roles in several of Barrie's plays and, most recently, in Flecker's *Hassan*.   *the poems*: TH was preparing his *Human Shows* volume.   *Bateson*: Edith Bateson (d. 1938), sculptor and painter (*CL*, vi. 23).

To Paul Lemperly

MAX GATE, | DORCHESTER.
8th April. [1925]

Dear Mr Lemperly:

Thank you for your letter which arrived today, & was read by my husband and myself with much interest.

We should much like a copy of Brennecke's "Life & Art" if you would be kind enough to send it to us. You are right in surmising that Brennecke's "Life of T.H." is unauthorized. In fact my husband sent a cable of protest. The young man who wrote it came here under false pretences, representing himself as a student of philosophy—& promised that he would write no personal details. The details he gives of T.H's life are mostly fictitious. He gives an absolutely false picture of our life here, & makes me say things I should never have dreamed of saying, e.g. he makes me say that we had been reading 'The Genius' by Dreiser, & that we thought it ought to be suppressed. Neither T.H. nor myself have ever read any book by Dreiser. He describes the manner in which T.H smokes a cigarette—T.H. has been a non-smoker all his life & detests the cigarette habit, & so forth. There are errors on almost every page—some quite ludicrous. He gives a most revolting photograph of myself at Oxford, which no one who knew me would even recognize. At this very moment a friend of my husband's is having an interview with his publisher to see if anything can be done.

Mr Brennecke came here first about three years ago, & had a brief interview—he was not invited to tea. Later he came to show a MS. "Thomas Hardy's Universe", & was asked to lunch.

The picture of me "serving plum-tart & custard" is too comic. We loathe plum tart & custard, & the sweets at our table are handed to each guest in the usual manner. He was thinking of his hotel lunch I expect. I disliked the man when I first saw him, & he must have realized this, which accounts for the way in which he writes of me.

I hope that you will get Colonel Lawrence's book, & that you will not be disappointed. I know more than one person who would buy it from you if you did not like it—only whether that would be fair, they having been 'turned down' by Colonel Lawrence, as unworthy to possess it, I do not know.

I have some proof sheets & they are wonderfully printed.

Our garden is looking most beautiful now with spring flowers, & a new gardener—who came 6 months ago—has worked wonders. We have masses of daffodils in the orchard—a sea of flowers under the apple-trees.

This afternoon my husband & I walked to Stinsford churchyard (Mellstock in 'Under the Greenwood Tree') to lay flowers on the family graves. Although it was a long walk my husband was not over tired. It was a lovely walk over green meadows.

I am posting you with this, with many regrets for the delay, the promised 1st edition, "No Bell-Ringing".

Thank you for the notice of the sale of the Hardy collection.

I believe there are only half a dozen copies of 'The Three Wayfarers" in existence—a small copy of the dramatized version. I do not know what they refer to by 'Songs of the Soldiers' Wives.'

Yours sincerely,
Florence Hardy.

Text   MS. (with envelope) Colby.   *Date*   From postmark.
"Life & Art": *Life and Art: Essays, Notes and Letters Collected for the First Time* (New York, 1925), an unsystematic vol. of TH's miscellaneous prose writings compiled by the American critic Ernest Brennecke, Jun. (1896–1969); see *CL*, vi. 322.   *"Life of T.H."*: Brennecke's *The Life of Thomas Hardy* (New York, 1925); for TH's cable see *CL*, vi. 304 n.   *any book by Dreiser*: the Hardys had in fact been sent a copy of Theodore Dreiser's *The 'Genius'*, but in a letter to the American scholar S. C. Chew (5 Sept. 1925, Adams) FEH again insisted that they had not read the book and that she would never be 'so foolish' as to say that any novel should be suppressed.   *friend . . . publisher*: Cockerell and Sir Frederick Macmillan jointly drafted a letter to *The Times*, 11 Apr. 1925, warning British publishers of the book's unauthorized and objectionable character; it never did appear in the UK (see *CL*, vi. 318–19).   *Universe"*: Brennecke was admitted to Max Gate as a student of TH's philosophy, the subject of his *Thomas Hardy's Universe: A Study of a Poet's Mind* (London, 1924), a book to which TH had responded in critical but friendly fashion (*CL*, vi. 259).   *Lawrence's book*: *Seven Pillars of Wisdom*.   *1st edition*: TH's *No Bell-Ringing: A Ballad of Durnover*, one of FEH's pamphlets, privately printed in Feb. 1925 (Purdy, 233–4).   *Hardy collection*: evidently the catalogue of the New York auction of the George Barr McCutcheon collection, 20–1 Apr. 1925.   *Wayfarers"*: i.e. the first (1893) printing for copyright purposes only (Purdy, 78–9); the McCutcheon copy is now in the Adams collection.   *'Songs . . . Wives.'*: the 's' on 'Songs' is an error; FEH was evidently unfamiliar with no. 63 in the McCutcheon catalogue, an offprint of the poem's first printing (Purdy, 109).

To Siegfried Sassoon

MAX GATE, | DORCHESTER.
15th April '25.

Dear Mr Sassoon:

T.H. has sent you a note (to your club I think) & as he always writes in such a restrained manner I must supplement it.

When he read your poems first he said in a *very* quiet—awed—tone. "Really these are very good," & he repeated that twice while reading.

I, of course, think them wonderful.

I hope you are well. T.H. is looking splendidly & working hard.

Yours very sincerely
Florence Hardy.

Text   MS. (with envelope) Eton.

restrained manner: TH's brief letter of this same date (*CL*, vi. 320) says only that Sassoon's privately printed *Lingual Exercises for Advanced Vocabularians* represented an 'advance' on his previous poems.

To Charlotte Mew

MAX GATE, │ DORCHESTER.
27th May. '25.

My dear Charlotte:

I am so sorry to hear about your sister's accident to her eye. It is most unfortunate, & I so hope it will not prove very serious. Anything to do with the eye is so alarming, & it is a great nuisance that her work should be interfered with.

It is so good of you to be so thoughtful & understanding about T.H. Most people are inclined to take up this attitude: 'Oh, I shan't tire him. Other people may do so, but its impossible that he should be tired of ME.' Our kind S.C.C. is rather like that, thoughtful as he is in other ways.

However I do think that once *next* week is over, everything will be all right, if only your sister is well enough to be left. The birthday week is always an exhausting one for T.H. & he still feels weak. A voluble lady came to tea yesterday, & in the midst of a perfect *spate* of egotistical non-sense, he jumped up & went away, to her indignation. I found him lying on the sofa in his study, & he said: "I feel absolutely exhausted."

However, I will write again, directly everything seems well—for I really am looking forward to seeing you most tremendously. Please give my love & best wishes to your sister,

Yours affectionately,
Florence Hardy.

Text   MS. (with envelope) Berg.
next week: TH was 85 on 2 June 1925.   *voluble lady*: unidentified.

To Virginia Woolf

MAX GATE, | DORCHESTER.
31st May: '25

Dear Mrs Woolf:

I have just been reading to my husband, to his great pleasure, your book of essays—The Common Reader—& this has reminded me that you were good enough, when you came to see me in the nursing home, to say that you would like a poem by him for The Nation.

I enclose one herewith. My husband says that if Mr Woolf does not think it suitable please do not hesitate to return it.

With kind regards,

Yours sincerely,
Florence Hardy.

Text   MS. Berg.
Woolf: [Adeline] Virginia Woolf (1882–1941), known to TH not only as a novelist and critic but as the daughter of Leslie Stephen, 'who influenced me in many ways when I was a young man' (*CL*, vi. 196). She and her husband Leonard Sidney Woolf, currently literary editor of the *Nation and Athenaeum*, visited Max Gate in July 1926.   *Common Reader:* Woolf's *The Common Reader* (London, 1925), her first collection of literary essays.   *nursing home:* according to Penelope Fitzgerald's *Charlotte Mew and Her Friends* (London: Collins, 1984), 199, V. Woolf and C. Mew met at FEH's bedside but were 'too shy' to speak.   *a poem:* TH had declined to contribute to the *Nation* in May 1923 but now sent 'Coming up Oxford Street: Evening', printed in the 13 June 1925 issue.

[The withdrawal of Gertrude Bugler had left TH free to make arrangements with Sybil Thorndike and her husband for a London production of *Tess*, but negotiations broke down over their insistence on changes he was unwilling to accept. In mid-July 1925 he was approached by a relatively unknown producer, Philip Ridgeway, who wanted to put the play on at the Barnes Theatre, unpropitiously distant from central London. Quickly pushed into a positive decision by the ever-urgent Ridgeway, TH soon found himself once more involved in—though not responsible for—the selection of the cast, and in a series of letters to Ridgeway he either hinted at or specifically advocated the choice of Gertrude Bugler as Tess. Ridgeway, however, was determined to have a fully professional company, and early in August announced, with much publicity, that the role would be taken by Gwen Ffrangcon-Davies, who had enjoyed an immense success in Rutland Boughton's *The Immortal Hour*. Although these developments were clearly satisfactory from FEH's point of view, they did not altogether restore her sense of security. Writing to Cockerell on 8 August 1925 she alluded ungenerously to the explanations Gertrude Bugler was offering for the decisions she herself had forced upon her, and later in the same month (20 August 1925, Beinecke) she begged Cockerell to persuade her husband to put an end to the Dorchester performances lest 'some terrible catastrophe' result from another 'Hardy play' with Gertrude Bugler in it.]

To Sydney Cockerell

MAX GATE, | DORCHESTER.
8th August. [1925]

My dear Sydney:

We are so pleased to hear that your little party are to be at Cerne after all, & I hope we shall see as much of them as possible. If you come down with them would you care to spend Wednesday or Thursday night here? We have promised to lunch with Dr & Mrs Head at Lyme Regis, on Thursday next, & go on to tea with Lady Pinney at Racedown, but that is our sole outing next week. We should be home, on the Thursday, not later than 7 I imagine, & of course on Wednesday we should be here all the time & until about 11.30 on Thursday morning.

I hope you approve of the arrangements about "Tess". Mrs Bugler's name was sent up to Mr Ridgeway, but, *thank Heaven*, he wasn't having any. Harley G-B. warned T.H. against experimenting with her, & so did Middleton-Murry. She (so Mr Tilley tells me) is now saying that *she* wouldn't think of appearing at a suburban theatre. If she did go to London it would be to a West End theatre or none. Her husband told Mr Tilley that the offer of two matineés a week at the Haymarket *"wasn't good enough"*.

T.H. is very pleased about 'Tess' being produced by professionals at last. It is long since I have seen him so happy about anything, & there is none of that un-natural excitement that there was about the former productions & the Haymarket scheme. He may fall in love with Miss Gwen as much as he likes, & the more the better.

Rutland Boughton writes to congratulate T.H warmly on having her as Tess. He says he daren't think what would have happened to 'The Immortal Hour" without her. And Newman Flower says that when he saw her last, as Cleopatra, he decided that she was the finest actress we have. You know he wanted to finance the play if it could be produced at the West End. I hope that Mr Ridgeway won't spoil it by any vulgarities. I am terribly afraid. There have been certain little things that have made me anxious, but Mr Golding Bright will look after things I hope.

They are coming here tomorrow—Miss Gwen F-Davies, Ridgeway, & Milton Rosmer, to discuss matters. T.H. has never seen the lady. I hope he won't be disappointed. Everyone speaks very highly of her as an actress & as a woman. I was never so much attracted by an actress as I was by her in 'The Immortal Hour.' She was actually a being from fairy-land, sweet & wistful, half lost in dreams.

I don't know whether Lawrence has gone or not. If he is still at Bovington I expect he will be in tomorrow. He is not likely to make a ceremony of leave-taking & he says he will often be at Cloud's Hill for week-ends, & see as much of us as he does now—though that is highly improbable.

Eden & Emily Phillpotts will be here to lunch on Wednesday—

Yours very sincerely,
Florence Hardy.

Text MS. Beinecke.   *Date* Year supplied on MS. by Cockerell.
little party: Cockerell's wife and children were holidaying on a farm near Cerne Abbas, N. of Dorchester.   *Head . . . Pinney*: the Heads were staying at Lyme Regis in order to be near Henry Head's sister, Lady Hester Pinney (the wife of Major-General Sir Reginald John Pinney), at Racedown, Dorset, a house occupied by William and Dorothy Wordsworth 1795–7.   *name was sent up*: by TH; see *CL*, vi. 342.   *Mr Ridgeway*: Philip Ridgeway (1891–1954), theatrical producer.   *Harley G-B.*: Harley Granville-Barker.   *matineés*: sic.   *Miss Gwen*: Gwen Ffrangcon-Davies (1891–1992); she had recently played Cleopatra in G. B. Shaw's *Caesar and Cleopatra*.   *Flower*: see letter of 1 Feb. 1921.   *Milton Rosmer*: actor and producer—but not, in fact, associated with *Tess*; FEH apparently misheard the name of A. E. Filmer, the actual stage-director and producer.   *gone or not*: T. E. Lawrence, leaving the Tank Corps and returning to the Royal Air Force, had been posted to Cranwell in Lincolnshire.   *Cloud's Hill*: see letter of 1 Dec. 1923.   *Emily Phillpotts*: née Topham.

To Gertrude Bugler

MAX GATE, | DORCHESTER.
Sunday morn. [27 September 1925]

Dear Mrs Bugler:

When I was last at the Barnes Theatre I was speaking to Mr Ridgeway about his reasons for not offering you the part of 'Tess', & he repeated all that he had told me before about it taking "years of training to make an actress," etc. etc. but he added that if you really wanted to take up a career on the stage he would hear you read the part & if he was satisfied would offer you the part in his first touring company which he intends to send out shortly.

Now please do not imagine that I recommend this to you, or that I think that you want to start a new career. I told Mr Ridgeway that I felt sure you wouldn't think of accepting such an offer if made. However, I think it fair to tell you of the suggestion. I hear that you are going to the Barnes Theatre on Thursday next, & if you wished to discuss the matter with Mr Ridgeway I would write to him at once.

All I can say in favour of his plan is that it would be the only *certain* way of beginning as an actress, & might lead to a triumph—and couldn't be a definite failure. But of course the life would be a very strenuous one, & probably absolutely impossible for a wife & mother. Still, there it is, & you will know now that he did make that offer, & you can use your own discretion about it. He is anxious also to send or take companies to South Africa & Australia to play 'Tess,' & Miss Ffrangçon-Davies couldn't go as she is under contract to go back to Sir Barry Jackson's company after the run of 'Tess' in London. With kind regards—

Yours sincerely—
Florence Hardy.

Text MS. Bugler. *Date* From internal evidence.
the part in his: 'of Tess' inserted in MS. following 'part' but apparently not in FEH's hand. *send out shortly*: *Tess* opened at the Barnes Theatre 7 Sept. 1925, but its successful transfer to the Garrick Theatre, in the West End, on 2 Nov. 1925 delayed the departure of the touring company until early 1926; see letter of 16 Mar. 1926. *going . . . Thursday next*: with the rest of the 'Hardy Players'; see letters of 5 and 22 Oct. 1925. *Ffrangçon-Davies*: the name appears to have been spelled without a cedilla. *Jackson's company*: the Birmingham Repertory Company, founded and led by Sir Barry Vincent Jackson (1879–1961); G. Ffrangcon-Davies returned Jan. 1926 to a revival of *The Immortal Hour*, which the company had originated in 1921.

To Sydney Cockerell

MAX GATE, | DORCHESTER.
5th October. [1925]

My dear Sydney:

Thank you so much for seeing to the pendant. It has been done so well, & the price *most* moderate. It will be a delightful trinket—if that word is now allowed.

T.H. has not been very well. Yesterday he was in bed until the evening when he insisted upon getting up & coming down to the dining room. He rather alarmed me after tea, as he had complained of weakness & a chill, by saying he was going to get up & go to Frome Hill to see the moon rise— with me. He didn't seem to be joking either, but a little rambling. However I took no notice & he was quiet for a time, & then said he would come down to the dining-room, & sit by the fire. And then he said he felt so unwell, & just as he used to when he was a little boy & very delicate. I realize now why Dr Head so strenuously urged me to keep him from all excitement. Today he is up, but looks unwell & says he does not feel equal to going for a walk. Thank you for your advice about the fires.

Mr Ridgeway writes that he must have another of his 'famous press stunts" & that in order to revive interest in the play T.H. must attend a performance either at Bournemouth or London. As if he could! The Hardy Players have all been up to see the play at Barnes, &, as I expected, say their own production was better. Well, I am glad they have that satisfaction.

I expect that you are both feeling very lonely now the children have gone back to school.

Always yours sincerely,
Florence Hardy.

Text　MS. Beinecke.　　*Date*　Year supplied on MS. by Cockerell.
the pendant: FEH (26 Sept. 1925, Beinecke) had asked Cockerell if he would get an earring of hers turned into a pendant by a London jeweller.

To Sydney Cockerell

MAX GATE, | DORCHESTER.
22nd. October '25.

My dear Sydney:

I send the photograph post-cards of Dorchester that Christopher asked for, and I hope they may be of some use, or at least of interest. I send also a guide which will have to go under separate cover as it is raining in torrents and I would not be able to post this letter if I sent that with it, as our post-box is so small and I cannot walk to the bridge. Also I return Margaret's very interesting letter which we were glad to see.

I never answered one question of yours about "Ariel". We did read it—in a translation of course. I have almost forgotten it but I know T.H's feeling was that he did not like a book in which fact and fiction were intermingled so that one was likely to confuse the real with the imaginary in thinking of Shelley's life after. A life of George Gissing was done in that way, and I remember he thought it unfair. I shall, however, get "Ariel" again from the Times Book Club and re-read it since you think so highly of it.

We have had a very bright letter from Miss Ffrangcon-Davies. She thinks that for a play to run six weeks at an outlying theatre like Barnes is a record. She says three weeks is the longest that any other play has run in similar circumstances. She is very hopeful of success when it goes to the West End, but it is not paying where it is at present, I think.

Everyone writes to us most warmly about her, and several friends have gone to see her a second time. Harley Granville-Barker wrote enthusiastically to T.H. about her and said that no-one could have served him better. He said "She has served you well". I must show you his letter someday.

T.H. says that it is not quite fair criticism to say she is unlike the Tess of the novel, as the play ought to be judged as a play and without reference to anything else. The Hardy players who went up from Dorchester found fault with nearly every other performer, but said that she was beyond criticism, and one of them said to me last Sunday "They (the Hardy Players) all admitted that she wiped Gertrude off the slate." You may not agree but it is rather a consolation to me to think so, and I think no good can be done by harping on the fact that she does not look like Tess.

Post just going—must hurriedly close,

Yours/

F.E.H.

Text MS. (typed) Beinecke.

"Ariel": *Ariel: ou la vie de Shelley*, by André Maurois (pseud. of Émile Herzog), first pub. in Paris 1923, trans. into English 1924.   *Gissing*: for TH's reaction to Morley Roberts's *The Private Life of Henry Maitland* (1912), see *CL*, iv. 234–5.   *confuse the real*: FEH typed 'confure the real'.   *enthusiastically*: FEH first wrote 'very warmly'.   *about her*: FEH typed 'zbout her'.

[TH never went to London to see Ridgeway's production of *Tess*, but Ridgeway, always eager for press attention, brought the cast from London to Dorchester on Sunday, 6 December 1925, to give a performance in the drawing-room of Max Gate—characteristically funding the publicity exercise by persuading TH to accept reduced royalties for that week. Although the play did not attract full houses at Barnes, it was more successful following its transfer to the West End and Ridgeway arranged for a provincial tour, with Christine Silver in the title role, to follow the end of the London run. He also made insistent requests to be assigned the American and other overseas rights to *Tess* and given permission to undertake dramatizations of other Hardy novels. Wilting somewhat under this pressure, TH increasingly relied on his wife to correspond with Ridgeway—many of her letters to him are now in the Frederick B. Adams collection—and to deal with theatrical matters generally.]

To Philip Ridgeway

MAX GATE, | DORCHESTER.

November 29th. 1925.

Dear Mr Ridgeway:

With reference to our conversation last Wednesday night, about the dramatization of "Jude the Obscure" I find, on looking through the correspondence relating to it, that my husband finally refused permission to the French dramatist who wished to dramatize it. This was after making enquiries as to the ability of the dramatist. However it is possible that if a really good English dramatist wished to dramatize it my husband would consent.

You asked if you might see a script of "Far from the Madding Crowd" as it was played down here, many years ago. I have just found a tattered copy which you might see if you wished. It is a pretty pastoral play with lots of rustic humour, and in parts as funny as "The Farmer's Wife"—only there is a tragedy towards the end—the shooting of Sergeant Troy. The great feature of it here was a sheep-shearing scene, with live sheep, which of course could not be done in London.

The general opinion is that "Trumpet Major" which was performed here thirteen years ago was the prettiest and most successful. There is pure comedy, with very amusing characters of an old miser and his loutish nephew, and the two chief characters, men, are a soldier and a sailor, who come in most effectively. The dramatic critic of the Times told me that this was his favourite of all the Hardy plays. However my husband, as you know, is not keen about any of these being put on the London stage and would only consent, I think, if he felt that you were satisfied with your production of "Tess". He would hate to think of your being involved in any loss over one of his plays. The other plays, of course, would not be exactly his, as he has not dramatized any except "Tess" and "The Three Strangers".

Thank you so much for the delightful evening I spent with you and Mrs Ridgeway last Wednesday. I hope that all is going well. We have not heard from Miss Ffrangcon-Davies. My husband says that it is possible that a little scene inserted, showing her being tried beyond her strength by Alec, might improve the play, if Alec was left in the confession scene. However he agrees with you that it would be a great pity for anything more to be put in the papers about it, so that the impression was given that it was a bad play that had to be patched up.

With kind regards,

Yours sincerely,
Florence Hardy.

Text   MS. (typed) Adams.
Ridgeway: see letter of 8 Aug. 1925.   *last Wednesday night*: when FEH attended a performance of *Tess* at the Garrick Theatre.   *French dramatist*: Claude Anet (pseud. of Jean
Schopfer); see *CL*, vi. 173–4.   *dramatize it*: FEH typed 'dranatize it'.   *played down here*:
see ELH letter of 21 Nov. 1909.   *Farmer's Wife*": play by Eden Phillpotts, currently running at the Court Theatre.   *thirteen years ago*: see ELH letter of 21 Nov. 1909; in her letter
of 1 Dec. 1925 (Adams), however, FEH told Ridgeway that TH was unalterably opposed to
the play's revival.   *critic of the Times*: Harold Child; see letter of 20 Aug. 1929.   *scene
inserted*: as G. Ffrangcon-Davies had suggested.

To Violet Hunt

MAX GATE, | DORCHESTER.

2. 12. 25

Dear Mrs Hueffer:

My husbands says he would be pleased to autograph a good portrait of himself for you, but he thinks the one enclosed too horrible for words. He looks like a conjuror—not in the least as he really looks—& he loathes the sight of the O.M. Of course he would never have consented to be taken wearing that, but it was a flash-light thing. And the spectacles!!! He only wears them for *small* print, & I remember on the occasion when this was taken he was reading a speech written in the *tiniest* script in a minute note-book.

But if you send a photograph that is really like him I'll see that he autographs it. Unfortunately we have not a single one left here.

We hope you are well—& with kindest regards,

Yours sincerely,
Florence Hardy.

Text MS. Berg.   *Date* Not certainly in FEH's hand.
Hunt: [Isobel] Violet Hunt (1862–1942), novelist and literary journalist, currently living with the novelist Ford Madox Ford (formerly Hueffer); TH had first met her in the 1890s. *husbands*: an error perhaps induced by FEH's awareness of V. Hunt's reputation.   *the one enclosed*: i.e. a press photograph (initially reproduced in the *Daily Graphic*, etc.) of TH, in dress suit with white bow tie, receiving the Freedom of the Borough of Dorchester, 16 Nov. 1910; ELH, elaborately dressed, also appears.   *I remember*: see FED letter of 19 Nov. 1910. *Unfortunately . . . here*: evidently squeezed in as an afterthought.

[FEH's surviving correspondence for the autumn of 1925 is so largely preoccupied with the London production of *Tess* that a more important event, TH's publication of a new collection of poems in his 86th year, seems to have passed relatively unnoticed. *Human Shows* received little mention even in TH's own correspondence, however, and he seems to have sent out fewer presentation copies than usual— perhaps because of a feeling that he had already been too much in the public eye. Writing to Cockerell on 24 November 1925 (Beinecke), four days after the publication date of *Human Shows*, FEH reported TH's resolution to 'keep very quiet now & publish no more poems for a year or people will be sick of him'. She added: 'I think he is wise: there has been too much booming. One review of his poems had this headline:—"Mr Hardy Again." He said that was very significant.']

To Siegfried Sassoon

MAX GATE, | DORCHESTER.
10th Dec. '25.

Dear Siegfried:

How delighted we are to hear that we may be seeing you soon.

T.H.'s message—*word for word.*

"Yes come to lunch next week certainly, as often as you can, & if you are good you shall have a nice cup of coffee afterwards." He says he does not mind what you say about him as a writer, but what the Americans want is not that, but whether his hair has been lately cut & whether his trousers are "knee-sy" etc. (His own words again).

He is very glad that you have moved to a more healthy spot—T.H. lived near there once, & says he felt very well all the time.

We are so glad you like the poems. You are responsible for one—but you would never guess which. It arose from something you once said here.

I must proudly point out that one of the poems is written to me: "Why do I go on doing these things". I was very surprised when T.H. told me & cannot resist telling all my friends.

T.H. says he meant to send you a book, but Macmillans were very mean about copies, & when we ordered some at our local bookseller he had sold out & has not yet been able to get the copies we ordered a fortnight ago. But he says he'll write in yours if you like, & if you will bring it.

How strange your being in that house, where there must be many ghosts. But they (the ghosts) will like your being there.

The "popular personage" is now listening with absorbed interest to his lovely broadcasting, or he would send a greeting—ie. a growl.

Always yours sincerely
FH. & T.H.

Text   MS. Eton.

"knee-sy": i.e. apparently, baggy at the knees.   *the poems*: *Human Shows, Far Phantasies, Songs, and Trifles*, pub. Macmillan, 20 Nov. 1925.   *ordered a fortnight*: FEH first wrote 'ordered from the local bookseller a fortnight' but then deleted the repetition.   *house, . . . ghosts*: Sassoon was about to rent a flat at 23 Campden Hill Square, the house Barrie had purchased in 1907 for the widowed Sylvia Llewelyn Davies and her five sons—whose guardian he became following Mrs Davies's own death in 1910; see Andrew Birkin, *J. M. Barrie and the Lost Boys* (London: Constable, 1979). The house was currently owned by the painter Harold Speed: see *Siegfried Sassoon Diaries 1923–1925*, ed. Rupert Hart-Davis (London: Faber & Faber, 1985), 292–3.   *"popular personage"*: the dog Wessex, subject of the poem 'A Popular Personage at Home' in *Human Shows*, was said to be a devoted radio listener.

To Sydney Cockerell

MAX GATE, | DORCHESTER, | DORSET.
Christmas-day 1925. | 7.0. p.m.

My dear Sydney:

Thank you so much for that beautiful book of poems. I shall love reading it when T.H. has done with it—but he has carried it off to his study & is enjoying it—which is, of course, what you would like, & what I like.

Here I sit alone in the drawing-room—not quite alone though, for Wessex is here, sulking, because he wants more broadcasting & I have called a halt. My mind goes back to a Christmas day—1910—when I sat here alone, & vowed that no power on earth would ever induce me to spend another Christmas day at Max Gate. T.H. had gone off to Bockhampton to see his sisters, after a violent quarrel with the first Mrs T.H. because he wanted me to go to see the sisters too, & she said I shouldn't because they would poison my mind against her—& then—oh dear oh dear, *what* a scene—& he went off, & she went up to her attic-study to write her memoirs until he came back at 8.30. It was the first Christmas of the kind I had ever spent, having always been with a party of cheerful people before that. She had only one more Christmas to live, poor thing. How different things might have been. If her ghost can read the latest volumes of poems published on earth I hope it is enjoying "Ten Years Since"—But if the ghost is anything like the living woman was I can imagine it saying——but no, it is better *not* to imagine.

After that I feel that my pen is hardly fit to write words of thanks for that beautiful portrait of your Katharine. What a beautiful calm & self-possession in her face for a girl of fourteen. We both like having it so much.

T.H. had an absolutely beautiful letter from Harley G-B- today. There is something that is *very* fine about him, is there not—& such kindness.

Again with all good wishes, & I am writing to Christopher (how well he designed that card) & to his fortunate mother—

Always yours sincerely
Florence Hardy.

Text MS. Beinecke.
book of poems: unidentified.   *more broadcasting*: see letter of 10 Dec. 1925.   "Ten Years Since": i.e. since the death of ELH; the poem, dated Nov. 1922, first appeared in *Human Shows*.   *Harley G-B-*: for the letter, dated 23 Dec. 1925, see Eric Salmon (ed.), *Granville Barker and His Correspondents* (Detroit: Wayne State Univ. Press, 1986), 384–5.

To Lady Pinney

MAX GATE, | DORCHESTER, | DORSET.
20th Jan. '26.

Dear Lady Pinney:

I have read with the deepest interest the story of that unhappy couple. What a story! One of the great Russian writers could deal with it—only it finishes off too completely for them.

The most terrible touch, & the most dramatic, is that account of Mary Davies, who was morally responsible for the whole tragedy, walking to see the hanging of the woman she had wronged. Horrible woman. I am so glad she was turned back.

Of course the account T.H. gives of the hanging is vivid, & terrible. What a pity that a boy of sixteen should have been permitted to see such a sight. It may have given a tinge of bitterness & gloom to his life's work.

However, he is bright & cheerful enough just now.

If you are able to come to see him some time again it would give him the greatest pleasure. I wish he were able to go over to see you, but the last two times he has been out to tea, after a longish drive, he has been very unwell the day after, & I think it is far more tiring for him, than seeing friends in his own home. One has to be so careful.

I am thankful of anything that keeps his mind a little bit off his own work (during his leisure hours), & the vivid account you sent of the Martha Brown tragedy was really most helpful. He is deeply interested in it—& so grateful to you for taking so much trouble.

Hoping that we may have the pleasure of seeing you soon.

Yours very sincerely,
Florence Hardy.

Text   MS. Bristol University Library.
Pinney: see letter of 8 Aug. 1925.   *the story*: TH, present in 1856 at Martha Brown's public execution for murder, became deeply interested in memories of the murder itself gathered by Lady Pinney from the inhabitants of the village, close to Racedown, where it had occurred; see *CL*, vii. 5, and Lady Pinney's pamphlet *Thomas Hardy and the Birdsmoorgate Murder 1856* (Beaminster, 1966).   *Mary Davies*: Martha Brown was said to have killed her husband after seeing Mary Davies sitting on his knee.

To Sydney Cockerell

Max Gate, | Dorchester. | Dorset.
23. I. 26.

My dear Sydney:

We are so very sorry to hear of your fall & hope that you are now better. No doubt you are in the hands of a really good doctor who will ascertain that there is no real injury to the shoulder. Mrs Hirst (the Queen of Cornwall) had a fall out hunting, & broke her arm, & then, after several weeks went to a London man, & found there was serious injury to her shoulder, & she thinks it will never be right again. And another friend fell downstairs & tore the muscles of her shoulder, & it was botched by a local doctor—another one—& the real nature of the injury was only discovered two months after, when her shoulder was Xrayed. This awful stories are by way of warning, but I know that a Cambridge doctor would be more efficient that a Dorchester one, & you would not, I hope, run any risks.

You must miss the children greatly. We are sorry to hear of the death of Mr Charles Doughty—a noble figure in the history of English Literature. You will miss him. I wonder if I am right in supposing you to be his literary executor?

I have just come in from a short walk with T.H. & Wessex. T.H. said he enjoyed the walk as the air was so fresh & pleasant. He is quite well, & his eyes seem stronger today. E. M. Forster is coming to Weymouth next week for a few days, & is coming over to see us. We shall enjoy his visits as he is so sympathetic & considerate.

I have just been put on our Borough Licensing Committee, the first woman who has ever been on that Committee for Dorchester, or Dorset I think. T.H., I fear, does not like the idea. He says there is such feeling always with the brewers & the publicans, but I was urged to accept as I could not be suspected of being 'got at', & I was properly elected by the votes of the magistrates. I do so like that work, & I suppose it flatters my vanity to be the only woman on three important committees. We have to set about closing a few public-houses in Dorchester where they abound to a disgraceful extent. I am sorry T.H. does not care for my taking up this work, but it is a real recreation to me, & takes up very little time.

I hope that Mrs Cockerell is well.

Yours very sincerely,
Florence Hardy.

Text MS. Beinecke.
Mrs Hirst: Kathleen Hirst, who played Iseult in the Dorchester production of *The Queen of Cornwall*. *This awful stories*: 'These awful stories' obviously intended. *efficient that*: 'efficient than' obviously intended. *Doughty*: Charles M. Doughty (see letter of 8 Aug. 1920) died 20 Jan. 1926; Cockerell, however, was not his literary executor. *the magistrates*: i.e. her fellow magistrates, since FEH was now a JP herself.

[One of the things that FEH had in common with her husband—and with Florence Henniker, Howard Bliss, and several other of their friends—was a passionate abhorrence of blood-sports and of all forms of cruelty to animals. She had also heard from TH of his first wife's courage in this cause—her readiness to challenge, then and there, acts of brutality of which she happened to be a witness—and while FEH removed several references to her predecessor when revising TH's autobiographical 'Life' for publication after his death, she allowed this aspect of ELH's character still to receive its due.]

To Howard Bliss

MAX GATE, | DORCHESTER, | DORSET.

5th March '26.

Dear Mr Bliss:

Thank you so much for your interesting letter which we were both so pleased to have.

I read, with great relief, the paragraph about the bull-fights: the abolition of the picador's turn. Just lately I read the opening chapter of D. H. Lawrence's latest novel—The Plumed Serpent—& the description there—of a bull-fight in Mexico—was horrible.

I can only hope that one day there will be an end to "blood" sport. In Dorset hunting is almost a religion, & I made many enemies by making a speech (a feeble little speech too) against it. And of course—*shooting*. But you know English country life. T.H. & I often discuss the bewildering plan of the Universe, & the only solution he can come to is that consciousness is a disease, & ought not to exist. But one would not give up many beautiful things—that could not exist if there were no consciousness.

I should much like to see "Uncle Vanya', but I am so rarely in Town & then only for a few hours, so I have very little opportunity to see plays.

The 'Balliol Players" are coming to us from Oxford early in July, to perform a Greek play in our garden, for T.H. If you should be anywhere near Dorchester at that time we do hope you will come to see it, but I hope that we may see you before then.

T.H. is very well & very busy. He went out for a walk with me today—though I fear it was too cold for him. 'The Dynasts' broadcasted—was not at all good. I am glad you did not hear it.

With our best regards

Yours sincerely,
Florence Hardy.

Text   MS. Princeton.
the paragraph: presumably a cutting sent by Bliss.   *The Plumed Serpent*: D. H. Lawrence's novel, first pub. 1926.   *"Uncle Vanya'*: the play by Chekhov, currently being produced by Ridgeway at the Duke of York's Theatre.   'Balliol Players": see letter of 9 July 1924; they returned to Max Gate, 29 June 1926, with a performance in English of Euripides' *Hippolytus.*   *broadcasted*: three extracts from *The Dynasts* were included in 'Napoleon Bonaparte: In Music and Story', broadcast by the London and Bournemouth stations of the BBC, 23 Feb. 1926.

To Philip Ridgeway

MAX GATE, | DORCHESTER.
16th. March 1926.

My dear Mr Ridgeway:

I was so sorry and disappointed that my husband did not feel equal to going to Bournemouth last Saturday. I had hoped he would do so, but he seemed to have made up his mind, and I cannot alter his decisions when once they are made. Moreover I have had such grave warnings from more than one doctor about his heart and blood pressure, and the danger of excitement, that I dare not upset him or even argue with him. If he keeps quiet all is well. He does very little now, and sees very few people. But I wish he could have seen Miss Silver who is excellent.

I rushed up to Town on Friday to see Sir James Barrie on a business matter—not about "Tess" of course—and he discussed Miss Davies performance which he praised very highly. As you know he thought her very good. He had not seen her act before he went to Barnes.

He said that in one instance particularly he though the girl who acted here her better. That was after the murder. Here she came back into the room dressed, in walking dress, but holding her hat. Her face was very pale. She stood before the mirror—sideways to the audience—and slowly coiled her hair—all this like one in a dream. Then she turned to the audience, and with an ecstatic smile said "I am coming my love". T.H. showed her how to do it, but it was really a wonderful bit of acting, and more than one who saw it Colonel T. E. Lawrence of Arabia—and others—thought her supreme in that.

Barrie said that the horror-struck eyes the terrified attitude were good acting—but acting. The other, he said, was just what Tess would have done had she committed the murder. However that is just a matter of opinion and the London way may be better for a general audience and for the provinces.

My husband was glad to hear that you agreed with him about the inadvisability of taking the play to America. He has decided definitely against it, also, as I told you, against the Ben Greet Company doing it in Paris.

I have given your letter to my husband and hope he will be able to find a photograph and write on it as you wish. I tell him he ought to.

Thank you so much for your kindness to my sister-in-law and myself at Bournemouth. Miss Hardy is my husband's only surviving sister and she has a terrible life in the country, and that little outing meant so much to her. She will remember it for years. In fact I don't think she ever had such a treat in her life. I thought you were so very good to her.

With kindest regards to Mrs Ridgeway and yourself from us both,

Yours very sincerely,
Florence Hardy.

Text MS. (typed) Adams.
disappointed: FEH typed 'disapponted'.　　*to Bournemouth*: to a matinée performance by the *Tess* touring company; FEH herself went, in company with Katharine Hardy, TH's surviving sister.　　*Silver*: Christine Silver (1884–1960) played the lead in the touring production; FEH told Cockerell (27 Mar. 1926, Beinecke) that she and Ridgeway agreed that C. Silver was a better Tess than G. Ffrangcon-Davies—'& looks the part'.　　*the girl*: G. Bugler, to whom FEH had reported Barrie's comments in a letter of 25 Nov. 1924 (Bugler).　　*mirror . . . smile . . . wonderful*: FEH typed 'mirrow', 'smilc', 'wondeful'.　　*Greet*: Ben Greet, actor-manager, currently associated with Edward Stirling (*CL*, vii. 8–9) in producing English plays in France.　　*such . . . life*: it appears from FEH to Cockerell, 18 Mar. 1926 (Beinecke), that this was K. Hardy's own phrase; FEH added that Ridgeway was 'really kind to her—box of chocolates—tea etc.'

To Maurice Macmillan

MAX GATE, | DORCHESTER, | DORSET.
18th April., | '26

Dear Mr Macmillan:

Some months back you wrote to me about the biography of my husband, & you were good enough to make a suggestion about the immediate printing of the first part. I discussed this with him, & he said he feared that, if it were set up in print, knowledge of he contents would leak out, through the printers. However, he is, at this present time, going over the MS. &

correcting it very carefully. This may be wise, or the reverse. However he is greatly interested.

Messrs Harper have asked our friend Mr Siegfried Sassoon to write the "authorized biography." Mr Sassoon told me that Mr Wells (the chairman) spoke as if they had every right to publish this. I explained to him the position, &, although I think he was disappointed, he understood.

Matters having reached this point I was wondering whether there is any likelihood of any member of your firm coming to see my husband some time this spring or summer on any business matter not connected with the biography. If so it would be an excellent opportunity to speak to him about the biography, so that you would have from himself instructions, or at least some statement of his own wishes. This would make everything much more simple. And, in addition, I can imagine few things that would give my husband more pleasure than a visit from Mr Daniel Macmillan or any member of the firm. I do not think that my husband is likely to be in London again. He knows, of course, that I mentioned the matter of the biography to you some months ago.

> Yours sincerely,
> Florence Hardy.

Text MS. BL.

Macmillan: Maurice Crawford Macmillan (1853–1936), publisher, younger son of Daniel Macmillan, co-founder of the firm.   *he contents*: 'the contents' clearly intended.   *greatly interested*: FEH told D. Macmillan (14 July 1926, BL) that TH had found 'so many fresh notes that he wishes put in, & then most of them have to be taken out again, so there seems no prospect of the work being completed'.   *Mr Wells*: Thomas Bucklin Wells (1875–1944) of Harper & Brothers, still TH's American publishers.   *Daniel Macmillan*: Daniel de Mendi Macmillan (1886–1965), M. Macmillan's son.   *visit . . . firm*: Sir Frederick Macmillan came to Max Gate with Charles Whibley (see letter of 19 Aug. 1919) a week later (FEH to Cockerell, 28 Apr. 1926, Beinecke), but it was in July that Daniel Macmillan talked with TH and 'heard from his own lips that he is not disinclined to the publication of the biography some day' (FEH to D. Macmillan, 14 July 1926, BL).

To Siegfried Sassoon

> MAX GATE, | DORCHESTER, | DORSET.
> 5th July. [1926]

Dear Siegfried:

We have thought a great deal about you lately—but we thought you were abroad. We were told so.

T.H. says he is sorry but he does not want any more of this MSS. to be auctioned. He hates the idea—& though several have been sold, by auction

& otherwise, for charities & for other people's benefit—it has never been with his approbation. And so many people have the idea that the money goes into his pocket, which makes him seem so grasping.

Moreover he says he is not in a position to know who is in the right in the dispute—& he will not do anything to give the impression that he approves of the strike. He thinks the miners are mislead.

I arranged to have a party of miners here (they were singing in Dorchester) but that had to be cancelled as he would not lend his name—but he *did* give them a good donation, through me—anonymously.

One of the Macmillans came down the other day to try to make some arrangement about an official biography. They are up in arms at the idea of Harpers publishing it, even in America. However nothing definite was settled—& T.H. would not let me show my MS—the second part of which is merely a mass of material—needing careful arrangement. The first part does not want so much done to it—but T.H. seems reluctant to come to any definite decision about it.

I should much like to see you some time but am so rarely able to get away—& then it is merely a rush to London, & a rush back. I nearly came on to try to find you at home one day in March, after I had been lunching with Barrie, but I wasn't sure of the way, & whether I could get there & back to Waterloo in time for my train.

It will be a very great thing for me to have the Heads so near. I hope they will not find Charminster very dull.

T.H. is very well, but of course his strength does diminish—very perceptibly—& he gets tired very very quickly. But he seems bright & happy now—more so than he was last year—by a long way. He often speaks of you—& always with affection.

We shall be delighted to see you whenever you are this way.

Always yours sincerely,
Florence Hardy.

Text MS. Eton. *Date* Year supplied on MS. by Sassoon.
this MSS.: 'his MSS.' presumably intended. *the dispute*: the coal miners' strike which precipitated, but did not end with, the General Strike of May 1926; Sassoon had evidently solicited one of TH's MSS. for auction in support of the miners. *singing in Dorchester*: the Penrhyn Glee Party gave a number of concerts in the Dorchester area to collect money for the miners' families. *official biography*: see letter of 18 Apr. 1926. *Charminster*: the Heads were moving to Forston House, NW of Dorchester.

[The London production of *Tess of the d'Urbervilles* had been sufficiently successful —running for more than a hundred performances before going on tour in the provinces—to interest Ridgeway and others in the possibility of adapting further Hardy novels for the professional theatre. These developments seem to have re-awakened FEH's sense of guilt at having deprived Gertrude Bugler of her opportunity to appear on the London stage, and when John Drinkwater's version of *The Mayor of Casterbridge* began to be seriously discussed she again offered to assist Mrs Bugler in obtaining a part, wrote to Drinkwater on her behalf (though perhaps with little real expectation of success), and went with her (at TH's prompting) to a performance of the play as produced.]

To Philip Ridgeway

MAX GATE, | DORCHESTER.
12th. September '26.

My dear Mr Ridgeway:

I posted to you yesterday the script of "The Trumpet-Major", as I thought it would be less trouble to do that than to carry it up. But unless "The Mayor" really succeeds I do not suppose either you or my husband will care to attempt another dramatization of one of his novels. He is certainly not anxious at the present moment, though he pays little attention to the critics, as those of his works which have proved most lasting and successful were the most violently condemned by critics when they first appeared. "Tess", for instance, and "The Dynasts".

However, the main thing is that we do not wish you to have any loss over this.

If you ever did think of producing another, and T.H. were willing, a pretty gay little comedy might succeed better, not a big tragedy.

I am much looking forward to seeing Mrs Ridgeway and yourself on Tuesday, and I will be at the Theatre quite early, by myself. My husband wished me to let Mrs Bugler (the Dorchester "Tess") see the play with me, as she does rather feel that she is now cast aside, there being no Dorset play this year, so I have asked her to meet me at the Box Office at 2.15. as she will be in London that day, and I know you won't mind her being with me, instead of the friend I asked, who has already seen the play, and prefers to wait a few weeks before seeing it again. You will find Mrs Bugler very gentle and aimable, and not in the least resentful towards you or the Barnes Theatre. I was very very angry with her some time ago, and I consider that she behaved very badly on several occasions, so I am not prejudiced in her favour—but I must say that I think her "Tess" was far better than that of Miss Ffrangçon-Davies, and so did several quite eminent men.

I will do my very best about the photograph—or it might be taken over to you at Weymouth.

With kind regards,

Yours very sincerely,
Florence Hardy

P.S. Mrs Bugler will be leaving quite soon after the performance as her husband is picking her up and taking her home to Dorset by car that same evening. F.H.

Text MS. (typed) Adams.

the script: evidently the text of A. H. Evans's Dorchester dramatization; see ELH letter of 21 Nov. 1909.   *the Theatre*: the Barnes Theatre, where Drinkwater's dramatization of *The Mayor of Casterbridge* opened 8 Sept. 1926.   *see the play*: as FEH first suggested in her letter of 28 July 1926 (Bugler).   *photograph*: see letter of 16 Mar. 1926.

[It was the custom at Max Gate for FEH to read to her husband every evening after dinner, an exercise which sometimes put a strain on her always delicate throat. To judge from the 5 March reference to Lawrence's *The Plumed Serpent*, the titles mentioned to Blunden on 31 October, and the 17 November comment on A. C. Benson's *Diary*, the Hardys kept up with the latest books—even the latest novels—to a surprising extent. They perhaps made few purchases at this date, but a good many books came by gift from the authors themselves and others were borrowed by mail from The Times Book Club. Not all their reading was new, however: on 26 May 1926 (Beinecke) FEH told Cockerell that she was currently reading aloud to her husband his favourite book of the year thus far, *Seventy Years a Showman*, the autobiography, first published in 1910, of 'Lord' George Sanger, the Victorian circus proprietor.]

To Edmund Blunden

MAX GATE, | DORCHESTER. | Dorset
31st October 1926.

Dear Mr Blunden:

I have just been reading—re-reading I mean—a delightful letter from you, dated Feb. 10th. & a terrible misgiving assails me. Was it ever answered? I cannot for the life of me remember. However, I believe you will forgive me if it was not, but I hope it was.

All your friends are eagerly looking forward to your return to England, ourselves among them. T.H. is pretty well, but of course the passing years take their toll of vigour. He still writes—poems only, of course, but he burns practically all that he writes, which is I believe the wiser plan. Anything is better than to put forth a quantity of work below his level.

I hope that you are well, and that you have good news of Mrs Blunden & your children. What an exciting re-union it will be when you return.

We have nothing of, or from, Siegfried Sassoon for several months, but had anything been amiss we should no doubt have heard, as his friends Dr & Mrs Head, have come to live a few miles from us. Robert Nicholls was there with his wife three weeks ago but we did not see them, though we were told that they suggested calling. I expect that Dr Head thought that a visit from them would be too much for T.H. but he would have been pleased to see them.

The Tomlinsons have just returned to London from their little home in Abbotsbury, & the Middleton Murrys go next week. The Tomlinsons are a most delightful family—& the M.M's have two attractive children, as no doubt you have heard.

We have read nothing good lately in the way of poems except one by you in the Adelphi. We are now reading H. G. Wells's latest, 'William Clissold'—a little tedious. Arnold Bennett's 'Lord Raingo' seemed to me so insufferably vulgar that I have not attempted to read it to T.H—but I am, also, reading to him Aldous Huxley's 'Jesting Pilate' which is good.

I hope that R. Hodgson & Mrs Hodgson are well. I wish I could have met them again before they left England—at least I have never met her, but met him one—in Tufton St—a pleasant memory.

I do not know how long this will take in reaching Japan—but if it is anywhere near Dec. 25th we send cordial Christmas greetings.

Yours very sincerely—
Florence Hardy.

Text   MS. Texas.

letter from you: not one of the two letters from Blunden preserved in DCM.   *return to England*: Blunden was currently teaching at Tokyo University.   *Mrs Blunden*: Blunden's first marriage, to Mary Daines, did not long survive his return from Japan.   *have nothing*: 'have heard nothing' presumably intended.   *a few miles from us*: see letter of 5 July 1926. *Nicholls*: correctly Nichols (see letter of 21 Apr. 1918); he preceded Blunden at Tokyo University.   *Tomlinsons*: see letter of 25 Nov. 1927.   *Murrys*: Middleton Murry, his second wife Violet (née le Maistre), and their two young daughters had spent the summer in the Old Coastguard Station near Abbotsbury.   *one by you*: Blunden's 'Ornithopolis', *Adelphi*, Nov. 1926.   *Clissold'*: Wells had sent a copy of the 3-vol. limited signed edition of *The World of William Clissold* (London, 1926); for TH's response see *CL*, vii. 40–1.   *'Lord Raingo'*: by Arnold Bennett (London, 1926).   *Pilate'*: Huxley's *Jesting Pilate: The Diary of a Journey* (London, 1926).   *Hodgson*: the poet Ralph Edwin Hodgson (1871–1962) taught in Japan, at Sendai University, 1924–38; he was married to Muriel Fraser.   *met him one*: 'met him once' clearly intended.   *Tufton St*: where Sassoon used to live.

November 1926

To Sydney Cockerell

MAX GATE, | DORCHESTER.
17th November. [1926]

My dear Sydney:

I return the letter you so kindly sent me to read. It is very delightful—simple & unaffected—which is the quality one likes best in children & their letters. Katherine is hardly a child now, though, is she? You are very fortunate.

T.H. is middling well. I think he is beginning to worry a bit about that trouble, & talked about putting a porous plaster on the swelling—at which Dr Head threw up his hands in horror. So I think he will soon have to have some sort of easy support. In all other ways he seems exceedingly well.

Between ourselves the award of the Nobel prize to G.B.S. was rather a blow to him I thought. He had not counted on it exactly, but had always had the feeling that he had been passed over for some unjust reason. If anyone else had to get it I am glad that it was G.B.S. I hope that John Galsworthy will have it some day.

Helen & Harley called here last Monday on their way to Southampton—as they were leaving that evening for France. They both were unusually gay, Helen obviously delighted at leaving England for a while.

I hope that Mrs Cockerell is now well.

I am reading to T.H. the Diary of Arthur Christopher Benson—a saddening book. T.H. says he liked him so very much, & wishes that he had seen more of him, & I think Benson liked T.H. What a pity that T.H. did not go to Cambridge more often. But he only discovers how much he liked people when they are dead, & can no longer be visited.

Dorothy Allhusen was here on Sunday for two hours—having motored from Basingstoke $3\frac{1}{2}$ hrs to get here, $3\frac{1}{2}$ hrs back. She is sad & lonely, but sweet & loveable as ever.

Yours very sincerely,
Florence Hardy.

Text MS. Beinecke. *Date* Year supplied on MS. by Cockerell.
that trouble: TH, diagnosed as having a hernia, had thus far refused to wear the light truss the Max Gate doctor had recommended (FEH to Cockerell, 27 Oct. and 7 Nov. 1926, Beinecke). *to G.B.S.*: the award to George Bernard Shaw of the (reserved) 1925 Nobel Prize for Literature had been announced a few days earlier. *some day*: Galsworthy did win it in 1932. *Helen & Harley*: Granville-Barker. *now well*: Kate Cockerell remained an invalid, however, for the rest of her life. *Benson*: *The Diary of Arthur Christopher Benson*, ed. Percy Lubbock (London, 1926); Benson (1862–1925) was Master of Magdalene College, Cambridge, of which TH was an honorary Fellow. *sad & lonely*: her husband, her only son, and one of her two daughters had all died within the space of a few years, and her remaining daughter was already married.

To E. M. Forster

MAX GATE, | DORCHESTER.
22nd November. [1926]

Dear Mr Forster:

We were glad to have news of you from Colonel Lawrence—on Sunday. He said, I think, that he would be seeing you before he left, & if so I wonder if you would be kind enough to give him this message—as we have not his address.

T.H. went into the porch to see him off—a ritual he always observes—& loves—when Col. Lawrence is in question. The motor-cycle was being started when T.H. felt cold & rushed indoors to get his shawl, & when he returned he saw that Col. Lawrence was just disappearing. He came to me, *greatly distressed*, to say that he did hope Col. L. did not think he was tired of waiting & went in. He said he always liked to have the last look—Col. L. always looks back he says, as he departs.

It is such a trifle to write about, but I think you will understand. Such trifles mean so much to T.H. & he felt very sad at parting from Lawrence.

We hope you are quite well. Everything is very happy & smooth here something generally happens when all seems so well—but I hope my superstitious fears are vain.

We hope that Mrs Forster is well, & that she has made up her mind to come to Dorchester next summer.

Our kindest regards to you both.

Yours sincerely,
Florence Hardy

Text MS. King's College Cambridge.   *Date* Year from internal evidence.
at parting from Lawrence: T. E. Lawrence, posted to India, did not return to England in TH's lifetime; this episode is narrated, and dated Nov. 1926, in *Life and Work*, 468.   *here something*: FEH, turning a page, failed to begin a new sentence.   *Mrs Forster*: Forster's mother, Alice Clara Forster (née Whichelo); FEH wrote at least one letter to her, 29 Dec. 1924 (King's College).

To Sydney Cockerell

MAX GATE, | DORCHESTER, | DORSET.
29th Dec. [1926]

My dear Sydney:

This is indeed a tragic letter. I need not tell you how I feel about it. But how wonderful they both are. I wish I could do something to help, but it is difficult, being here, & T.H. as he is, & my hands are already full to overflowing.

It has been a most appalling Christmas—one letter after another with serious news. My little nephew Tommy has swellings in his neck, & the doctor (in Canada) warns my sister that it may mean T.B. if he does not have special treatment. All would be so easy to arrange for if he were here—in England. However I must not pile on one sorrow after another.

I am almost ashamed after this to mention poor Wessie—who was put to sleep on Monday. Of course he was merely a dog, & not a good dog always, but *thousands* (actually thousands) of afternoons & evenings I would have been alone but for him, & had always him to speak to. But I mustn't write about him, & I hope no one will ask me about him or mention his name.

Yes—we shall be very pleased to see you on the 11th. It is a kind thought of yours to come on that day.

We have 'The Seven Pillars', a beautiful book of course. T.E.L told me that he felt obliged to go to India as Jonathan Cape would arrange a campaign of publicity with the publication of the *unlimited* edition.

I wish you a happy New Year & all the family.

By the way I [*remainder of letter absent*]

Text MS. Beinecke.   *Date* Year supplied on MS. by Cockerell.
tragic letter: from Charlotte Mew to Kate Cockerell, reporting the dangerous illness of her sister (Cockerell diary, 28 Dec. 1926, BL); Anne Mew died in June 1927.   *the 11th:* of January, FEH's birthday.   *Seven Pillars':* i.e. a copy of the privately printed limited edition of Lawrence's *The Seven Pillars of Wisdom.*   *unlimited edition: The Revolt in the Desert* (1927) was in fact an abridged version of *Seven Pillars*; the trade edition of the complete work appeared only in 1935, after Lawrence's death.

[Relatively few of FEH's letters seem to have survived from the year 1927, and there are grounds—for instance, the wide intervals between her letters to Cockerell—for suspecting that fewer than usual were actually written. The chief factor was perhaps the increasingly settled character of life at Max Gate. TH was 87 at the beginning of June, his wife more than ever saw it as her task to shield him from unwanted intruders and excessive excitements, and the greater part of the year seems to have passed almost without external incident. The Soundy family in Canada at last appeared to be on a sounder economic footing, removing some of FEH's acuter worries about her sister and nephew, and it was only at year's end that TH's health began to give cause for anxiety: 'T.H. I am glad to say is *very* well,' Cockerell was told on 23 May (Beinecke), and other correspondents received similar assurances.]

To Siegfried Sassoon

Max Gate. | Dorchester. | Dorset.
29th January '27.

Dear Siegfried:

I have read the poems to T.H., some of them several times. The one he liked best (as did I) was 15. 'Alone I hear the wind.' I had to mark that with two crosses in the notes I took for him: a sign of great excellence. Next to that he liked 6. 'While I seek you' which he thought Elizabethan. After that 23, with one cross. Then 13, 14, 19 & 26.

He was immensely struck by one line, though he certainly had read it before in the printed volume:

'Today you own the eternal overplus.'

he said that was a perfect line & the best in the book. Finally, he thinks this the best collection of your poems he had seen & thanks you for letting us read it. I took it to the Heads on Thursday but had no time to talk about it as Sir Reginald arrived very muddy from hunting, demanding a hot bath, & poached eggs, after, & they were expecting people to tea, so I fled.

Thank you for sending Mrs Blunden's letter. I do so hope that they will be happy when he returns. We are much looking forward to seeing Lady Gosse & her daughter to tea tomorrow. T.H. sends his affectionate greetings.

Aways yours sincerely—
Florence Hardy.

Text MS. Eton.

the poems: apparently the final proofs of the limited edition of *The Heart's Journey* (New York: Crosby Gaige; London: William Heinemann, 1927), containing only twenty-eight poems as against the thirty-five of the first trade edition; Sassoon later sent FEH an inscribed copy of the limited edition itself.   *took for him*: FEH first wrote 'took with him'.   *23, . . . 13, 14, 19 & 26*: assuming consistency of numbering between proofs and book, these represent, respectively, 'It has been told', 'When Selfhood can discern', 'Grandeur of Ghosts', 'To One in Prison', and 'The wisdom of the world'.   *'Today . . . overplus.'*: from 'To An Old Lady Dead'.   *he had seen*: 'he has seen' evidently intended.   *Sir Reginald*: Sir Reginald Pinney; see letter of 8 Aug. 1925.   *Mrs Blunden's*: see letter of 31 Oct. 1926.   *Lady Gosse*: Nellie Gosse, née Epps, wife of TH's friend Edmund Gosse, knighted 1925; she had two daughters, Tessa and Sylvia.   *Aways*: 'Always' clearly intended.

To Sydney Cockerell

MAX GATE, | DORCHESTER.
Sunday. [24 July 1927]

My dear Sydney:

Thank you so much for your suggestion about printing the little speech. I sent off the telegram as we had yesterday two applications from strangers —one a dealer—J. A. Allen—16 Grenville St. W.C.1—& another a private person, apparently, living at Manchester. Both of these wished to print it so that they might benevolently distribute free copies, like poor old Shorter. Philanthropic beings!

I enclose a copy of the speech with a few words added afterwards.

Thank you so much for letting me know about the hour glass. I went immediately to Weymouth & brought it back. The wooden part was rather worm-eaten, but I have treated it with Hope's wood-worm destroyer. We are so pleased to have it. I have wanted an hour glass for years, & yet I never had the sense to go to that shop to inquire.

My mother went back on Friday very much better for the fortnight's rest & change of air. But it was so difficult for me to go down to see her. T.H. seemed to think that I had done my duty by getting her to Weymouth, & that I need not go to see her, nor need she come here. However I took her for two glorious drives, without saying anything about it here. One was to the top of White Nore—a cliff 600 feet high. We saw sea-birds floating beneath us, & a lovely sea, & on the left a little deserted beach, with grey shingle, to which access can only be had through a smuggler's passage. Llewelyn Powys told me that noone ever goes there. The view was mar- vellous—the best I have ever seen in Dorset. There is an old smugglers' boat there, the last one used, so it is said.

Then I took my Mother to Abbotsbury, to see Middleton Murry & his dear little children. That too was delightful, & she was enchanted with the long stretch of deserted beach with the view of Portland Bill on one hand, & Lyme Regis on the other, & wild country at the back. Middleton Murry looks very ill, but was very nice, & seemed so grateful to me for going, that I felt ashamed for being able to do so little. However H. M. Tomlinson & family are there now & he & his wife will be a great help. They are all coming over to see us next Wednesday.

T.H. is working tremendously hard. I enclose a line from him.

With regard to Lawrence's relationship to the Fetherstonhaughs & the Framptons I can only say that Lawrence himself told me that he was related to Teresa *on both sides*—& that the families had intermarried more than once. Also that T.F. told me that her father & Lawrence's father were first cousins. Also she asked me if I did not see a strong likeness between herself & T.E.L. I did. The smile was exactly the same, colour of hair & so on— that was before Teresa had a stroke & had all her teeth taken out. I also think that Beryl Fetherstonhaugh-Frampton is like him—her eyes & arch expression, when she is in a mischievous mood. Once Lawrence said to me, speaking of family likenesses: "I am like my grandmother in appearance. She was a Fetherstonhaugh." or words to that effect. I distinctly remember his telling me that.

Always yours sincerely—

F.E.H.

Text MS. Adams. *Date* Supplied on MS. by Cockerell.
little speech: TH's address, 21 July 1927, at the laying of the commemoration stone of the new buildings for the Dorchester Grammar School (*Life and Work*, 472–3); for FEH's printing of the speech in pamphlet form and the unauthorized printing by Joseph A. Allen, see Purdy, 248–9. FEH's telegram of 23 July (Adams) read, 'PLEASE PRINT SPEECH OTHER APPLICATIONS RECEIVED FLORENCE HARDY'. *poor old Shorter*: died in 1926. *My mother*: Emma Dugdale had been ill for several years. *Powys*: Llewelyn Powys (1884– 1939), writer, second youngest of the Powys brothers; he lived on the Dorset coast and was on friendly terms with FEH both before and after TH's death. *a line from him*: CL, vii. 72. *Lawrence's . . . Framptons*: T. E. Lawrence was the natural son of Thomas Robert Tighe Chapman, later the 7th and last holder of the Chapman baronetcy; the 4th baronet had married Maria Fetherstonhaugh, an aunt of FEH's friend Teresa Fetherstonhaugh (1856– 1939). See Jeremy Wilson, *Lawrence of Arabia* (London: Heinemann, 1989), 742–3, 941–4. The family assumed the additional surname of Frampton in 1887, and Beryl Galfrida Violet Fetherstonhaugh-Frampton (1896–1941) was also a friend of FEH's; after TH's death she assisted FEH in making a catalogue of his incoming correspondence.

To Marie Stopes

MAX GATE, | DORCHESTER, | DORSET.

10th August. [1927]

Dear Dr Marie Stopes:

We shall be so pleased if you & Mr Roe would have tea with us at 4.30. on Sunday next—August 14th. I fear there will be merely a depressed charwoman to answer the door to you, as it is the h.p.maid's Sunday out. Please forgive these petty domestic details. How glad you must be to get rid of your large house & estate, beautiful though they must have been. I think

I am really a disciple of the Mahatma Gandhi. I want to get rid of worrying possessions.

I hope that you are well, both of you, & your boy flourishing.

Yours very sincerely,
Florence Hardy.

P.S. If Sunday is not convenient to you would Monday or Tuesday suit you? F.H.

Text MS. BL. *Date* Supplied on MS. (by M. Stopes?).
estate: Givons Grove (see letter of 14 Sept. 1923); M. Stopes and her husband seem not in fact to have sold it at this date. *Gandhi*: Mohandas Karamchand Gandhi (1869–1948); temporarily withdrawn from active politics, he was living with the utmost simplicity, advocating rural crafts, and attaining a kind of sainthood.

To Marie Stopes

MAX GATE, | DORCHESTER, | DORSET.
19th August. [1927]

Dear Dr Marie Stopes:

If we really wouldn't be too great a nuisance Lady Head & I would like so much to motor over to see you on Saturday the 27th inst. This is the only free day she has next week.

We were so pleased to see you both last Sunday.

Yours very sincerely,
Florence Hardy.

P.S. I hope that I didn't seem argumentative about birth control, for I know you are right, but I always like to hear arguments for & against. F.H.

Text MS. BL. *Date* From internal evidence.
Lady Head: Ruth Head; her husband was knighted in Jan. 1927. *to see you*: at the Old Lighthouse on Portland Bill (see headnote to letter of 14 Sept. 1923).

To Howard Bliss

MAX GATE, | DORCHESTER.
23rd October '27.

Dear Mr Bliss:

It was with great disappointment that I found myself obliged to refuse to take the chair at the suggested meeting for the Prevention of Cruel Sports,

& I would like to explain to you my reasons, if it is not taking up too much of your time.

Had I only my-self to consider I would gladly take the chair at such a meeting even though it involved severe mental strain. But I found my husband very strongly opposed to my doing anything of the kind & he would have been seriously annoyed had I done so. He has written against blood-sports as you know, & I hope will do so again, but he does not like the idea of my appearing on a platform.

Moreover the few friends in Dorset that he cares to visit now are all, I am sorry to say, given to hunting & shooting. It seems cowardly to give this as an excuse, but at his age he does not want to feel that I am doing anything that would cause his friends to cold-shoulder us. Personally I would not care if I lost every friend I had in Dorset if I could further the cause but I could not go away for a month or two until the storm blew over, if I thought that desirable. As you know, I am never away now for a single night. But I should have taken the chair nevertheless had my husband been willing.

I think the sights you describe at the Zoo must be *sickening*. We hope you are well, & with kindest regards

Yours very sincerely—
Florence Hardy

Text   MS. (with envelope) Princeton.
suggested meeting: if planned for Dorchester, it seems not to have taken place.   *against blood-sports*: most recently in a letter pub. in *The Times*, 5 Mar. 1927.   *sights . . . Zoo*: the feeding of live animals to large snakes.

To H. M. Tomlinson

MAX GATE, | DORCHESTER, | DORSET.
25th Nov. '27.

Dear Mr Tomlinson:

It was indeed a pleasant surprise to have your letter awaiting me when I returned to Max Gate from London yesterday. I had just rushed up & back in the day. We thought you were in America until next summer. We both thank you so much for your valuable & greatly prized gift of that lovely edition of "Gallion's Reach". I had already read half of it aloud to T. H. & we finished it from your edition. We both thought it a great achievement. The storm is most wonderful—only I expect you are tired of being told that. We both felt that we were in that storm. It is one of the finest pieces of prose I have ever read—& T.H. agrees.

Of course we shall be most delighted to see you & Mrs Tomlinson, & also Mr & Mrs Wells, whenever you are able to come—only please give us a day or two's notice so that we may be alone. It is impossible to talk properly with a tablefull. We are disengaged all next week with the exception of Monday, tea-time. T.H. is fairly well, but he feels very tired today, for no reason apparently, which always rather worries me.

My love to Mrs Tomlinson, & so much looking forward to seeing her & you—

Yours very sincerely—

F. E. Hardy

Text   MS. Texas.

Tomlinson: Henry Major Tomlinson (1873–1958), writer.   *your edition*: a presentation copy (lot 195 in the Hodgson sale of TH's library) of the limited signed American edition of Tomlinson's just-published *Gallions Reach: A Romance*; the Hardys seem to have been already reading a copy of the English trade edition.   *Mrs Tomlinson*: Florence Tomlinson, née Hammond.   *Mr & Mrs Wells*: for Wells, of Harper & Brothers, see letter of 18 Apr. 1926; his wife Harriet, née Sheldon (d. 1961, aged 87), was a women's suffrage leader.   *able to come*: they arrived on 10 Dec.

[Hardy's tiredness, mentioned in the letter to Tomlinson, was in reality an early signal of the decline which led to his death a few weeks later. In other respects, however, he seemed to his wife to be in exceptionally good health—'Not a cloud in the sky', she reported to Cockerell as late as 1 December 1927 (Beinecke)—and she felt able to devote a good deal of her time to seeking financial and other assistance for Middleton Murry, his sick wife, and their two children and visiting them by car in their remote cottage on the Dorset coast. One of Hardy's greatest pleasures earlier in the year had been a visit from Edmund (now Sir Edmund) Gosse and the active renewal of their long-standing friendship, and in November it was Gosse, with his characteristic energy and diplomacy, who was instrumental in obtaining substantial grants for Murry both from the prime-ministerial Privy Purse and from the Royal Literary Fund.]

To Edmund Gosse

MAX GATE, | DORCHESTER, | DORSET.

29th November. 1927.

Dear Sir Edmund:

I have just returned from Abbotsbury & wish you could have seen the change in the atmosphere of that little cottage—due to the arrival, three days ago, of the splendid cheque which you so kindly caused to be sent. It arrived at a very critical moment, when it was most needed, & there is no doubt about Middleton Murry's deep gratitude.

Almost as soon as I arrived he asked if it would be wrong if he were to write to you. When I expressed my astonishment at the question he said that he had understood that he was not supposed to know that it was your application to the Prime Minister, on his behalf, that had caused the cheque to be sent.

So that I hope you have received a letter from him.

Although he has received such a generous amount I cannot help feeling that the £250 will melt away pretty quickly. The bills at the chemist's for her medicines are enormous. I know, because I so often have to order things for them in Dorchester. The fees at the sanatorium took every penny that he had. Mrs Murry seemed a little better today—I thought I had never seen anyone looking so beautiful, & such a child—and she may live on for months. Murry now believes that she is going to get better, & she thinks so too, but I am afraid there is not the slightest hope of that. I am quite certain that any sum from the Royal Literary Fund would be useful. There is no sort of extravagance in the home, & I know that Murry would not take a penny unless he were in absolute need of it. He is certainly not a cadging man, but has tried to hide his money difficulties from us.

Please excuse this long rambling letter, but I have tried to explain how matters stand with the hapless pair.

Again thanking you for the trouble you have taken—

Yours very sincerely,
Florence Hardy.

Text   MS. (with envelope) Leeds.
caused to be sent: by the Prime Minister, Stanley Baldwin.   *letter from him*: Gosse replied 30 Nov. 1927 (Adams) that a 'very nice' note from Murry had just arrived.   *sanatorium*: at Midhurst, Sussex.   *Mrs Murry*: see letter of 31 Oct. 1926.   *Literary Fund*: Gosse had already made the necessary application (*CL*, vii. 81).

To Sydney Cockerell

MAX GATE, | DORCHESTER.
December 5th 1927.

My dear Sydney:

I have posted to you today the copies of the pamphlet that I said I was sending. One is for you. If you think that there is anything against my selling the others to Maggs, then please do not do so. I am quite sincere in this. And any time will do: after Christmas, next year, anywhen that suits you.

T.H. is very well, but is tired today & did not go out. This is rather unusual with him. Of course he has not the strength he had, which is but natural, & he very soon becomes tired, especially when he has been talking. But he seems always very contented & cheerful. I am more thankful than words can express that there has been no so-called 'Hardy' Play this autumn. He really couldn't have stood it: moreover he did not wish for one.

We are expecting Siegfried Sassoon tomorrow to lunch, & he is bringing with him a friend, Stephen Tennant, the son of Lady Grey. No doubt you know him. We wish that S.S. would come by himself, but it cannot be helped, & we'd rather put up with his bringing a stranger, that not see him at all.

Dorothy Allhusen was here on Saturday, sweet & affectionate as ever. She & T.H. were talking of old times, of the pranks she used to play when she was a child, & he stayed with her mother. And now she is a widow & has lost two of her three children, & very sad & lonely.

We hope so much that by now Mrs Cockerell is pretty nearly well, & the nurse gone, & also that the three children are well. I asked T.H. if he had any message for you, & he said none, except that he was dreaming of you last night.

I see it is two minutes to post-time—

Always yours sincerely
FEH.

Text MS. Beinecke.
pamphlet: FEH's privately printed pamphlet of TH's 'G. M.: A Reminiscence' (Purdy, 250–1).   *Tennant*: Stephen Tennant (1906–87), poet, painter, and aesthete; he kept up an active friendship with FEH after TH's death. FEH told Cockerell (8 Dec. 1927, Beinecke) that she and TH had liked Tennant 'exceedingly', TH saying he was 'the only man he ha[d] ever met who walked like Swinburne'.   *Lady Grey*: Lady Pamela Grey (née Wyndham), wife since 1922 of Lord Grey of Fallodon (see letter of 16 May 1920); S. Tennant was the youngest child of her first marriage, to Lord Glenconner (d. 1920).   *that not*: 'than not' clearly intended. *sad & lonely*: see letter of 17 Nov. 1926.

To Edmund Gosse

MAX GATE, | DORCHESTER.
15th December 1927.

Dear Sir Edmund:

T.H. & I were both quite overwhelmed when we read your kind letter of this morning. You have indeed been most generous to the poor Murrys, & I should think he will remember you always with deepest gratitude. I hardly like to think of what their position would be at the present moment had it not been for your help. As it is you have done all that is humanly possible to save him anxiety. I expect that she has been told & her last days are being made happier. What a splendid sum you have obtained for him— far beyond any thing we had hoped for.

I had intended going to see them yesterday but T.H. has been in bed the last few days. He became over-tired last Saturday, & this has affected his heart. His doctor hopes, however, that he will be all right in a day or two, but must keep quiet. I will certainly go to see the Murrys tomorrow or on Saturday, if T.H. is able to get up. My last news was that Mrs Murry had had "a set-back," & was too weak to see anyone, though last week she was asking if I might be sent for as she wanted to see me.

Again thanking you so much. T.H. sends his love to you all, & says what wonderful things you are able to do.

Yours very sincerely,
Florence Hardy.

Text   MS. Leeds.
splendid sum: Murry was granted £250 by the Royal Literary Fund on 14 Dec. 1927; Gosse, a member of the committee, seems to have been largely responsible both for the size of the award and the rapidity of the decision.   *last Saturday*: 10 December, the date of the visit by the Tomlinsons and Wellses (see letter of 25 Nov. 1927).

To Sydney Cockerell

MAX GATE, | DORCHESTER.
25th December '27.

My dear Sydney:

Thank you so much for your beautiful present. I am so pleased to have it. T.H. has been in bed for three weeks & is very weak, but not alarmingly ill. He has seen no-one during that time, except the doctor, & not written a word until this morning, when he is attempting a line to you & to Gosse. He did admire your portrait exceedingly.

He asked me not to tell you he was not well as you might be needlessly anxious, & want to come down. I think the visit of the American publisher was too much for him. He dreaded it, & seemed to collapse directly after.— Since I wrote that, I have been to his bedroom & he told me that he has not strength to write even a pencilled line, so that must wait. I asked the doctor what really was the matter, & he said: 'Old age'. His brain is tired for he cannot follow when I read aloud to him—the first time this has happened. But with rest & quiet he may get quite well again. Dorothy Allhusen wished to come to see him tomorrow, but he said he couldn't talk to her so I asked her not to come. Just before he was ill everyone was saying that he was better than he had been for years.

We were so very pleased to hear of the improvement in Mrs Cockerell's health, & hope that she may steadily gain strength, & that the coming year may bring her, & all the family, many joys.

Always yours sincerely—
F.E.H.

Text   MS. Beinecke.

to you & to Gosse: TH's letter to Cockerell seems not to have been completed.   *American publisher*: see letter of 25 Nov. 1927.

To Edmund Gosse

MAX GATE, | DORCHESTER.
Christmas day— | 1927.

Dear Sir Edmund:

It was exceedingly kind of you to write that letter, as the only thing that gives T.H. pleasure now is appreciation of his poems by those whose literary judgement he trusts. He has pencilled you a reply: he has written no other word than these since he went to bed, three weeks ago.

Between ourselves he overtired himself on Dec. 10th by talking rather too energetically & at too great a length to his American publisher—Mr Wells of Harpers—& Mrs Wells. I have been warned by his doctors against letting him over-tire himself but he said he must see Mr Wells, whom he had not met before, & he seemed so well that I thought the visit would do no harm.

The doctor says he is just over-tired, mentally & physically.

We are so very sorry to hear of your bronchial cold & hope you will take very great care of yourself.

Thank you so much for the box of delicious chocolates you so kindly sent.

Since I wrote the above our invaluable friend Sir Henry Head has called & confirms what our doctor says. The only cause for anxiety is that the heart is feeble. With all good wishes—

Yours very sincerely—
Florence Hardy.

Text   MS. (with envelope) Leeds.

that letter: Gosse wrote 24 Dec. 1927 (DCM) to praise as 'marvellously fine' TH's poem 'Christmas in the Elgin Room', pub. in that day's issue of *The Times*.   *a reply*: *CL*, vii. 89; it was TH's last letter.   *on Dec.*: FEH first wrote 'on Sept'.   *care of yourself*: Gosse had been seriously ill during the late summer of 1927 and died in May 1928.

To Lady Hoare

MAX GATE, | DORCHESTER, | DORSET.
Tuesday. [27 December 1927]

Dearest Alda:

We thought of you much on that sad anniversary last week, but I did not write as I had not any good news. T.H. has been in bed over three weeks, & is very unwell. He is, naturally, very weak. However he is making a good fight & I do trust that he will soon be much better. I will send you a line. His mind is clear & vigorous, but his body is so frail. He sends you his love—& so do I. May the New Year bring you many blessings.

Ever your affectionate,
Florence Hardy.

Text MS. Wiltshire R.O.　　*Date* From internal evidence.
sad anniversary: of the death of the Hoares' only son, of war wounds, 20 Dec. 1917; FEH had sent similar messages to Lady Hoare in previous Decembers (Wiltshire R.O.).

To Sydney Cockerell

Max Gate— | Dorchester—
Friday. [30 December 1927]

My dear Sydney:

The doctor has just left. T.H. is about the same; not any weaker fortunately. Of course the weather is all against his recovery at present. I think the doctor is more anxious about T.'s heart than he admits. He has given me pills to strengthen the heart—but I think Sir Henry Head disapproves of that—though I am not sure. Thank you so much but I can manage all the nursing at present. My sister Eva telephoned last night & begged to be allowed to come but I asked her not to, though she is really a good nurse. The doctor says that T.H must not see *anyone* at present. His brother & sister do not offer to come, & perhaps that is better for him. It is only naturally that the heart—at that age—should be rather feeble. The doctor is *not* alarming but says it will be a long time before he is well, & that is quite obvious. Since writing the above he has made quite a good lunch— the first time for nearly three weeks—pheasant & champagne—so I think he may be getting on. He told me, before I received your letter, that if you offered to come I was to thank you, & ask you to come later, when he was able to talk to you. But I will use my own discretion & send you all news, & if he were in a dangerous condition I would let you know at once.

Yours very sincerely,
Florence Hardy.

P.S. I am sure the doctor is quite good, & T. has taken to him immensely.
F.H.

Text MS. Beinecke. *Date* Supplied on MS. by Cockerell.
the doctor: the new Max Gate doctor was Edward Weller Mann (d. 1971, aged 84). *only
naturally*: 'only natural' evidently intended.

To Sydney Cockerell

MAX GATE, DORCHESTER.

[1 January 1928]

My dear Sydney—

T.H. much about the same, but do not be alarmed by reports in papers.
Dr Mann is having a specialist down tomorrow for his & my satisfaction—
as he remains weak. T. knows I am writing & tells me to be sure to give
you his best New Year wishes. I told him of your kind offer to come, & he
does not think it necessary as he would not be able to talk to you, & the
doctor does not wish him to see anyone not even his sister. In case a nurse
is necessary my sister Eva is ready to come at a moment's notice. Will write
or telegraph tomorrow—

F.H.

Text MS. Beinecke. *Date* Supplied on MS. by Cockerell.
anyone not: 'but his sis' struck through before 'not'.

To Siegfried Sassoon

Max Gate. | Dorchester—

4th January '28.

My dear Siegfried:

I know that you will be glad to have a line direct from Max Gate giving
news of T.H. He is certainly better, but still so very weak. I am afraid that
it will be several weeks before his normal life can be resumed. He has been
in a state of utter exhaustion, mental & physical, & is hardly able to sit up
for half an hour daily—even now. But it is a great relief to know there is
an improvement, & a good doctor who came from Bournemouth made a
careful examination, & said his organs were all sound, & his arteries like
those of a man of 60. So we may feel very hopeful.

Your letters about his poems give him *real* pleasure, & he values them
exceedingly.

I am sending you tomorrow if possible a privately printed copy of the

Times Christmas Eve poem, which you liked. It is not done quite as I wished, but I had to leave it to the printers, owing to T's illness.

We were *very* sorry to hear of the death of your friend, Mr Schuster—and we hope that you are quite well yourself, & not overtaxing your strength.

In times of sickness & trouble it is a great help to think of your true friendship.

T.H. sends his love. I am writing this at his bedside.

Always yours sincerely,
Florence Hardy.

Text MS. (with envelope) Eton. *Date* '4' written over '5'.
doctor . . . Bournemouth: E. How White. *the printers*: a Dorchester firm, Henry Ling Ltd., printed the 'Christmas in the Elgin Room' pamphlet (Purdy, 251). *Mr Schuster*: Frank Schuster (1840–1928), described by Rupert Hart-Davis as a 'wealthy music-lover and giver of parties'; for Sassoon's own 'appreciation' see *Siegfried Sassoon Diaries 1920–1922*, ed. R. Hart-Davis (London: Faber and Faber, 1981), 293–4.

To Sydney Cockerell

[5 January 1928]

Thank you so much, but it would be nicer I think if you could come when T. is well. He is worried if I am talking to anyone down stairs while he is upstairs, & sends for me if he hears anyone is here with me. He is still pitifully weak, & very ill indeed, I think—though the doctors are reassuring. They admit though it will be many weeks before he can get up. He cannot see anyone yet, of course, nor is he well enough to be read to even—*Very many thanks*

Text MS. Beinecke. *Date* Supplied on MS. by Cockerell.
Very many thanks: FEH included neither salutation nor signature in this hastily written note.

To Sydney Cockerell

Friday evening. [6 January 1928]

All much the same—a trifle stronger perhaps—but not very much. Dr has today stopped the digitalis he was giving as he thought it would otherwise lose effect. He eats & sleeps moderately well. The doctor today warned me once more, very strongly, that he must see no one—until he gave permission—

F.E.H.

Text MS. (lettercard) Beinecke. *Date* From postmark.

To Sydney Cockerell

Sunday morn. [8 January 1928]

Am afraid T. is in a very critical condition, but we are clinging to hopes. Fluid at base of lungs—what they feared through recumbent position— heart too weak to allow him to sit up, may cause hypo-static pneumonia— but this is no worse this morning than it was last night but heart rather weaker. If you think it well to be in Dorchester *come*—only T. must not see you, or even know you are there.

F.H.

Text MS. (lettercard, marked 'Urgent') Beinecke. *Date* Supplied on MS. by Cockerell. *come:* FEH sent Cockerell a telegram, 'PLEASE COME AT ONCE = HARDY' (Beinecke), early the next morning.

[Although TH had been growing progressively weaker, his actual death, on 11 January, came quickly and unexpectedly at the end of a day in which he had rallied to the extent of dictating sardonic epitaphs on G. K. Chesterton and George Moore. Mourning for the man long regarded as the greatest of living English authors was on a national and even an international scale, and the intense press scrutiny was only one among many pressures upon FEH as she confronted a series of difficult de- cisions about funeral arrangements and the disposal of her husband's body. It was Cockerell, supported by Barrie, who pushed for TH's burial, after cremation, in Westminster Abbey, and it was the decision for interment in the Abbey that prompted in its turn the locally inspired proposal for TH's heart to be removed prior to cremation and buried at Stinsford. Overwhelmed by grief, weariness, confusion, and the sheer force of male argument, FEH yielded to arrangements she subse- quently deplored, and it was only after her husband's funerals—one in the Abbey, the other at Stinsford—on 16 January 1928 that she was able to begin responding to the condolences of friends and assuming the responsibilities incumbent upon her as TH's widow. If the most pressing task was the publication of *Winter Words*, Hardy's final gathering of poems, by far the more demanding was the realization of her husband's plans for the 'Life'. Sharply illuminated in letters that follow are some of the difficulties she encountered in bringing what she now began to call the 'biography' (rather than the 'notes' or 'materials') to completion and publication as Florence Emily Hardy's *The Early Life of Thomas Hardy 1840–1891* (London: Macmillan, 1928) and *The Later Years of Thomas Hardy 1892–1928* (London: Macmillan, 1930).

To Dorothy Allhusen

MAX GATE, | DORCHESTER, | DORSET.
17th January. [1928]

Dearest Dorothy:

I am sitting alone at Max Gate, for the first time, with all my memories. It is the hour when I used to sit & read to him—& the house is silent, save for the ticking of the clock. I feel that he is here, & thinking of us both, of you & of me. You were so good to him, & he loved you. Your flowers were at his bedside when he died, & he spoke of you with love so many times during his illness.

You of all people will understand what life seems to me now—without him. You knew him many years before I did, & you must have brought much joy into his life.

Thank you again & again—& I hope I have not dwelt selfishly of my sorrow when your own is so great.

Always your affectionate,
Florence.

P.S. It has comforted me so to write to you dearest Dorothy.

F.H.

Text MS. Beinecke. *Date* Year from internal evidence.
of my sorrow: 'on my sorrow' clearly intended.

To Daniel Macmillan

Max Gate. | Dorchester.
19th January '28

Dear Mr Macmillan:

I have had your kind message from Mr Cockerell, & I thank you for your sympathy.

Also I thank you for the perfect way in which all the arrangements at the Abbey, & in connection with the distribution of tickets were carried out.

I shall be going to London very shortly & would like to see you then, as my husband gave me so many verbal instructions the last few weeks before his death that I feel you should be acquainted with them. He had so hoped to bring out a new volume of poems on his 90th birthday, & we were both so confident that he would reach that age. We had made plans for spending that day. He was going through his biography with me a few days before he went to bed with this last illness. His death seems still so untimely.

Yours sincerely,
Florence Hardy.

Text MS. (mourning stationery) BL.
Daniel Macmillan: see letter of 18 Apr. 1926; FEH wrote a similar letter to George A. Macmillan 18 Jan. 1928 (BL).

January 1928

To Sydney Cockerell

Max Gate. | Dorchester.
25th January. [1928]

Dear Sydney:

The enclosed came today & I am sending it to you before replying. I shall not ask Barrie or anyone else to write for them unless you think I ought. But *not* Barrie.

With regard to the Men of Letters volume I am sure that Siegfried Sassoon would do it well. He told me he had been working hard at prose lately, & one who is so careful with his poetry would write good prose—and he was a good critic of T.H.'s work, & we can be sure that he write nothing that T.H. would have disliked. I couldn't bear Squire to do it himself, & E. M. Forster is a little bit precious & niggling.

Then about the poems to be submitted to Walter de la Mare & Siegfried Sassoon. You did not mean, I suppose, that they were to alter or revise, for that would never do. All the poems in that envelope, so T.H. told me, could go to press as they were, at a pinch. I was thinking over this for several hours last night. It is the last work of an old man, but a great poet, & must be accepted as such—everyone knowing that he could not give the final revision. No tinkering of his last work must be permitted. But perhaps it is only arrangement you are thinking about—though he had arranged them himself. However, you can think this over.

I hope that Mrs Cockerell is better. I am glad to hear of the slight improvement. Please give her my love.

Always yours sincerely,
Florence Hardy.

Text MS. (mourning stationery) Beinecke.   *Date* Year supplied on MS. by Cockerell. *The enclosed*: unidentified but perhaps a request for an obituary article of some kind.   *Men of Letters*: Sassoon seems to have begun but later abandoned the Hardy vol. in the English Men of Letters series, eventually written by Edmund Blunden (London, 1941); see letter of 28 Nov. 1930.   *he write*: 'he would write' clearly intended.   *Squire*: John Collings Squire (see letter of 2 Apr. 1922), general editor of the series.   *to press*: for inclusion in the posthumous *Winter Words* volume.

To Rebekah Owen

MAX GATE, | DORCHESTER, | DORSET.
26th January. [1928]

My dear Betty:

It is all too terrible, like a dreadful nightmare.

I thank you so much for your kind words of sympathy. Life seems absolutely at an end for me—& I wish it actually we. Poor Wessie died a year before his master—Dec. 27th. 1926. He never quite got over the loss. He had been growing weaker for some months—& was very *very* tired.

I hope you are well, & I send my loving thanks.

Florence.

Text MS. (mourning stationery, with envelope) Colby. *Date* Year from internal evidence.
actually we: 'actually were' clearly intended.

To Sydney Cockerell

MAX GATE, | DORCHESTER, | DORSET.
27th January '28.

Dear Sydney:

The enclosed will do very nicely, but I don't think I shall use very many of them. Some letters from real friends I *must* answer. Will the forms do to send to various societies? I suppose not.

My Mother has been ill with a sharp heart attack, & I had to go home yesterday. She is better now.

With regard to the poems we can discuss those when you are here. Thinking the matter over I feel sure that he considered all in that packet ready for printing, & would have included them all in a volume. He never wrote on that better paper until the poem was ready. Anyhow the collection will have *far* more value coming straight from his hand, than if it had been rearranged or selected by any other poet. Little scraps of unfinished poems of course are different.

I am so glad that Mrs Cockerell is getting better. Please give her my love. It is a good thing, for her sake, that you are not coming here this week-end.

The Mayor is very pleased with your letter.

I have been down to Talbothays. Kate says she has told Henry, but he will not mention the legacy. When I approach the topic he sheers off. They will never use it for themselves, nor leave any to any charity.

The Czech translations do not amount to much. We have had lots of correspondence about them, & only tiny sums at long intervals. T.H. always said they were hardly worth troubling about.

I remember now that he told me to join the Society of Authors—& so I will. It will be most useful to have their advice—although I know that Macmillans will always be true friends as well as publishers.

Yours very sincerely,

Florence Hardy—

Text   MS. (mourning stationery) Beinecke.

The enclosed: printed acknowledgements of messages of sympathy.   *The Mayor . . . letter*: Wilfrid Hodges (1873–1952), wine merchant and current mayor of Dorchester; Cockerell had presumably written about the projected Thomas Hardy Memorial Fund. For this and other issues confronting FEH in the wake of TH's death see Michael Millgate, *Testamentary Acts: Browning, Tennyson, James, Hardy* (Oxford: Clarendon Press, 1992), 148–52, etc.   *told Henry*: of the contents of TH's will.   *Czech . . . troubling about*: TH, approving a Czech translation of *Jude* in Dec. 1926, had declared himself 'more interested in having the book well-translated than in getting money from it' (*CL*, vii. 52).   *Society of Authors*: TH was an early member of the Incorporated Society of Authors, Playwrights, and Composers, founded by Walter Besant in 1884, and had succeeded George Meredith as its president in 1909.

To Daniel Macmillan

MAX GATE, | DORCHESTER, | DORSET.

27th January '28.

Dear Mr Daniel Macmillan:

When thinking over our talk yesterday it occured to me that I might have given you a wrong conception of Mr Wells's visit to my husband on December 10th. I am glad to say no business whatever was discussed with him then, as I had stipulated before that the visit was to be merely a friendly one. Mr & Mrs H. M. Tomlinson accompanied Mr & Mrs Wells, & the only business proposal was made to me before my husband came down to see them.

I had endeavoured to persuade my husband to remain in his study, & not to see any visitors that day, and I thought I had succeeded, but, to my dismay, he walked into the drawing-room half an hour after the visitors had arrived.

But I expect also intense cold had much to do with his illness, & his doctor says that he dates the beginning of his loss of strength from the day when he laid the Foundation stone of the Grammar School on July 21st of last year—that effort & the speech he made in the open air being too much for a man in his 88th year.

But all my seeking for causes is fruitless now. I feared I might have been unjust to Mr Wells.

Yours sincerely,
Florence Hardy.

Text   MS. (mourning stationery) BL.
Mr Wells's visit: see letter of 25 Dec. 1927; FEH's letter to D. Macmillan of 24 Jan. 1928 (BL) shows that Wells had further annoyed her by 'writing & telegraphing at great length' about the American rights to the 'Life'.   *Grammar School*: see letter of 24 July 1927.

To Sir Owen Seaman

MAX GATE, | DORCHESTER, | DORSET.
1st February '28.

Dear Sir Owen Seaman:

I feel that I must write & thank you for the exceedingly tender & beautiful verse in Punch that you wrote about my husband's burial in the Abbey & at Stinsford.

You could hardly realize what comfort those four lines gave me, & I wished so much that my husband could have read them.

It was a difficult, &, in some ways, terrible, decision to have to make.

Some day, if you will allow me, I would like to have those lines engraved in some suitable place.

With deepest gratitude

Yours very truly,
Florence Hardy.

Text   MS. (mourning stationery) DCM.
Seaman: Owen Seaman (1861–1936), satirist, parodist, and editor of *Punch* 1906–32; he was knighted in 1914.   *verse in Punch*: 'The Nation's Temple claims her noblest Dead; | So to its care his ashes we confide, | But where his heart would choose a lowlier bed | There lay it, in his own loved countryside' (*Punch*, 18 Jan. 1928). Seaman, writing to a friend 5 Feb. 1928 (Cheltenham College), expressed pleasure at FEH's letter and observed that separate heart burial, a very ancient practice, simply meant preserving the heart from the flames.

To Edmund Gosse

MAX GATE, | DORCHESTER, | DORSET.
February 5th. 1928.

My dear Sir Edmund:

I thank you so much for your very kind letter of advice. It was very good of you to write.

But it was a great shock to me to learn of your great anxiety about Lady Gosse's health, and I hope most sincerely that you have had a good report of her & that all is much better that was anticipated. How grieved T.H. would have been had he known. I hope that you keep well.

I have been very worried & made quite ill by a preposterous book that has just been published, written by a young man who paid us several visits under the pretext of being a mere admirer of T.H's work, and who actually gave me a promise that he would write nothing about T.H. or Max Gate.

With regard to the biography of my husband I have for many years been collecting material which has been put somewhat roughly into shape. T.H. allowed me to take a great many extracts from his diaries & note books, & supplied all the information that I required. Sir James Barrie is coming to see me tomorrow, & he has been considering the matter & will, no doubt, have many helpful suggestions. Just at present I feel I could not write about him. We are just completing the agonizing task of going through his papers & books—& there is much business to be done. But later I may find a great relief in a different kind of work. T.H. left written directions about the biography—clearly stating that he wished it to be written by me—& I am *most* thankful to find that you think I am capable of the task.

Again thanking you & with my earnest wishes for the speedy recovery of Lady Gosse.

Yours affectionately—
Florence Hardy

Text MS. (mourning stationery, with envelope) Leeds.
Lady Gosse's health: she had been in a nursing-home for some months but survived her husband (see letter of 12 May 1928) by more than a year.   *better that*: 'better than' clearly intended.   *preposterous book*: Vere H. Collins's *Talks with Thomas Hardy at Max Gate 1920–1922* (London, 1928).   *We . . . completing*: not FEH and Barrie, as might appear, but FEH and Cockerell, her fellow literary executor.

To Daniel Macmillan

MAX GATE, | DORCHESTER, | DORSET.
8th February 1928.

Dear Mr Macmillan:

Many thanks for your letter. In reply to

1. I should be most grateful for suggestions from you about the biography. This is, indeed, what my husband advised.

Sir James Barrie brought me back the copy I had lent him on Monday. He agreed with me that certain slight omissions are desirable, but he did not give anything like a detailed criticism. He says that it is a great book and unlike any other life that has ever been published. This is, of course, entirely due to the long extracts from my husband's diaries, and his assistance all through.

Whether I shall be able to write the concluding chapters I do not know. At present it is difficult for me to write anything, but I may be able to do so later with some assistance.

2. I am now having the poems left by my husband typed. As soon as this is done I will forward to you the original manuscript. I am willing for you to publish the poems in the same way and on the same terms as "Human Shows" and previous volumes. Mr Cockerell suggested a portrait of him as a frontispiece.

I leave the date of publication in your hands. If June 2nd. is a convenient day, publication then would be a tribute to his memory—although as he did not live to see his 88th. birthday the point of the preface is unfortunately lost.

It would be very kind if you would arrange with Messrs A. P. Watt for the publication of a limited number of the poems in magazines.

3. *Film rights.* These I shall leave entirely to you.

4. I can see no objection to two short stories from "Life's Little Ironies" being published in "The Outline". But in this, as in all other matters I prefer to be guided by your decision.

With many thanks,

Yours sincerely,
Florence Hardy—

Text   MS. (typed) BL.

your letter: FEH's numbered paragraphs correspond to those in Macmillan's letter to her of 7 Feb. 1928 (copy, BL).   *the biography*: copies of the entire typescript as it currently stood had been sent to both Macmillan and Barrie at the end of Jan. 1928; Macmillan in his letter promised to suggest some possible omissions.   *poems . . . typed*: for *Winter Words*. *frontispiece*: FEH typed 'frontsipiece'; no frontispiece was in fact included.   *Watt*: literary agency founded by Alexander Pollock Watt; Macmillan had suggested it might place 'a limited number' of *Winter Words* poems in periodicals ahead of book pub.   *leave entirely to you*: Macmillan had offered to deal with film rights without commission.   *two short stories*: 'Old Andrey's Experience as a Musician' and 'Absent-Mindedness in a Parish Choir', both pub. in the 11 Feb. 1928 issue of *The Outline* weekly.

To A. E. Housman

MAX GATE, | DORCHESTER, | DORSET.
12th February 1928.

Dear Professor Housman:

I thank you for your kind words of sympathy with me in my heavy loss, and I thank you for acting as Pall Bearer at the Abbey burial.

My husband always spoke of you with real affection, and he had a passionate admiration for your poetry—especially 'Is my team ploughing'. I know that you understood him, as few people could have done, & that you realize how empty life will be for me henceforth.

Again thanking you.

Yours sincerely,
Florence Hardy.

Text MS. (mourning stationery) Adams.
Housman: Alfred Edward Housman (1859–1936), poet and classical scholar; TH had known him since 1899, and he spent a weekend at Max Gate in August 1900. *'Is . . . ploughing'*: from Housman's *A Shropshire Lad* (1898); TH's copy is in DCM.

To Daniel Macmillan

MAX GATE, | DORCHESTER, | DORSET.
16th. February 1927. [1928]

Dear Mr Macmillan:

I was astonished to see the paragraph, half invented, in today's Times. I spoke to no-one in London yesterday except yourself, Mr Cockerell and an official at the National Portrait Gallery. After my return home, sometime after ten, I was called up by a stranger from London, who said he had authentic information that I was to write Mr Hardy's biography. I hesitated, and then thought you might have given out the news, though that was not likely, or that the contents of my husband's "Instructions to my Executors" which are now filed in London, and which we are not allowed to have back, had become public as they must do in a day or two. I said that was correct and he began to ask me questions and I said that I could not tell him any more and hung up the receiver. The telephone was very indistinct. I should not have told him that I had not begun the book. A week ago Sir James Barrie suggested that he should write to the Times and say that I was going to write the biography as his doing so might prevent other publishers publishing unauthorized books, though it would not prevent writers from attempting them. I wish that he had done so now as it would have been much better than the news being given out in this fashion.

I forgot to say that there is a verse faintly pencilled in against one of the poems which is very good. I had this typed in the poem. The title to one of the poems is pencilled in and this might stand.

I am sorry about the paragraph in the Times, but I hope it will make no difference.

Yours sincerely,
Florence Hardy.

Text   MS. (typed) BL.   *Date*   Year corrected from internal evidence.
paragraph: in *The Times*, 16 Feb. 1928; headed 'Biography of Thomas Hardy', it read in its entirety, 'Mrs. Thomas Hardy stated yesterday that she was preparing a biography of her husband. She has already done preliminary work in getting the material together, but has not yet started on the book.' An earlier report had appeared in the *Evening Standard*, 15 Feb. 1928, and Macmillan (17 Feb. 1928, copy BL) told FEH that it was probably the *Standard's* correspondent who had telephoned.   *verse faintly pencilled in*: the rough draft TH wrote in the margin of 'To a Tree in London'; see *The Complete Poetical Works of Thomas Hardy*, ed. Samuel Hynes (Oxford: Clarendon Press, 1982–95), iii. 322.

To Edmund Gosse

MAX GATE, | DORCHESTER, | DORSET.
21st February '28.

My dear Sir Edmund:

I am much relieved to know that dear Lady Gosse has not had to undergo any operation at present, and I trust that she will soon be well enough to leave the nursing-home.

You must all have had a time of terrible anxiety, as also the many friends by whom she is so much beloved.

It is with satisfaction and gratitude that I learn of your consent to edit a volume of letters. Your views about that undertaking co-incide with mine in every respect. By the younger colleage I think that you must have Siegfried Sassoon in your mind, & I agree that noone could be better.

In my husband's will you are named as literary executor after Mr Cockerell. Your name would have stood first, as it did once, but he fully anticipated, as did I, that he would live to be over ninety, and he thought that by that time you would have found the very arduous duties of a literary executor beyond your strength.

I have, upon Mr Cockerell's strong insistence, written to the Times a very brief letter about the biography. I think that now all will be well and that I shall not be disturbed again. Thank you so much for your kind offer.

With deep gratitude—

Yours very sincerely
Florence Hardy—

Text MS. Leeds.

volume of letters: when FEH (19 Feb. 1928, Leeds) invited Gosse to edit a projected vol. of TH's letters, he recommended in his reply (20 Feb. 1928, Univ. of St Andrews) that the edition be selective rather than comprehensive.   *colleage*: i.e. 'colleague'; Gosse also suggested the participation of 'a younger colleague, equally sympathetic to you and to me, who would lighten the work'.   *brief letter*: pub. in *The Times*, 23 Feb. 1928, it acknowledged that she had been 'for some time' preparing a biography of TH, 'with his approval and with the assistance of his early note-books'.

To Daniel Macmillan

MAX GATE, | DORCHESTER, | DORSET.
22nd. February 1928.

Dear Mr Macmillan:

I am sorry that I was so precipitate in writing to Sir Edmund Gosse. I should not have done so had not Sir James Barrie thought him so much the most suitable person. However I am going to ask him to allow me the right to withdraw any letter or part of a letter that I would prefer not to be published, and perhaps when he hears that he will not wish to do the book.

I heard that he was rather hurt that he had not been consulted about the biography, and considered that Mr Cockerell ought to have communicated with him, so perhaps it was better to ask him to edit the letters. He is named in the will as Literary Executor after Mr Cockerell, and if Mr Cockerell resigns Sir Edmund would have the option of taking his place.

I shall be very pleased to hear from Mr Whibley. I do not think it necessary for anyone to collaborate with me as I can see for myself a great deal that must be altered. The biography as it stands is just as it left my husband's hands after a lengthy revision and correction. I should not like it to be pulled to pieces and rewritten, which is what he warned me would happen if I had a too-eminent literary man to help me. But I shall be grateful for assistance.

Yours sincerely,
Florence Hardy.

Text MS. (typed) BL.

so precipitate: D. Macmillan (21 Feb. 1928, copy BL) hoped FEH would not commit herself to an editor for the letters until 'the question of the biography is finally settled'; he subsequently explained (24 Feb. 1928, copy BL) that his only concern was that some letters might be needed in the biography.   *Whibley*: Charles Whibley (see letter of 19 Aug. 1919) was one of Macmillan & Co.'s most trusted readers. D. Macmillan's 21 Feb. letter spoke of Whibley's having 'very kindly agreed to help you with regard to your biography of Mr Hardy'; on 24 Feb. he assured FEH that Whibley would act only as a friend, not as a collaborator.

To Siegfried Sassoon

MAX GATE, | DORCHESTER, | DORSET.
24th February '28.

Dear Siegfried:

It was very good of you to write, for I had feared that the stroke which robbed me of my husband might also, indirectly, rob me of one of my most valued friends.

I am so sorry that my letter to Mr Tomlinson hurt you. If I had reflected I might have known that, for I knew he was certain to show it to you. Some men wouldn't have done so—I know some who would have said: 'Well—she accuses me wrongly, but she's lost her husband anyhow, & I won't do anything to rob her of a friend as well."

I've been trying to get into the mood to write to Mr Tomlinson & say I am sorry I wrote, & most likely I was mistaken about T.H's illness, but I cannot do it yet—something boils up within me when I think of what I could say. Those eyes that observed, the pen that noted down the evidences of old age—& then calmly cabled them off to America, for money, while he was lying dead here—as a result of that visit so cold-bloodedly described. Oh—my God *no*—not yet can I take back *anything*; wrong though I may be.

You were probably right about Newman Flower's article. Cockerell didn't like it. I have purposely not read it, for I only want to remember that Newman Flower was the last person to give T.H. any real pleasure. A present of grapes—wonderful bunches—came the afternoon of the day T.H. died. He was as pleased as a child about them—he would have them shown to the doctor, & told him who had sent them, he eat some & said gaily 'I'm going on with these', he called my sister to have some. And it was the same at Christmas with a present from Newman Flower—& it was always done so nicely & kindly. I thought T.H. was certainly going to get well when I saw him so interested & pleased with Newman Flower's present,

& I scribbled a line from the bedside to tell him so—& I believe a bit of that was printed—but I shouldn't like to see it. No wonder poor T.H. said, a few weeks before his death, that if he had his life over again he would prefer to be a small architect in a little country town, like Mr Hicks. He would have been a much happier man.

I will try to remember what you say about charity—I know it is the greatest of all things—& later, when I am calmer, I may be able to feel regret for what I have written & said.

Yesterday the rehearsal of Egdon Heath was wonderful, but it was almost too much for me—& afterwards Gustav Holst took my arm & walked up & down the empty corridors with me. The music was *his* tribute to T.H. & a beautiful one.

Thank you again for your letter, & forgive me for my lack of self control.

Yours ever—

F.E.H.

Text MS. (mourning stationery, with envelope) Eton.

letter to Mr Tomlinson: the violence of FEH's response to H. M. Tomlinson's 'Hardy at Max Gate' (*Saturday Review of Literature*, 11 Feb. 1928) was clearly related to her belief that the December visit of the Tomlinsons and the Wellses (see letters of 25 Nov. and 15 Dec. 1927) had led directly to TH's death. *Flower's article*: Flower's obituary article, 'In His Wessex Home. A Sheaf of Memories', *Sunday Times*, 15 Jan. 1928, referred particularly to FEH's having protected TH against intrusive visitors and quoted from an optimistic note she had written the day of his death. *Mr Hicks*: John Hicks (1815–69), the Dorchester architect with whom TH served his architectural apprenticeship. *Egdon Heath*: the first London performance of Gustav Holst's *Egdon Heath*, an orchestral work dedicated to TH, was given by the Royal Philharmonic Society in the evening of 23 Feb. 1928; FEH went up to London for a rehearsal that afternoon. For Holst's Aug. 1927 visit to Max Gate see *Biography*, 566. *empty corridors*: of the Queen's Hall.

[By the beginning of March 1928 FEH was beginning to pick up strands of her life that had been essentially let go during the traumatic period of her husband's death and its immediate aftermath: on 2 March 1928 (Princeton), for example, she told Howard Bliss that if he wished to acknowledge her gift of Hardy's cello he could send some money to help the Middleton Murrys. Many practical problems still confronted her, she was finding the 'Life' difficult to finish, and in the same letter to Bliss she expressed the hope that she would not live long, 'the pain & loneliness are almost unbearable'. A day later (Texas) she told Leonora Ervine, St John Ervine's wife, that she felt 'almost paralysed by misery.... *Nothing* has been spared me. And of course the loneliness, after fourteen years of the closest companionship, is terrible.' By 27 March (Princeton), on the other hand, she was telling Bliss that she hoped to have 'volume 1. of the biography finished this week' and asking whether he had in his collection 'any intimate & interesting letters' that might be included in the second volume.]

To E. M. Forster

MAX GATE, | DORCHESTER, | DORSET.
2nd March '28.

Dear Mr Forster:

Many thanks for your letter. It was very kind of you to think of writing to me. I had hoped to have been able to complete the biography, but I feel completely numb with misery—which today is worse than it has ever been. It may be the effect of medicine which I have been taking to make me sleep, but it cannot be altogether that. If I cannot get on with it in a week or two perhaps I had better resign it into other hands. If I read any part of what is already written, or look over any letters of his, I feel crushed to the earth. It is not possible to write under such conditions.

I am so pleased to hear that Mrs Forster keeps well: it is very kind of her to think of me. I heard that you had not been very well, & was sorry. I know that particular trouble can be very painful.

Please forgive me for writing so much about myself.

Yours very sincerely,
Florence Hardy.

Text MS. (mourning stationery) King's College Cambridge.
that particular trouble: not confidently identified.

To T. E. Lawrence

MAX GATE, | DORCHESTER, | DORSET.
5. 3. 28.

Dear Mr. Shaw,

Your letters were very kind and both of them helped me. But, besides my loneliness, which will never be less, I have to suffer remorse, almost beyond expression, because I know I failed him at every turn. Indeed, had it not been that he left work for me to do, I would not have lived on.

I do not think he had a chill, though the papers said so. He was worn out. His heart was very weak, and it was from that he died. The doctor said it was like a clock running down. For the last few months he grew very weary of life, though at the end he made an effort to live, except that once he said: "What is the good of trying to patch up this worn out old body?" His brain was clear, clearer than mine was, to a few minutes before the end, when he became unconscious. He thought only of poetry during the last few days, and dictated two verses, epitaphs on two living writers. I will send you these. He was devoted to you. Somehow I think he might have lived had you been here.

You say the news struck you as a triumph. When I saw him after he had been laid out I was spell bound. On his face was a radiant look of *triumph*. Never on any other face have I ever seen such a look, nor could I ever have believed it possible. Cockerell used the same word, "triumphant", and one journalist who—without my knowledge or consent was allowed to see him after, used the same word in a short article I saw only yesterday: "a *triumphant* smile on his pale face'. It is the only word that can describe it. I wish I could understand it.

In his study your portrait is on the wall where he placed it. I wanted him to see you again. He and I both thought he would live to be over ninety. All our plans were arranged for that—only, as I said, towards the end he grew very tired. On November 28th. he told me that he had done all that he meant to do, but that he did not know whether it had been worth doing.

Time will not help me for I know my own nature, and I shall miss him more and more. The thought of years that may have to be lived through without him fills me with terror. There was really nothing in my life except T.H. nor will there ever be.

There are things of his I should like you to have, only I don't like sending them to India and if you were nearer I would implore you to take over the biography altogether. You seem nearer to him, somehow, than anyone else, certainly more akin. Beryl and Miss Fetherstonhaugh have been very good.

Again thanking you,

Florence Hardy.

Text   Photocopy of typed transcript (see below) Ronald D. Knight.
your letters: Lawrence's letters of 15 Jan. and 16 Feb. 1928, both written from Karachi, were first pub. in David Garnett (ed.), *The Letters of T. E. Lawrence* (London: Jonathan Cape, 1938). Three of FEH's letters to Lawrence seem to have survived, but only as carbon copies of typed transcriptions; see Ronald D. Knight (ed.), *T. E. Lawrence and the Max Gate Circle* (Weymouth: R. D. Knight, 1988), 102–3, 106–7, 135.   *living writers*: G. K. Chesterton and George Moore; see *Complete Poetical Works of TH*, ed. Hynes, iii. 308–9.   *a triumph*: Lawrence used the phrase in both his letters.   *journalist . . . article*: unidentified.   *The thought of*: the transcript reads 'The though of '.   *Beryl . . . Fetherstonhaugh*: see letter of 24 July 1927.

To Sydney Cockerell

MAX GATE, | DORCHESTER, | DORSET.
8th March 1928.

My dear Sydney:

I hope that you were not too tired when you reached Cambridge, for you really had a far more strenuous time than I had. It is rather amusing about the Macmillans. A letter came this morning from J.M.B. but he did'nt mention business.

I was rung up by a newspaper this morning to tell me that Miss Teresa Hardy died last night. Dr Mann called this morning to tell me about it. He is a kind hearted man & seemed angry with Kate Hardy. He said he had told her how things were, & Miss Teresa had sent for her, but she didn't go until yesterday afternoon when her cousin was unconscious. The undertaker came to me to ask about the funeral—& who was going to pay if she had an oak coffin. I said that he was to give her a proper coffin etc. & if there wasn't enough money of hers I would pay. Her niece, a widow, arrived yesterday, & Dr Mann tells me that she, too, is very angry—with K. Dr Mann had told me not to go as Miss Teresa was so angry with *me*, & the sight of me would only upset her. She held me responsible for the Abbey burial, & the heart burial. Isn't it all terrible?

I will send the proofs by registered post tomorrow.

Thank you so much for all that you are doing with the Macmillans—but if it worries you let them take what they want.

Always yours sincerely—

F.E.H.

Text   MS. (mourning stationery) Beinecke.
strenuous time: Cockerell had been at Max Gate, sorting (and often destroying) TH's papers and arranging the books in his library.   *about the Macmillans*: with whom Cockerell was arguing over the division of the royalties generated by the *Daily Telegraph*'s advance pub. of fifty poems from *Winter Words*.   *J.M.B.*: J. M. Barrie.   *Teresa Hardy*: TH's first cousin (1844–1928), the youngest child of his uncle James Hardy; she had remained at Higher Bockhampton all her life and played the organ at Stinsford Church from 1880 to 1914.   *Dr Mann*: see letter of 30 Dec. 1927.   *Her niece*: Emily Charles (née Hardy), daughter of TH's cousin Augustus Hardy.   *the proofs*: of *Winter Words*; see letter of 13 Mar. 1928.

To Sydney Cockerell

MAX GATE, | DORCHESTER, | DORSET.
13th March 1928.

My dear Sydney:

I am so sorry that you are still not well, & I feel rather guilty as I know that you have had a fearful strain upon you for the last few months—two months rather. I think upon the whole it would be well to postpone your visit for a week or so, until you are stronger. I have no engagements after this week—but of course people want to come, & worry me to go out to tea. Barrie comes this evening. I had half a mind to send him a telegram to ask him not to come because of the cold. Your coming will not interfere with the memoir, because I must get things right in the study, & would help you there. I have an idea about the biography but will write to you later.

I agree with you about the change you wish—on slip 34. T. had omitted the commas & quotes. The fault was not the printers.

I had not noticed anything at all wrong. Your proof reading is wonderful.

I did not like 'Aristodemus the Messenian', & am afraid I annoyed T.H. by saying so. He actually thought it was suitable for performance here.

Did you want the manuscript sent to you? I will send it if you like. I will go through them again.

I am so pleased to hear that Mrs Cockerell continues to improve. I send my very best wishes to Christopher.

Yours very sincerely,
Florence Hardy.

P.S. Would you ask someone's advice—preferably A. E. Housman's—as to whether we should exclude 'Aristodemus'?   F.H.

Text   MS. (mourning stationery) Beinecke.
on slip 34: of the proofs of *Winter Words*.   *T. had . . . printers.*: a late insertion.   *for performance here*: the poem is in dialogue form.   *exclude 'Aristodemus'?*: it was, however, included when *Winter Words* was pub., 2 Oct. 1928.

To Siegfried Sassoon

MAX GATE, | DORCHESTER, | DORSET.
May 12th. 1928.

My dear Siegfried:

It was very good of you to write: I did not intend to draw a letter from you.

I am glad that your long book is finished, & look forward with eagerness to seeing it in print. I am sorry that you were tired & I hope that you are well now. You must be terribly anxious about Gosse.

I still feel my life to be intolerably & unalterably lonely, but I begin to realize that the close of that wonderful & precious life was not so untimely as it seemed at first. He knew that he was nearing the end, & I think he did not regret it.

I was very rushed by publishers & the agent about the first volume of the biography, which is now in the printer's hands. The second part is at present chaos, but I shall be able to get that in order later.

Strange complications seem to come into my life and unreal situations. I often wonder where I am drifting—& why. Some time later I should so like to have a talk with you.

On the 21st. I go to Oxford, to take the MS. of a volume of poems that I am presenting to them, in memory of T.H. The fellows & their wives are having dinner with me in the Common Room. On the 22nd I hope to go to London, for one night or perhaps two, to stay with the Hornbys, at Shelley House—& then back to Max Gate, & I hope I shall be able to remain here quietly for the rest of the summer.

I hope so much that E. Blunden is now quite happy & settled. I am sorry that he is overworked.

I had a long talk with the Heads this morning. He is no better, of course, but as much of an angel as ever. She too is wonderful, the darling. They loved your poems. I lent them the Mercury. The more often I read them the more wonderful I think them.

Always yours sincerely
Florence Hardy.

P.S. I forgot to say that I have not sent you a book as requested by T.H—thinking you would rather choose one for yourself when you come. But I will send one if you prefer—F.E.H

Text   MS. (mourning stationery, with envelope) Eton.
long book: Memoirs of a Fox-Hunting Man, pub. anonymously later in 1928.   *about Gosse:* who died 16 May 1928.   *to Oxford*: FEH presented the MS. of *Winter Words* to Queen's College, of which TH had been an honorary Fellow.   *Hornbys*: Charles Harry St John Hornby (1867–1946) and his wife Cicely, née Barclay; Shelley House, on the Chelsea Embankment, was their London address. Hornby was a distinguished printer, both commercially (as a partner in W. H. Smith & Sons) and privately (as founder of the Ashendene Press), and a close friend of Cockerell's.   *no better*: Henry Head suffered from Parkinson's disease (on which he was a leading authority) for many years prior to his death in 1940.   *the Mercury*: i.e. Sassoon's 'Three Sonnets', *London Mercury*, May 1928.

To Sydney Cockerell

MAX GATE, | DORCHESTER, | DORSET.
Monday—May 29th | 1928.

My dear Sydney:

I *am* sorry about the proofs, but I feel so horribly unwell, & *extremely* worried. I find it so difficult to concentrate, & though I read over the proofs time after time I cannot see any mistakes. I know the whole by heart almost. Mr Forster is abroad now I think. In any case it would be injudicious to rely on his help too much.

T.H. spent not only weeks, but *months*, in going over & over this biography, altering & revising copiously. If he were satisfied, then I think we may be, at least so far as Part I is concerned—unless we adopt George Moore's theory, that he couldn't write good prose—which I don't feel inclined to do. Personally I rather like a passage from a diary coming in abruptly, rather than being clotted up with woolly sentences of introduction.

I admit that a very great deal must be done to Part II—as a matter of policy. Much of what is written there would do T.H. harm.

I send some more proofs for you just to see the alterations. I am ashamed to admit that I don't know whether it should be 'lay' or 'laid' on 89. I suppose 'laid'. Of course I know it should be *amiable*. (84)

I sat up last night long after eleven looking over the proofs, but it seemed time wasted, as I could not take in properly what I was reading.

Yours ever—
F.E.H.

I am so glad that Mrs Cockerell is feeling better. F.H.

Text MS. (mourning stationery) Beinecke.
the proofs: of *Early Life*.   *George Moore's theory*: Moore, in *Conversations in Ebury Street* (see letter of 30 Mar. 1924), had been especially critical of TH's style.   *I suppose 'laid'*: *Early Life*, 182, reads 'They lay down'.   *89 . . . (84)*: galley proof, or 'slip', numbers.   *amiable*: in 'a most amiable woman' (*Early Life*, 172); FEH, however, consistently spelled it 'aimable' (e.g. letter of 12 Sept. 1926).

[In appointing FEH and Cockerell as joint literary executors TH doubtless believed that he would be guaranteeing to his widow the friendly support of a wise and exceptionally experienced collaborator. In practice the two were quickly driven apart by the always latent antagonism between them and by FEH's need to resist Cockerell's automatic assumption of authority. Disagreements arose early over relations with publishers, custodianship of TH's literary remains, proposals for a national memorial, and correction of the proofs of *Early Life*. FEH's letter to Cockerell of 31 May 1928 (Beinecke) both apologized for her 'peevishness' and sought to excuse it, but her 2 July 1928 letter to Forster reflected her anger at the discovery that Cockerell and Barrie (whom she regarded as her closest ally) had met together to discuss the final proofs of *Early Life* before either of them had gone over them with her. She also sought to strengthen her hand by getting a favourable opinion from Forster on two points over which she and Cockerell were currently at odds.]

To E. M. Forster

MAX GATE, | DORCHESTER, | DORSET.
2nd July 1928.

Dear Mr Forster:

It was a great pleasure to see your writing. I was thinking of you as I walked home from Dorchester this morning, & came in to find your letter on the hall table. I hope you are better for your tour abroad. I am so sorry I am unable to be in London this week or I should like to have seen you. I have had a trying week-end here with Mr Cockerell, my co-literary executor, & I am seriously thinking of resigning my executorship—if it would not be an act of faithlessness to the trust my husband reposed in me.

I have a short story which my husband told me once I might publish after his death. It is founded on fact. But I do not wish to publish anything, naturally, that would not reach a high enough standard. May I send it to you, & will you give me an opinion? It is a very short story.

Also do you see any harm in the second paragraph on the first page of the proof sent herewith?

I am glad the rose blooms. Ours here has done so well this year. I hope that Mrs Forster is well & her rheumatism quite disappeared.

Yours very sincerely
F. E. Hardy—

Text MS. (mourning stationery) King's College Cambridge.
short story: 'Old Mrs Chundle' (Purdy, 267–8); Forster's unhelpfully indecisive opinion was quoted in FEH to Cockerell, 11 July 1928 (Beinecke). See letter of 24 July 1928 for FEH's continuing disagreement with Cockerell over the story and, for a full account, *Thomas Hardy: The Excluded and Collaborative Stories*, ed. Pamela Dalziel (Oxford: Clarendon Press, 1992), 215–23.   *second paragraph*: it appears from FEH's letter to Cockerell of 6 July 1928 (Beinecke) that Forster recommended retention of the paragraph about George Eliot ('not a born storyteller by any means') in *Early Life*, 129.   *herewith?*: the MS. has two question-marks, the second having been left untouched when FEH deleted the original ending to the sentence, 'under separate cover?'

To Sydney Cockerell

MAX GATE, | DORCHESTER, | DORSET.
24th July '28.

Dear Mr Cockerell:

Thank you for the lettering for the tomb. I have sent the one you prefer—B—to the mason, & a copy to Mr Cowley as I understand this has to be done before any inscription is made on any tomb in the churchyard. I saw the stone mason also, yesterday afternoon, & gave him the instructions about pasting paper to the stone, & on a board etc. He seemed bewildered, & said he had not done that when he carved the other inscriptions—he has done them all—but I asked him to follow the instructions. He promises to begin next week.

I had two letters this morning, one from Curtis Brown in America, & another from his London agent. Would you let me know the position?

I can positively affirm that my husband gave me that MS. with instructions that it might be printed. He copied it out carefully himself, & fastened the pages together, thus showing that he did *not* consider it valueless— though he certainly did not wish it published during his lifetime. I agree that it would be unwise, perhaps, to publish it in a separate & expensive volume—but as a literary achievement I do not think it falls much behind, if at all, some of the short stories already published. Might I have your views upon this?

Thank you for the proofs with the corrections. I find that '*bemeaned*' is a good Dorset word, that was once in common-use. I notice it came in an extract from my husband's diary—& this was either copied out, or quoted by himself. It is a word to be found in the Oxford Dictionary, & to my mind infinitely preferable to "*lowered*" which is a very commonplace word, having not half the force of '*bemeaned.*' Also I regretted the alteration of '*practically*', his own word, to '*pathetically*'. The meaning of the phrase was altered—& not, I thought, for the better. The other alterations were most valuable—being, of course, errors in typing or omissions. I am sorry for a carelessly written letter, but it is a very hot afternoon—

Yours sincerely,
Florence Hardy.

Text MS. (mourning stationery) Beinecke.

Mr Cockerell: FEH's abandonment of 'Sydney' was not immediately repeated. *the mason*: Walter Hounsell, local stonemason (*CL*, iv. 262). *Mr Cowley*: vicar of Stinsford; see letter of 6 Feb. 1919. *done them all*: i.e. the tombs for TH's parents and sister and for ELH. *Curtis Brown*: [Albert] Curtis Brown, the American literary agent seeking publication permission for 'Old Mrs Chundle'; the manager of his London office was Michael Joseph, later an independent publisher. *that MS.*: 'Old Mrs Chundle'; see letter of 2 July 1928. *'bemeaned'*: restored to *Early Life*, 281. *'practically'*: restored to *Early Life*, 283.

[Richard Little Purdy, author in later years of *Thomas Hardy: A Bibliographical Study* and co-editor of *The Collected Letters of Thomas Hardy*, was at this period working towards a doctorate at Yale University. Already an enthusiastic and knowledgeable student of TH's work, he had organized at Yale in the spring of 1928 an impressive memorial exhibition of books and manuscripts, based in part upon his own collection. FEH's appreciation of this gesture became the starting-point for a close working and personal friendship which began with Purdy's first visit to Max Gate in 1929 and lasted until FEH's death.]

To Richard Purdy

MAX GATE, | DORCHESTER, | DORSET.
28th July 1928.

Dear Mr Purdy:

I must apologize most deeply for the long delay in acknowledging the copies of the Hardy Catalogue of that most interesting exhibition. I am delighted to have them, & thank you most warmly for your kindness in sending them. I wish it had been possible for me to be at the meeting held in memory of my husband, & also to have seen the exhibition. I am grateful to Yale University and yourself for the tribute to my husband. Nothing of the kind took place in England—at least so far as I know.

Again my most grateful thanks,

Yours very sincerely,
Florence Hardy.

Text MS. (mourning stationery, with envelope) Beinecke.
Purdy: Richard Little Purdy (1904–90), American Hardy scholar and collector.

To May O'Rourke

MAX GATE, | DORCHESTER, | DORSET.
7th September 1928.

My dear Miss ORourke:

Thank you so much for sending the copy of 'The Month', with the article about my husband. It is exceedingly well written. My only criticism —& I don't know whether you care to have it—is that it seems to me to be rather too much of an apology for him—though you say many beautiful things about his work. I should not, myself, have thought there was a line in his work that could be called "a frenzied out burst of unbelief." He always seemed to me so sane & well balanced in his judgement of other people's religious views nor do I know of anyone who has entered this house who is mentally capable of sitting in judgement on his beliefs, the result of many years deep thought & honest self-examination. Of course it is difficult to disentangle the two elements of your article—the praise & what seems to me (forgive me if I misjudge you) a carefully veiled attack which does not come gracefully from *you*. He never criticized your religious views, & it seems to me that you were not called upon to express your opinion on his—though after what Anatole France suffered at the hands of his secretary one cannot but be thankful for small mercies. Somebody else, I think, might have taken on that job. But I suppose 'The Month' would not have printed your article had it not contained something of the sort.

I may tell you now that in his lifetime he wondered several times whether something of this sort might not happen—but finally decided that he might trust your honour.

Yours sincerely—
Florence Hardy.

Text   MS. (mourning stationery, with envelope) R. Greenland.
ORourke: i.e. O'Rourke (see letter of 27 July 1918); she was currently living in a Catholic convent in SW London.   *the article*: O'Rourke's 'Thomas Hardy, O.M. 1840–1928', *The Month*, 152 (Sept. 1928), 205–12.   "*a frenzied . . . unbelief.*": quoted from p. 207 of O'Rourke's article. Although extravagantly phrased, the sentence in its entirety seems intended to win sympathy for TH from the magazine's Catholic readership: 'His was indeed a mind in pain, and it is as the ravings of a man in pain that we should rank those frenzied outbursts of unbelief, which to too many people represent all they know of the man or his works.'   *Anatole France . . . secretary*: FEH's reference to Jean Jacques Brousson's sensational *Anatole France Himself: A Boswellian Record*, trans. John Pollock (London, 1925), was deeply resented by O'Rourke, who retorted on 9 Sept. 1928 (copy, Greenland) that FEH had in fact read and approved the article in manuscript.

To Marie Stopes

MAX GATE, | DORCHESTER, | DORSET.
16th September 1928.

Dear Dr Marie Stopes:

Thank you so much for your kind letter, & also for the most highly appreciated gift of your novel "Love's Creation"—which I ought to have acknowledged before. At the time you sent it I seemed to be suffering from severe nervous strain & found it impossible to concentrate on any novel. I read page after page & all the time my mind was a blank, & I couldn't grasp what I was reading. Now, however, I have read it with great interest. I do so admire your versatility. You seem able to do everything. Passages in it are exceedingly fine, & I like the part about scientific work—only (pray forgive me) I don't much appreciate the love-making. I seem unable to enter into that: a lack of real feeling on my part I suppose.

I am so sorry to hear of your troubles with regard to the smallpox in the village—but one must be thankful that your boy did not get it or yourself or Mr Roe. I was a Portland Bill the other day & looked towards your lighthouse, & was told you were not there.

Also I have made searching enquiries about the MS. of 'The Well-Beloved" & can not discover its present whereabouts. It may have been pulped, but more likely, someone has it who has no right to it, & is keeping it hidden, lest I should claim it.

I hope the Museum will be a success. When my life seems to be normal again I must see what I can do about it. Even now I seem to be living in a sort of evil dream, & my loneliness is terrible—I have such sleepless nights.

I hope you are quite well, & your most enchanting boy flourishing.

Again thanking you for your letter & the book.

Always yours sincerely
Florence Hardy.

Text MS. (mourning stationery) BL.

novel: *Love's Creation: A Novel* (London, 1928).   *a Portland*: 'at Portland' clearly intended. *claim it*: the MS. has never surfaced and was presumably destroyed.   *the Museum*: the Portland Museum, incorporating 'Avice's Cottage' (associated with TH's novel *The Well-Beloved*), was very much M. Stopes's personal creation.

[In September 1928 FEH rented an apartment in Adelphi Terrace, the famous but subsequently demolished Adam block near Charing Cross. The actor David Garrick once lived in the building and in the 1860s TH himself worked there as an architectural assistant to Arthur Blomfield, but what weighed most with FEH at this particular moment was the fact that one of her neighbours in Adelphi Terrace would be Sir James Barrie. Increasingly dependent on Barrie's advice and support during the difficult months since Hardy's death, she seems for a time to have interpreted his attentiveness in romantic terms—to the point of anticipating a proposal of marriage. Taking the apartment reflected in any case an impulse to escape from Max Gate and from some of the more pressing of her new responsibilities and to enjoy a more sociable London existence on the basis of her new affluence and freedom. A brief return from London to Max Gate taught her, according to her letter to Cockerell of 22 October 1928 (Beinecke), that 'I cannot possibly live on here during the autumn & winter in gloom & solitude. My three weeks in London have shown me that life there would be happier & fuller.' Her mood later changed—as it would change repeatedly during the succeeding years—and she was in any case forced back to Dorchester at the beginning of December 1928 by the death of Henry Hardy, long prey to a series of real and imagined illnesses.]

To Sydney Cockerell

8, ADELPHI TERRACE, | STRAND, W.C.2.
Monday. [10 December 1928]

Dear Sydney:

It is a very kind thought of yours to wish to be present at Henry's funeral, & you must do exactly as you think best. One never quite knows how Kate takes things: she might be deeply gratified; on the other hand she might not. If you think it right that you should be there certainly go. I will put you up at Max Gate, of course, & you will be met at the station. I *must* go there early tomorrow. I would have gone today but I felt compelled to see how my Mother was before starting. She is no worse—possibly a little better. The funeral is to be on Thursday I understand.

Gordon Gifford has just rung me up, & he wishes to be at the funeral. *That* will not suit Katie, I fear, though a more harmless & well meaning man could not exist. He will sleep at Max Gate on Wednesday night, but there will be a room for you also, of course. When I arrive at Talbothays tomorrow if I find K. definitely opposed to the presence of any one except near relatives at the funeral I will send a telegram instantly to you & Gordon Gifford. But she may be very pleased at the idea of you being there.

If you come by the 4.30 from Waterloo on Wednesday the car will be meeting that train at Dorchester—7.50 (or 40)—but if you are coming by an earlier train please let me know.

Yours ever—

F.E.H.

Text   MS. Beinecke.   Date   Supplied on MS. by Cockerell.
Henry's funeral: Henry Hardy, TH's younger brother, died on 9 Dec. 1928, and was buried at Stinsford on 13 Dec.   *Kate*: Katharine Hardy was now the only survivor among TH's siblings.   *your being there*: both Cockerell and Gordon Gifford attended the funeral.   *the car*: one of FEH's recent indulgences had been the purchase of a car and the hiring of a chauffeur.

To Sydney Cockerell

as from— | 8—ADELPHI TERRACE | STRAND, W.C.2.

Christmas Eve. [1928]

Dear Sydney:

Thank you so much for your kind letter. I ought to have written before but have, as you rightly observed, been dejected & worried, & also I have a heavy cold—the result I think of getting up at 2.15 to make tea for Sir James, & sitting talking to him, to soothe his nerves. I have promised to remain here for Christmas but am over at my own flat a great deal.

I hope that you all will have a tolerably happy Christmas together, & that Mrs Cockerell will be free from pain.

Early in the New Year I see that it will be necessary for me to very carefully consider my position & make a decision as to the way in which I must best live in the future. I cannot go on as I am doing at present— keeping on Max Gate & living at Adelphi Terrace. Even if I could afford it

I would not do it. Perhaps a holiday later would be a good thing, when I have given up this flat. We must have a long talk & come to some definite decision.

Again with every good wish—to Mrs Cockerell, yourself & the family—

Ever yours,

F.E.H.

Text MS. Beinecke.   *Date* Year supplied on MS. by Cockerell.
as from: FEH, writing from Barrie's flat, had adapted his headed stationery to show the address of her own flat nearby.   *tolerably happy:* i.e. despite Kate Cockerell's continuing illness.

[Howard Bliss was welcomed at Max Gate in TH's lifetime, both as a musician and as a serious student and collector of Hardy's works, and was even allowed to purchase the manuscript of *The Woodlanders*. Following TH's death FEH relied a good deal on Bliss's well-informed advice in matters relating to the books and manuscripts for which she was now responsible, and she encouraged him in the development of a collection that she saw as honouring her husband and contributing to the long-term preservation of his memory and his achievements. She gave Bliss letters, manuscripts, and memorabilia, entrusted still other items to his care, and at one point named him—so she told St John Hornby on 14 September 1929 (Beinecke)—as 'a trustee of Max Gate, its contents, the royalties, MSS, books etc—after my death'. Bliss became less important to her, however, once she had access to the scholarly expertise of Richard Purdy, and her confidence in him was perhaps shaken by the realization that she no longer remembered just what she had given him and that his promise to leave his collection to an institutional library was no guarantee against his selling such gifts at times of financial exigency. Her eventual repurchase of *The Woodlanders* manuscript seems to have occurred at just such a moment of difficulty for Bliss but may well have been facilitated by Bliss's sensitivity to FEH's uneasiness over the original sale.]

To Howard Bliss

8, ADELPHI TERRACE, | STRAND, W.C.2.
15th January 1929.

Dear Mr Bliss:

Many thanks for your letter. I shall certainly not mention to *anyone* the purchase of the MSS. nor any of the business we discussed concerning the literary executorship. I am convinced that the latter may well kept between ourselves for the present. I had a letter from Mr Cockerell this morning concerning the appointment of a successor to himself in the event of his death. The right to do this belongs to me, solely, & I do not wish to be co-erced. I have had legal advice on this matter & I can appoint anyone I like.

I am bringing back from Max Gate next Monday or Tuesday, my copy of my husband's will, so that you can see how the matter stands.

Also I have this morning received a request from a charitable society—a "mission"—for my husband's old piano—the only one he & his first wife ever possessed. I suppose this has no value as a relic, has it? It is worm-eaten in parts. Our drawing-room is over-crowded, & the piano is hopelessly out of tune. What had I better do about it? Of course it is, in a way, a relic, but such a one as nobody I imagine would care to possess.

I go to Max Gate on Friday & will make all arrangements, if possible, for your going down in February.

I will hand you the letters to my husband from Gosse, when next I see you. Would it be too much to ask you if I might have typed copies of the Tinsley letters etc—this quite at your leisure. Or written copies would do equally well.

Also I have another 'Blue Eyes' relic here for you, to take back with you at any time—perhaps when you come to go through the rest of the letters.

I expect to see Mr Cockerell here tomorrow if it is possible for him to get here about 12. as I have to go out at 12.30. If he asks for information I will tell him to apply to you.

Yours sincerely,
Florence Hardy.

Text   MS. Princeton.
purchase: FEH first wrote 'sale'.   *well kept*: 'well be kept' evidently intended.   *care to possess*: the piano's fate is unknown.   *Tinsley letters*: in recognition of Bliss's purchase of the (incomplete) MS. of *A Pair of Blue Eyes* at the George Barr McCutcheon sale in 1925, FEH had lent or perhaps given him (see letter of 9 Nov. 1932) the surviving William Tinsley to TH letters about the novel, together with ELH's miniature and earrings and other associated items. The letters are now in the Taylor collection at Princeton, the novel MS. and relics at the Berg.

To Sydney Cockerell

8, ADELPHI TERRACE, | STRAND, W.C.2.
16th January 1929.

My dear Sydney:
I am so *very* sorry that I missed you today. I waited until 12.30. & then thought that because of the weather & your cold you would not be coming up. Had I really known that you would certainly have called I would have put off my engagement. But I hope that I shall be able to see you soon, for there is a great deal to talk about. I have got Mr Curtis Brown to stop, at

any rate until we have talked over the matter—the publication in the limited edition of 'Old Mrs Chundle". I have taken back his cheque, & please do not sign any agreement if any is sent to you. I find I was misled—& I also very deeply regret the publication in 'The Ladies Home Journal.' It will not be published in England in any case. About the publication of letters etc, & the few unpublished poems I intend to leave everything in your hands as I fear I am liable to make very serious mistakes—partly due, I think, to my present state of health. Please let all this be entirely private.

Then the question of my will is very urgent. Will you think out some scheme concerning Max Gate & its contents, & the royalties. The question of mere money is not so important. Also it is better to consider the question of the printed books at Max Gate as well as the remaining MSS.

Will you let all this, "Old Mrs Chundle" etc—be absolutely private & between ourselves.

If I do not go to Dorchester on Friday I would be here all day on Monday or could go to see you at Cambridge. Or I could see you here to lunch, or any time until 3. o'clock on Tuesday—or *any time* on Thursday or Friday, if I know beforehand. If the weather is fine enough to allow me to go to Dorchester on Friday I would return on Monday & be here on Tuesday until 3. o'clock. I would let you know either by letter or wire at the Museum on Friday mid-day, if I decide *not* to go to Dorchester. If you haven't heard by then I shall have gone to Max Gate until Monday morning. I fear that all this is *very* confusing. If I do *not* go to Dorchester I have all Saturday free.

Please forgive this very confused letter—

Yours ever—
F.E.H.

Text   MS. Beinecke.
Brown . . . Chundle": see letters of 2 and 24 July 1928; the limited edition of 755 copies by Crosby Gaige of New York is dated January 1929 and had perhaps already been printed.

[Early in 1881 Arthur Wing Pinero's play *The Squire* had been attacked as a plagiarization of TH's *Far from the Madding Crowd*, but any hostility that may have existed between the two men dissipated over the years—so that TH, in 1914, is to be found responding warmly to Pinero's congratulations on his second marriage. It is not clear to what extent, if at all, Pinero encountered the Hardys in person either before or after his own wife's death in 1919, but in the earliest known letter (11 January 1929, Beinecke) from FEH to Pinero her acceptance of an invitation to lunch is already affectionately phrased.]

To Sir Arthur Pinero

8, ADELPHI TERRACE, | STRAND, W.C.2.

15th March 1929.

Dear Sir Arthur:

It was so kind of you to write & so kind also of you to go to my little lunch. I am afraid that I ordered all the wrong things though.

I am pleased that you liked my friend Adelaide Phillpotts—& she told me that she felt it to be a great honour to meet you & Barrie. Her father was much gratified also.

I have never told you—& I hope you will not think this mere flattery— how very much your plays meant to me when I was younger & a keen theatregoer. How well I remember seeing 'Letty'—'His House in Order' & others, & can even now recall the thrill—& also I love to read them. I have never seen any other plays that came near them. I hope that you will not mind my saying this, but I am sure you will not misunderstand.

This, *of course*, requires no answer.

Always yours sincerely,

Florence Hardy.

Text   MS. Beinecke.
Sir Arthur: Sir Arthur Wing Pinero (1855–1934), playwright, knighted 1909.   *Phillpotts*:
[Mary] Adelaide Eden Phillpotts, later Ross (b. 1896), daughter of the novelist Eden Phillpotts
and his first wife; a novelist, playwright, and poet in her own right, she was in London for
the opening of her play *The Mayor*. Her recollections of a 'woebegone' FEH, an 'unknowable'
Barrie, and a stone deaf Pinero suggest that FEH's lunch, at the Boulestin restaurant, was
a somewhat melancholy occasion: Adelaide Ross, *Reverie* (London: Robert Hale, 1981), 113–
14.   'Letty'—'His House in Order': plays of Pinero's first performed in, respectively, 1903
and 1906 (revived 1914).

To William Lyon Phelps

8, ADELPHI TERRACE, | STRAND, W.C.2.

26th March 1929.

Dear Professor Lyon-Phelps:

I hope that you do not think me very ungrateful for not having written before this to thank you for your kind letter & the most generous reviews of my 'Early Life of T.H.". I am sure these helped the work greatly.

My reason for not writing at once I am sure you will understand when I tell you that I have had many losses during the last few months. Early in December my husband's only brother died. He was the kindest soul imaginable, & devoted to me, & I loved him. Then my mother died early in

February—& you will understand what that loss meant—& other relatives have died since.

I hope that you & Mrs Lyon-Phelps are both well. I often think of our pleasant meetings. Sir James Barrie was not well at Christmas—a sharp attack of bronchitis—but he is well now—indeed I lunched with him today. He has been the kindest friend possible during the sad days.

I go back to Max Gate at the end of March when I have to give up this little flat. I shall miss the kind literary friends I have been seeing during the past six months but perhaps I shall be able to take a little house or small flat in London later.

I am afraid that the first part of my biography has not had a large sale in England. The publishers hardly advertised it at all—although it had a splendid press. I am hoping that when Part II appears, which I hope will be in the early autumn, people will want to read the whole book.

I am so glad that you liked 'Winter Words". Some of the poems I think are poignant beyond anything else that I have ever read, notably 'He resolves to say no more.' They tear my heart, because I think that if he could have recovered from that illness he could have written more. I miss him more than ever: the thought of returning to Max Gate to live alone there is almost more than I can bear.

With every good wish & my affection to Mrs Lyon-Phelps & yourself, & my most grateful thanks,

Ever yours sincerely,
Florence Hardy.

Text   MS. Beinecke.
Phelps: William Lyon Phelps (1865–1943), Yale professor and prolific literary commentator; he had praised *Early Life* in his regular *Scribner's Magazine* column, Feb. 1929, calling it 'very close to what an ideal biography should be'.   *pleasant meetings*: Phelps and his wife Annabel (née Hubbard) had visited Max Gate in 1928 and also dined with FEH at Barrie's flat.   *'Winter Words"*: also praised in Phelps's column.

[One of the semi-public controversies in which FEH was uncomfortably involved during much of 1929 related to the projected national memorial to her husband's memory. An appeal for funds launched in February 1928 produced only dismal results, and subsequent planning by a committee including Cockerell, St John Hornby, Lady Ilchester, Harley Granville-Barker, Augustus John, and the Mayor of Dorchester was able to go forward only on the expectation of very substantial financial contributions from TH's widow and surviving sister. Cockerell strongly advocated the erection of a tower on 'Egdon' heath, insisting (in a letter to *The Times*) that Hardy had once expressed approval of such a memorial, but projects of that scale and character were effectively ruled out by the shortage of funds and by the local

Dorset preference, which FEH increasingly shared, for a statue located in Dorchester itself.]

To Sydney Cockerell

8, ADELPHI TERRACE, | STRAND, W.C.2.
12th April 1929.

Dear Sydney:

With regard to the proposed public memorial to T.H. I have been told by one old friend of my husband's that it is a matter in which I should stand aside, & this has been confirmed by others to whom I have submitted the matter. I am told that it will be quite fitting to do what I can for the hospital (according to the written instructions which T.H left) & possibly for the Grammar School (I have already done something there) but that I should not be prominent in raising what it to be regarded as a *public* memorial. Of course I shall give a subscription, & what I consider will be an adequate one, but I cannot pledge myself to any fixed amount until the estate is wound up. His sister, so I am assured, stands in a different position. I think this reasoning is sound.

Had a sufficient sum been forthcoming from outside a tower, as at first proposed, would have been quite a good memorial, & possibly the best. But I am told that £6,000 would not be nearly sufficient to build a good tower. I think that Henry Hardy was prepared to spend the whole of what my husband left him in building a tower if he could have done it by himself, & according to his own ideas. He had no intention of subscribing to a tower designed by someone else.

The last time that I was in Dorchester I realized that public feeling there was in favour of a statue. I think that my sister-in-law would like this, & JMB. was telling me yesterday that he thought it quite natural that the Dorset people should want something actually in Dorchester. He certainly seemed inclined to a statue.

I know that my husband liked that statue of Barnes & said it was a good memorial, though he never said he wanted a statue of himself standing in Dorchester, any more than he ever said he wished for another Hardy tower to be built. He thought them both good memorials, & that was all. I should have no objection to either—but I think the tower is out of the question at present on account of the cost—just as a Hardy chair of Literature, which idea gave him great satisfaction, is also out of the question, unless I choose to leave sufficient money to endow one.

In thinking of the statue of Bunyan at Bedford, of Samuel Johnson at

Litchfield & of Gainsborough it seems to me that these are not unfitting memorials, though a tower would appeal to more imaginative people.

I shall be at Max Gate from Wednesday evening until Friday morning, & if you are still at Chantmarle I could go over to see you on Thursday or could see you at Max Gate—whichever is convenient to Mrs Hornby.

I should like to know exactly what Mr Hornby thinks—

Yours very sincerely—

F.E.H.

Text MS. (with envelope) Beinecke.
what it to: 'what is to' clearly intended. *JMB.*: J. M. Barrie. *statue of Barnes*: by Roscoe Mullins, outside St Peter's Church, Dorchester. *another Hardy tower*: i.e. in addition to the existing tower, SW of Dorchester, erected to the memory of Admiral Sir Thomas Masterman Hardy. *Hardy chair*: as had been proposed by University College, Southampton, shortly before TH's death. *statue . . . Bedford*: by Sir Joseph Boehm, erected 1874. *Litchfield*: correctly Lichfield; statue by R. C. Lucas erected 1838. *of Gainsborough*: by Sir Bertram Mackennal, erected in 1913 in Sudbury, Suffolk, Thomas Gainsborough's birthplace. *Chantmarle*: a Jacobean house N. of Dorchester, home of St John Hornby and his wife (see letter of 12 May 1928).

To Sir Arthur Pinero

MAX GATE, | DORCHESTER, | DORSET.

2nd June 1929.

My dear Sir Arthur

You have been so kind & sympathetic about my affairs that I must write to tell you that my negociations about the little Westminster house have fallen through, as the owner wants half as much again as the surveyor who valued it for me says its worth. Perhaps it is as well, as a friend of ours once had a house quite near this one—Siegfried Sassoon—& my husband was always urging him to sell it & move to a healthier part, which he eventually did. So please if you hear of an attractive little house for sale will you let me know. I feel sure that I cannot live here alone indefinitely. Everything has begun to go wrong. Two years ago today my little cat was given to my husband on his birthday, & today our stable was turned into an operating theatre & the poor little creature had an abscess opened by a veterinary surgeon aided by my chauffeur—both very imposing in white overalls— but its very melancholy & I hope I'll never be weak enough to have another pet. And the nightingale has either departed or turned into a garden-warbler, which is much less romantic.

My work—Part II of the Biography—will be finished by the end of July I hope, but I am going about too much, to see friends, to escape from the solitude here, & I am opening a Hospital Fête next week—all of which rather hinders. I hope that you are well & that your birthday celebration did you no harm. I expect that London is very gay & delightful now. Please remember that this letter does not require an answer, that your letters are so charming that I love to receive them.

> Your affectionate friend
> Florence Hardy.

Text MS. Beinecke.

Westminster house: writing to Pinero 25 May 1929 (Beinecke) FEH had mentioned her possible purchase of a house off Smith Square. *little cat*: Cobweb, or 'Cobby', given to TH on his 87th birthday; FEH was writing on what would have been his 89th birthday. *the nightingale*: mentioned in the 25 May letter as singing in the Max Gate garden. *Part II*: pub. as *The Later Years of Thomas Hardy*. *Hospital Fête*: organized by the nurses of the Dorset County Hospital on 12 June; FEH made a short speech. *that your letters*: 'though your letters' probably intended.

[Philip Ridgeway's decision to revive *Tess of the d'Urbervilles* for West End production at the Duke of York's Theatre unexpectedly placed FEH in a position to offer Gertrude Bugler precisely that opportunity of an appearance on the professional London stage she had effectively denied her a few years earlier—her lingering guilt over those past events showing clearly in the speed and decisiveness with which she now acted. The intervening years could not, of course, be brought back, and it was probably too late for Gertrude Bugler, whatever her talents, to embark on a career as a romantic actress, but even she seems to have been impressed and somewhat mollified by the wholeheartedness with which FEH sought to encourage, protect, and support her during her belated London campaign.]

To Gertrude Bugler

> 52 Portland Place | London. w.i.
> Thursday. [4 July 1929]

Dear Mrs Bugler:

You will, no doubt be surprised to hear from me, but I have just been asked by Mr Ridgeway if I will allow 'Tess' to be revived at the Duke of Yorks Theatre London.

Remembering your disappointment in the past I feel that I must, in fairness to yourself, ask you if you would care to take the part. Everything is now in my hands. I do not say that it would be a wise step for you to take, nor do I say it would be an unwise step. You may feel, & your husband also, that it is not worth thinking about. It would be a proper revival—not matineés only—& you would be paid properly. However do not think I an advising you. I return to Dorchester tomorrow. Could you see me at Max Gate or telephone to me after 4. o'clock? There is no time to be lost as Mr Ridgeway wants to start almost immediately.

I hope that you & your husband & little girl are well.

Yours very sincerely

Florence Hardy.

Text MS. (with envelope) Bugler.   *Date* From internal evidence.
think I an: 'think I am' clearly intended.

To Sydney Cockerell

MAX GATE, | DORCHESTER, | DORSET.

8th. July 1929.

Dear Sydney:

Like yourself I did not feel enthusiastic about Mr Ridgeway's proposal when I received his telegram, which was forwarded to me in London. However I was able to consult Sir James and also Mr Golding Bright, and both thought there could be no harm in the production if Ridgeway were compelled to produce it properly and Mr Golding Bright has promised to see to that. He understands that I would not like the play produced at all unless it can be well done. Mr Golding Bright was in favour of asking Miss Gwen F–D– to do it again, but Mr Ridgeway did not seem to care for the idea and proposed other names which Mr Bright thought impossible. I suggested asking Mrs Bugler and they both thought it a good idea. All this was done at express speed. I wrote to Mrs Bugler and on my return home found her waiting here. I spoke to Mr Ridgeway on the telephone and Mrs Bugler went to London next day to see him. Last evening I had her and her husband here for two hours, and now she is going up tomorrow to commence rehearsing. It is only by a chance that the Duke of York's Theatre is available. Mr Ridgeway is wildly enthusiastic about Mrs Bugler's acting— she went through a scene or two with him—and telegraphed to me that she was magnificent and he expects a terrifically big success. Let us hope so. The play is to be produced, I understand, in about a fortnight. Mrs Bugler's husband is much against her going but the child is older now and able to be left with a servant.

I have asked Mr Golding Bright to restrain Mr Ridgeway's press stunts if that is possible. Unfortunately they are what Mrs Bugler loves. Her husband feels with me that it is fair that she should have her chance, and otherwise she will be disappointed all her life. She is as young-looking as ever and has distinctly improved in looks. You will go to the first night I suppose. I will see that you have tickets. Or you may prefer to go later. Or ought you to go to a rehearsal?

I am not sure how you really feel about the proposed printing of the little play, and so I will not reply to Mr Thorne until the day after tomorrow which will give you a chance to telegraph if you have changed your mind, for I have no feeling about the matter. Mr Thorne is a young man who took the part of Timothy Sommers in a production at Oxford, and that is how he became possessed of the acting version. He is agent for this New York Fountain Press. So far I have agreed to nothing.

I went to tea with Augustus John last Thursday and he is very anxious for Epstein to do the Memorial. Sir James went with me to the Academy to see the sculpture and then to Mr McMillan's studio where we saw the maquette he has made for the memorial to Earl Haig. Unfortunately Kate Hardy will not say what she is going to subscribe until she knows what the statue is going to be or sees some sketch or maquette, but I feel sure she will do all that is necessary when she is satisfied that the statue will be all right. She says she is not going to give a penny to anything but a statue.

Yours very sincerely—

F.E.H.

Text   MS. (typed) Beinecke.
Bright: TH's dramatic agent (see letter of 10 Mar. 1925).   *Miss Gwen F–D–*: Gwen Ffrangcon-Davies.   *found her . . . went through . . . in about*: FEH typed 'found here', 'went though', 'an about'.   *the child*: Diana, now Diana Toms.   *little play*: TH's *The Three Wayfarers*; Eric Anthony Thorne, later the author of several novels, had sought, and was eventually granted, permission for the Fountain Press of New York to pub. the revised version of the play performed at Keble College Oxford, in 1926 (Purdy, 79–80).   *a chance*: FEH typed 'a ahance'.   *Timothy Sommers*: the reviewer for the Keble College *Clock Tower*, though unimpressed by TH's play, had described Thorne's performance as 'very fine'.   *John*: see letter of 10 Mar. 1925.   *Epstein*: Jacob Epstein (1880–1959), sculptor, a controversial figure at this date.   *the Academy*: i.e. the Royal Academy's Summer Exhibition.   *Mr McMillan's . . . Haig*: William McMillan (1887–1977), sculptor; the statue of Field Marshal Earl Haig was commissioned by Clifton College Bristol.

To Gertrude Bugler

MAX GATE, | DORCHESTER.
11th July. [1929]

Dear Mrs Bugler:

Thank you for writing to me. I am afraid you are having a trying time in many respects, but I hope you will also have a great deal of pleasure later. I honestly think you are sure of a success.

Mr Golding Bright wrote me a most kind & sensible letter. He says he has warned Mr Ridgeway that he will spoil the production if he goes in for too much "circusing." However no harm has yet been done I hope.

I hope you will not alter the way you played the murder scene. Keep that quiet determined way. You were better in that than Miss G. F–D.—men whose judgement is beyond question told me that—emphatically. I am sure it is a mistake to show *terror* after the murder.

I was afraid after I had recommended Batts Hotel that it might not be quite the right place. If there is anything I can do for you let me know— or go to Mr Golding Bright. Three of the leading critics have promised me to do their best for you—& as they are personal friends of many years I can depend upon them.

I am taking in press cuttings & can send them to you, if you like, or to your husband if you let me know. I hope that you are quite comfortable. Don't let them do the 'country girl' stunt too much or it may stand in your way if you want to do anything else of a different kind.

With all good wishes

Yours sincerely
Florence Hardy.

Text MS. Bugler.   *Date* From internal evidence.
Batts Hotel: in a letter dated Monday [8 July 1929] (Bugler) FEH told G. Bugler that if Batts Hotel proved too expensive she would 'gladly help' with the bill.

To Siegfried Sassoon

MAX GATE, | DORCHESTER, | DORSET.
11th July 1929.

My dear Siegfried:

I thank you so much for your delightful present, which I value greatly. I have put it in our drawing-room on a little table, in front of a bust of T.H. I value it as a token of your continued friendship which is most helpful to me, & a source of comfort in depressed moments.

I am sorry to hear that Mr S. Tennant has been so ill. I hope you are well and that we shall soon have another fine volume from your pen—& a poem or two. I am just finished Part II of the biography of T.H. It is a painful task as I live over again all the occasions of which I write. I would give all my life that is to come, however long it may be, or how prosperous, for one half hour of that past back again—indeed, I think for five minutes.

I am going on here as usual, friends being most wonderfully kind. I do not think I shall take a house in London, or make any change in my life.

I feel that I belong to Max Gate where I can visit Stinsford, & go to see my husband's sister every few days. I shall be so very pleased to see you here again.

You may have seen in the papers that "Tess" (the play) is to be revived, & Mrs Bugler is to take the leading part. It was my idea as I felt she might all her life be regretting that she had never had a chance to show what she can do on a London stage. If it is a failure & her married life upset I fear I shall be responsible. She is very pleased & seems grateful—but her husband isn't either.

I am writing this in T.H.'s chair at his writing-table in the study: the pines stand black against the mysterious blue of a summer night, & a late blackbird has only just ceased whistling. The spirit of T.H. seems all around, & lately I have had a feeling that all is well.

Again *thank you* so much

Always your affectionate friend
Florence Hardy.

Text MS. Eton.

present: from FEH's letter to Sassoon of 16 Sept. 1929 (Eton) it appears that he sent a photograph of himself together with Stephen Tennant (letter of 5 Dec. 1927).

To Sir Arthur Pinero

MAX GATE, | DORCHESTER, | DORSET.
1st August 1929.

My dear Sir Arthur:

I must write to you again because I am afraid that you think it was not very kind of me not to be at Mrs Bugler's first night, to support her. I would gladly have gone only it meant sitting with Mr Philip Ridgeway & his mother & his wife, in a box, & having reporters brought in to talk to me with the result that misleading paragraphs would have appeared everywhere. Barrie realized this, & thought it would be better for me not to go. I should so like to talk to you one day about that play of 'Tess' & various incidents, some very painful, connected with it. I have always thought that my husband's heart was weakened by excitements connected with the production here in Dorset, & had it not been for that I think he might have been alive now. However I may be wrong. Had it not been that I wished Mrs Bugler to have a chance of showing what she could do on a London stage I should not have allowed it to be revived.

I am going to London tomorrow to see her & return on Saturday. I thought I had finished Part II of the biography, but now I think there must be another short chapter—a summing-up as it were. The last chapters were incredibly difficult, & painful to write, but the two friends who have read them say that I have not failed.

Dieppe sounds *very* gay. I think you *must* be having a cheerful time. My friends are so kind in looking me up that I have very little spare time—& there is rarely a day that someone does not come from a distance, to see me. It is only in the winter that Max Gate is dreary. If I were nearer London, say within a two hours journey, I should not dream of changing my abode.

I hope that you will gain very much benefit from your visit to Dieppe. My kind regards to your step-daughter if she remembers me.

Ever your affectionate friend
Florence Hardy.

Text MS. Beinecke.
by excitements: FEH first wrote 'by various excitements'.　　*two friends*: Barrie and Harold Child (see letter of 20 Aug. 1929).　　*were nearer*: FEH first wrote 'were only nearer'.　　*step-daughter*: Myra ('Tina') Neville, née Hamilton.

[The Dorset associations of the Powys brothers were of long standing and they had lived in Dorchester itself from 1879 to 1885 while their father was curate at St Peter's. John Cowper Powys, Llewelyn Powys, and probably other members of the family had called at Max Gate during TH's lifetime, and FEH subsequently kept up connections that were facilitated by Theodore Powys's move to the village of East Chaldon, Gertrude Powys's to a house not far from East Chaldon, and Llewelyn Powys's to White Nose. John Cowper Powys lived in the United States until 1934 but paid a number of visits to his siblings in Dorset during the early 1930s and spent a year in Dorchester in 1934–5 while working on his novel *Maiden Castle*. See Charles Lock, *The Powys Family in Dorset* (Dorchester Dorset Natural History and Archaeological Society, 1991).]

To John Cowper Powys

MAX GATE, | DORCHESTER, | DORSET.
Thursday evening. [15 August 1929]

My dear Mr Powys:

Thank you so very much for sending me that very kind inscription to put in my copy of "Wolf Solent." I am so proud of it, & I shall always treasure your gift.

I send you my very best wishes for the voyage to New York, & for your future. I feel sure that you will have many more literary triumphs.

I shall be very proud to have a letter from you when you are back in the United States. It is just possible that I may go to America later, when Part

II of the biography is in the printer's hands. I hardly know what to do with the remnant of my life that is left. I am writing this in my husband's study, seated in his chair, at his writing table, & I feel that I am in a world of ghosts—& the grandfather clock in the hall has just struck ten, which was always the signal, in the old days, for me to stop reading aloud. Sometimes I feel that nothing could induce me to leave Max Gate, & at other times I feel that it will be death to remain here.

Again every good wish & very many thanks,

Always yours sincerely,
Florence Hardy.

Text   MS. (with envelope) Adams.   *Date*   From postmark.
Powys: John Cowper Powys (1872–1963), novelist; FEH had acknowledged his gift of *Wolf Solent* (London, 1929) in a letter misdated 5 July (for 5 Aug.) 1929 (Adams).   *to New York*: to resume an extended lecture tour.

To Harold Macmillan

MAX GATE, | DORCHESTER, | DORSET.
20th August 1929.

Dear Mr Macmillan:

I am sending herewith the main part of Part II of the biography of my husband, which I think may be called "The Late Years of Thomas Hardy." I have finished the work, but the last few chapters are now being retyped, and as soon as I have made final corrections I will post them to you at the end of the week. I do not know whether there ought to be appendices giving interesting letters, and material which does not seem to belong to the body of the work. It seems to me that there will have to be a small volume of letters published later, as I have so many interesting ones, and more would be forthcoming, no doubt, if required.

With the help of Sir James Barrie I have selected several photographs that seem suitable for illustration. I should be glad to know whether to post these to you direct? I shall not be having the help of Mr Cockerell this year but no doubt you will be kind enough to arrange with Mr Emery Walker.

Two friends, Sir James Barrie, and Mr Harold Child have been through the complete MS. in accordance with instructions left by my husband, and they profess themselves completely satisfied, but if you care to have some other man of letters of your own choice, go through the MS. for a fee I shall be very pleased if you will arrange this.

Yours sincerely,
Florence Hardy.

Text MS. (typed) British Library.

Macmillan: [Maurice] Harold Macmillan, later 1st Earl of Stockton (1894–1986), publisher and statesman; currently without a seat in the House of Commons, he had been handling most of the firm's correspondence with FEH since early May 1929. *"The Late . . . Hardy."*: pub. as *The Later Years of Thomas Hardy*. *Walker*: Emery Walker (1851–1933), pioneer process-engraver and typographer, knighted 1930; his firm, Emery Walker Limited, executed the illustrations for both *Early Life* and *Later Years*. *Child*: Harold Hannyngton Child (1869–1945), author and critic; his *Thomas Hardy* first appeared in 1916 and he had more recently written the description of TH's obsequies pub. as Appendix 1 of *Later Years*. *arrange this*: George Macmillan, writing in H. Macmillan's absence, replied that since Barrie and Child had seen the MS. it would not be sent out to another reader (21 Aug. 1929, copy BL).

To St John Hornby

Private.

MAX GATE, | DORCHESTER, | DORSET.
2nd September 1929.

Dear Mr Hornby,

I have been studying Mr Kennington's work in 'The Seven Pillars' & thinking a great deal about some of those photographs, especially those of nude figures. I must confess I begin to feel very nervous lest Mr Kennington should be far too modern for the type of statue we want, & for the place where it is to stand.

I liked the head of T. E. Lawrence & of the child, but they were done from life. I wonder what hand Mr Kennington would be at a *statue*, & one of a man he had never seen.

That symbolic work of his I thought rather horrible, though there were touches of beauty. It would be appalling if a statue were produced that gave a suggestion of evil. On the other hand it is possible that Mr Kennington might give us something very beautiful, as Lawrence & Squire both declare. It is a question of whether we care to run a risk, or go for safety first.

I feel that after all I have had to endure since my husband's death it would be the climax if there were any bitter controversy about this memorial.

I am so sorry to have to give you all this trouble—& thank you for what you have done—

Yours sincerely
Florence Hardy

Text MS. Beinecke.

Hornby: see letter of 12 May 1928; he was currently chairing the Hardy Memorial Committee sub-committee responsible for recommending a sculptor for the Dorchester statue of TH (see Millgate, *Testamentary Acts*, 150–2). *Mr Kennington's*: Eric Henri Kennington

(1888–1960), artist; he had been art editor of T. E. Lawrence's *Seven Pillars of Wisdom.* **might give us**: FEH first wrote 'might produce'.   *Squire*: J. C. Squire (see letter of 25 Jan. 1928). *safety first*: FEH's 14 Sept. 1929 letter to Hornby (Beinecke) concurred with Barrie's advice that the commission be given to Kennington 'if he would agree to do a simple portrait statue, & nothing symbolic'; the selection of Kennington was approved by the full Memorial Committee at its final meeting on 16 Sept. 1929.   *controvery*: i.e. 'controversy'; FEH refers not to disagreements within the Committee but to possible public disapproval of the completed memorial.

To Howard Bliss

KING ARTHUR'S CASTLE HOTEL | TINTAGEL. CORNWALL.

29th Sept. '29.

Dear Mr Bliss,

I shall be back at Max Gate I expect before you receive this—for I leave early tomorrow morning. Any time in October that you choose for your visit will suit me, as I have no fixed engagements after Tuesday—although I shall be going to London for a night or two sometime soon. Please fix your own time for coming, & let me know when convenient to yourself.

Yesterday I visited St Juliot, to the great pleasure of the solitary little clergyman who lives there. It seems so strange that the whole place—both Church & Rectory—should have remained so unchanged. The very stones & flowers seem the same, & there is an atmosphere of romance.

But it is a wholly unfitting place for any valuable MSS. The few sketches that my husband gave the clergyman before this one do not seem well-cared for, & no one sees them. Also they are liable to be carried off some day, as no one is responsible for them.

'The Pair of Blue Eyes' is a companion MS. I should say to 'The Queen of Cornwall'. Although this hotel is so very modern, the moment one steps outside the whole coast before one is totally unspoiled, & I look out from my bedroom window on to the ruins of King Arthur's Castle, the drawings of which, as my husband imagined it, in its original form, are at Max Gate. The last time I was here was with my husband, in September 1916. Of that little group of people he mentions in the dedication to 'The Queen of Cornwall' I am the only one left, & I do not think that I shall visit these scenes again. I sat on the seat in the garden of the Rectory where he used to sit, & it was all very sad.

With kind regards

Yours sincerely,
Florence Hardy.

P.S. I find I have forgotten your address so must post this in Dorchester tomorrow.   F.H.

Of course I will gladly rewrite the description of those articles.   F.H.

Text   MS. (hotel stationery, with illustration of building) Princeton.

St Juliot: where TH had first met ELH in 1870.   *clergyman*: the Revd David Rees Morris, rector of St Juliot with Lesnewth 1925–32.   *carried off some day*: they survived, however, and are now in DCM.   *at Max Gate*: one was reproduced in the first edition of *The Famous Tragedy of the Queen of Cornwall* (London: Macmillan, 1923).   *the only one left*: the others, identified by their initials only, were ELG, her sister Helen Holder, and Helen's husband, the Revd Caddell Holder, then rector of St Juliot.   *those articles*: presumably the items associated with ELG and *A Pair of Blue Eyes*; see letter of 15 Jan. 1929.

To Siegfried Sassoon

52 Portland Place—

as from— | Max Gate. | Dorchester.
17th December 1929.

Dear Siegfried,

I was so delighted to have your letter: it was good of you to write to me —as I know you have many friends & your correspondence must be heavy.

I am in London now for a few days, but return to Max Gate for Christmas & the New Year which I shall probably spend there alone—& after that I may return to London for a few weeks—or not. I am unable to decide as yet. In February I should love to go to Rapallo, as I feel just as you do about the angelic Maxes. But I have never travelled & feel rather nervous about taking that long journey alone.

I was delighted to have Mr Tennant's kind message. The hours I spent at his home—Wilsford (?)—my memory is quite appalling now—are the pleasant I have spent this year, & I realized why you have such an affection for him.

I was reading R.G's book when your letter came, & I knew, before you told me, that the anecdote on page 290 referred to your mother & yourself, & I was shocked by it.

He says that T.H. criticized Edmund Gosse for making fun of Henry James. T.H. did *nothing of the kind*. He would never have criticized Gosse before a young man, almost a stranger. I was the culprit & I am sorry about it. I remember saying that I did not know what Henry James would have said if he could have seen his dear friend E.G. imitating him eating soup

—one of the careless statements that one so regrets have made when one sees them in print. However it might have been worse. I so dislike that way of describing T.H.—as a rather comic old gentleman—just as much as I hate any description of his personal appearance when he had grown old—baldness, wrinkles etc.

I think it was abominable of Graves to write of you as he did, & yet I think he gives the impression all the time that he really admired you, which makes it perhaps not so bad. He might have written as if he hated you. I have heard a great deal about him from Eric Kennington who was at Max Gate four days last week making a little model for the statue of T.H. (which I think will be really fine). I have not seen T.E. for some months but he told his cousin (my friend Miss Fetherstonhaugh) that he thought Graves was really a little mad. But that is rather too easy an excuse. One can divide one's friends into two classes—one which will gladly make copy of its friends & the other which will not.

In my biography of T.H. I so many times could have written amusing anecdotes about friends who visited us there but I didn't do it—& consequently it will be regarded by many as a dull book—a failure, in fact.

I have just had a visit from Lowes-Dickenson—E.M. Forster says he is the best human being he knows, & certainly I felt lifted to a higher plane while he was here. He is so absolutely unworldly, & so charitable in his judgements.

I hope that Mr Tennant's chill has not increased since you wrote. Will you give him my kindest regards, & every possible good wish to you both for the New Year. May it bring you another great literary triumph. You have certainly added to the glory of English letters—

Yours ever sincerely,
F.E.H.

And of course of very merry Christmas to you both.

Text   MS. (with envelope) Eton.

52 Portland Place: the address (lightly struck through in MS.) of Lady St Helier (see letter of 20 June 1915), who was now totally incapacitated.   *angelic Maxes*: Max and Florence Beerbohm, whom FEH did later visit in Rapallo.   *Mr Tennant's*: Stephen Tennant lived at Wilsford Manor, near Salisbury.   *the pleasant*: 'the pleasantest' or 'the most pleasant' evidently intended.   *R.G's book*: in *Goodbye to All That* (London: Jonathan Cape, 1929), 289–90, Robert Graves speaks of staying at the home of 'a First Battalion friend who had recently been wounded' and being kept awake by shrieks and rapping noises that his friend's mother attributed to a hysterical maid; the reference to TH and Gosse is on p. 376. *regrets have made*: on the MS. a hand other than FEH's has supplied the missing 'to' before 'have'.   *T.E.*: T. E. Lawrence.   *Lowes-Dickenson*: correctly, Goldsworthy Lowes

Dickinson (1862–1932), historian and philosophical writer.   *literary triumph*: i.e. in addition to his much-praised *Memoirs of a Fox-Hunting Man* (letter of 12 May 1928).   *course of very*: 'course a very' evidently intended.

To Howard Bliss

MAX GATE, | DORCHESTER.
11th March 1930.

Dear Mr Bliss,

Thank you so much for your letter. I think I must leave you to deal with the letters as you suggest, and of course you must have those that belong to your collection. It was suggested to me the other day, by a literary friend of my husband's, that a good book could be made out of letters written to him. But it might be difficult to obtain the copyright of many of the letters. However even the seemingly unimportant ones might be of great interest a century hence.

If it is inconvenient for you to keep the letters & the black trunk at your flat you must let me know, so that I can fetch them away, but of course you can keep them as long as you care to do so. I am at 52 Portland Place from tomorrow until Friday or Saturday if there were anything important about which you wish to see me. Lady St Helier's in the telephone-book.

I am sorry to say I have heard nothing of poor Cobby, & I fear he is dead. I miss him so much; the house is almost unendurable to me now.

I am so glad that you have secured those other MSS. I wish that T.H. could have known—perhaps he does know. What a marvellous collection yours is now.

Again thanking you—

Yours sincerely,
Florence Hardy.

P.S. I did not intend to return to this painful topic, but I feel obliged—I asked J. M. Barrie whether he could recall the circumstances of the Abbey burial, & whether Cockerell was against it, as he now represents himself to have been. J.M.B's reply, as nearly as I can quote it was:

"Why, he was the one who was all for it. I remember that he walked to the station with me the night before Hardy's death, and he was *urging it on me* all the way." Cockerell knew that I did not wish it.   F.E.H.

Text MS. (with envelope) Princeton.

Cobby: see letter of 2 June 1929.   *Abbey burial*: see headnote to letter of 17 Jan. 1928 and Millgate, *Testamentary Acts*, 143–7.

[The final stages of work on the first part of the 'Life', published in November 1928 as *The Early Life of Thomas Hardy*, had been distressing for FEH, its ostensible author, but not especially demanding, in that she was working with material that TH had himself revised to what he considered a finished state. Completion of the second part, however, involved a good deal of new writing—Hardy having left only notes for the last ten years of his life and no account, naturally enough, of his own death—and the difficulty FEH experienced in putting together the final chapters was compounded by a depressive sense that *Early Life* had been both critically and commercially unsuccessful and that *The Later Years of Thomas Hardy* would inevitably seem even less interesting than its predecessor. Nor did the actual publication of *Later Years* in April 1930 lead her to different conclusions. On 21 September 1930 (Eton) she told Siegfried Sassoon: 'My biography of T.H. has been, from the publishers' point of view, a dire failure: perhaps it was published at the wrong time of the year, or perhaps it was too expensive. . . . I suppose people think that a man's widow is the wrong person to write his biography, & perhaps they are right.']

To Daniel Macmillan

MAX GATE, | DORCHESTER, DORSET.

25th June 1930.

Dear Mr Macmillan,

Thank you so much for your letter & for your explanation of the sales etc. of 'The Later Years of Thomas Hardy.'

I would be quite willing to pay another hundred pounds or so for advertising, but if you think it is not worth while it would be a pity to waste the money. I am sure you know best about this.

I had been rather misled by reports from friends—Mr E. M. Forster, for instance, & Colonel T. E. Lawrence—who said that 'everyone was talking about the book' & that it must be selling largely. I expect the price—18/- for half a book,—is really too high just at present when people are not spending freely. However I know you have done your best with it & I am much obliged,

Yours sincerely,

Florence Hardy—

Text MS. BL.

for advertising: *Later Years* was pub. by Macmillan 29 Apr. 1930; on 9 May FEH wrote to D. Macmillan (BL) and offered to share in any additional advertising costs, 'as I consider this biography a memorial to my husband'.

To Lady Ottoline Morrell

MAX GATE, | DORCHESTER, DORSET.
Sunday. [Mid-July 1930]

Dear Lady Ottoline,

I am just off for eight or nine days to visit old friends of my husbands &
workmen are to be here painting & making all right. As soon as they have
finished I shall make strenuous efforts to let this house for the winter, &
then I shall feel more easy about taking a flat—which I hope to be able to
do early in the autumn, unless I go to America, or Italy or Tunis. It is
terrible to feel like a straw on a current of water, tossed hither & thither—
but I must come to rest somewhere at last.

I know how you feel about E. M. Forster. I have had such-like experiences with so many of T.H.'s friends—so much kindness & sympathy at
times, & then silence & long neglect. I often wonder whether selfishness is
not at the back of most friendships. I see now why T.H. never poured
himself out in friendship to many who flocked around him. At the end of
this month I hope to be in London & shall love to see you again if possible.

Ever sincerely,
Florence Hardy.

Text MS. Texas. *Date* From internal evidence.
Morrell: Lady Ottoline Violet Anne Morrell (1873–1938), half-sister of the 6th Duke of Portland, wife of Philip Edward Morrell, and a central figure in the literary and intellectual world
of her time; she visited Max Gate, and photographed TH, in Sept. 1924 (*CL*, vi. 274–
5). *old . . . husbands*: Sir George Brisbane Douglas, Bt. (1856–1935), Scottish landowner
and author (*Biography*, 222, etc.), and his sister, Mary Helena Henrietta Douglas (d. 1932);
they lived in Kelso.

To Sir Arthur Pinero

MAX GATE, | DORCHESTER, DORSET.
10th October 1930.

My dear Sir Arthur,

It was so pleasant to meet you again, & I do thank you so much for
taking me to such a cheerful restaurant, & giving me that splendid lunch.
I hope you were none the worse for our little outing.

I wonder whether you care for going out to dinner & if so whether
you would give me the pleasure of your company at St James's Court on
November 6th, to meet Mr & Mrs Leonard Rees & perhaps one or two

other friends. He is a genial little man—editor of the Sunday Times—& I expect he knows many of your friends. He has always the latest political information. Dinner $\frac{1}{4}$ to 8.

I hope your friend is better. I should much like to have invited her here now, only Max Gate is so dark & depressing—the gloomiest time of the year is before the leaves fall, & the house seems so cold & damp. In the spring & summer it is different. I should her & her friend to come here then.

I have just been reading my husband's will over again to find out, if I can, what he really wished done with Max Gate. There is no doubt that he left it *in trust* but never stated for what purpose.

When I arrived home last evening I found Somerset Maugham's novel awaiting me, & I read a few chapters, though I had intended not to read the book at all. I wish I had read those chapters before I met you on Tuesday, so that I could have talked to you about it.

No one who knew my husband would ever believe that the offensive old creature about whom the book is written was in the least degree a portrait of him, but readers who never met him, having been instructed by so many reviewers that 'this is an easily recognisable portrait of Thomas Hardy" will wonder how much is true, & whether he did tipple in Dorchester public houses & so forth. I never knew him enter a public house, nor did anyone else since I have known him. The poisonous part of the book is the mingling of a few actual facts of T.H.'s life with so much that is grotesque. For instance he did cycle about the county with a young friend, a clergyman's son, who was taking rubbings of old brasses in various Dorset churches. It is possible that Mr Maugham had some of his information from this man, who later turned out to be a thorough bad lot & had to leave the country for a time. He returned however some four or five years ago & called here, but my husband refused to see him. There is so much I would like to tell you—only I should go on writing till mid-night if I let myself go.

Again thanking you,

Ever affectionately—
F.E.H.

Text MS. Beinecke.

St James's Court: a large apartment block in Westminster; see letter of 5 Dec. 1930. From FEH's letter to Pinero of [26 Oct. 1930] (Beinecke) it appears that she did not move in until 14 Nov. and that the planned dinner did not take place.   *Rees*: Leonard Rees (1856–1932), editor of the *Sunday Times* 1901–32.   *your friend*: unidentified.   *should her*: 'should like her' presumably intended.   *Maugham's novel*: Somerset Maugham's *Cakes and Ale, or The Skeleton in the Closet* (London, 1930).   *young friend*: perhaps to be identified with John Everett, artist son of the Revd Henry Everett, a former rector of Holy Trinity, Dorchester, and his wife Augusta (*CL*, vii. 42).

To John Cowper Powys

MAX GATE, | DORCHESTER, DORSET.
26th Oct. 1930. Sunday evening | 10.5. p.m.

Dear John Cowper Powys,

It was a great delight to see your attractive handwriting again but the second paragraph of your letter fills me with sadness, for I had hoped you were quite well by this time. What cruel things those 'tearing ulcers' must be. I have heard they are very painful. By the time this letter (but I am afraid it will hardly be a letter, merely the promise of a letter) reaches you I trust that you will feel considerably better. Will you give a message to Miss Alyse Gregory & thank her so much for her kind letter to me before they left White Nose. I ought to have answered it, but I shall hope to write to her in a day or two—and I will write you a longer letter very soon. It is late at night—or what I call late—in this silent house—a clock ticking near me—in the room where we have so often sat together with T.H. & it is rather like a grave. Do you know his poem 'The House of Silence', which begins 'This is a quiet place'? It described Max Gate then, & even more aptly describes it now—when I am the phantom left alone.

But—lest that should sound too complaining—I am going to London tomorrow for a few days.

I am so pleased to hear about the new book, which I hope will be quite as long as you intend it to be. Don't let any one persuade you to take out *one* line. I have a feeling that it will be even finer than 'Wolf Solent'—if that be possible. And the other book of yours I see advertised I shall read immediately. I hope next week to go to see your brother Theodore & his wife. Lately I have been going backwards & forwards, like a tennis-ball over a net—with no profit to myself or any one else.

I am glad that your new book is about Glastonbury. I connect it in my mind, not with the Holy Grail, but with my husband's play 'The Queen of Cornwall' which was performed there some years ago. This is just the beginning of a letter—more will follow soon—

Always admiringly & affectionately,
Florence Hardy

Text MS. Texas.
Gregory: Alyse Gregory (1883–1967), American-born writer, wife of Llewelyn Powys (see letter of 24 July 1927), with whom she had been living in a former coastguard cottage at White Nose, on the Dorset coast; they left for the United States in August 1930. *of Silence'*: first pub. in *Moments of Vision* (1917); all editions read '"That is . . .' *the phantom*: line 5 of the first stanza reads, 'Why, a phantom abides there, the last of its race'. *new book*: A Glastonbury Romance, first pub. 1933. *'Wolf Solent'*: see letter of 15 Aug. 1929.

Other book: presumably *The Meaning of Culture* (London, 1930).   *Theodore & his wife*:
Theodore Francis Powys (1875–1953), novelist, and his wife Violet (née Dodds) lived in the
Dorset village of East Chaldon.   *some years ago*: see letter of 29 June 1924.

To Francis Brett Young

as from / Flat 128A. | St James' Court | Buckingham Gate
November 28th. [1930]

Dear Mr Brett Young—

How ungrateful you must think me for not having written before this to
thank you for your kind letter & the trouble you took in speaking to Mr
Charles Morgan about the volume in the "English Men of Letters" series
which is to be written about my husband.

I wrote to J. C. Squire immediately, putting the proposal before him. As
you know, he is the editor of the series. I had a brief note in reply promising
to come to lunch with me at St James' Court, Buckingham Gate, where I
have a little flat in which I am writing this letter. Hearing nothing further
I went, two days ago, to his office to hear what he really thought. Although
the errand involved going into a pub next door & drinking a cocktail with
J.C. & meeting the greatest living etcher, whose name I have forgotten, &
the greatest (to be) living poet—quite young—my mission was not wholly
unsuccessful for I found that J.C.S. thought Charles Morgan lacked humour,
& though he would deal most splendidly with the tragedy in T.H.'s works
he would not do justice to his humour. He suggested Edmund Blunden,
who would not do at all, to my mind. And *where* is *Blunden's* humour?
Anyhow the matter is, for the moment, laid aside until we meet to discuss
it again on Dec. 9th—at lunch, here. I could, of course, ask Mr Daniel
Macmillan to persuade J.C.S. to ask Mr Morgan, as the latter is one of their
authors, but I am sure that Mr Morgan would prefer the offer to come
voluntarily from J.C.S.

There is no great hurry as a cheap edition of my biography of T.H. is to
be brought out, I hope, next year—although J.C.S. says the volume in the
E.M. of L. series would help that.

I hope you are finding life pleasant & happy at Capri. I think often of you
both, & of the delightful hours I spent with you at Esthwaite.

I have been reading & *re-reading*, three times your new novel. You can
draw such a thoroughly decent man, who is never a prig. I hope it is going
well. I saw a huge pile in Harrods yesterday.

I hope that I shall be able to prevail upon Mrs Brett Young & yourself
to spend a few days at Max Gate when you are next in England. It would

give me such pleasure, & I could show you lovely spots in the county that are very little known.

Florence & Max Beerbohm are in London now—I see much of them, to my great joy. Again thanking you so much, & with kindest remembrances to Mrs Brett Young—

Yours very sincerely,
Florence Hardy.

Text   MS. (Max Gate headed stationery) Univ. of Birmingham.   *Date*   Year supplied on MS., presumably by Young.

Young: Francis Brett Young (1884–1954), novelist; he and his wife Jessica (née Hankinson) had lived on Capri for many years but appear to have visited Max Gate in Oct. 1923.   *Morgan*: see letter of 26 Nov. 1922; he had recently contributed to *Later Years* an account of TH's 1920 visit to Oxford (*Life and Work*, 524–8).   *cheap edition*: see letter of 2 Jan. 1934.   *Esthwaite*: Esthwaite Lodge, in the Lake District, where FEH had visited the Youngs the previous summer.   *new novel*: *Jim Redlake* (London, 1930).

[Very few communications, and those of the stiffest kind, now passed between FEH and Sydney Cockerell, even though their formal relationship as co-literary executors of Hardy's estate still continued. When Richard Little Purdy visited England in the summer of 1929 to begin working towards his goal of a comprehensive Hardy bibliography, he called first on Cockerell at his house in Cambridge, winning his confidence and obtaining access to his considerable TH collection. Eight days later Purdy met FEH at Max Gate, finding her already well disposed towards him on account of the memorial exhibition he had mounted at Yale shortly after TH's death. Purdy's formal request, in the summer of 1930, for permission to embark on the bibliography was therefore positively received on both sides, although Cockerell raised the question, subsequently taken up by FEH, as to whether the American collector Carroll A. Wilson might not have a prior claim.]

To Sydney Cockerell

Flat 128 A. | ST. JAMES' COURT, | BUCKINGHAM GATE, | S.W.I.

[2 December 1930]

Dear Mr Cockerell,

In my reply to Mr Purdy's previous letter I said that I was quite willing to give my consent to his undertaking the definitive bibliography, but I thought it better to raise the question of Mr Carroll Wilson possibly wishing to compile one—in order to prevent any misunderstanding or disappointment afterwards.

It is most satisfactory to know that Mr Carroll Wilson is willing to lend his assistance.

Mr Purdy's project has my complete approval.

Yours sincerely,
Florence Hardy.

P.S. I am here for a few weeks but I go to Max Gate on Saturday until Monday.   F.H.

Text   MS. (with envelope) Beinecke.   *Date*   From postmark.
bibliography: Purdy (letter of 28 July 1928) was beginning the research which resulted in his *Thomas Hardy: A Bibliographical Study* (Oxford, 1954).   *Wilson*: Carroll Atwood Wilson (1886–1947), American lawyer and book collector, with a particular interest in TH; Purdy had assured both FEH and Cockerell that Wilson, though too busy to undertake the bibliography himself, 'would lend me such assistance as he is able' (Purdy to Cockerell, 16 Nov. 1930, Beinecke).   *complete approval*: Cockerell had written 30 Nov. 1930 (draft, Beinecke) to ask what response FEH had made to Purdy's request.

To Sir Arthur Pinero

Flat 128 A. | ST. JAMES' COURT, | BUCKINGHAM GATE, | S.W.I.
5th Dec. 1930.

Beloved Sir Arthur,

Indeed I am not lost so easily. I have been thinking about you much these last few days & hoping the fog was not affecting you. I am longing to see you again, &, unless I hear to the contrary I will present myself at your hospitable door at 1.15 on Wednesday next—or Thursday will suit me if you prefer.

Tomorrow I run down to Dorset for the week-end & on Tuesday I have an engagement but the rest of the week is fairly free. I love being in this spot for a little while, though I should not like to be here always. When my friends ask why I choose to be here I tell them it because I cherish a hopeless passion for King George, & like to be near Buckingham Palace. I like to be near buildings that seem permanent—Westminster Abbey—the Houses of Parliament—

Ever affectionately, & so much looking forward to Wednesday—

F.E.H.

Text   MS. Beinecke.
it because: 'it is because' clearly intended.   *near Buckingham Palace*: Buckingham Gate leads directly from Victoria Street to the SE corner of Buckingham Palace.

To Howard Bliss

MAX GATE, | DORCHESTER, | DORSET.
10th January | 1931.

Dear Mr Bliss,

I hoped to be able to go to Westminster Abbey tomorrow but am absolutely unable. I shall however go to Stinsford—& Bockhampton. If you are in London & if it is quite convenient I should be more grateful than words can say if you would go to the Abbey just for a minute or two. It will mean much to me if I think that someone who knew T.H. & cared for him visits that spot.

With regard to the letters written by T.H. to E.L.G—afterwards ELH— it was *she* who burned his letters, & he told me he much regretted that at the time, & since. She asked him for her letters to him which he had carefully preserved, & she burned those too. He told me he thought the letters quite as good as the Browning letters, & they might have been published. The note I sent to you shows a very personal domestic side that appeals to me—but whatever you do will be right I am sure.

I do hope your affairs are now less worrying. I wish I could help. I have a great deal to do here in the way of clearing up before the books can be catalogued—if they ever are—but at *any* time if you want to look through the papers etc. do please come down. I am in London from Feb. 3rd for about ten days, & if you wished to be alone here then you could come. However you know you can always do as you like. I do hope this year will be a good one for you. I feel so grateful for all you have done—

Yours very sincerely,
Florence Hardy.

Text MS. Princeton.
tomorrow: the anniversary of TH's death.   *The note*: TH's letter to ELH of 23 Oct. 1900
(*CL*, ii. 270–1), now in the Berg collection.

To Lady Hoare

MAX GATE, | DORCHESTER.
7th September '31. | (after post).

Dearest Alda—

It was such a comfort to have your dear letter. I feel now as if there had been a general 'wind up', & that everything that mattered was ended. However one has to carry on.

I felt you were there, and I thought I saw your faces.

The owner of the house to which you went is Dr Nash Wertham—partner to the doctor who attended T.H. in his last illness. I was so amused at your account of your conversation with him—it was so *true*, & I imagine he (Dr. N.W) hardly ever hears, or *faces* the truth: few do.

The little account of T.H. in the booklet given away is by J. W. Mackail, a true & valued friend of T.H.'s. I hope you liked it. He married Margaret—daughter of Burne-Jones. They were there—great friends of the Hornbys.

I am glad you liked the statue—I thought, really, there were some beautiful things in his speech. In the pocket of the last coat T.H. wore I found, after his death, just an old knife—an unfinished poem, & a piece of string—

F.H.

Text MS. (with envelope) National Trust (Stourhead).
were there: at the unveiling of Eric Kennington's statue of TH at Top o' Town, Dorchester, 2 Sept. 1931. *Nash Wertham*: F. L. Nash-Wortham, Dorchester surgeon, partner to Dr F. W. Mann (see letter of 30 Dec. 1927). *the booklet*: *Order of Proceedings at the Unveiling of the Memorial Statue of Thomas Hardy, O.M. Mackail*: for both Mackails see letter of 12 Aug. 1916. *his speech*: i.e. Sir James Barrie's, in performing the unveiling.

To Howard Bliss

MAX GATE, | DORCHESTER, DORSET.
14th October. [1931]

Dear Mr Bliss—

Things have been in a state of turmoil here. Cook left to get married—parlourmaid giving notice—workmen all over the house—& the friend I was going to stay with has had to go into a nursing home suddenly—for an operation.

I talked with Mr Lock the Dorchester solicitor who drew up the will & manages my sister-in-law's affairs. He took Mr Cockerell's point of view—that it was a great risk to let any stranger catalogue the library—for he might pass on information—even innocently. Anyhow I feel that, *just for the time being*, with a new cook coming & another parlourmaid I would rather not have *a stranger* in the house yet awhile—& I cannot see that we shall be settled here for some weeks. If you cared to come—say for the week-end—or when you liked I'd be glad, & indeed thankful—for you to look over any papers—& just see what books there are & what the cataloguing would be? There is no very immediate hurry & I am so tired & worried with domestic affairs & servants that I would rather avoid having a stranger in the house if possible—& I could not leave new servants here alone with a stranger.

You would be another matter altogether & could come here at any time & be alone, if you so wish. I had hoped to be in London for several weeks before Christmas but I see now that is impossible. The royalties on the books issued by Macmillan are down over £1,000 for year ending June 30th 1931—so I heard a few days ago when the returns were sent me—& so I shall not have a flat in London this year—but as I feel so terribly run down I shall try to get away for a little while when the workmen are out of the house & the servants all settled down quietly—whenever that may be.

Yours very sincerely,
Florence Hardy.

Text MS. Princeton.   *Date* Year from internal evidence.
workmen: electric lighting was being installed at Max Gate.   *the friend*: identifiable from FEH's letter to M. Stopes, 16 Oct. 1931 (BL), as Vivien Gribble (Mrs Doyle Jones), the wood engraver and book illustrator (*CL*, vi. 292); she died in 1932.   *stranger*: FEH told Bliss, 12 Oct. [1931] (Princeton), that Cockerell had made 'a *violent* protest' against the suggestion that H. A. Martin, an auctioneers' clerk (see letter of 3 Dec. 1913), might catalogue the Max Gate library.

To Thomas Soundy

MAX GATE, | DORCHESTER, DORSET.
30th December [1931] | Wednesday.

My dear Tommy,

I was so pleased to have your nice letter and that beautiful handkerchief which I value more than any other of my Christmas presents. I had one sent to me by an American lady from Detroit. I do hope that you and Mother & Father are well. You must be very pleased to think you have a dear little sister. What a splendid present for Christmas. I am longing to see her—but I do hope you will be over to see me this summer. You would love my little French bull-dog, and the cat, Tozie, has grown to be a beauty—especially now he has a winter coat. Do tell Mother that Mrs H. O Lock has a little girl & her name is to be Susan Ann—and they will call her Sally.

Much Love
F.H.

Text MS. (with envelope) Barbara Jones.   *Date* Year from internal evidence.
Soundy: Reginald Soundy, Thomas's father, was currently serving with the Royal Canadian Air Force at Camp Borden, Ontario.   *sister*: now Barbara Jones.   *bull-dog*: FEH owned two such dogs, Toby and Tobina, at different periods during the 1930s.   *Tozie*: perhaps the stray cat mentioned in one or two of FEH's 1930 letters.   *little girl*: FEH's goddaughter Susan Ann Lock (later Baker), youngest daughter of TH's solicitor and his wife.

[Rarely reflected in FEH's surviving correspondence is the leading role she played during the early 1930s in the work of the Mill Street Housing Society, a voluntary organization devoted to the provision of better housing in the poorer areas of Dorchester and Fordington — Mill Street roughly corresponding to the 'Mixen Lane' of Hardy's *The Mayor of Casterbridge*. She also took very seriously her duties as a magistrate and as a member of the management committee for the local hospital, finding in their performance not just occupation but a satisfying if limited sense of social purpose and achievement. FEH's politics, though far from ideologically consistent, were certainly left of centre, and in writing to Rutland Boughton she knew that she was addressing someone much further to the left.]

To Rutland Boughton

MAX GATE, | DORCHESTER, DORSET.
4th Jan. 1932.

Dear Mr Boughton—

How kind of you to write to me. I have been thinking a great deal about you lately & your letter seemed an answer to my thoughts. I am so glad that some of your exquisite music to 'The Queen of Cornwall" is to be broadcast & I look forward much to hearing it. I often wish that I could see, & hear 'The Queen of Cornwall" again.

I hope you are well. My chief work at present is trying to build (with the help of others) a few good cottages in a slum near here—to show what *could* be done if people would only realize their responsibilities.

With all good wishes—

Yours sincerely,
Florence Hardy.

Text MS. BL.
broadcast: the overture and three songs from *The Queen of Cornwall* were performed as part of a 'Rutland Boughton Programme' on the London and Midland regions of the BBC, 8 Jan. 1932.

To Howard Bliss

MAX GATE, | DORCHESTER, DORSET.
Nov. 9th. [1932]

Dear Mr Bliss—

I am so sorry to hear that you have had a chill. I hope that you are now feeling quite well. I am glad to hear that you are staying on at your flat for another two years.

With regard to the promise of the British Museum to exhibit a letter & small MS. I think that may be left to your discretion, since you know so much better than almost anyone else I know whether such a course is advisable. There would be no harm in it, I should think.

There is a new curator at the Dorchester Museum—a much younger man—& a great admirer of T.H's work, which the late curator—Captain Acland—was not. This new curator Mr Charles Prideaux was well known to my husband and liked by him. He asked me yesterday to go round the Museum with him & advise about allotting a certain part of it to a *Hardy* collection, which he thought might be opened on the 5th anniversary of his death. He tells me that American, & other, visitors, complain that there is so little there connected with T.H. & nothing personal. Mr Prideaux asks me to lend a table that he used, or a chair, or something of that kind. I should like to talk the matter over with you. I hope to be in London from Wednesday evening next—the 16th until Dec 1st. at 16 Half Moon Street, in quiet rooms, & if you could come there some time, to discuss the affair, that would be most kind & helpful. I thought of one writing-table in the study, at which the earlier novels were written—but I do not want to alter Max Gate at present more than I can help. I enclose a letter which I received today. You will see by that that this house does hold attractions—but at the same time I do think there should be a proper Hardy collection in the Dorset County Museum.

Thank you so much for arranging the letters. They are here at your disposal at any time. The Tinsley letters should, I suppose, go with the Blue Eyes MS. & so you had better keep them. Some day we must set about cataloguing & putting all papers etc. into complete order. I have not been away from Max Gate for a whole week for more than a twelve-month, I think. I am leaving in charge my youngest sister with her two children. Her husband has had bad times in Canada & they have had to return & he, an ex-airman—flying officer in the Canadian Air Force—was discharged with 168 other officers & men in March last & has been unable to find a job— no pension—& the younger child an infant in arms. The elder boy— Tommy—goes now to the Dorchester Grammar School & is in 'Hardy' house there. You may remember that T.H. laid the foundation-stone.

With kind regards,

Yours sincerely,
Florence Hardy.

Text MS. Princeton. *Date* Year from internal evidence.
Acland: John Edward Acland (1848–1932), curator of the Dorset County Museum 1904– 32. *Prideaux*: Charles Sydney Prideaux, dental surgeon and amateur archaeologist; his curatorship of the Museum was cut short by his death in 1934. *Tinsley letters*: see letter of 15 Jan. 1929. *find a job*: Reginald Soundy was subsequently employed as a pilot by Scottish Motor Tractor Co. and, from early 1935, by Imperial Airways. *foundation-stone*: see letter of 24 July 1927.

November 1932

To The Editor of *The Times*

MAX GATE, DORCHESTER.

[Late November 1932]

Sir,

I have read your leading article of November 2 on "Productive Expenditure" with great interest. It follows along the lines of Mr. C. H. St John Hornby's appeal, "Spend wisely rather than save money should be our motto to-day." And this appeal was prompted by the very sane letter from Mr. P. W. Petter, of Yeovil, headed "The Time to Spend."

As chairman of a small organization formed in this town in October of last year (registered under the Industrial and Provident Societies Acts) and known as the Mill Street Housing Society, Limited, may I be permitted to give one or two details of the work of the society as a practical illustration of what can be done?

It started with a modest scheme of four houses, and all the men engaged thereon were previously unemployed, receiving a total of £11 19s. 3d. weekly for unemployment benefit. This is being saved, the men are having remunerative work, and overcrowded families are being properly housed at a rent they can pay (5s. 6d. weekly, excluding rates, for a three-bedroom, non-parlour, well-built house, with bathroom, copper, scullery, larder, and indoor lavatory). Further, the subscribers for loan stock at $2\frac{1}{2}$ per cent will have their money returned in due course and in the meantime have as much interest as is at present allowed on Post Office accounts.

This little society wants to continue its operations, and will do so if the necessary finance is forthcoming, and therefore, by reason of what I have now discovered can be done, I welcome the suggested cooperation of larger bodies who have the money but cannot use it to its fullest extent. Someone once said "Money is like muck, not good except it be spread," and the late Mr. Commissioner Booth Tucker observed, "Take the waste labour and put it on the waste land by means of waste capital, and convert the Trinity of Waste into a Unity of Production." He was referring to agriculture, but the same principle operates in other spheres. The work of this and similar societies surely combines the trinity of overcrowding, unemployment, and wise spending. I merely submit the above statement of fact for consideration and encouragement.

I am, Sir, yours faithfully,
Florence Hardy.

Text The Times, 1 December 1932, 8 (editorial heading, 'Wise Spending'). *Date* Inferred from date of publication.

Hornby's appeal: *The Times*, 11 Oct. 1932.   *sane letter*: *The Times*, 7 Oct. 1932.   Mill . . .
Limited: see headnote to letter of 4 Jan. 1932.   *necessary finance*: in another letter to *The
Times*, 30 Aug. 1933, 11, FEH reported that local difficulties and the withdrawal of an anticipated government subsidy had forced the Society to 'shelve' a scheme for a further fourteen houses.   *Someone once said*: cf. Francis Bacon's 'Money is like muck, not good except
it be spread' ('Of Seditions and Troubles').   *Booth Tucker*: Frederick St George de Lautour
Booth Tucker (1853–1929), Commissioner in the Salvation Army; quotation untraced.

[A mere handful of FEH's letters to her relatives survive from the years of her
widowhood, and one or two of them have been included here as a reminder of
her continuing involvement in the intense and not always easy relationships that
prevailed within the Dugdale family. Her deepest emotional and practical commit-
ment was to her youngest sister, Margaret (or Marjorie) Soundy, and her two
children, but she was supportive of her other sisters in times of difficulty—well
knowing that she was financially better off than any of them—and sought, so far as
her circumstances would allow, to take her share of responsibility for the care of her
elderly and ailing father. The touch of asperity detectable in the following letter to
her niece Monica Richardson perhaps reflected a perception that the bride and
bridegroom had chosen, in Easter Saturday, a day doubtless convenient for themselves but distinctly inconvenient for someone thus obliged to drive to and from
North London over a holiday weekend.]

To Monica Richardson

NEW CENTURY CLUB, | 12, HAY HILL, W.I.
Wednesday. [1 February 1933]

My dear Monica,

I am so sorry you have been ill. I hope you are now well. Marjorie
showed me your letter. I quite see that the day you have chosen for your
wedding is the best possible one for you & Arthur, which is what matters
most—& it may a very convenient day for the majority of your friends. I
certainly hope to be able to attend—if invited—& probably Marjorie &
Tom, if they are still at Max Gate, will be able to go up in the car with me.

Could you & Arthur have dinner with me here on Friday—you both
coming on as you are—from business no evening dress of course. There
are many things I shall like to discuss with you. But could you let me know
by FIRST post Friday whether you can come—or telephone or wire (I will
refund) so that I know in good time.

What would you like for a wedding present?

1. Something strictly personal—a dressing-case—fitted—or dress-coat &
hat for going away—from Harrods?

or.

Combined tea-breakfast & dinner service—good quality & design.

or
a cheque
or
anything else.

Love to Mother & all.

Affectionately.

F.E.H.

Text MS. (with envelope) Daphne Wood.   *Date* From postmark.
Richardson: [Emily] Monica Richardson, daughter of FEH's sister Ethel (see letter of 7 Feb. 1914); her marriage to Arthur Laing took place at Southgate, near her home in Palmers Green, on 15 April (Easter Saturday) 1933. FEH was reported in the local press as having 'happily and neatly' proposed the health of the bride and bridegroom.   *it may a*: 'it may be a' clearly intended.   *in the car with me*: FEH seems in the event to have gone alone; her letter to M. Richardson of 5 Apr. 1933 (D. Woods) explained that Barbara Soundy could not be left at Max Gate and that FEH's sister Constance, still living with their father in the family house at Enfield, felt that neither she nor the servants could cope with a young child.   *dinner with me here*: the New Century was a London club for women.   *a cheque*: evidently the alternative chosen; FEH's 5 Apr. letter enclosed 'a small cheque with my love to buy something personal'.

To Richard Purdy

MAX GATE, | DORCHESTER.

5th November '33.

Dear Mr Purdy—

(I would have written 'Professor' but Mrs Wharton told Dorothy Allhusen that it was not 'the thing' to do so).

I am ashamed of not having replied before this to your kind letter. You are very much present in spirit at Max Gate—I fear that is wrongly expressed—I mean that you are remembered here with great regard.

Please do not think I minded the proofs coming here. Far from it.

I hope you are well. I am sending on some of the seed of the night-scented stock for your mother. It must not be planted until the spring however, being a quick growing annual.

The letters are all being most beautifully arranged, according to your directions, & a cross-index being made. I think the job will be completed in about a week. It is a load off my mind to know that they are done. I find, however, that a good many important letters I thought were there are missing. I know Mr Bliss had the box unlocked in his flat for over a year, but one would hardly expect any ardent collector to go there—& purloin letters—though such things have been done. I think however that I did say he might have such letters as properly belonged to his collection, i.e. letters of thanks for books given by T.H. to friends, who sold their copies which were purchased later by Mr Bliss. However it does not really matter.

I am wondering whether you still have an idea of coming to Max Gate next summer for some weeks, as tenant? Later on perhaps you will let me know whether there is a chance of that. I am having a great deal of tidying done, and if you do come you will find, I hope, a very much improved house; but, of course, no structural alteration.

I expect your rooms at Yale look very beautiful.

The poem, the MS. of which I gave you, is one of the E.L.H. series, written soon after her death. The incident was a pathetic one. It was the last time she went out—she was going to tea with some friends at Puddletown— where we saw the old church, with the roof being restored. T.H. said he felt sorry when he saw the car drive off that it was such an old one—a hired one—the leather & mica flaps would not fasten properly, & when she returned she said how cold it had been. It was just about this time of the year. He said he was so sorry afterwards that he had not gone with her.

With all good wishes,

Sincerely yours
F.E.H

Text   MS. (with envelope) Beinecke.
Mrs Wharton: the American novelist Edith Newbold Wharton (1862–1937), whom Purdy had met.   *proofs*: of Purdy's Clarendon Press edition of Sheridan's *The Rivals*; FEH's assistance is acknowledged in the preface.   *The poem*: TH's 'A Leaving', first pub. *Human Shows*; the MS. (now Beinecke) has the title 'A Last Leaving' (Purdy, 246–7).

To Siegfried Sassoon

MAX GATE, | DORCHESTER, DORSET.
8th November 1933.

My dear Siegfried,

Just a line to let you know how sincerely I wish you every happiness. I hope that your life, from now onward, may have all that is good—& although I do not know Miss Gatty I am sure that you could not have chosen anyone who was not rare & beautiful & sweet.

I think of you often, & of the days that are no more. During the last month I have been arranging many letters to T.H. & yours are among the best—or possibly the best. I am so pleased to think he received them.

I have made many mistakes in the past, & no doubt have forfeited your friendship, but I am always grateful for what I had of that, & think of you with affection & deepest regard.

Ever sincerely,
F.E.H.

Text   MS. (with envelope) Eton.
every happiness: on his forthcoming marriage (18 Dec. 1933) to Hester Gatty, daughter of Sir Stephen Gatty, a former chief justice of Gibraltar, and his wife Katharine.

To Daniel Macmillan

MAX GATE, | DORCHESTER, DORSET.
2nd January 1933. [1934]

Dear Mr Macmillan,

You may remember that I wrote to you some time ago about a collection of letters written by my husband to the Hon. Mrs Arthur Henniker. I have had these typed—also Mrs Henniker's letters to my husband, & Lord Crewe has written a preface, which I fear is not interesting, but he gives permission for it to be 'cut' as much as I like.

Before sending you these MSS., for your inspection, I have been wondering whether you cared to undertake the publication. My biography of Thomas Hardy has not been, I imagine, a financial success. I do not know whether the cheaper edition has yet been published, as I have seen no allusion to it in the press—or any advertisement.

Should there be a danger of this book—the letters of T.H.—falling flat & being un-noticed I would far rather with-hold it from publication for some years. I should only wish it to be published if it were very well advertised—& if it appeared at the most favourable time of the year for such a book: which, I suppose, would be early October.

You said something about an editor. I would gladly agree to that, only I should have to supply information for footnotes—& also I would not like the letters to be much cut about—that is to say T.H.'s—for only a very few paragraphs from Mrs Henniker's letters are worthy of publication as they are so slight, & obviously carelessly written—not revealing in the least her truly delightful personality & sense of humour.

If you do feel disinclined to consider the publication I shall not be in the least offended.

Yours sincerely,
Florence Hardy.

Text MS. BL.   *Date* Correction of year from internal evidence.
some time ago: specifically, FEH to D. Macmillan 28 Nov. and 14 Dec. 1933 (both BL).   *Crewe*: Robert Offley Ashburton Crewe-Milnes, 2nd Baron Houghton, Marquess of Crewe (see letter of 10 Apr. 1923), was Florence Henniker's brother; FEH (to D. Macmillan, 28 Nov. 1933) reported him as 'strongly in favour of the publication as he knew it was his sister's wish'. *cheaper edition*: *Early Life* and *Later Years* were reissued in 1933, shorn of all illustrations save their frontispieces, as *The Life of Thomas Hardy*, vols. i and ii.   *with-hold it from publication*: FEH's projected edition never appeared.   *worthy of*: FEH first wrote 'suitable for'.

To Hamilton Marr

MAX GATE, | DORCHESTER, DORSET.
8th January 1934.

Dear Mr Marr,

I am very pleased to give my permission to the reading of the short chapter—"A Tree Planting" from "The Woodlanders" by Thomas Hardy on January 12th, subject to the payment of a fee of £2–5–0.

May I take this opportunity of asking you whether you think there would be any possibility, later on, of my broad-casting, or reading. I have had some experience of speaking, & an American agent for lecturing—the best the is I was told—wanted to engage me for a series of lectures when he had heard me speak. Also in the Journal of Arnold Bennett" Vol. II p. 202, when he describes his first meeting with me he writes of my 'vibrating attractive voice'. However, that was many years ago—& my voice may have changed.

After the 17th of this month I shall be for a time at 5, Adelphi Terrace Strand. W.C.2. & could go to Broadcasting House to have my voice tried, if necessary. I expect, however, that your list of speakers is more than full.

Yours sincerely,
Florence Hardy.

Text MS. BBC Written Archives Centre.
Marr: Hamilton Marr (1900–40), a staff member in the BBC Copyright Section.   *reading . . . Planting"*: i.e. chapter 8, although only its final portion is likely to have been read (by Najda Green) in the 5 minutes allocated.   *best the is*: 'best there is' evidently intended. *'vibrating . . . voice'*: accurately quoted from the 25 July 1917 entry in *The Journals of Arnold Bennett*, ed. Newman Flower (London: Cassell, 1932), ii. 202; Bennett there describes FEH as 'a very nice woman' and TH as 'very lively; talked like anything'.   *more than full*: it is not known what response, if any, FEH received to this proposal.

To Richard Purdy

Dear Professor Purdy,

Yes indeed—this sketch is by T.H. I remember it quite well, & his explanation of it—to me. When I took it out of the envelope & looked at it before reading your letter I had quite a shock, for it seemed as if he (T.H.) had just handed it to me. I return it herewith.

This flat is wonderful. When J. M. Barrie came first to see it he walked up & down uttering exclamations of admiration. Eden Phillpott's daughter tells me the library-sitting room, overlooking the river, is the nicest London room she has ever seen—& E. M. Forster who was here yesterday sat looking round silently for a long time, & then said in his quiet, emphatic way—'It is a beautiful room'. The furniture, nearly all genuine period, looks so well. But in taking the flat I also took Garrick's ghost, who was so much in evidence on the 155th anniversary of his (Garrick's) death—that my Dorset h.p. maid, very alarmed, decided to return to Max Gate.

My plans as to the future are uncertain—except that I know I shall not be able to keep on this flat, Max Gate & my car permanently, & must decide which is to be given up. The car costs me roughly £1 a day which includes chauffeur's wages, petrol, oil, tax insurance etc—*not* allowing for depreciation of car. This allows long journeys. The wages of the servants at Max Gate varies according to the ones I have. A good cook, as I have at present, costs £5 a month, h.p. maid £1 a week—& betweenmaid 10/- a week. Two should be able to work the house—but they will not.

Gardener's wages & rent of his house—taxes—etc. £2–12–6 a week—I have to supply him with a house, & pay his rates etc. In July he's working pretty hard in the garden—& then the fruit & vegetables are at their best. Food I would put at £1 a head, as there are vegetables, eggs etc from garden—or 25/- if you live well. Heating, lighting, cleaning materials roughly 25/- a week.

Unfortunately, though Max Gate covers a large space & has many passages, it has only three bedrooms & one dressing-room on the first floor. The rooms on the 2nd floor are attics & box-rooms—& the servants sleep up there—6 rooms in all—2 fit for box rooms only. There is a terrible accumulation of lumber at Max Gate—boxes of letters & bills even which belonged to the first Mrs Hardy, who died 1912. T.H. always meant to sort them, but never did.

With kind regards & many thanks—

Sincerely yours,

F. E. Hardy

Text MS. (with envelope) Beinecke.
this sketch: not confidently identified; Purdy owned four sketches by TH (all now Beinecke). *This flat*: FEH was now renting (furnished) part of the centre house of Adelphi Terrace, once occupied by David Garrick (1717–79), the actor. *Phillpott's daughter*: see letter of 15 Mar. 1929. *three bedrooms*: this calculation excludes TH's study.

[Among the papers of Wilfred Partington in the Huntington Library is a series of letters from FEH, the earliest—a belated, hence apologetic, response to a formal 'permissions' request—dated 24 May 1934. It is not known how FEH and Partington first encountered each other, but since she was currently spending a good deal of time at her Adelphi Terrace flat and he, as author, literary journalist, and omniverous bookman, knew many people in the London literary world, it seems likely that they met as lunch or dinner guests—perhaps at Barrie's, Partington having recently edited two selections from the correspondence of Sir Walter Scott. The current scandal over the alleged forgeries of Thomas James Wise was to both of them of more than common interest: FEH had had dealings with Wise and Partington was later to write the popular account of the Wise forgeries for which he is now best remembered.]

To Wilfred Partington

MAX GATE, | DORCHESTER.

3rd October 1934.

Dear Mr Partington,

Thank you so much for so kindly sending me the book 'An Enquiry into the Nature etc.' I am reading it with interest—and *amazement*. It leaves no loop-hole of escape for poor T.W.—or so it seems to me. I will return it to you very soon. I go to 5 Adelphi Terrace tomorrow, but expect to return here on Sunday morning. I so much enjoyed the very pleasant dinner I had with you, & as soon as I can find a daily cook in London I hope you will come to dinner with me at my flat & meet some congenial friends.

I am afraid I talked much too much, but you were such a kind & sympathetic listener that I talked as freely as if I had known you all my life—I don't think I often talk as much as I did that evening.

I was much amused by your delightful 'mot' concerning the pamphlets. The second was the better but both were good.

With kind regards and again thanking you.

> Yours very sincerely,
> Florence Hardy.

Text MS. Huntington Library.
Partington: Wilfred Partington (1888–1955), literary journalist, author of *Thomas Wise in the Original Cloth*, pub. in the US as *Forging Ahead*; he listed his recreations in *Who's Who* as 'friendship, walking, talking, books, manuscripts, paintings, and objets d'art'.   '*An Enquiry . . . Nature etc.*': John Carter and Graham Pollard, *An Enquiry into the Nature of Certain Nineteenth Century Pamphlets* (London, 1934), a systematic exposure of Thomas J. Wise's activities as a literary forger.   *poor T.W.*: although Wise had 'courted' both TH and FEH (see letter of 25 Nov. 1917) no genuine friendship seems to have developed, Wise in November 1929 describing FEH to Richard Curle as 'the most *unreasonable* person I ever came into contact with' (J. Stevens Cox (ed.), *T. J. Wise, Mrs Hardy & Hardy's Manuscripts* (Guernsey: Toucan Press, 1969), [3]).   *the pamphlets*: those Wise was accused of forging.

To Richard Purdy

MAX GATE, | DORCHESTER, DORSET.
3rd February 1935.

Dear Professor Purdy,

I feel very guilty at not having written to you before this to thank you for your interesting & pleasing Christmas presents, & also for that really beautiful card, showing Salisbury Cathedral.

I do not know where that Constable is? I have never seen a reproduction of it before. If the original is in England I shall try to see it some time. When I next visit Salisbury, which may be within the coming week, I will the card with me & find the spot where it must have been painted & see the changes that have been made; very few I think. It is a familiar & be-loved view.

You cannot think how much I valued the kind message written therein. It came on a morning when I was feeling particularly desolate—& the whole aspect of affairs immediately brightened.

The cook-book is certainly amusing, & I hope it will be useful to my cook. She thinks some of the receipts are rather extravagant, but I tell her that Americans feed more luxuriously than English people.

I was exceedly pleased to have a book of views of the colleges at Yale. How beautiful some—in fact *all*—of them are. I am particularly interested in the photographs of Berkeley College, for I can now picture you in your surroundings.

I have let my flat to an exceedingly nice tenant—a diplomat—brother to a Dorset neighbour at Corfe Castle. He pays enough to cover rent & taxes—no more—but I am glad to be saved that expense, & I have plenty to do here. There are masses of papers in the attics, and these must all be sorted & the best part of them burned. Every time I begin to go through them I find something of interest or value—& so I do not like to destroy them en masse—but often I feel I shall die & leave them much as they are.

The cataloguing of the letters as you suggested—with a subject index—has been of immense value to a Mr William Rutland who was at Lausanne & is now at Oxford writing something about T.H. & Barnes. When the cataloguing was finished I discovered in a cupboard several bundles of early letters—of great interest. However my friend—Miss Inglis—& I felt we must leave those for the present. Mr Rutland now asks if these early letters may be sent to the Bodleian Library, where the authorities have promised to look after them, & allow Mr Rutland access to them—and, I suppose, copy any passages from them that are suitable for his work.

I like Mr Rutland well enough, & admire his zeal, but I am wondering whether it is not too cheapening altogether to allow anyone to have access to T.H's letters & private papers. I wish you were in England that I might consult you on this matter. Indeed were you domiciled in England I would ask you to take charge of all the papers & library & do with these as you thought fit. That would relieve me of much anxiety so it is a purely selfish wish on my part.

Last night I read with amused amazement, which ended in indignation, Hamlin Garland's account of a visit to Max Gate. His story of T.H's criticism of Barrie is absolutely false—also his account of my complaint about never going to London. The absurd phrase 'one of my crosses' is one that I am sure I have never used in my life. I remember my surprise when Mrs Garland began to sympathise with me for never being able to leave Max Gate. I had made no complaint. I believe I did tell them that J.M.B. had invited us to go to stay at Stanway, but T.H. had felt unequal to the visit. That was because they were bragging so intolerably about this visit to 'Sir James Barrie at his *Castle*".

I remember my amusement when, on leaving, Mr Garland bowed coldly to a little man in the uniform of a private in the Tank Corps who had been all the time sitting quietly in a further corner of the room watching & listening with an expressionless face. I thought: 'You little know.' Private Shaw as he was then, formerly Colonel T. E. Lawrence, had dropped in a little while before the Garlands arrived, & put us on our guard by telling us that Hamlin Garland was the worst kind of interviewer; one who came in the guise of a friend. He sat & listened to every thing with intense amusement, & had I said 'one of my crosses' it would have been with the intention of making him laugh aloud.

Ever sincerely,
Florence Hardy.

Text MS. (with envelope) Beinecke.
that Constable: evidently—from Purdy's draft reply (Beinecke)—*Salisbury Cathedral from the South-West* in the Victoria and Albert Museum.   *will the card*: 'will take the card' evidently intended.   *cook-book*: unidentified.   *exceedy*: sic.   *book . . . College*: Purdy, a Fellow of the recently opened Berkeley College, presumably sent a copy of *The Yale Residential Colleges* (reprinted from the *Yale Alumni Weekly*) with its bound-in supplement, an illustrated article on Berkeley College reprinted from the *Yale Alumni Weekly* of 28 Sept. 1934. *tenant . . . neighbour*: unidentified.   *Rutland*: William Rutland, an Oxford-trained literary scholar who lived and worked mostly in Switzerland; his *Thomas Hardy: A Study of his Writings and their Background* (Oxford, 1938) was based largely on his researches at Max Gate.   *Miss Inglis*: Kitty Inglis, presumably a daughter or other relative of FEH's friend Ethel Inglis (see letter of 23 July 1917), was assisting FEH in rearranging and cataloguing TH's incoming correspondence (now DCM) along lines suggested by Purdy; in a letter to Frederick B. Adams of 25 June 1958 (Adams), however, Purdy spoke of Beryl Frampton (see letter of 24 July 1927) as having done most of this work.   *Garland's account*: Hamlin Garland (1860–1940), American novelist, visited Max Gate with his wife Zulime (née Taft) 11 Aug. 1923; his meagre diary entry (MS. Huntington) is much expanded in his *Afternoon Neighbors: Further Excerpts from a Literary Log* (New York: Macmillan, 1934), 86–93.   *Stanway*: a house in the Cotswolds often rented by Barrie during the summer months from 1921 onwards; see Lady Cynthia Asquith, *Portrait of Barrie* (London: James Barrie, 1954), 132–5 and, for the Garlands' visit, 157.   *interviewer*: FEH first wrote 'reviewer'.

To Llewelyn Powys

MAX GATE, | DORCHESTER.
Thursday even—[1935?]

My dear Mr Powys,
  With very great pleasure I have written & posted the letter you suggested to Mr Taylor, & I do sincerely hope he'll get the job. Why mind a white lie for a good purpose when the whole of modern life is more or less a lie, & for no purpose at all, unless perhaps a bad one. I have heard of Mr Taylor from your brother Mr Theodore Powys. I am exceedingly glad that you are so much better—I hope you will go on getting better & better & be able to come here to see me—& I'll love to go to see you some time. My warmest & most affectionate greeting to Miss Alyse Gregory. After Saturday I hope to be here all the next three months—or longer—I have had enough of London. Am I happy? No—not quite. I think my nature

only allows me to be happy at rare intervals—for a short time—but *when* I am happy I *am* happy—filled to the brim, with an ecstacy that the generally cheerful person can never know.

My best greetings

Ever sincerely,
Florence Hardy.

Text MS. Adams.   *Date* Speculative only.
Mr Taylor: presumably Bernard Taylor, addressee of three letters (from 1935, 1937, and 1938) in Louis Wilkinson (ed.), *The Letters of Llewelyn Powys* (London, 1943).   *Gregory:* see letter of 26 Oct. 1930.

[The estrangement between TH's two literary executors continued and deepened, and in such matters as the granting or withholding of permission for stories and poems to be broadcast by the BBC or included in anthologies FEH became accustomed to act alone. It was only when Cockerell became aware, in March 1935, of her private printing of Hardy's uncollected novella, *An Indiscretion in the Life of an Heiress*, that he decided to reassert his position. FEH's action was prompted by the prospect of an American edition which she (mistakenly) believed to be in the nature of a piracy, but from Cockerell's point of view, publicly and forcefully expressed in a letter to *The Times Literary Supplement*, *Indiscretion* was, like 'Old Mrs Chundle', a substandard work which TH himself had deliberately chosen not to reprint but which had now been revived without the consent or even the knowledge of one of the literary executors. Instead of backing down, however, FEH seized the occasion of Cockerell's open attack upon her to seek a clarification and possible resolution of the situation, chiefly by seeking an expert legal interpretation of TH's will but also by ensuring that Daniel Macmillan—who had encountered an aggrieved Cockerell while on a Mediterranean cruise—was fully apprised of her side of the story.]

To Daniel Macmillan

MAX GATE, | DORCHESTER, DORSET.
10th May 1935.

Dear Mr Macmillan—

Thank you for sending the two books—I am anxious to have a complete set of every kind of edition of Thomas Hardy's works.

I quite agree with what you say about Mr Powley. I did not like to say anything against him as an anthologist, because I understood that his claims were supported by my valued friend Mr Walter de la Mare, but in a letter received today from Mr de la Mare it does not appear to be so, particularly.

I had an interview with Mr Medley last Tuesday, and I found him most helpful, though of course unbiassed. I assured him that I was quite ready to resign my literary executorship in favour of Sir Sydney Cockerell, & also to let him have the whole of the royalties from my late husband's works. I refuse to work with Sir Sydney Cockerell. Mr Medley said that was out of the question and he is endeavouring—or will endeavour—to persuade Sir Sydney Cockerell to resign the literary executorship in favour of Mr St John Hornby, if a sufficiently large payment is made to him. There is nothing I should welcome more than this, as it was by my request that my husband mentioned Mr St John Hornby in his will, as possible literary executor to succeed Cockerell & Gosse. My relations with Mr Hornby have been of the happiest. He helped me with regard to the two Dorset memorials to my husband, & I have implicit faith in his judgement in all things, literary or otherwise. I would accept his decision without question, in any matter. Also I am willing to be guided by Mr Medley who is most sympathetic and wise. I enclose a letter received from him today.

I must also thank you for advising me to see Mr Medley. He had my letter before he saw Sir Sydney Cockerell at Cambridge, on Saturday last, & it was well that he should have known I wished him to help me in this painful & unpleasant business. He seemed glad to hear that I wished to make another will, and he said that he never liked the will he drew up for me some years ago. When the Cockerell business is settled a new & more satisfactory will is to be drawn up.

With apologies for all the trouble you have been caused—

Yours sincerely,
Florence Hardy.

Text MS. BL.

two books: copies of *Stories and Poems of Thomas Hardy* in the New Eversley series—not sent earlier, according to D. Macmillan's letter of 7 May (copy, BL), because differing from the existing Scholar's Library issue only in omitting the final pages of questions.   *Powley*: although Edward Barzillai Powley (1887–1968) had already pub. at least two anthologies, Macmillan's letter called him 'worthy' but 'comparatively unknown', hence perhaps not the ideal editor for a selection of TH's poems.   *Medley*: Charles Douglas Medley (1870–1963), solicitor, of the London firm of Field Roscoe & Co.; he specialized in literary estates.

[Although T. E. Lawrence seems to have been an infrequent visitor to Max Gate in the early 1930s, he and FEH remained in fairly frequent correspondence, Lawrence's letters being among the very few that she preserved from her annual bonfires. The relationship meant much to her—enhanced as it must have been by the extra-ordinary excitement and mystique that still attached to Lawrence in the popular imagination—and his death on 19 May 1935, six days after a motor-cyling accident, was the bitterest blow she had suffered since the death of TH himself.]

To E. M. Forster

MAX GATE, | DORCHESTER, DORSET.
23rd May '35.

Dear Mr Forster,

I know how you feel. I know that for most of T.E's friends life will never be quite the same again. Perhaps it was as well that you were not at the funeral. In some ways I wish I had not gone—but I did have one word with Siegfried—I wanted so much to talk to him for a few minutes—but the doctor who looked after T.E. for those last six days had my arm & was marching me off like a policeman & I couldn't resist. But he was really meaning to be kind—though I longed to escape. I should like very much to see you sometime for I want to tell you about my last conversation with T.E. less than a fortnight before his death—& of something very strange that happened. He thought so much of you, as of course you know. *What* a friend he was—unchanging.

T. H. used to feel sometimes as you do about occasions being preserved—but then he thought that if the beautiful moments were preserved—moments of horror—& torture—would be preserved also—which spoiled the thought.

My present instinct is to give up Max Gate & get away from Dorset—all the friends I cared for here have died lately—more or less tragically. I have let my London flat, & mean to give it up in September. I do not want another London flat.

Yours sincerely,
Florence Hardy.

Text MS. King's College Cambridge.
the doctor: Captain C. P. Allen, of the Royal Army Medical Corps.   *a friend*: writing to Rutland Boughton 21 May 1935 (BL), FEH called Lawrence 'my best friend on earth'. *tragically*: FEH's letter to Purdy, 24 Apr. 1925 (Beinecke), shows that she had particularly in mind the death of her Dorset friend Alice Patterson (whom Purdy had met) and the subsequent suicide of Myles Patterson, the dead woman's brother.

To Wilfred Partington

MAX GATE, | DORCHESTER, DORSET.
28th June 1935.

Dear Mr Partington,

I was very pleased to receive your letter, but am sorry I have not replied to it before. I have indeed been busy, but have not yet been able to do any original writing—that is to say I have not been able to start the book I contemplated.

I wish you had replied to Cockerell's letter. It was most unjust as he did not say that the story 'An Indiscretion' was printed merely to prevent an American—a stranger—making a first edition. It was being published, anyhow, in America. Had it not been so I would not have published it. Also the first story 'Mrs Chundle' was published because Mr Curtis Brown made the arrangements & when I asked him to stop them he said it was too late. I regretted the matter very much, but was not to blame. Anyhow I think Cockerell's letter has had the effect of gaining me the sympathy of many friends who, before that, did not realize the way he had been behaving to me. An American friend—a Professor at Yale—wrote to me that we have no right to judge for posterity. Certainly Cockerell has to claim to decide which of T.H.'s stories are to be published, & which not. He lost a very valuable picture by his letter. When Colonel T. E. Lawrence read it he went to the Fitzwilliam Museum & took away a painting of himself by Augustus John which was there on loan. He told me that he thought that was the first time anyone had got back from the Fitzwilliam any thing lent to it.

I hope your new flat is what you like. I have let mine until July 25th—I find I have so much to do here, & really the country suits me better than London. It is really lovely here now. I have never known the county so beautiful. I should be so pleased to see you if you are able to come down at any time. I have an invalid father coming next week for a fortnight, & a sister & her two children with me now—leaving tomorrow—so that I find plenty to do. I am writing this late at night in the study feeling rather exhausted after a heavy day, so please excuse any slipshod writing.

I hope that you are quite well. It was very good of you to write me such an interesting letter which I thoroughly enjoyed reading.

The 'Thomas Hardy' to whom William Cobbett wrote was a rather fine man I think. Several amusing incidents have occured through people thinking my husband was meant when that T.H. was alluded to.

Kind regards & all good wishes

Yours very sincerely,
Florence Hardy.

Text   MS. Huntington.

book I contemplated: perhaps a selective edition of TH's letters.   *Cockerell's letter*: headed 'Early Hardy Stories', *The Times Literary Supplement*, 14 Mar. 1935.   *an American*: Carl Jefferson Weber (1894–1966), of Colby College; for his edition of *Indiscretion* see letter of 7 Mar. 1937 and headnote.   *Curtis Brown*: see letter of 24 July 1928.   *at Yale*: Purdy.   *has to claim*: 'has no claim' clearly intended.　　*painting . . . John:* unidentified, but perhaps the portrait of Jan. 1935 listed as unlocated in Jeremy Wilson, *T. E. Lawrence* (London: National Portrait Gallery, 1988), 222–3; see also Wilson, *Lawrence of Arabia* (London: Heinemann, 1989), 921.　　*invalid father:* Edward Dugdale, a constant source of anxiety at this time, died a year later, in June 1936.　　*sister . . . children:* Margaret Soundy, with Thomas and Barbara; Tom Soundy had been living at Max Gate while attending school in Dorchester.　　'*Thomas Hardy*': Thomas Hardy (1752–1832), shoemaker and radical politician; for TH's response to Cockerell's gift, in 1913, of *Memoir of Thomas Hardy . . . Written by Himself,* see *CL,* iv. 325. The Cobbett letter has not been identified.

To Wilfred Partington

5, ADELPHI TERRACE, | STRAND, W.C.2.
18th Sept. [1935]

Dear Mr Partington,

You are very kind. I am going to the country for a week-end & I have the cold that I always get when I come up to London. But I'll be back, & quite well I hope, some time on Monday.

Would you come to tea on Tuesday? I shall be so pleased if you would. And any film will be delightful to me, except the one at the Tivoli—Wings of Song—which I've seen, & do not care for.

What about 'Peg of Old Drury', the film about Garrick? But anyone you like to see will please me.

Kind regards,

Sincerely yours.
Florence Hardy.

Text MS. Huntington.　　*Date* Year supplied on MS. by Partington.
Wings of Song: On Wings of Song (US title *Love Me Forever*), a film about opera and crime, directed by Victor Schertizinger and with Grace Moore in the principal role.　　'*Peg of Old Drury*': directed by Herbert Wilcox and starring Anna Neagle, it focused on the relationship between David Garrick and the actress Peg Woffington.　　*please me*: they saw *Peg of Old Drury* and FEH wrote 26 Sept. (Huntington) to thank Partington both for the film, which she 'greatly enjoyed', and for 'the box of very delicious chocolates'.

To Richard Purdy

MAX GATE, | DORCHESTER, DORSET.
17th November 1935.

Dear Richard Purdy,

In my foregoing letter to you I forgot to thank you for the article on T.E (Lawrence of Arabia). I was exceedingly glad to read it, as it was a finely expressed tribute—& I was especially glad to be able to give it to his mother—poor Mrs Lawrence—who asked me to save for her anything I read about 'Ned', as she calls him. She is still most unhappy & unsettled. A week ago I drove her from Bournemouth to Moreton to visit the grave a second time. It is almost bewildering to think that this is the end. I was reading a little book by E. V. Lucas, & the concluding sentences might be said by those who loved T.E.

"Nothing but silence. Nothing but a world made drab by the absence of him."

The book is 'The Old Contemporaries'.

After the above it seems a little ridiculous to continue by saying how much I appreciated two very delightful visits paid by your friend, F. B. Adams Junior, & his beautiful little wife. Certainly he is one of the most interesting & likeable young men I have ever met—& I only wish I had met him before as I understand he has been to Dorchester several times before. He has, with much kindness, sent me copies of T.H.'s letters to Gosse— those, at least, that T. J. Wise was willing to sell. I read them aloud to Major F. Yeats Brown (Bengal Lancer) who was here when the copies arrived, & we both found them most interesting—& I, very moving. One could read so much behind the lines. As I have often said to you before I wish all the documents in this house were in your hands. But the Atlantic is so wide—if only it were as narrow as the Frome then all would be easy for I could refer to them when I wished.

With best wishes—

Ever sincerely,
Florence Hardy.

The election went exactly as I thought it would. I am sorry for Ramsay MacDonald & for his son Malcomb, both friends—but there again I am not surprised—F.E.H.

Text MS. (with envelope) Beinecke.
article on T.E.: not identified.   "*Nothing . . . of him.*": quoted from E[dward] V[errall] Lucas, *The Old Contemporaries* (London: Methuen, 1935), 169, with the alteration of 'her' to 'him'.   *Adams . . . wife*: see letter of 1 Nov. 1936.   *Brown*: Francis Yeats-Brown (1886–1944), soldier and author, best known for his *Bengal Lancer* (1930); he had apparently asked FEH if he might finish writing one of his books—presumably *Lancer at Large* (1936)—in TH's study.   *MacDonald*: James Ramsay MacDonald (1866–1937), Prime Minister 1929–35, first of a Labour and then of a so-called National government; he lost his seat in the Nov. 1935 general election but won a by-election in 1936. He had been on friendly terms with TH and was a pall-bearer at his funeral.   *Malcomb*: i.e. Malcolm John MacDonald (1901–81), who had also temporarily lost his seat as a National Labour MP; he later had a distinguished diplomatic career.

To Wilfred Partington

MAX GATE, | DORCHESTER, DORSET.
13th February 1936.

Dear Mr Partington,

I am absolutely ashamed of my long negligence in returning the enclosed article, which I read with much interest. At the same time I did feel rather terrified at the thought that some one might come here some time & write a similar article about Max Gate—though of course this modest dwelling could not compete in interest with Brackenburn. Containing so many treasures. I do understand there *is* material for a *good* article here—but one of a very different kind—& I turn cold when I contemplate that vision. Because of that I hesitated to ask you to pay that long promised & often deferred visit—for it would be a dull affair after a visit to Brackenburn. Mr Walpole is so kind, & so generous that I am sure he *loved* your article, & certainly it does give a pleasant picture of his home. Here alas there is much of a different kind to be notice—dining-room carpet wearing into holes, paper peeling off the walls in sundry places etc. etc—& many things here that came by accident which I haven't had the heart to cast overboard yet.

I hope you are well & that the cold weather is not trying you. I hate it—London is a strange city to me now—I find so much to do here—& really I am better in health away from the fogs & the smoke.

With kind regards—

Sincerely yours—
Florence Hardy.

Text MS. Huntington.
enclosed article: evidently Partington's 'Hugh Walpole's Library of Affections', *Bookman's Journal* (edited by Partington), 3rd series, 17 (1929), 59–66. Somewhat fulsomely written, it concludes: 'Running brooks and running books. Yes! Brackenburn is the place for a library.'   *that vision*: Partington's brief reply of 16 Feb. (typed copy, Huntington) vehemently rejected 'the suggestion that any private visit would be forthwith turned into copy'.   *Walpole*: Hugh Seymour Walpole (1884–1941), novelist, knighted 1937; his important collections of books, manuscripts, and works of art were kept at his house, Brackenburn, near Keswick.   *to be notice*: 'to be noticed' clearly intended.

To Howard Bliss

MAX GATE, | DORCHESTER, DORSET.
April 21st. 1936.

Dear Mr Bliss,

Thank you so much for your letter. I think I told you how much I liked Mr Adams, & I have no objection to any Hardy material being in his possession. But, at the same time, I see your point about the letters. I am afraid that I have neglected my duty in not having arranged for the publication of a volume—or two volumes—of collected letters of T.H. The unfortunate break between S. Cockerell & myself is the cause of this. Certainly I do not want an unauthorized American edition to be published. I wish that you could or would edit this, but I am sure your business affairs are too worrying for you at the present time to attempt any such task.

With regard to the letters you mention I do admire more than I can say your delicacy of feeling in being willing to destroy them—but you must not think of this. I do not mind their being published, in due course. I had seen a copy of the letter to Gosse about Miss Helen Paterson. I had also heard the story from T.H. himself, who told it me in a most amusing way. I think he felt 'quite romantical' about several young ladies in those far off days. He had a similar story to tell about Miss Thackeray—afterwards Lady Ritchie. I think Mrs S. (in the letter) must be Mrs Sturgis—Meredith's daughter, whom I knew years after. To go back to the story of Lady Ritchie—the feeling there was, he implied, more on her side than his. But I know you hate gossip & feel rather ashamed of writing this.

I wish Colonel T. E. Lawrence were alive for I feel he would know exactly what should be done. I have always felt I would like to add my collection to yours, with yourself as custodian—but, as you say, the future is so vague. It was hinted to me some time ago that *Yale* might possibly be prepared to purchase your collection. If only my husband had arranged that the large proportion of his estate which was left to his brother & sister would come back after the death of the survivor to endow Max Gate & pay a custodian then all might be easier, & I could buy, at the proper market price, your collection, to remain here. I do *not* think I shall give anything else to the Dorset County Museum. The things I have already given are not valued.

I hope you are well. I fear all this trouble must be *very* bad for your health. Yes—the country is beginning to look lovely.

Yours sincerely,
Florence Hardy.

Text   MS. Adams.

Mr Adams: see letter of 1 Nov. 1936.   *American edition*: FEH, writing to Bliss, 22 Feb. 1936 (Princeton), expressed concern at the possibility that Carl J. Weber (see letter of 28 June 1935) might pub. 'a small volume' of TH's letters. Weber's later *The Letters of Thomas Hardy* (Waterville, Maine, 1954) was restricted to TH letters in the Colby College library.   *letter . . . Paterson*: TH's letter, dated 25 July 1906 (*CL*, iii. 218), spoke of his feeling ' "quite romantical" . . . (as they say here)' about Helen Paterson, the illustrator of *Far from the Madding Crowd*, who married William Allingham, the poet, at about the same time as TH married ELG.

Lady Ritchie: Anne Isabella Thackeray (1837–1919), novelist, later Lady Ritchie; she was Thackeray's elder daughter and TH first met her in 1874 when visiting Leslie Stephen, who had married her sister.   *Mrs S.*: correctly identified by FEH as George Meredith's daughter Marie, wife of Henry Parkman Sturgis.

[Richard Purdy's friendship with FEH, sustained by frequent correspondence and Purdy's transatlantic crossings, continued and deepened throughout the last years of her life. She also met and befriended another young American, Frederick B. Adams, Jr., who was to become an important figure in the subsequent development of Hardy studies. Adams, later Director of the Pierpont Morgan Library in New York, was a former student of Purdy's at Yale whose early interest in the study and collection of books and manuscripts has resulted over the years in a personal collection of exceptional quality, in significant scholarly contributions of his own, and in the attainment of a position of acknowledged pre-eminence within the international bibliophilic community.]

To Frederick B. Adams

MAX GATE, | DORCHESTER, DORSET.
1st November 1936.

Dear Mr Adams,

I was so pleased to receive your letter—a particularly delightful one. I rejoiced to learn that 'Precious Bane' and 'Seven for a Secret' are in your collection. Indeed I would rather you had them than myself as I am afraid I do not appreciate Mary Webb's work as I ought.

I have heard no more from Mr Bliss. I hope all is well with him. I think he should let me know what becomes of his collection as so many items were *given* to him by me on the understanding that they would eventually form part of a Hardy collection in some museum. I certainly did not anticipate that they would ever be sold.

I am writing this in the room where we first met, & where we had tea. I am alone in the house & the silence & gloom are profound. How much I wish I could summon courage to break away from Max Gate. I think if it were not for the books & papers in the study I would be able to do so. However as my income is rapidly decreasing I may soon find that I cannot afford to live here—& in that case I suppose it would be advisable for me to store the books & MSS in one or two rooms—or ask the Dorset County Museum to take charge of them. Unfortunately the present curator, though a most charming man, is not really interested in literary relics—nor in my husband's work. All his interest is given to the excavations at Maiden Castle. Years ago J. M. Barrie advised me not to give any more MSS. to Dorchester.

He said they would not be valued. I have lent four MSS—including that of 'Under the Greenwood Tree" to an exhibition in Canada—(or America?). My publishers have sent them. And several interesting relics (I rather hate that word) to the Book Exhibition which opens in London tomorrow.

What you say about the terrible state of affairs in Spain is so true. Where is it going to end? Perhaps I ought to cling to Max Gate in spite of the gloom & silence—for bombs may be raining down on London before long, & after all my garden here does provide some kind of food—chicken, vegetables & fruit. Well do I remember the shortage of food in the last war—& I heard, too, the noise of bombs dropped by a Zeppelin & the anti-aircraft guns, once when I was paying a visit to my parents.

My love & good wishes to Mrs Adams & your little Gillian.

Yours very sincerely
Florence Hardy.

Enclosed a little gift—but I fear you will not find it very interesting.

Text MS. (with envelope) Adams.
Adams: Frederick Baldwin Adams, Jun. (b. 1910), American collector and bibliographer, director of the Pierpont Morgan Library 1948–69.   *in your collection*: Adams was interested in the novels of Mary Webb (1881–1927), who had presented TH with inscribed copies of her *Precious Bane* and *Seven for a Secret*, the latter dedicated to him. When Adams visited Max Gate he persuaded FEH to seek out these vols. (they were in a servant's room), subsequently purchasing them from her through John Carter, the bookseller and bibliographer.   *curator*: Lieutenant-Colonel C. D. Drew.   *Maiden Castle*: the excavations of this massive Iron Age hill-fort just SW of Dorchester were being conducted by the archaeologist R. E. M. Wheeler (1890–1976), later famous as Sir Mortimer Wheeler.   *exhibition in Canada*: the Canadian Book Week Fair.   *Book Exhibition*: organized by the *Sunday Times* in Dorland Hall, Lower Regent Street; displayed were TH's travelling desk, his watch, his OM, and the pen with which he wrote *The Dynasts*.   *in Spain*: the Spanish Civil War had begun 17 July 1936 and the battle for Madrid was currently at its height.   *Mrs Adams . . . Gillian*: Gillian (born Dec. 1934), Adams's daughter by his first wife, Ruth (née Potter). *little gift*: tentatively recalled by Adams as a Max Gate Christmas card.

To Ethel Richardson

MAX GATE, | DORCHESTER, | DORSET.
Wednesday. [25 November 1936]

My dear Ethel,

I thoroughly approve of the inscription you suggest. It is well to have a record of the long & useful years of teaching. It is just a historical fact to keep his memory from oblivion. It is my wish also that this should be put on the stone—& I will *gladly* bear all the expense. As to the size of the grave

I do not know what I think. In a way I do understand Connie's wish—but no one knows what the future may hold. Tom was genuinely fond of Father, & Father of Tom—only it may be more than half a century—I am sure I hope so—before thought need be given to a grave for Tom—& also I hope Margaret will live to old age.

I asked Connie here for Christmas, during conversation. I felt that no other member of the family would care to come. I should be *most delighted* if Pamela cared to come. Monica & Arthur, I imagine, cannot get away from their offices until late.— or I could put them up as well as Connie. I can put up two singles—or one single (Connie) & a double—as there are now two single beds in best spare room. But it will be a dull Christmas here—no festivities or entertaining. I wish I were nearer you. I asked Connie—just as I go to see so many invalids. I've been to see an old friend, Miss Fetherstonhaugh—this afternoon, who has had a stroke, & her mind & her speech are affected. I went, not for my own pleasure, but because I thought it the right thing to do—& it is so with Christmas—a most depressing time to me now.

With love to all,

Affectionately,

F.E.H.

Text MS. (with envelope) Daphne Wood.   *Date* From postmark.
Richardson: FEH's eldest sister; see letter of 9 Feb. 1914.   *inscription*: for the tombstone of their father, Edward Dugdale, in Enfield cemetery.   *Connie's*: Constance Dugdale; see letter of 3 Dec. 1913.   *Tom . . . Margaret*: Tom Soundy (Edward Dugdale's grandson) died in Australia in 1988, but his ashes were interred in the grave of his mother, Margaret Soundy, at Stinsford.   *Pamela*: Pamela Richardson, E. Richardson's daughter.   *Monica & Arthur*: see letter of 1 Feb. 1933.   *in best spare room*: 'in the best spare room' obviously intended.

To Richard Purdy

MAX GATE, | DORCHESTER, DORSET.
30th November 1936.

Dear Richard Purdy,

The sight of your writing was delightful—a letter from you is like a letter from a very favourite nephew. And the first words were so cheering 'I've thought of you so often these last few days'—then when I read on I wondered in just *how* you had been thinking of me, as I, too, have listened to Mrs Belloc Lowndes' stories—some of them about her best friends,—& I have watched other people listening—with awed faces. I have been told that her stories are harmless, because no one believes them, but that is absurd because the majority of listeners are ready to believe any scandal about people in the public eye. However, as you say, she *is* very friendly. J. M. Barrie told me that she was always so affectionate to him when she met him—but she has never been inside his flat. Quite a good few of her stories are about J.M.B.

As I am writing this letter news comes on the radio that the Crystal Palace is on fire; I suppose that conveys little to you, but to me it seems one of the most fantastic things I have ever heard on the radio.

Today I went to the D.C.C. office & looked up that letter, which I found easily. It *is* rather staggering, & might well have been written by T.H. in his youth. But I know of no association he may have had with Wareham in those days. He certainly told me his letter was about the clock on Napper's Mite. He & other pupils at Mr Hicks's office used to put their heads out of the window to see the time by it, so it was great grievance when it was taken away. The clock was taken away also a few month's after T.H.'s death, & I remember how dismal it looked in South St. without it. I even sent a cheque to help pay for repairing the clock.

I never knew T.H. make a mistake. He was so accurate—& so truthful. My own memory is very bad now, but I certainly seem to remember his telling me about *the clock*. I'll think it over, & read the letter again, & write to you. A few pages before was an account of the hanging of poor Martha Brown, which T.H. witnessed. It is rather late now—I will post this letter, & write a continuance in a day or two.

Affectionately—

F.E.H

Text   MS. (with envelope) Beinecke.
wondered in just how: FEH evidently began to write 'wondered in just what way' but lost track of the construction in turning the page.   *Lowndes'*: Marie Adelaide Belloc Lowndes, née Belloc (1868–1947), wife of Frederic Sawrey Archibald Lowndes, of *The Times*. She was a prolific author, chiefly of detective stories; her *The Merry Wives of Westminster* (London: Macmillan, 1934), the first of an eventual three volumes of gossipy memoirs, contains several otherwise unsubstantiated anecdotes about TH.   *Crystal Palace*: the huge glass-covered building erected by Joseph Paxton in Hyde Park for the Great Exhibition of 1851 and subsequently moved to S. London.   *that letter*: 'A Pump Complaining', a humorous letter (as from the pump itself) pub. in the *Dorset County Chronicle* and the *Southern Times* on, respectively, 6 and 1 Mar. 1856. Purdy had suggested it as a possible basis for TH's youthful recollection (*Life and Work*, 37) of publishing a mischievous letter about the removal of the clock which hung (then as now) outside Napper's Mite, a former almshouse in South Street, Dorchester—across the street from the office of the architect John Hicks, to whom TH was apprenticed in 1856. See Purdy, 291, and *Biography*, 53–4.   *Martha Brown*: see letter of 20 Jan. 1926.

To Richard Purdy

MAX GATE, | DORCHESTER, DORSET.
7th Dec. 1936.

Dear Richard Purdy,

This is really a continuation of my other letter—written while the Crystal Palace was blazing. Is that disaster symbolic—& does it mean the end of an age—& of a dynasty. If Galsworthy were living, & had not finished the chronicle of the Forsytes, he might have made Soames die in the blaze of the Crystal Palace—rescuing heaven knows what—a bust of the Prince Consort perhaps.

A young man from one of the universities visiting me a few weeks ago said that all the stories one heard were amusing yet the time might come when the nation would be tired of a comic Royal Family. Tonight I hoped there would be some definite news but apparently we are to go on waiting.

I hope you will have a happy Christmas & a very good new year.

I hope I was not indiscreet in my remarks about the English literary lady visiting the U.S.A.

What a lot we would have to talk about, were you here—

Affectionately,
F.E.H.

Text MS. (with envelope) Beinecke.
other letter: of 30 Nov. 1936. *Soames*: Soames Forsyte, the central figure in John Galsworthy's narrative sequence *The Forsyte Saga*, first pub. in its completed form in 1922. *young man*: Henry Reed; see letter of 25 Dec. 1936 and headnote. *definite news*: of the anticipated abdication of King Edward VIII following his decision to marry the divorced Wallis Simpson; he signed the actual instrument of abdication on 10 Dec. 1936. *literary lady*: Mrs Belloc Lowndes; see letter of 30 Nov. 1936.

To Frederick B. Adams

MAX GATE, | DORCHESTER, DORSET.
20th December 1936.

Dear Mr Adams,

I wrote the heading to this letter, & then just waited for the photograph of Gillian to arrive. I am longing to see it—but if I don't write off tonight this letter may not reach you by Jan. 1st as I had wished. In fact I'm not sure that it will do so even now—but you have my good wishes always, & I hope you will be having a happy Christmas while this letter is on its way to you

My husband must, I think, have read those novels by Mary Webb, for remember one criticism of his—that she did not really know the life of the farm labourer (agricultural worker they prefer to be called now). When I told her that, she (Mary Webb) told me something rather sadly that showed me she *did* know the life of the wife of a poor working-class man. I think the farm workers in Dorset are of a more noble type than those Mary Webb wrote about. My husband used to say they had better manners than any other class of Englishman.

When our late King Edward VIII was here years ago, in the very room where I am now writing, I noted with surprise how difficult & obstinate he was with two of his secretaries, Sir Godfrey Thomas, & Walter Peacock, over a little question of answering a telegram. I thought then that there might be trouble later on. And yet he was so very kind & friendly one *had* to like him. My gardener, a very uneducated man, said to me simply. "He was simply worshipped by the whole country." And now everyone is so angry with him. The western approach to Dorchester which was very pleasant, has been quite ruined lately because the Duchy of Cornwall has sold so much land by the roadside to speculating builders, & there are now rows of hideous little villas where there used to be fields & trees. The solicitor who who has been negociating for the Duchy, said to me rather bitterly "I suppose that money was to go into the pocket of Mrs Simpson." And when one hears of a fortune spent in jewels for Mrs S. one is inclined to think his warmly expressed sympathy for the unemployed is rather a sham. I never heard that he really *did* any thing for them.

The late Lawrence of Arabia (T.E. we called him) said once, years ago, that if ever the Duke of York came to the throne there would be a revolution, as he was so unpopular. However, everyone seems thankful to have him on the throne now. Had Mrs Simpson not been married before, & had she had a good reputation the country would have been *overjoyed* to have her as our queen. The fact of her being an American would have been a great advantage.

I am spending Christmas here alone (I expect) and quietly, and I will try to begin sorting papers—& burning some. I often think it is time for me to begin my packing. My husband's last surviving cousin died two days ago. She had lived for over sixty years with his mother & sisters—& now one sister is left—but she is very frail. With regard to the Gosse letter I think it must have been congratulations upon a silver wedding, or something of that sort—certainly not on an honour conferred as T.H. thought so little of honours. Gosse himself thought so much of them, which explains the O.M. but most people put O.M after his name when they addressed envelopes to him. Now a hazy memory comes back to me—T.H. wrote to tell Gosse how much he had enjoyed hearing him broadcast. T.H. used to be much amused & pleased when he heard his friends broadcasting—in the early days of that great invention.

Reading this letter through my grammar seems wobbly—but you must forgive it as I am writing late at night—

My love to you all, & best wishes—

Florence Hardy.

Text MS. (with envelope) Adams.   *Date* '20' written over original '15'; envelope postmarked 21 Dec. 1936.

just waited: hence the altered date.   *Gillian . . . Mary Webb*: see letter of 1 Nov. 1936.   *late King*: FEH means 'former King', Edward VIII having abdicated but not died.   *Thomas . . . Peacock*: when Edward VIII (then Prince of Wales) visited Max Gate in July 1923 (*Biography*, 548–9) his entourage included his private secretary Sir Godfrey Thomas, Bt., and Walter Peacock (knighted 1924), Keeper of the Records of the Duchy of Cornwall. The Duchy was, and is, conducted as the private estate of the Prince of Wales.   *My gardener*: Bertie Norman Stephens was the Max Gate gardener from 1926 until after FEH's death; his recollections appear in the pamphlet, *Thomas Hardy in His Garden* (Beaminster, 1963).   *solicitor who who*: FEH turned the page at this point.   *Duke of York*: younger brother of Edward VIII, whom he had succeeded as King George VI.   *advantage*: FEH first wrote 'assett'.   *cousin*: Mary Elizabeth ('Polly') Antell, daughter of TH's mother's sister Mary, was 83 years old at her death; other first cousins with whom TH had lost touch were still alive in Canada.   *Gosse letter*: not confidently identified; for TH's reference to Gosse's broadcasting see *CL*, vii. 33.   *the O.M.*: Order of Merit, conferred upon TH in 1910; Gosse had evidently added the 'O.M.' when addressing an envelope to TH.

[Henry Reed, best known as a poet and radio dramatist, came from a working-class background, won a Classics scholarship to Birmingham University, transferred to English studies, and by 1936 had completed an impressive MA thesis on Hardy. He subsequently embarked on an assiduously researched but never completed Hardy biography, endured the war service that provided the subject-matter for his best-known poems, and wrote, together with translations from French and Italian, a series of highly successful radio plays, one of them, *A Very Great Man Indeed*, prompted by his researches into Hardy's life and friendships.]

To Henry Reed

MAX GATE, | DORCHESTER, | DORSET.
25th Dec. [1936]

Dear Mr Reed,

I have been thinking very long & seriously about the book we discussed when you were here, and the more I think about it the more impossible it seems. My own memory is not good & becomes worse & worse, & probably I have exaggerated in my own mind much that was told me, &, as for Miss Hardy, she is an old lady in bad health, who has, during the last few days lost her nearest surviving relative & she will not see any stranger, nor will the doctor allow her to do so. Moreover she would refuse to discuss any member of her family with anyone. It is possible that I built up a great deal on a few careless remarks from prejudiced persons. I should be very sorry to put into print more than is in my biography as there is not a scrap of documentary evidence to go upon.

Also, with regard to a stage version of 'The Dynasts'—I find that my husband left very special instructions about that, & any performance by amateurs, except the O.U.D.S, is prohibited. I am sorry to be so negative on both these points, but I hope you will understand.

With seasonable wishes,

Yours sincerely,
Florence Hardy.

Text   MS. (with envelope) Millgate.   *Date*   Year from postmark.
Reed: Henry Reed (1914–86), poet and radio dramatist.   *the book*: Reed, perhaps encouraged by the freedom with which FEH talked to him about her husband, had apparently suggested the possibility of a book based on conversations with her and with Kate Hardy, still living at Talbothays.   *relative*: Polly Antell; see letter of 20 Dec. 1936.

To Seymour Adelman

MAX GATE, | DORCHESTER, DORSET.
January 3rd 1937.

Dear Mr Adelman,

I am greatly obliged for your interesting letter. It is always a pleasure to me to know that association copies of the works of my husband are in the keeping of someone who cares to possess them. Of all contemporary English poets I think that A. E. Housman was nearest to my husband in thought & expression. I should say *undoubtedly* the volume you bought must have been sent to Mr Housman at the request of my husband. I believe he had a copy of every volume of poetry he published sent to Professor Housman. In England we just say A. E. Housman.

I have looked through a small collection of letters sent to my husband by A.E.H. & unfortunately there is not one there acknowledging the gift of 'Poems of the Past and present', though there is a *most* interesting one acknowledging the gift of "Satires of Circumstance," naming the poems which most appealed to A.E.H. A list of the titles of poems marked in your volume would be of great interest to me, and I should be much obliged if you would send it to me, as you so kindly suggest.

Certainly if I ever hear of any letter from my husband to A. E. Housman being put up for sale I would let you know immediately.

Unfortunately I allowed a trusted friend to take from the collection of letters written to my husband certain of the most interesting, as he wished to insert these in volumes he had bought. These were NOT SOLD but given, as the friend had promised to give the collection to some Hardy Museum should such be formed. Unfortunately this friend had heavy financial losses & I fear some of the letters were put upon the market.

Again thanking you for the letter & most interesting information, & with all good wishes for 1937,

Yours sincerely,
Florence Hardy.

I fear this is a badly composed letter; written late at night.   F.H.

Text   MS. Bryn Mawr College.
Adelman: Seymour Adelman (d. 1985), American collector of books, manuscripts, and works of art; see *The New Yorker*, 23 Apr. 1979, 38–40.   *the volume*: Housman's copy of TH's *Poems of the Past and the Present*, now in the Bryn Mawr College Library.   *interesting one*: dated 27 Nov. 1914 (DCM); Housman picked out 'In Death Divided', 'At Castle Boterel', 'Regret Not Me', and 'Seen by the Waits'.   *trusted friend*: Howard Bliss.

To Paul Lemperly

MAX GATE, | DORCHESTER, | DORSET.
7th March, 1937

Dear Mr Lemperly,

I had not learned about your operation & the hospital and I am exceedingly sorry to have the news. I trust that soon you will feel absolutely well, & that the feeling of having "aged" will be a thing of the past. I hope that you did not suffer much: even a small operation is a horrible thing. Mrs Lemperly must have been very anxious. I hope that she is well.

I have received the two numbers of "Littell's Living Age" which you so kindly sent me. I hardly like to keep them—& if this forms a gap in your collection I shall feel guilty. But I am most interested to see them, as I had no idea that "An Indiscretion" had been printed in an American magazine—& this being so of course Professor Carl Webber was within his legal rights in printing that little book—but not, of course, in selling it in England, as he tried to do. That printing, by me, of "An Indiscretion" was an unfortunate step indeed. You may know that Sydney Cockerell—whom my husband appointed as co-literary executor with me—wrote a violent letter to the Times Literary Supplement attacking me—to the amazement of even his own friends. This made it quite impossible for me ever to have anything to do with him again—& it is very difficult for me to carry on the work of literary executor unaided. Also, I suppose to revenge himself upon me for not allowing him to sell his books in England, Professor Webber printed in an American periodical—'The Colophon' an article, & extracts from correspondence of many *many* years ago, accusing my husband of plagiarism—of which he always had the greatest horror. It is so easy to read something, then forget it, &, years after recall it, & believe it to be an original thought. In one of George Moore's most brilliant essays—in 'Memoirs of My dead Life'—the one called 'Bring in the Lamp'—he (no, I have just been to look it up & it is the last paragraph—a long one—of the concluding essay 'Resurgam')—he quotes a long passage from 'Fantastics' by Lafcadio Hearn—without quotation marks. Certainly he would never have done such a stupid thing deliberately.

I want to send you a little book—or something that belonged to my husband—as a token of gratitude for many many kindnesses received from you—& I hope you will soon be well. I am writing this, late on Sunday evening, in the dining-room where I used to sit and read to my husband. How quickly the years are slipping away.

Sincerely yours—
Florence Hardy

Text   MS. (with envelope) Colby College.
Lemperly: see letter of 7 Mar. 1919.   *"Living Age"*: TH's 'An Indiscretion in the Life of an Heiress', *Littell's Living Age* (Boston), 5 and 12 Oct. 1878; neither Lemperly nor FEH seems to have known of the earlier and more clearly authorized US printing in *Harper's Weekly*, 29 June–27 July 1878 (Purdy, 274–5). For Lemperly's own interest in 'An Indiscretion' see Dalziel (ed.), *Excluded and Collaborative Stories*, 82–3.   *Webber*: correctly, Weber; his edition of *An Indiscretion* was pub. in Baltimore by the Johns Hopkins University Press in 1935.   *printing, by me*: see letter of 4 July 1935.   *violent letter*: see letter of 28 June 1935; also Dalziel (ed.), *Excluded and Collaborative Stories*, 83–4, and Millgate, *Testamentary Acts*, 166–7.   *amazement of even*: FEH first wrote 'amazement of evening'.   *an article*: Weber's 'A Connecticut Yankee in King Alfred's Country', *The Colophon*, NS 1 (Spring 1936); see also letter of 30 Aug. 1937.   *without quotation marks*: the passage by Moore (whom FEH had known) is certainly reminiscent of Lafcadio Hearn's essay 'Metempsychosis' but seems less directly derivative than FEH suggests.

To Morris Parrish

MAX GATE, | DORCHESTER, DORSET.
3rd April 1937.

Dear Mr Parrish,

I was interested in the little note, written by my husband, which I return to you herewith.

The Mr Foster—J. J. Foster—to whom the letter was sent—was born in Dorchester a few years later than my husband was born, four miles away, at Higher Bockhampton. The father of J. J. Foster, was a bookseller in Dorchester, & the shop is still a bookseller's shop, but now kept by someone named Longman. In this shop little J. J. Foster used to watch Thomas Hardy in the early teens, reading books at his father's counter. He read many books through in this way, & the good-natured bookseller never complained. The little boy J.J.F. used to welcome T.H. because he took to the child some particularly good eating apples, a variety known as 'Bockington Sweet'—no longer to be found. J. J. Foster told me this himself, & he was the only person I ever spoke to who remembered T.H. at that early age.

My husband always spoke of him as 'Jossy' Foster so I imagine his name was Josiah John—or Joshua John. He became an authority on miniatures & wrote a large two volume book about them. He was connected with some Fine Art shop in London.

The book referred to in the letter was 'Some Dorset Worthies'. I think J.J.F. sent my husband the proofs—or at any rate the preface—to correct. I feel certain that T.H. did not write a preface as I fear he was always a little bored by good Mr 'Jossy' Foster. I have spent several hours, not unpleasantly, in looking for the book on *Dorset Worthies*, but with no success. I am afraid that someone may have removed it from the study—but if I find it I will send it to you. Meanwhile I send you all the letters from J. J. Foster that have been preserved. If you care to keep one of them please do so, & then would you kindly return the others. The pencil writing was T.H.'s reply, written by himself for me to copy.

I think Mr Foster died just before my husband—I think he was about six or seven years T.H.'s junior.

I hope you are well and I look forward greatly to seeing you in the autumn if you come to England. I should like much to go to America; there is nothing to prevent me, except that I dislike the idea of the long sea journey.

Sincerely yours,
Florence Hardy.

Text MS. Princeton.

Parrish: Morris Longstreth Parrish (d. 1944), stockbroker and book collector; his important collection of Victorian books and documents is at Princeton.   *Foster*: Joshua James Foster (1847–1923), Dorchester-born art historian and antiquary; his father, James Foster, is listed in the 1861 census as a bookseller and printer employing five men and two boys.   *Longman*: the shop, in Cornhill, Dorchester, is now owned by Blackwell's.   *'Bockington*: i.e.

Bockhampton.   *two volume book*: Foster in fact pub. two 2-vol. works on miniature painting, but FEH's reference is probably to his *Miniature Painters, British and Foreign* (London,
1903).   *Fine . . . London*: Dickinson & Foster, of Bond Street.   *Worthies'*: correctly,
Wessex Worthies (London, 1920). FEH wrote again, 5 Apr. 1937 (Princeton), to report that she
had found TH's copy of *Wessex Worthies* and that he had in fact contributed an Introductory
Note: 'I might have known he would not refuse a few lines.'

[Despite the cheerful tone of Florence Hardy's letter to Morris Parrish, she was
already ill, and by late April or early May 1937 the deterioration in her health had
become unignorable. Tests and consultations followed, a diagnosis of bowel cancer
was confirmed, and by the date of her letter to Christine Wood Homer she had
accepted her doctors' recommendation that she go immediately to London for an
operation. She made a new will, signed and witnessed on 18 May, and added a
codicil, dated 8 June, while she was in the same Fitzroy Square nursing-home to
which she had gone at the time of her previous operations. In the event, the cancer
was deemed inoperable, and she returned to Max Gate a dying woman—addition-
ally saddened by the loss of Barrie, who had come to see her at Fitzroy Square just
a day or two before his own death on 19 June.]

To Christine Wood Homer

MAX GATE, | DORCHESTER.
Friday. [11 May 1937]

My dear Miss Wood Homer,

Thank you so much for your kind letter. I am glad that you liked the
R.S.P.C.A lorry etc. I think more attention is being paid to its work in
Dorchester.

I haven't been much better, thank you for asking. Next week I go to
London for an abdominal operation that I have been fighting against for
some time—NOT appendicitis. But I have had the *best* advice, was Xrayed
in London—& had down a surgeon who was head surgeon at the London
Hospital for many years, and whom I believe in more than any other medical
man—& now I do realize it is *inevitable*. The symptoms are such that I
could not go on much longer—& I am very weak. Please don't mention this
to anyone—as I have to keep quiet & I want to get papers etc a little in
order before I go up. I have told *very few* people & sworn those to secrecy.
How nice of little John Antell. I am glad he is a humane child. I thought he
was a nice boy. So many thanks for your letter. With love to both

Affly—
F.E.H.

(They do not hide the fact that the operation is a heavy one. It is my *fourth*!)

Text MS. (with envelope) Eton.   *Date* From internal evidence and partially legible postmark.
Homer: Eleanor Christine Wood Homer (1884–1975), daughter of farmer and landowner George Wood Homer and his wife Eliza; her pamphlet, *Thomas Hardy and His Two Wives* (Beaminster, 1964), is more concerned with ELH than with FEH.   *R.S.P.C.A*: Royal Society for the Prevention of Cruelty to Animals; the 'lorry' presumably carried displays designed to generate interest in the organization.   *surgeon*: Ernest Charles Lindsay (1883–1943); FEH inscribed to him 'with affectionate gratitude' a copy of *Early Life* (Millgate) and dated it, pathetically, 'October 1938', a year after her death.   *Antell*: John Antell (b. 1931), a grandson of TH's cousin John Antell (see *CL*, i. 92); long active in local politics, he was mayor of Dorchester in 1994.

To Thomas Soundy

MAX GATE, | DORCHESTER, | DORSET.
17th May. [1937]

My dear Tom,

I send you a cheque for the railway fares for June. Please give it to your mother. Also write and tell me about Coronation Day, & what you did. I hope you were not very much overworked—I often wish I could think of something else for you—other than the Carlton, though no doubt the training you are now having will be invaluable to you later—& might help you to any number of good jobs. I wish you could learn more of actual hotel management—but that may come later. Anyhow I don't want you to make yourself ill & miserable.

Your affec. aunt—
Florence.

Text MS. Barbara Jones.   *Date* Year from internal evidence.
railway fares: presumably for him to visit her in Dorchester.   *Coronation Day*: of King George VI, 12 May 1937.   *the Carlton*: he was currently training as junior chef at the Carlton Hotel, Pall Mall.

To Monica Laing

MAX GATE, | DORCHESTER.
Tuesday. [July 1937?]

My dearest Monica—

I wish all blessings to fall on your dear little daughter & yourself & Arthur. If only I were strong I would try to do some thing more for her, & her future—but I may, *even now*, be gaining a little strength. I had a *very* bad turn over the week-end. I hope Pamela will be well soon. I'd love her

to come for a holiday to Weymouth only I can see very very few people—
one person a day should be the limit.

With love—
Your Aunt Florence.

Text   MS. Daphne Wood.   *Date*   From internal evidence.
Laing: née Richardson; see letter of 1 Feb. 1933.   *daughter*: Daphne (now Wood), born 27
June 1937. FEH's letter to M. Laing of 15 May 1937 (D. Wood) enclosed a cheque 'to help with
the expenses—or to buy yourself & the baby some pretty clothes—or anything you like';
on 22 May (D. Wood) she sent a second cheque from the nursing-home, explaining, 'I felt
I might have made the last cheque a bit larger'.   *Arthur*: her husband (see letter of
1 Feb. 1933).   *Pamela*: her sister (see letter of 25 Nov. 1936).

[Florence Hardy spent the last months of her life at Max Gate, always ill and in pain
but supported by her sister Margaret and by professional nurses. Richard Purdy,
visiting Max Gate on 9 July 1937, found her in the drawing-room, lying on a hospital
bed that could be wheeled into the conservatory or the garden; when he came
again on 1 August she was outside, under a marquee, walking a little and seeming
altogether stronger and in better spirits—mildly triumphant, indeed, at having already
survived longer than her doctors had predicted. She lived, in fact, until 15 October
1937, but seems to have written no letters—other, perhaps, than to members of
her own family—later in date than the one which follows. It is, in any case, a
complexly valedictory document—dictated to and typed by someone else, devoted
to the belated restoration of a broken friendship, and voicing a final regretful tribute
to Max Gate itself and all that it had come to represent.]

To Wilfred Partington

MAX GATE, | DORCHESTER, DORSET.
30th. August, 1937.

Wilfred Partington, Esq.,
21. Barons Court Road,
London. W.14.

Dear Mr. Partington,

Thank you so much for sending me a copy of "The Colophon".

Someone in America is sending round articles and letters to detract from
my husband's reputation as a writer. I think it must be an American professor who wanted permission to sell in England copies of copyright work
which of course I could not allow. He was very angry when I refused. Do
what you like about it.

I am glad you wrote again because I wish to tell you that I am so sorry
for that irritable letter I last wrote you. It was the result of the beginning

of a very serious illness which I am told causes that irritability. Three months ago I had a very serious operation and am still very ill indeed. But it seems to me that I have been preserved in a miraculous manner for the past three months. Though I am in bed and looked after by two excellent nurses.

To go back to the letter you might tell Sir Hugh Walpole—that is if you told him about my letter which I have no doubt you did—that I feel I was utterly wrong.

I wish the pleasant hours we spent together had been more in number but this illness has been coming on for quite two years.

I wish I could see you for a few minutes but I suppose that is impossible. Certainly send me anything which I shall read with very great pleasure.

Max Gate seems more beautiful than ever. I feel sorry that a home which has taken over fifty years to build up must so soon be broken up but it is inevitable.

My best wishes to you and I hope your health is good.

With compliments and regards,

Yours sincerely,
Florence Hardy.

Text   MS. (professionally typed) Huntington.

Colophon": evidently the July 1937 issue, containing Carl J. Weber's 'Plagiarism and Thomas Hardy'; see also letter of 7 Mar. 1937.   *American professor*: FEH's obliquity is puzzling (given that the articles are signed) but perhaps reflective either of her enervated condition or of her ambiguous feelings towards Weber, whom she had never met.   *irritable letter*: of 13 Feb. 1936.   *broken up*: after FEH's death, and as directed in her will, first the contents of Max Gate and then the house itself were sold at auction, the purchaser on the latter occasion being Kate Hardy, TH's surviving sister, who in her own will left Max Gate to the National Trust.

Index

Where several entries are listed for a single person, *italic* may be used to identify the principal location of biographical information; the abbreviation 'h.' indicates a reference to one of the editorial headnotes introduced at intervals throughout the volume. In the indexing of letters only the initial page reference is given.

Acland, John Edward 316 & n.
Adams, Frederick B. xxi, 230 h., 333–6, 336 h.,
    337 n.
  FEH letters to 336, 340
Adams, Gillian 337 & n., 340
Adams, Katharine (Webb) 118, 119 n., 129,
    167 & n.
Adams, Ruth 337 & n.
Adelman, Seymour 344 n.
  FEH letter to 343
Adelphi Terrace 284 h., 285, 323, 324 n., 326
Alexandra Club 4 n.
Allbutt, Sir Clifford 81, 82 n., 190, *192 n.*
Allen, C. P. 330 & n.
Allen, J. A. 249
Allhusen, Dorothy xxi, 143, 144 *n.*, 187, 191, 202,
    203 n., 245 & n., 256–7
  memories of TH 255
  FEH letters to 202, 261
Allhusen, Elizabeth 191, 192 n., 202
Allhusen, Henry Christian Stanley 191, 192 n.
Allingham, Helen, *see* Paterson, Helen
Alma, Roger 48 n.
Antell, Gertrude 170 n.
Antell, John (sen.) 170 n.
Antell, John (jun.) 347, 348 n.
Antell, Mary ('Polly') 341, 342 n., 342
Arc, Joan of 39, 139
Archer, William 102, 103 n.
Arnold, Matthew:
  'Poor Mathias' 72 & n.
Arnold, Thomas 24, 26 n.
Ash, Caroline 23 & n., 34
Asquith, Herbert Henry 45 h., 45 & n., 71 n.
Asquith, Lady Cynthia 327 n.
Atkins, Norman 213, 214 n.
Austen, Jane:
  Emma 167
  Northanger Abbey 167
  Persuasion 167

Bain, Francis William:
  A Digit of the Moon 153, 154 n.
Baldwin, Stanley 254
Balfour, Lady Frances 45 h., 49 & n.
Balliol Players 208, 209 n., 237
Baring-Gould, Revd Sabine 6, 7 n.

Barker, Harley Granville- 77 n., 160, *160 n.*, 182,
    188, 198, 234, 234 n., 245, 290 h.
  and *Dynasts* 103 n.
  and Hardy Players 189
  and *Tess* play 226, 229
Barker, Helen Granville- 160 & n., 188, 189, 198,
    245
Barnes, Emily 5 & n.
Barnes, Revd William 5 n.
  statue 291
Barnes, Revd William Miles 5 & n.
Barrie, James M. ix, *128 n.*, 128, 156, 184, 185 n.,
    218 n., 233 n., 241, 263, 276, 289 & n., 313,
    323, 324 h., 326, 329, 347 h.
  and FEH xx, xxi, 271, 284 h., 285, 290 & n.,
    291
  and TH dramatizations 127, 174–5, 205, 215,
    217–18, 218 n., 221, 238–9, 294
  and TH 'Life' 267–8, 269, 279 h., 298, 299,
    300 n.
  and TH's obsequies 261 h., 301 n., 304
  Dear Brutus 135
Bartelot, Evelyn 55 n.
  ELH letter to 54
Bartelot, Revd R. G. 35 n., 55 n.
  ELH letters to 35, 55
Bateson, Edith 221 & n.
Baughan, Edward 174, 175 n.
Beerbohm, Florence and Max xxi, 200 & n.,
    302, 310
Bennett, Arnold:
  on FEH 322 & n.
  Lord Raingo 244
Benson, Arthur Christopher 245 & n.
  Diary 243 h., 245
Benson, Edward Frederic:
  An Autumn Sowing 136, 137 n.
Bible 3, 19, 21, 32 & n., 33, 42, 43, 51, 55, 96, 167,
    168 n., 210
Birkin, Andrew 233 n.
Birrell, Augustine 166
Björk, Lennart 41 n.
Blanche, Jacques-Émile 173 & n.
Bliss, Howard *176 n.*, 237 h.
  as FEH's advisor xxi, xxii, 286 h., 313, 315–16
  given Max Gate items 287 & n., 302 & n.,
    304, 320, 336, 344

Bliss, Howard (*cont.*):
  and *Woodlanders* MS. 286 h., 286
  FEH letters to 175, 217, 237, 251, 286, 301, 304,
    312, 313, 315, 334
  FEH letters cited 273 h., 314 n., 335 n.
Blomfield, Sir Arthur 148, 149 n., 284 h.
Blunden, Edmund 146 h., 185–6, *186 n.*, 244 &
  n., 263 n., 278, 309
  FEH letter to 243
Blunden, Mary 244 & n., 248
Blunt, Wilfrid Scawen 118, 119 n., 186
Blyth, James, Lord 169, 170 n.
Boer War, *see* South African War
Boscastle 80, 119
Boughton, Rutland 208 *n.*, 226, 330 n.
  The Immortal Hour 225 h., 226, 227, 228 n.
  Queen of Cornwall (musical setting) 208 & h.
  FEH letters to 207, 315
Brennecke, Ernest, jun. 222, 223 n.
Bridges, Robert 160 & n.
Bridgman, Laura 39, 41 n.
Bright, Reginald Golding 221 & n., 226, 294, 296
British Broadcasting Company 322 n., 328 h.
British Museum xvi, 315
  FED letter to 59
Brontë, Charlotte 95, 106 h.
Brooke, Rupert 148, 149
Brousson, Jean Jacques 282, 283 n.
Brown, Curtis 281 & n., 287–8, 331
Brown, Martha 235 & n., 339
Browning, Elizabeth Barrett 3 h., 13, 14 n., 182,
  312
  'To Flush, My Dog' 72 & n.
Browning, Robert 3 h., 155, 312
Bugler, Diana (Toms) 294, 295 n.
Bugler, Ernest Frank 128 n., *171 n.*, 226, 243, 294,
  297
Bugler, Gertrude 126–7 h., *128 n.*, 193, 243, 297
  Barrie on 127, 174–5, 217–18, 218 n., 238–9
  and FEH xix, 127 h., 175 n., 182 h., 183 n.,
    214 h., 218 h., 221, 242 h.
  and TH 171, 172, 212 h., 214 h.
  in *Return of the Native* 171, 172, 174, 175 n.
  as Tess 212 h., 213, 225 h., 227–8, 238–9, 242
  as Tess in London 293 h., 293–6
  FEH letters to 174, 182, 183, 188, 214, 217, 219,
    227, 295
  FEH letters cited 218 n., 218 h., 243 n., 296 n.
Bulkeley, Henry Charles 126 & n.
Buller, Lady Audrey 18, 20 n.
Buller, Sir Redvers 18, 20 n.
Bunyan, John:
  statue 291, 292 n.
Burne-Jones, Edward 313
Burne-Jones, Philip 205 n.
Burns, John 173 & n.
Bury, John Bagnell 79 & n.

Butler, Samuel 165 & n., 192
  The Way of All Flesh 191–2, 192 n.
Butterfield, Harry Greenwood 132, 133 n., 137,
  139

Carr, J. Comyns 46 n.
Carter, John 337 n.
  (and Graham Pollard) *An Enquiry into the
  Nature of Certain Nineteenth Century
  Pamphlets* 324, 325 n.
Casson, Lewis 215, 216 n.
Cecil, Lady Evelyn 209, 210 n.
Chadwick, Esther Alice 95 & n.
  In the Footsteps of the Brontës 95 & n.
Channing, Mary 157 & n.
Chant, Mrs Ormiston 6, 7 n.
  Why We Attacked the Empire 7 n.
Charles, Emily 276 & n.
Chekhov, Anton 133 & n.
  Uncle Vanya 237
Chesterton, Gilbert Keith 261 h., 274, 275 n.
Chew, Samuel C.:
  FEH letter to, cited 223 n.
Child, Harold 231, 298, 299, 300 n.
Chopin, Frederic 22
Churchill, Elizabeth 28 n.
  ELH letter to 27
Clifford, Sophia Lucy (Mrs W. K.) 177, 178 n.
Clodd, Arthur 82 n., 122
Clodd, Edward xi–xii, xvii, *12 n.*, 115, 118
  and Aldeburgh 12 n., 31 & n., 60 h., 62 n.,
    65–6, 66 n., 68, 74 n., 77, 78, 80, 81, 82 n.,
    84 & n., 156
  Enfield lecture 73, 74 n., 75–6, 77 n.
  Memories 113, 121, 122
  Pioneers of Evolution 11–12, 12 n.
  ELH letter to 11
  FED letters to 60, 65, 66, 68, 73, 75, 76, 78,
    80 (2), 82, 83, 86, 91
  FED letter cited 59 n.
  FEH letter to 121
Clodd, Phyllis 122 & n.
Cobbett, William 331
Cockerell, Christopher 106, 107 *n.*, 133, 210, 229,
  234, 277
Cockerell, Kate (Mrs S. C.) 82, 83 n., *94 n.*, 116,
  126, 173, 209, 234, 245 & n., 255, 257, 263,
  264, 277, 285
  and ELH's bath-chair 134 & n.
  FEH letter to 93
Cockerell, Katharine 106, 107 n., 133, 181, 234
Cockerell, Margaret 106, 107 n., 152, 229
Cockerell, Sydney Carlyle 82, 83 n., *85 n.*, 112 h.,
  262, 272, 284–5, 299, 332 n.
  and FED 85 h., 88
  and FEH viii, xvii, xxi, xxiii–xxiv, 113, 122 h.,
    124, 128, 178, 210 h., 219, 224, 299, 329

assists FEH xviii, 119, 125, 132, 133 n.,
156–7, 190, 221, 228, 229 n., 249; *see also*
Hardy, Florence, privately printed
pamphlets
and TH xvii, 122 h., 124, 162, 163 n., 173,
223 n., 255
and TH 'Life' 139, 270–1, 276–7, 278–9, 281
as TH's literary executor xviii, 115, 116, 267,
271, 279 h., 280, 281, 286–8, 288 n., 310 h.,
313, 328 h., 329, 331 & n., 344–5
and TH memorial 290 h., 291–2, 295
and TH proofs 170, 181, 193
and C. Mew 142, 143 n., 146 h., 148, 153,
201 n., 204
Book of Hours of Yolande of Flanders 93, 94 n.
FED letter to 85
FEH letters to 93, 106, 114, 117, 119, 120, 125,
129, 130, 131, 133, 137, 139, 140, 142, 144, 147,
151, 152, 154, 155, 161, 162, 164, 167, 172, 179,
181, 186, 190, 192, 194, 195, 197, 199, 200,
204, 209, 213, 220, 226, 228, 229, 234, 236,
245, 246, 249, 254, 256, 258, 259, 260, 263,
264, 275, 276, 278, 280, 284, 287, 291, 294,
310
FEH letters cited 137 h., 154 h., 160 n., 173 n.,
175 n., 197 h., 201 n., 203 h., 207 n., 208 n.,
225 h., 229 n., 232 h., 239 n., 240 n., 243 h.,
245 n., 247 h., 253 h., 255 n., 279 h., 284 h.,
250 n.
FEH telegrams cited 250 n., 261 n.
Coleridge, Sir John Duke, Lord 21, 22 n.
Coleridge, Samuel Taylor 34, 35 n., 52
Collins, Vere H. 267 & n.
Colophon, The 345 & n., 349
Colville, Sir Stanley 83 n.
Colvin, Sidney:
John Keats 137, 138 n., 140
Compton, Fay 221 & n.
Congreve, Madeleine 202 & n.
Connolly, James 125
Conrad, Jessie 209
Conrad, Joseph 178, 179 n., 198–9, 209
Constable, John 325, 327 n.
Corbett-Winder, Revd Edmund 157 & n.
Corelli, Marie (Mary Mackay) 10, 11 n.
Cornhill Magazine 3 n., 95
Cosens, Dr William Burroughs 151 & n.
Courtney, William 153, 154 n.
Cowley, Ethel 157 & n.
Cowley, Revd Henry 157 & n., 167, 280
Cox, J. Stevens 325 n.
Crabbe, George 31 & n., 155
Crackanthorpe, Blanche 153, 154 n.
Crewe, Robert Offley Ashburton Crewe-Milnes,
Lord 196, 197 n., 321, 322 n.
Crippen, Hawley Harvey 68, 69 n.
Crossley, Florence, Lady 137

Daily Chronicle 17 n., 23 h.
ELH letters to 16, 24
Daly, Augustin 4 n.
Dalziel, Pamela xiii & n., 280 n., 345 n.
d'Arville, Anne 47, 48 n.
Darwin, Charles 11
Davies, Sylvia Llewelyn 233 n.
Davray, Henry D. 141, 142 n.
Dean, Basil 216 & n.
Debenham, Ernest 173 & n.
de Bunsen, Sir Maurice and Lady 209, 210 n.
de la Mare, Constance 198, 199 n., 199
de la Mare, Walter 177, 178 n., 198, 199, 205 n.,
263, 328
Detmold, Edward Julius 95 & n.
Dickens, Charles 103 h., 152, 153 n.
Dickinson, Goldsworthy Lowes 148, 149 n.,
303 & n.
Dickinson, Revd. John Harold 119, 120
Don, Archibald 148 & n.
Dorchester xx, 34, 47, 76, 87, 346
Dorchester Debating and Dramatic Society
46 h., 47, 52, 53 n., 65 n., 73 n., 74 h., 126 n.,
126 h., 138 & n., 231
literary competition judged by FEH 192,
194 n.
see also Hardy Players
Dorchester Grammar School 291, 316
Dorset County Chronicle:
ELH article in 44 h.
ELH letter to 49
Dorset County Hospital xx, 291, 293 & n.
Dorset County Museum ix, 316, 335, 336–7
Douglas, Sir George 306 & n.
Douglas, Mary Helena 306 & n.
Doughty, Charles Montagu 168 n., 192, 236, 237 n.
Mansoul 167, 168 n.
Doughty, Dorothy 167, 168 n.
Doyle, Lady Conan 29 n.
Dreiser, Theodore:
The 'Genius' 222, 223 n.
Drew, Charles D. 336, 337 n.
Drinkwater, John 188, 188 n., 203 h., 205, 242 h.,
243 n.
Duchy of Cornwall 341
Dugdale, Constance 71 h., 87, 89 n., 91, 92 n., 92,
319 n., 338
Dugdale, Edward 71 h., 92, 93 n., 150, 152, 153 n.,
318 h., 319 n., 331, 337–8
Dugdale, Emma 61, 62 n., 67, 69, 70, 167, 249,
264, 289–90
Dugdale, Eva 123, 125 n., 152, 159, 162, 163 n., 174,
175 n., 178, 184, 190, 258, 259, 272
DUGDALE, FLORENCE EMILY (later Hardy, q.v.)
viii, xiii, 91
and ELH xvi–xvii, xxii, 50 & n., 52 h., 60 h.,
60–4, 64 h., 66, 68, 71 h.

DUGDALE, FLORENCE EMILY (*cont.*):
and TH xiii, xvii, 59 h., 59–61, 66, 68, 73–4,
74 h., 75, 77, 78, 85 h., 86–7, 88, 90 h.,
92–3
and TH/ELH marriage 66, 71 h., 76
political views 70
religious views 70, 71 n., 72, 90
WRITINGS 69
book reviewing for *Sphere* 85, 86 n.
journalism 60 h., 60
stories in *Cornhill* 95, 95 n.
The Book of Baby Beasts 70 n., 95 n.
'The Silver Bell' 71 & n.
Dugdale, Margaret (later Soundy, q.v.) *119 n.*
marriage of 118, 123, 130 & n., 132

Edgcumbe, Sir Robert Pearce 145 & n.
Edis, Olive 98, 99 n.
Edward, Prince of Wales 197 h.
as King 340 & n., 341
at Max Gate 201 & n., 341
Ellenborough, Cecil Henry Law, Lord 157 & n.
Eliot, George 106 h., 280 n.
Elliott, Gertrude (Lady Forbes-Robertson)
216 & n.
Ellis, Stewart Marsh 155 & n.
George Meredith 155, 156
Epstein, Jacob 295 & n.
Ervine, Leonora:
FEH letter to, cited 273 h.
Euripides:
Hippolytus 238 n.
Oresteia 209 n.
Evans, Alfred Herbert 46 n., 65 n., 170 h., 243 n.
ELH letter to 46
Evans, Laura 46 & n.
Eves, Reginald 203 h.
Everett, Augusta 307 n.
Everett, Revd Henry 307 n.
Everett, John 307 & n.

Fairfield, Cicily Isabel, *see* West, Rebecca
Fare, Ethel 193, 194 n.
Fawcett, Henry 39, 41 n.
Fawcett, Millicent 38 h., 41 n., 45 h.
Felkin, Elliott 148, 149 n.
Fetherstonhaugh, Teresa 250, 250 n., 275, 303, 338
Fetherstonhaugh-Frampton, Beryl 250, 250 n.,
275, 327 n.
Ffooks, Dorothy 198, 199 n.
Ffrangcon-Davies, Gwen 225 h., 226–7, 227 n.,
228 & n., 294
as Tess 229–31, 238, 239 n., 242, 296
Filmer, A. E. 227 n.
Fisher, William W. 82, 83 n.
Fitzgerald, Edward:
The Rubáiyát of Omar Khayyám 19, 20 n.

Fitzgerald, Penelope 225 n.
Fitzwilliam Museum 85 h., 331
Flecker, James Elroy:
Hassan 216 n.
Fleming, Albert 112 h., 116 n.
Fletcher, Sir John Samuel 69, 70 n.
Flower, Newman 174, 175 n., 200, 226, 272–3,
273 n.
Forbes-Robertson, Sir Johnston 216 & n.
Ford, Ford Madox 232 n.
Fordington St George:
Amazon Society 49
Children's Guild 55 & n.
Forster, Alice 246 & n., 274, 280
FEH letter to, cited 246 n.
Forster, Edward Morgan 176 h., 178 n., 187, 303,
305, 323
and FEH xx, xxi, 213, 236, 263, 278, 306
and TH 186
Pharos and Pharillon 206 & n.
FEH letters to 177, 206, 246, 274, 279, 330
FEH letter cited 279 h.
Foster, Joshua James 345–6, 346 n.
Wessex Worthies 347 n.
Fox-Strangways, Lady Mary 157 & n.
France, Anatole 282 & n.
Freeman, Mary Wilkins:
'The Cat' 21, 22 n.
Frohman, Charles 215, 216 n.

Gainsborough, Thomas:
statue of 292 & n.
Galpin, Stanley 174, 175 n.
Galsworthy, Ada:
FEH letter to, cited 214 n.
Galsworthy, John xvi n., 166, 195, 245
Forsyte Saga 340
Gandhi, Mohandas 251 & n.
Garland, Hamlin 326–7, 327 n.
Garnett, David 275 n.
Garrick, David 284 h., 323, 332 & n.
Gatty, Hester 320, 321 n.
George III, King 120
George V, King 311
George VI, King 341
George, Frank 109, 109 n., 142 n.
Gifford, Charles Edwin 52, 53 & n.
Gifford, Edwin Hamilton (Archdeacon) 75, 76 n.,
80, 81, 87, 148
GIFFORD, EMMA LAVINIA (later Hardy, q.v.) viii,
x, xiii, 4 h.
courtship correspondence ix–x, 3 h., 3, 312
Gifford, Gordon 13, 14 n., 18–19, 80 & n., 161, 285
Gifford, Helen 33 & n., 148
Gifford, John Attersoll 36, 37 n., 78, 88, 89 n.
Gifford, Leonora 53 n.
ELH letter to 51–3

Gifford, Lilian *14 n.*, 27 h., 28 n., 55 n., 75, 81,
　86–8
　in asylum 159 h., 159–60, 161
　on ELH 84
Gifford, Randolph 88, 89 n.
Gifford, Richard Ireland 88, 89 n.
Gifford, Walter ix, 14 n.
Gillon, Stair Agnew 126, 127 n.
Gissing, George 229
　see also Roberts, Morley
Gittings, Robert 67 n., 72 n., 74 n., 159 h.
Glastonbury Festival 208 & n., 209–10
Gordon, Charles George 152–3, 154 n.
Gosse, Edmund ix, 116, *116 n.*, 141, 142 n., 187,
　201, 277, 302, 341
　correspondence with TH 287, *333*, *335*
　death of 257 n.
　and M. Murry 253 h., 253–4, 255–6, 256 n.
　and G. Moore 207 & n.
　as potential literary executor 329
　and projected edition of TH letters 270,
　271 n., 271, 272 n.
　The Life of Algernon Charles Swinburne 130,
　131 n.
　FEH letters to 253, 255, 257, 266, 270
　FEH letter cited 271 n.
Gosse, Nellie 248, *248 n.*, 267 & n., 270
Gowring, Dr Benjamin 190–1, 192 n.
Graham, Derrick 83 & n., 122
Graham, Edith 78, 79 n., 88, 122
Grahame, Elspeth xii, 16 n.
　ELH letter to 15
Grahame, Kenneth xii, 15, 16 n.
Grand, Sarah (Frances Elizabeth M'Fall):
　Babs the Impossible 23 & n.
Graves, Robert 145 h., 303
　Goodbye to All That 302–3, 303 n.
Gray, Thomas 34, 35 n., 191
Great War, The, *see* World War I
Green, Mary 102, 103 n.
Green, Peter 16 n.
Greet, Ben 239 & n.
Gregory, Alyse 308 & n., 327
Grey, Lord Edward 166, 167 n.
Grey, Lady Pamela 255 & n.
Gribble, Vivien (Doyle Jones) 314 n.
Grove, Lady Agnes 30 h., *32 n.*
　and TH 30 h., 36 h.
　'How Time Began to Count' 31–2, 32 n.
　The Social Fetich xi–xii, 36 h., 36–7, 37 n.
　ELH letters to 31, 36
Grove, Sir Walter 32 n., 37

Haggard, H. Rider 84 & n.
Haig, Field-Marshal Earl:
　statue of 295 & n.
Hanbury, Caroline Fox 209 & n.

Hanbury, Cecil 129 n., 167, 168 n.
Hanbury, Effield Dorothy 111, *112 n.*, 129 n., 167,
　168 n., 179
Hardy, Emma Lavinia (née E. L. Gifford, q.v.)
　xxii, 21, 33, 104 n., 115, 134 n., 232, 302 n.,
　348 n.
　and animals xii, 10, 12, 16–17, 17 n., 49–50,
　50 n., 72, 237 h.
　on authors 10, 26–7, 48
　and children 3 n., 19, 24–5, 28–9, 31–2, 49–50,
　54, 55 n., 55, 142
　as correspondent viii, ix–xii, xvi, 312, 323–4
　and cycling 12 h., 13
　death of xiii, 74 h., 79, 158, 193, 205, 320 & n.
　on Devon 18, 23, 52
　on Dorchester and Dorset 23, 48, 52
　and FED xvi–xvii, 50 & n., 60 h.
　on evil-speaking 8, 21, 23, 34–5
　and Gifford family history 35–6, 36 n.
　and TH ix–x, xi–xiii, 4 h., 6, 10, 13, 15–16,
　18–19, 33, 38, 42, 47, 48 & n., 75, 77, 78,
　80, 86–8, 91–2, 106 h., 114, 134, 160 n.
　and TH's family 7 h., 7–8, 15, 27 & n., 30 h.
　and TH's writing 4 h., 175–6, 176 n., 217 & n.
　health 7 h., 9, 13, 21, 32, 34, 35, 36 n., 41, 45,
　48, 61 & n.
　reading 9–10, 11, 13, 21, 23, 31, 36, 38
　religious views xvii, 11–12, 16, 19, 23, 32, 33,
　42 h., 42–3, 51, 52
　social views 21, 23 h., 24–6, 33
　and women's rights xii, 6, 7 n., 38 h., 39–41,
　45 h., 45, 48, 49, 50, 53 & n., 54
　writings xii, xvi–xvii, 30 h., 32, 38 h., 44 h., 50
　　'The Acceptors' 50 n., 61–2, 63, 63–4, 67
　　Alleys 55 n., 68 n.
　　diaries 75, 77, 78, 114
　　'The Inspirer' xvii, 63 & n., 64
　　'The Maid on the Shore' 30 h., 62 & n.,
　　62–3, 63 n., 67
　　poems 21, 22 n., 30, 31 n., 67 & n., 69
　　Some Recollections 76 n., 85, 86 n.
　　Spaces 55 n., 64 n.
　　'The Trumpet Call' 63
　　FED letters to 61, 61, 62, 63, 67, 69, 70, 72
Hardy, Florence Emily (née F. E. Dugdale,
　q.v.) 111, 285 n., 297, 322, 342–3, 343 n.
　and animals 237 h., 237, 251–2, 347
　　see also Max Gate, animals *and* Wessex
　　(dog)
　and bereavement 262, 264, 273 h., 274, 277,
　290, 296, 297, 299, 308
　and children 106 h., 106, 108, 208, 218, 263
　as correspondent viii–ix, xv–xvi, xx
　emotional states xix & n., 102, 135, 173, 219,
　234, 247, 283, 284, 327–8
　financial concerns 314, 323, 336
　　see also Max Gate

HARDY, FLORENCE EMILY (*cont.*):
and Gifford family 134, 148, 159 h.
on ELH 175–6, 193, 217, 234, 237 h.
and TH xiv, xxii, 98–9, 104, 105, 111, 112 h.,
152 & n., 184, 193, 214 h., 247 h., 275, 303,
307, 313, 339, 341–2
health 107, 108, 132, 135, 137, 162, 163 n., 164,
176 n., 190–1, 206, 210 h., 210–12, 213, 225
final illness 347 h., 347, 348–9, 349 h., 350
and literary executorship 279 h., 280, 299, 326
see also Hardy, Thomas, wills *and*
Cockerell, Sydney Carlyle, as TH's
literary executor
as magistrate xx, 149 h., 208 & n., 236
political and social views 100 h., 100, 106 h.,
125, 169, 192, 203, 208 & n., 251, 315 h.,
337, 340
and privately printed TH pamphlets 119, 121,
125, 126 n., 133–4, 140 & n., 144, 158,
159 n., 162, 163, 164, 170, 171 n., 176 & n.,
180, 181 n., 198, 223 & n., 249, 250 n., 254,
255 n., 259–60, 260 n.
reading aloud to TH 136, 137, 146–7, 152, 153,
165, 170, 191–2, 192, 195, 225, 229, 237,
243 h., 244 & n., 245, 248, 252
religious views 102
secretarial assistance to TH xiv, xv, 99,
106 h., 112 h., 136, 168
travel plans 298–9, 306, 346
voluntary work 315, 317
see also Dorset County Hospital *and* Mill
Street Housing Society
wills 132, 133 n., 288, 329, 347
work on TH's 'Life' xiv, 131 h., 133, 137 h., 137,
139, 143, 152, 154 h., 157, 164 & n., 213,
237 h., 239–40, 241, 262
WRITINGS 95, 99, 213
articles for *Weekly Dispatch* xiv & n.,
190 & n.
book reviews for *Sphere* 86 n., 95, 124
stories for *Sunday Pictorial* xiii & n., 106 h.,
108 & n.
The Early Life of Thomas Hardy: completion
of 261 h., 266 n., 267–71, 271 n., 272 n.,
273 h., 274, 277, 305 h.; proofs of 278–9,
279 h., 280 & n., 281; reception of 289,
290 & n., 309, 321, 322 n.; *see also* work
on TH's 'Life' (above)
The Later Years of Thomas Hardy ('Part II'):
completion of 261 h., 279, 290, 292,
293 n., 296–9, 303, 305 h. & n.; reception
of 35 & n., 35 h., 309, 321, 322 n.; *see also*
work on TH's 'Life' (above)
Hardy, Henry 73 n., 78, 99, 136, 166, 171, 212,
258, 264
death of 284 h., 284–5, 285 n., 289
and C. Dugdale 71 h.

health 94, 96, 193
and L. Gifford 87, 88, 92
and TH memorial 291
and M. Hardy's death 110
FED postcard to 73
FED postcards cited 64 h.
Hardy, Jane 79
Hardy, Jemima 8, 16 n., 79, 104 n., 156
Hardy, John 79, 99 & n.
Hardy, Katharine 8, 64 n., 71 h., 75, 99, 110, 112,
130, 165, 166, 171, 264, 276, 297
and ELH and Gifford family ix, 78, 88, 92,
96, 234, 285
health 341, 342–3
and TH's death 258, 259
and TH memorial 291, 295
at performance of *Tess* 239 & n.
and purchase of Max Gate 350 n.
FED postcard to 64
Hardy, Mary (TH's grandmother) 79
Hardy, Mary (TH's sister) 8 n., 16 n., 99
death 109 h., 110, 193
and ELH ix, 7 h., 7–8, 16 n., 88, 96, 234
and TH's writings 115
ELH letter to 7
FED postcard to 72
FED postcards cited 64 h.
Hardy, Teresa 276 & n.
Hardy, Thomas (TH's grandfather) 79, 99 & n.
as 'ghost' 165 & n.
Hardy, Thomas (TH's father) 4 h., 79
Hardy, Thomas (radical politician) 331, 332 n.
HARDY, THOMAS:
and animals 65–6, 74
see also Wessex (dog)
and architecture 202 & n., 203 n., 273 & n.,
339 n.
and children 28–9, 29 n., 141, 142, 203
correspondence xviii, 316, 319–20, 321, 322 n.,
326, 333, 335 & n., 343
see also Hardy, Florence, secretarial
assistance to TH
and criticism 180, 242, 257, 259
death and obsequies 253–61, 261 h., 262,
264–6, 266 n., 269, 272–3, 273 n., 274–5,
297, 304, 313
destroying MSS. 138, 154 h., 155, 156
see also *The Poor Man and the Lady* (below)
on Dorset and its people 141, 341
English Men of Letters vol. on 263 & n., 309
sees ghosts and visions 165, 120–1
health 75, 78, 79, 81–5, 94, 113, 118, 124, 132,
133 n., 150, 168–9, 171, 177, 179, 180, 186–7,
194, 195, 203, 208, 220, 224, 228, 235, 238,
241, 245 & n.
on himself 133, 157, 189, 233, 273, 346
honours 68, 69 n., 97, 98 n., 160 & n., 193, 232

as magistrate 149 h., 151 & n.
memorials to 265 n., 290 h., 291–2 295, 300,
301 n., 303, 305 n., 312–13, 313 n., 329
and Nobel Prize 245, 278 & h.
personal traits 73, 76–7, 129–30, 140, 162–3,
194, 202, 203, 210, 236, 252
on poetry 129, 140, 145, 263, 264, 274
political views 125, 131, 192, 208 n., 241 & n.
portraits 173, 203 h.
as professional author 68, 74, 165–6, 171, 180,
195, 198, 220, 225 & n., 232 h., 249, 264,
345
religious views 167, 188, 209 & n., 282
in wartime 100 h., 100, 117, 126, 140
see also Max Gate, in wartime
wills 112 h., 115, 116, 187, 188 n., 264, 270, 271,
278, 287, 307, 313, 329, 335
see also Cockerell, S., as literary executor
ELG letters to 3
ELH postcards to 44
NOVELS:
Desperate Remedies 4 h.
dramatization (*A Desperate Remedy*)
185 & n., 189, 191, 193
Far from the Madding Crowd 3 & n., 6 n.
manuscript 137, 138 n., 139
dramatizations 46 & n., 47, 231
projected film 90
Jude the Obscure xiii, 10 & n., 71 h., 105, 156,
157, 203
projected dramatization 230–1
The Mayor of Casterbridge 315 h.
dramatization 242 h., 243 & n.
A Pair of Blue Eyes 3 n., 175, 176 n.
manuscript 287 n., 301, 316
The Poor Man and the Lady:
manuscript 118, 119 n., 129, 130 n., 137–8
The Return of the Native:
dramatization 170 h., 171 & n., 172, 174,
175 n.
Tess of the d'Urbervilles 6, 35 n., 45 n., 102, 242
dramatization (by Stoddard) 9, 10 n.
The Trumpet-Major:
dramatization 47 & n., 231 & n., 242
Two on a Tower 23 & n.
Under the Greenwood Tree 65 n., 79, 223
manuscript 118, 337 & n.
dramatization (*The Mellstock Quire*)
65 & n., 68, 69 n., 138 & n.
The Well-Beloved 9, 10 n.
lost manuscript 283–4
The Woodlanders 322
manuscript 175–6, 176 n., 217 & n.
dramatization 86, 89 h., 96, 126 h., 127
STORIES:
A Changed Man 84 & n.
Life's Little Ironies 268

'Absent-Mindedness in a Parish Choir' 268 n.
'The Distracted Preacher' (dramatization)
52, 53 n., 73 n.
'The Duke's Reappearance' 84 & n.
'The Fiddler of the Reels' 189
An Indiscretion in the Life of an Heiress
328 h., 344, 345 n.
'Old Andrey's Experience as a Musician'
268 n.
'Old Mrs Chundle' 280 & n., 281, 288,
328 h., 331
'On the Western Circuit' 189
'The Romantic Adventures of a Milkmaid'
90 & n.
'The Three Strangers' 189, 231
'A Tradition of Eighteen Hundred and
Four' 162, 163 n.
'A Tragedy of Two Ambitions' 189
OTHER PROSE:
Early Life of Thomas Hardy, see Hardy,
Florence, WRITINGS
Later Years of Thomas Hardy, see Hardy,
Florence, WRITINGS
Life and Work of Thomas Hardy ('Life'), *see*
Hardy, Florence Emily, work on TH
'Life'
Dorchester Grammar School address 249,
250 n., 265
'G. M.: A Reminiscence' 255
Preface to J. J. Foster's *Wessex Worthies*
346, 347 n.
Preface to TH's *Late Lyrics and Earlier* 180,
181 n.
South Street clock letter 339 & n.
VERSE:
Human Shows 220, 221, 232 h., 233
Late Lyrics and Earlier 180–2
Moments of Vision 141, 142 n.
Satires of Circumstance 103 h., 103–5, 343
Winter Words 261 h., 262–4, 268 & n.,
276 n., 290
MS. and proofs 270 & n., 276, 277
'And there was a great calm' 170, 171 n.
'Aristodemus the Messenian' 277 & n.
'At Castle Boterel' 344 n.
'Before and After Summer' 96 & n.
'Before Marching and After' 109, 141
'Channel Firing' 96 & n.
'Christmas in the Elgin Room' 257 & n.,
260 & n.
'Coming up Oxford Street: Evening' 225 & n.
'The Dark-Eyed Gentleman' 157 & n.
'The Dead and the Living One' 112 h.
'The Death of Regret' 105
'Domicilium' 138, 140, 144
Epitaphs (on Chesterton and Moore)
261 h., 274

HARDY, THOMAS, POEMS (*cont.*):
  'Friends Beyond' 79
  'Haunting Fingers' 180
  'He resolves to say no more' 290
  'The House of Silence' xxi, 308 & n.
  'I need not go' 79
  'In Death Divided' 344 n.
  'In Time of "the Breaking of Nations"' 141
  'The Ivy Wife' 19, 20 n.
  'A Leaving' 320
  'The Oxen' 116 & n.
  'The Pity of It' 107, 108 n., 116, 117 n., 129,
    130 n.
  'Poems of 1912–13' xxii, 89 n., 103 h.
  'A Popular Personage at Home' 233
  'Regret not me' 344 n.
  'The Roman Gravemounds' 68, 69 n., 74
  'Seen by the Waits' 344 n.
  'The Singer Asleep' 152 n.
  'Song of the Soldiers' 116 n.
  'Ten Years Since' 234 & n.
  'To Meet, or Otherwise' 88, 89 n.
  'To Shakespeare After Three Hundred
    Years' 118, 120, 121, 141, 142 n.
  'The Torn Letter' 193
  'The Vanished Choir' 79
  war poems 18
  'Wessex Heights' 104, 105
  'Why do I go on doing these things' 233
  'Winter Night in Woodland' 198, 199 n.
  see also Hardy, Florence, privately printed
    pamphlets
  PLAYS:
  The Dynasts xvi, 59, 154 h., 165, 238 & n.,
    242
    staged 102, 103 n., 343
  The Play of St George 153, 154 n., 171
  The Queen of Cornwall 120 & n., 206, 301,
    302 n.
    staged 204, 205 & n.
    musical setting 208 & n., 315 & n.
  Tess of the d'Urbervilles xix, 212 h., 214 h.,
    214–20
    in London 225 h., 226–30, 230 h., 231, 238
    London revival 293 h., 293–6, 297
  The Three Wayfarers 52, 53 n., 73 & n.,
    223 & n., 295 & n.
  Wessex Scenes from The Dynasts 125, 126 n.,
    127 h., 128, 129 n., 174–5
Hardy, Sir Thomas Masterman 120, 121 n.,
  292 n.
Hardy Players, The xix, 153, 170 h., 207, 212 h.,
  229, 230, 255
  see also Dorchester Debating and Dramatic
  Society *and* Hardy, Thomas, novels *and*
  stories *and* plays
Harper & Brothers 64 n., 240 & n., 241, 253 n.

Harper's Magazine 22 n.
Harrison, Frederic 87–8, 89 n.
Harrison, Frederick 215, 216 n., 216, 219, 220 n.
Hart-Davis, Rupert 233 n., 260 n.
Haweis, Rev. Hugh 7 n.
Haweis, Mary 7 n.
  ELH letter to 6
Hawes, Margaret ix
Hawkins, Sir Anthony Hope 166
Hawkins, Desmond 32 n., 37 n.
Hayne, Mrs Henry 101 & n.
Head, Henry 180, 181 n., 226, 241, 244, 248,
  278 & n.
  medical advice of 210 h., 219, 228, 245, 257,
  258
Head, Ruth 181 n., 212, 226, 241, 244, 248, 251,
  278
  Pages from the Works of Thomas Hardy 181 n.
Hearn, Lafcadio:
  Fantastics 345 & n.
Heelis, Mrs. William, *see* Potter, Beatrix
Hémon, Louis:
  Maria Chapdelaine 195, 196 n.
Henniker, Arthur 74 n.
Henniker, Florence ix, 11 n., 30 h., 74 n., 110, 132,
  191, 237 h.
  and dogs 102, 182
  and ELH 50 n.
  and FED/FEH 79 & n., 113, 123, 196 h., 196
  and TH 73, 104 & n., 105, 168, 198, 200 & n.,
  321
  last illness 187, 196 h., 196–7
Herkomer, Sir Hubert von 90 & n.
Herkomer, Siegfried von 90 & n.
Hicks, John 273 & n., 339 & n.
Higher Bockhampton 64 h., 64, 82, 90 & n., 98,
  312
Hirschmann, Anna 187, 188 n., 196 h.
Hirst, Kathleen 236, 237 n.
Hoare, Lady Alda ix, xx, 48 n., 97 h., 97, 110,
  136, 161
  ELH letter to 47
  FEH letters to 97, 98, 103, 104, 109, 141, 258,
  312
  FEH letters cited 103 h., 106 h., 112 h., 147 n.
Hoare, Sir Henry 48 n., 103, 161
Hoare, Henry Colt 97 h., 100 h., 105, 109, 141,
  142 n., 258 & n.
Hodges, Wilfrid 264, 265 n., 290 h.
Hodgson, Muriel 244
Hodgson, Ralph 244 & n.
Holder, Revd Caddell 3 n., 81, 302 n.
Holder, Helen 3 n., 81, 302 n.
Holst, Gustav 273 & n.
  Egdon Heath 273 & n.
Homer, Christine Wood 348 n.
  FEH letter to 347

Hone, Joseph 180 & n.
Hopper, Nora 21, 22 n.
Hornby, Charles St John 278, 278 n., 290 h., 292, 317, 329
  FEH letter to 300
  FEH letters cited 286 h., 301 n.
Hornby, Cicily 278 & n., 292 & n.
Houghton, Lord (Richard Monckton Milnes) 197 n.
Hounsell, Walter 280, 281 n.
Housman, A. E. 269, 269 n., 277, 343, 344 n.
  FEH letter to 269
Howe, Ena Hay 220 & n.
Hunt, Gladys Mulock Holman 20 & n.
Hunt, Violet 232 n.
  FEH letter to 232
Huntington, Helen, see Barker, Helen Granville-
Huxley, Aldous:
  Jesting Pilate 244 & n.
Hyatt, Alfred H. 73–4, 74 n., 101–2, 103 n.
Hyndman, Rosalind 143 & n.
Hynes, Samuel 270 n.

Ibsen, Henrik 9
  John Gabriel Borkman 9, 10 n.
Ilchester, Helen, Lady 111, 112 n., 119, 123, 157, 290 h.
Incorporated Society of Authors, see Society of Authors
Inge, William Ralph 165 n.
  Outspoken Essays 165 & n., 192
Inglis, Ethel xx & n., 132, 133 n., 136, 138, 152
Inglis, Colonel Henry 133 n., 134
Inglis, Kitty 326, 327
Institute of Journalists 31 & n.

Jackson, Sir Barry 228 & n.
James, Henry ix, 302
Jeune, John Frederic Symons 112 n., 179, 179 n., 209 n.
John, Augustus 221, 221 n., 290 h., 295, 331, 332 n.
Johnson, Diana viii
Johnson, Samuel:
  statue of 291, 292 n.
Jones, Henry Festing:
  Life of Samuel Butler 192

Kavanagh, Arthur 39, 41 n.
Kaye-Smith, Sheila 169, 170 n.
Keats, John 177, 178 n., 186
Keble College, Oxford 295 & n.
Kennedy, Daisy 203 h., 205 & n.
Kenney, Annie 38 h.
Kennington, Eric 300 & n., 303
Keppel, Sonia 111, 112 n.
Kipling, Rudyard ix, 23 n., 67, 68 n., 100, 101 n., 160

Kitchener, Field-Marshal Lord 19, 20 n.
Knight, Ronald D. 275 n.

Laing, Arthur 318, 319 h., 338, 348
Laing, Daphne 348, 349 n.
Laing, Monica 338
  FEH letter to 348
  FEH letter cited 349 n.
  see also Richardson, Monica
Lane, John 50 n., 84
  ELH letters to 50, 51
Lang, Andrew 121, 122 n.
Lawrence, D. H.:
  The Plumed Serpent 237, 243 h.
Lawrence, Sarah 333
Lawrence, T. E. 176 h., 197 h., 227 & n., 238, 303, 341
  and Cloud's Hill 204, 205 n., 227
  family relationships 249–50
  and FEH xvi n., xx, xxi, 305, 329 h., 330, 332–3, 335
  at Max Gate 199, 203 h., 246 & n., 326–7
  Seven Pillars of Wisdom 206 & n., 222, 247 & n., 300
  FEH letter to 274
Lea, Hermann 87, 89 n., 90 & n., 98, 106, 120, 132, 161
Le Gallienne, Richard 9–10, 10 n.
  The Quest of the Golden Girl 9, 10 n.
Lemperly, Paul 130 & n., 159 n.
  FEH letters to 158, 222, 344
Le Neve, Ethel 68, 69 n.
Leslie, Revd Edward 101 n.
Leslie, Margaret 101 & n.
Lindsay, Ernest Charles 347, 348 n.
Linton, Eliza Lynn 19, 20 n., 21, 122, 123
Littell's Living Age 345 & n.
Lloyd George, David 150
Lock, Charles 298 h.
Lock, H. O. 188 n., 213 n., 313, 314
Lock, Joan 314
Lock, Susan Ann 314 & n.
London Society for Women's Suffrage xii
  ELH letters to 45, 49, 51, 53, 54
  ELH postcard cited 49 n.
Lowndes, Marie Belloc 338–9, 339 n., 340
Lucas, E. V. 333 & n.

MacCarthy, Desmond xi, 26, 27 n.
MacCarthy, Lillah (Granville-Barker) 77 & n., 160 & n., 215
MacCarthy, Louise xi, 27 n.
  ELH letter to 26
MacDonald, Malcolm 333 & n.
MacDonald, Ramsay 333 & n.
McDowall, Arthur 138, 138 n., 167 n., 179
McDowall, Mary 84, 84 n., 138, 148, 167 n., 179

McEwan, John 59 n,, 77 n.
McIlvaine, Clarence W. 64 & n.
Mackail, Clare 118, 119 n., 145
Mackail, John William 118, 119, 119 n., 154 n., 156,
313
Life of William Morris 85 & n., 130
Mackail, Margaret 118, 119 & n., 313
Macmillan & Co. 189–90, 198, 233, 265, 276 & n.
royalties from 314
Macmillan, Daniel 240, 240 n., 241, 309, 328 h.
FEH letters to 262, 265, 267, 269, 271, 305, 321,
328
FEH letters cited 240 n., 266 n., 305 n., 322 n.
Macmillan, Sir Frederick 94, 95 n., 148, 164 n.,
223 n., 240 n.
FEH letter to 164
Macmillan, George A. 300 n.
FEH letter to, cited 262 n.
Macmillan, Harold 300 n.
FEH letter to 299
Macmillan, Maurice 240 n.
FEH letter to 239
McMillan, William 295 & n.
M'Taggart, Margaret 126 & n.
Magdalene College, Cambridge 97, 245 n.
Maggs Bros. 134, 140, 144, 254
Major, Ethel 213, 214 n.
Mann, Dr Edward Weller 256–8, 259 n., 259–60,
265, 272, 274, 276
Mansel, Clara 136, 137 n.
Manton, Jo 67 n., 74 n.
Marie Louise, Princess 187, 188 n.
Markham, Violet 53 & n.
Marr, Hamilton 322 n.
FEH letter to 322
Masefield, John xvi n., 102, 177, 201
Massie, John 39, 41 n.
Massingham, H. W. 38 h.
Masterman, C. F. G. 100, 101 n.
Maugham, W. Somerset:
Cakes and Ale 307 & n.
Maurois, André:
Ariel 229, 230 n.
Max Gate viii, ix, xiv, xxi–xxii, 5 n., 12 h., 31 &
n., 52, 183, 184, 230 h., 284 h., 292, 298, 308,
349 h., 350
alterations to 6, 14, 28, 43 h., 88, 96 & n., 313,
314 n.
animals 13, 14, 18, 22, 27, 28 n., 29–30, 30 n.,
31, 38 & n., 65 & n., 68, 292, 304, 314; *see
also* Wessex (dog)
books and papers 313, 314 n., 316, 323–4, 326,
336, 341, 347
condition of 80, 158, 197 h., 320, 334
future of xxi, 286 h., 307, 316, 335, 350 n.
garden 18, 20–1, 22, 129–30, 136, 222, 297
piano 194, 208, 287

running costs 99, 285, 306, 323
servants 9, 27–8, 52, 72, 78, 96, 100–1, 123, 132,
137, 143, 163, 169, 181, 187, 313, 323
TH's study 9, 135, 195, 299, 316
in wartime 123, 125, 128, 129, 131, 148, 151
Meachin, Dr Norman 67 & n.
Medley, Charles Douglas 328–9, 329 n.
Meredith, George 19, 121, 122, 156, 335
Merrick, Leonard 147 & n.
Mew, Anne 178, 178 n., 205 n., 211, 224, 247 n.
Mew, Charlotte 143 n., 146 h., 199 & n., 204,
205 n., 246–7
Civil List pension 153, 200–1, 201 n.
and FEH xvi n., xx, 144, 146 h., 210 h., 211,
225 n.
and TH 144, 146 h., 148, 151–2
The Farmer's Bride, poems from 142–3, 144,
146, 153, 155, 178 & n.
The Rambling Sailor, poems from 211 & n.
FEH letters to 146, 178, 211, 224
Meynell, Viola:
(ed.) *Friends of a Lifetime: Letters to Sydney
Carlyle Cockerell* xxiii–xxiv, 114 n., 168 n.
Mill Street Housing Society xx, 315 h., 315, 317,
318 n.
Mills, A. Wallis 134 & n.
Milnes, Richard Monckton, *see* Houghton, Lord
Moore, George 207 n., 261 h., 274, 275 n.
Conversations in Ebury Street 207 & n., 279
Memoirs of My Dead Life 345 & n.
Morgan, Charles 193, 194 n., 309, 310 n.
Morgan, W. W. xx n.
Morley, John:
Recollections 136, 137 n.
Morrell, Lady Ottoline 306 n.
FEH letter to 306
Morris, Revd David 301, 302 n.
Morris, William 85 & n., 88, 89 n., 113, 130,
143 & n., 158
Moule, Henry Joseph 14 & n., 101 n.
Moule, Horace 145 & n.
Mudie's Select Library 9, 10 n., 19
Murry, John Middleton 207 n., 226, 244 & n.,
249
financial assistance to 253 h., 253–4, 255–6,
273 n.
defends TH 207
FEH letter to 207
Murry, Violet 244 & n., 249, 254, 256

Nash-Wortham, Dr F. L. 313 & n.
Nation, The xii, 38 n., 41 n., 42
ELH letter to 39
National Society for Women's Suffrage 6, 7 n.
Nelson, Horatio, Viscount 120, 121 n.
Neville, Myra 298 & n.
Newbolt, Henry 100, 101 n., 160

Newby, Revd Thomas 102, 103 n.
Newcombe, Bertha 49 & n.
Newsome, David 149 n.
New Weekly 96 & n.
Nichols, Robert 141, *142 n.*, 244 & n.
   Ardours and Endurances 141, 142 n.
Nietzsche, Friedrich Wilhelm 39, 41 n.
Northcliffe, Alfred Harmsworth, Lord 148,
   149 n., 151

Old, George 6 & n.
O'Rourke, May xiv n., xv, 145, *145 n.*, 208
   article on TH 282–3, 283 n.
   FEH letter to 282
Ouida (Marie Louise de la Ramée) 113, 114 n.
Ouless, Catharine 123, 125 n.
Outline, The 268 & n.
Outlook, The 9, 10 n.
Owen, Catharine x, *5 n.*, 10, 22, 101–2, 103 n.
   ELH letter to 41–2
Owen, Rebekah xiv, xx, 4 h., *5 n.*, 10 n., 89 h.
   converts to Catholicism 42 h., 42–3, 43 n.
   death of sister 101–2
   dog (Pietro) 96, 102, 123, 136, 169
   as gossip 112 h., 115, 116 n.
   and ELH x, xi
   and TH x–xi, 94, 96
   and Ruskin 14 & n., 115
   ELH letters to 5, 9, 13, 18, 20, 22, 34, 41, 42
   ELH letters cited 17 n., 30 h., 41 n.
   FED letter to 89
   FEH letters to 94, 95, 110, 113, 122, 128, 135,
      168, 264
   FEH letters cited 122 n., 122 h.
Oxford English Dictionary 281

Pallin, Miss ('lady gardener') 123–4, 125 n., 129,
   136
Parrish, Morris 346 n.
   FEH letter to 345
Partington, Wilfred xxi, 324 h., *325 n.*, 334 n.
   FEH letters to 324, 330, 332, 334, 349
   FEH letter cited 332 n.
Paterson, Helen (Allingham) 335 & n.
Patmore, Coventry 32 & n., 175, 176 n.
Patterson, Alice 330 n.
Patterson, Myles 330 n.
Peacock, Sir Walter 341, 342 n.
Phelps, Annabel 290 & n.
Phelps, William Lyon 290 n.
   FEH letter to 289
Phillpotts, Adelaide (Ross) xxi, 289 & n., 323
Phillpotts, Eden xxi, 84, *84 n.*, 132, 227, 289
   The Farmer's Wife 231 & n.
   The Joy of Youth 94
   My Garden 94
Phillpotts, Emily 227 & n.

Pinero, Sir Arthur Wing xxi, 288 h., 289, *289 n.*
   FEH letters to 289, 292, 297, 306, 311
   FEH letters cited 288 h., 307 n.
Pinney, Lady Hester 226, 227 n.
   and Birdsmoorgate murder 235 & n.
   FEH letter 235
Pinney, Sir Reginald 248
Pitt, William 120, 121 n.
Plymouth 78, 134
Pocock, Reginald 195, 196 n.
Poe, Edgar Allan 13, 14 n.
Pollard, Graham, *see* Carter, John
Pope, Alfred 55 n.
Portsmouth, Isaac Newton Wallop, Lord 47–8,
   48 n.
Potter, Beatrix (Heelis) 20 n., 136 n.
Pouncy, Thomas 90, *90 n.*, 96 & n., 213 & n.
Powley, Edward 328, 329 n.
Powys, Gertrude 298 h.
Powys, John Cowper xxi, 298 h., *299 n.*
   A Glastonbury Romance xxi, 308
   Maiden Castle 298 h.
   The Meaning of Culture 308, 309 n.
   Wolf Solent 298, 299 n., 308
   FEH letters to 298, 308
   FEH letter cited 299 n.
Powys, Llewelyn 249, *250 n.*, 298 h., 308 n.
   FEH letter to 327
Powys, Theodore Francis 298 h., 308, *309 n.*, 327
Powys, Violet 308, 309 n.
Puddletown 99 & n.
Pretor, Alfred ix, 9, *10 n.*, 30, 31 n., 64 n.
   Ronald and I 19, 20 n.
Prideaux, Charles 316 & n.
Purdy, Richard Little xvi, xxi, 281 h., *282 n.*,
   286 h., 310 h., 310–11, 331, 336 h., 349 h.
   Sheridan edition 319, 320 n.
   and Yale exhibition 281 h., 282
   FEH letters to 282, 319, 323, 325, 332, 338, 340
   FEH letter cited 330 n.
Putnam, George Haven 78, 79 n.

Queen's College, Oxford 278 & n.
Quiller-Couch, Sir Arthur 137, *138 n.*, 139,
   140 & n.
Quinton, Arthur 65 & n.

Racedown 226, 227 n.
Rapallo xxi
Reed, Henry 340, 342 h.
   FEH letter to 342
Reed, William Wilton 115, 116 n., 187
Rees, Leonard 306–7, 307 n.
Rehan, Ada 4 n.
   ELH letter to 4
Rhys, Ernest 190 n.
   FEH letter to 189

Richardson, Ethel 93 n., 154, 155–6, 167
  FED letter to 92
  FEH letter to 337
  FEH telegram to 93
Richardson, Henry William 92 & n.
Richardson, Monica (later Laing, q.v.) 142,
    143 n., 318 h.
  FEH letter to 318
  FEH letter cited 319 n.
Richardson, Pamela 338 & n., 348
Ridgeway, Philip 227 n., 242 h.
  produces London *Tess* 225 h., 226–9, 230 h.,
    238 n.
  revives London *Tess* 293 h., 293, 296, 297
  FEH letters to 230, 238, 242
  FEH letter cited 231 n.
Rivière (book bindery) 137, 139
Roberts, Frederick, Field-Marshal Lord 19, 20 n.
Roberts, Morley:
  The Private Life of Henry Maitland 229, 230 n.
Roe, Humphrey Verdon 204 n., 250, 283
Rogers, M. F. 96 & n., 111
Rolland, Madeleine 45 n., 215, 216 n.
  ELH letters to 44, 46
Rosmer, Milton 226, 227 n.
Ross, Adelaide, *see* Phillpotts, Adelaide
Rousseau, Jean-Jacques:
  Julie, ou la nouvelle Héloïse 13, 14 n.
Royal Academy 131, 295
Royal Literary Fund 253 h., 254, 256 & n.
Royal Society for the Prevention of Cruelty to
    Animals 347, 348 n.
Ruskin, John 14 & n., 115, 154
Russell, Arthur 205–6, 206 n.
Rutland, William 326, 327 n.

St Helier, Lady (Mary Jeune) 107 n., 108, 110, 113,
    132, 144 n., 255, 303 n., 304
St Juliot 3 h. & n., 81, 87, 119, 301
  TH revisits 78, 80
Saint-Saëns, Camille:
  Danse Macabre 108 & n.
Saleeby, Caleb Williams 107–8, 108 n.
  FEH letters to 107, 116
Salmon, Eric 234 n.
Sanger, 'Lord' George:
  Seventy Years a Showman 243 h.
Sassoon, Siegfried Loraine 140, 144, 145 n., 162,
    176 h., 177, 187, 191, 244, 255, 263 & n., 321 n.
  and FEH xvi n., xx, xxi, 158, 213, 270, 330
  and TH 150, 160 n., 240, 292
  poems 140, 141 n., 278 & n.
  The Heart's Journey 248 & n.
  Lingual Exercises for Advanced Vocabularians
    224 & n.
  Memoirs of a Fox-Hunting Man 277, 278 n.
  Recreations 206, 207 n.

FEH letters to 180, 185, 211, 223, 233, 240, 248,
    259, 272, 277, 296, 302, 320
Schuster, Frank 260 & n.
Scott, Sir Walter 52, 53 n., 324 h.
Seaman, Sir Owen 266 n.
  FEH letter to 266
Shakespeare, William 4 & n., 15, 16 & n.,
    23 & n., 77 & n., 121, 141, 155
Shaw, Charlotte 218 & n.
Shaw, George Bernard 113, 114 n., 191
  and Nobel Prize 245 & n.
  Caesar and Cleopatra 226, 227 n.
Shellabear, E. 27, 28 n.
Shelley, Harriet (Westbrook) 10, 11 n.
Shelley, Mary (Godwin) 10, 11 n.
Shelley, Percy Bysshe 10, 152, 155, 229
Sheridan, Mary 19, 20 n., 88, 95, 121
Sherren, James 210 h., 212, 219
Shorter, Annie Doris 172 & n., 176
Shorter, Clement King xiv, 22 n., 29 n., 115
  and FED/FEH 71 & n., 102, 113
  and TH 77 & n., 82, 118, 124–5, 136, 144, 155,
    176, 187, 249
  ELH letters to 28, 29, 30, 38
Shorter, Dora Sigerson 31, 38 & n., 102
Silver, Christine 230 h., 238 & n.
Simmonds, William (puppeteer) 192, 194 n.,
    195 n.
Simpson, Wallis 340 n., 341
Sinclair, May 66, 67 n.
Smerdon, Dr Edgar 205 & n., 213
Smith, Goldwin 39, 41 n.
Smith, Reginald 95 & n.
Snaith, Madeleine Ruth 152 & n.
Society of Authors 67 n., 265 & n.
Society of Dorset Men in London 219, 220 & n.
  Year-Book 174, 175 n.
Soundy, Barbara (Jones) 314, 319 n., 331, 332 n.
Soundy, Margaret (formerly Dugdale, q.v.)
    141–2, 144, 150, 159, 314, 316, 318 h.
  in Canada 172 & n., 173, 184, 188, 247 h.
  at Max Gate xvi, 318, 331, 332 n., 349 h.
Soundy, Reginald 118, 119 n., 132, 136 n.,
    172 & n., 314 & n., 316 & n.
Soundy, Thomas 150, 151 n., 172, 197 n., 247,
    338 & n.
  at Max Gate 316, 318, 331, 332 n.
  FEH letters to 314, 348
South African (Boer) War 18 h., 18–19
Spanish Civil War 337
Sparks, Tryphena 104 n.
Speed, Harold 233 n.
Spencer, Herbert 12 n.
Sphere, The xiv, 21, 22 n., 30 n., 38 & n., 71 & n.,
    88, 112 h.
  FED/FEH reviewing for 86 n., 95, 124
Squire, John Collings 182, 182 n., 263, 300, 309

Standard 60 h., 60
Stephen, Leslie 336 n.
Stephens, Bertie 341, 342 n.
Stephens, James:
   The Insurrection in Dublin 125, 126 n.
Stephens, Winifred 66 & n.
Sterne, Laurence:
   A Sentimental Journey 9, 10 n.
Stinsford 75, 91–2, 96, 98, 121, 165, 167, 181, 223,
   261 h., 280–1, 297, 312
   as 'Mellstock' 79 & n.
Stoker, Bram 67 n.
Stoker, Sir Thornley and Lady 66, 67 n., 78–9,
   110–11
Stopes, Marie 203 h., 204 n., 284 & n.
   Love's Creation 283
   FEH letters to 203, 208, 250, 251, 283
   FEH letter cited 314 n.
Stourhead 48 n., 97
Strachey, Lytton:
   Eminent Victorians 152–3, 154 n.
Strachey, Philippa 49 n.
Strang, William 82, 83 n.
Strauss, Richard:
   Der Rosenkavalier 108 & n.
Sturgis, Henry Parkman 20 n.
Sturgis, Marie 19, 20 n., 335, 336 n.
Swinburne, Algernon Charles 130, 131 n.,
   152 & n., 156, 182, 255 n.
Sunday Pictorial xiii & n., 106 h., 108 & n.
Symonds, John Addington 138 & n.

Talbothays 75, 82, 101, 165, 186, 264, 285
Tatler, The:
   'Pretty Children Competition' 28–9, 29 n.
Taylor, Bernard 327, 328 n.
Taylor, Edith 69, 70 n., 123, 162, 163 n.
Taylor, Florence 69, 70 n., 123
Taylor, John 70 n.
Taylor, Richard H. 3 n.
Tennant, Stephen xxi, 255, 255 n., 296, 297 n.,
   302, 303
Thackeray, Anne (Ritchie) 335, 336 n.
Thomas, Sir Godfrey 341, 342 n.
Thomson, Winifred 16 n.
Thorndike, Revd Arthur 214–15, 216 n.
Thorndike, Sybil 214–16, 216 n., 221, 225 n.
Thorne, Eric Anthony 295 & n.
Thornycroft, Agatha 170 n.
Thornycroft, Hamo 170 n.
Thwaite, Ann 142 n.
Tilley, Thomas 170 h., 171, 171 n., 174, 205, 219,
   226
Times, The 53, 54 n., 174, 175 n.
   FEH letter to 317
   FEH letter cited 318 n.
Times Book Club, The 229, 243 h.

Times Literary Supplement, The:
   S. Cockerell letter to 331 & n.
Tintagel 119, 120
Tinsley, William 287 & n., 316
Tolstoy, Count Leo 113, 114 n.
   Resurrection 21, 22 n.
Tomlinson, Frances 249, 253 & n., 265
Tomlinson, Henry Major 244, 249, 253 n., 265
   article on TH 272
   Gallions Reach 252
   FEH letter to 252
Trench, Herbert:
   Napoleon 162, 163 n.
Treves, Sir Frederick 211 n.
Trollope, Anthony 27 & n.
Trollope, Frances 27 & n.
Tucker, Frederick Booth 317, 318 n.
Turner, Charles Tennyson 31, 32 n.
Tyndale, Walter 213 n.

Vaughan, Eleanor Mary 138 & n.
Vickery, Bessie Adelaide 166, 167 n., 168
Victoria, Queen 9, 10 n.
Vizetelly, Henry 11 n.

Walker, Emory 299, 300 n.
Walpole, Hugh 334 & n., 350
Ward, Mary Augusta (Mrs Humphry) 153, 154 n.
   Eleanor 21, 22 n.
Watkins, William 182, 183, 183 n., 184, 185, 188,
   209–10, 220
Watt, A. P. 268 & n.
Watts-Dunton, Clara:
   The Home Life of Swinburne 182 & n.
Webb, Katharine, *see* Adams, Katharine
Webb, Mary 336, 340–1
   Precious Bane 336, 337 n.
   Seven for a Secret 336, 337 n.
Weber, Carl J. 4 h., 331 & n., 335 n., 344, 345 n.,
   349, 350 n,
Weekly Dispatch xiv & n.
Wells, Amy 147
Wells, Harriet 253 & n., 257, 265
Wells, Herbert George 102, 147 n., 203 h.
   Joan and Peter 146–7, 147 n.
   Love and Mr Lewisham 147 n.
   Mr Britling Sees It Through 147 n.
   The World of William Clissold 244 & n.
   FEH letter to 146
Wells, Thomas Bucklin 240, 240 n., 253, 256, 257,
   265, 266 & n.
Wessex (dog) xxi, 90 & n., 102, 131, 136,
   182 & n., 186
   and broadcasting 233 & n., 234
   combativeness of 123, 169, 184, 206
   death of 247, 264
   TH's indulgence of 114, 164–5

West, Rebecca 155 & n., 203 h.
Westminster Abbey 261 h., 262, 311, 312
Whale, George 66 & n.
Wharton, Edith 319, 320 n.
Whibley, Charles 161, *162 n.*, 240 n., 271, 272 n.
Whibley, Ethel 161, 162 n.
White, E. How 259, 260 n.
Whittaker, Emily 98, 99 n.
Wilkins, Mary E., *see* Freeman, Mary Wilkins
Wilkinson, Louis 328 n.
Williams, Edward Wilmot 102, 103 n., 115–16, 116 n.
Williams, Sir Robert 150, 151 n.
Willis, Irene Cooper ix
Wilson, Carroll A. 310 h., 310–11, 311 n.
Wilson, Jeremy 250 n., 332 n.
Wilson, Woodrow 152, 153 n.
Wise, Thomas J. *135 n.*, 144, 324 h., 324, 325 n., 333
  FEH letter to 135
Woman at Home, The 38 h.
Woolf, Leonard 225 & n.
Woolf, Virginia 225 n.
  The Common Reader 225 & n.
  FEH letter to 225

Wordsworth, William 50 & n.
World War I 100 h., 100, 105, 109, 117, 123, 125, 126, 128, 131 & n., 140, 142, 151, 337
Worthing 52 & n., 71 h., 72 & n.

Yale University:
  colleges 320, 325, 327 n.
  TH memorial exhibition 281 h., 282, 310 h.
Yearsley, Louise 151 n., 190
  FEH letters to 150, 159, 171, 196
Yearsley, Macleod 107 n., 108, 132, 150, 151 n., 166 *n.*, 190, 191, 193, 206, 210 h.
  FEH letter to 165
Yeats, William Butler 160
Yeats-Brown, Francis 333 & n.
Young, Francis Brett 310 n.
  Jim Redlake 309
  FEH letter to 309
Young, Jessica 309, 310

Zangwill, Israel 33 n.
  The Mantle of Elijah 21, 22 n.
  ELH letter to 33
Zola, Émile 10, 11 n., 155